Conservation
of Historic Buildings

Bernard M. Feilden
Kt, CBE, D Univ, FSA, FRSA, AA Dipl(Hons), FRIBA

Formerly Director, International Centre for the Study of the Preservation and the
Restoration of Cultural Property (ICCROM), Rome

Butterworth Architecture
An imprint of Butterworth-Heinemann
Linacre House, Jordan Hill, Oxford OX2 8DP
225 Wildwood Avenue, Woburn, MA 01801-2041
A division of Reed Educational and Professional Publishing Ltd

ℝ A member of the Reed Elsevier plc group

OXFORD BOSTON JOHANNESBURG
MELBOURNE NEW DELHI SINGAPORE

First published 1982
Published in paperback 1994
Reprinted 1995, 1996, 1997, 1998

British Library Cataloguing in Publication Data
Fielden, Bernard M.
    Conservation of Historic Buildings. –
    New ed
    I. Title
    363.69

ISBN 0 7506 1739 X

**Library of Congress Cataloging in Publication
Data**
Fielden, Bernard M. (Bernard Melchoir)
    Conservation of historic buildings/Bernard
    M. Feilden.
    p. cm.
    Includes bibliographical references and index.
    ISBN 0 7506 1739 X
    1. Historic buildings – Conservation and
    restoration.   I. Title.
    NA105.F44
    720′.28′8–dc20   93–43653
                                        CIP

Printed in Great Britain by
St Edmundsbury Press Ltd, Bury St Edmunds, Suffolk

Conservation of Historic Buildings

Frontispiece   Ospizio di San Michele, Rome, Italy, before conservation

This state of affairs was due to lack of maintenance resulting from planning blight. The rainwater outlets were allowed to become blocked, so the gutters overflowed causing rot in the ends of the main beams which in due course collapsed taking the roof structure with them

Contents

Contents

vi

Preface

The conservation of our historic buildings demands wise management of resources, sound judgement and a clear sense of proportion. Perhaps, above all, it demands the desire and dedication to ensure that our cultural heritage is preserved. Modern long-term conservation policy must concentrate on fighting the agents of deterioration. Our industrial economy cannot and should not be halted, but by combating waste, uncontrolled expansion and exploitation of natural resources, and by reducing pollution of all types, damage to historic buildings can be minimized. Conservation is, therefore, primarily a process which leads to the prolongation of the life of cultural property for its utilization now and in the future.

Historic buildings have the qualities of low energy consumption, loose fit and long life, so the lessons learned from their study are relevant to modern architecture which should aim at the same qualities. They teach us that buildings work as spatial environmental systems and must be understood as a whole. There is no dichotomy between modern buildings and historic buildings — they both are used and abused, and have to stand up. However, it is still not realized how sophisticated traditional building techniques were. Since they have failed to understand buildings as a whole, designers using modern technology have now to relearn many lessons. It is an advantage to every architect's practice to have at least one member of the design team knowledgeable about the conservation of historic buildings.

This book is based mainly on my own experience. It surveys the principles of conservation in their application to historic buildings and provides the basic information needed by architects, engineers and surveyors for the solution of architectural conservation problems in almost every climate.

The book is organized into three parts. First, the structural elements of buildings are dealt with in detail. The second part focuses on the causes of decay which are systematically examined from the point of view of the materials which they affect. The third deals with the role of the conservation architect, starting with surveys and including the organization of work and control of costs, and some special techniques are reviewed. There is a valuable appendix, by R. J. Mainstone, which assesses historic buildings as structures.

Although I have used the best sources known to me for recipes and specifications of chemical treatments, I must advise that these be tested on small inconspicuous areas before wholesale use. Also, as we have become more aware of the toxicity of chemicals and their effect on flora and fauna we must be cautious in their application, since there may be risks in some of the chemical preparations.

Conservation work is multi-disciplinary, involving many skills which contribute to a balanced solution. The value of an historic building and the messages contained therein must be assessed and put in an agreed order of priority before the architect undertakes any project. In executing a conservation project the architect has a role similar to that of the conductor of an orchestra. The building is his musical score — not a note may be altered yet his artistic skill in presenting the building should make its architectural music a joy to the beholder. To do this, he must understand its totality.

The methodology of conservation applies to all workers in the field and is based on visual inspection which leads to specific investigations to the justified depth before a diagnosis is made. As in medicine the needs of the patient must come first and the architect should not hesitate to obtain second opinions when necessary and should have the right to receive scientific support. All practical alternatives should be explored and then evaluated in the light of theory in order to find the 'least bad' solution, which must respect the qualities in the historic building.

Note on the softcover edition

The objective of this softcover edition is to offer my major work *Conservation of Historic Buildings* to students at a price they can afford. Recognizing the merits of the Ashursts' *Practical Building Conservation* in five volumes I have omitted the four chapters dealing with Building Repairs. The Bibliography has been updated but also pruned. The section on Pollution and chapters on Earthquakes and Fire have been completely rewritten and an Appendix on Security has been added.

Wells-next-the-Sea, Norfolk   B.M.F.

Acknowledgements

One difficulty of writing this book has been that I have been learning so much all the time from my working experiences — so my first acknowledgement must be to those who have entrusted the conservation of the historic buildings in their care to me; in particular the Deans and Chapters of St. Paul's Cathedral (London), York Minster, Norwich Cathedral, the Minister of St. Giles (Edinburgh) and also to all the numerous Parochial Church Councils in the Diocese of Norwich who employed me under the 1955 Inspection of Churches Measure, the application of which in England laid the foundations of an approach to the scientific conservation of historic buildings. My other corporate clients included the University of York, Trinity Hall, Cambridge, Magdalen College, Oxford, the owners of historic houses and the Department of the Environment.

Clearly a book such as this depends on information, verbal and written, formal and informal, gathered from many sources. Inclusion in the Bibliography is an indirect form of acknowledgement, but where long quotations are made, these are acknowledged in the text. Sometimes sources have been used, but the content has had to be altered or adapted to make it relevant to historic buildings and for this reason cannot be directly acknowledged.

As author I owe a great debt to many persons with whom I have had a professional contact, but it is impossible to nominate all such persons. In particular I would like to acknowledge the assistance and generous advice I have received over many years from Poul Beckmann who, together with David Dowrick and Norman Ross of Ove Arup, Robert Potter, Patrick Faulkner, Frank Hall, Derek Philips and 'Steve' Bailey, were my collaborators on the consolidation of the foundations of York Minster, my involvement in which major conservation work provided the impetus to write this book. This remarkable experience of collaboration by a conservation team of architects, archaeologists, art historians, engineers, quantity surveyors, builders and craftsmen working together was stimulated by the urgent task of preventing the Minster's collapse, which could not have been carried out without the help of Messrs. Shepherds of York, whose manager Ken Stevens made an invaluable contribution. Messrs. Shepherds have kindly provided many of the technical photographs, for which I am most grateful. No excuse is made for referring to the work on York Minster, or to other historic buildings for which the author has had responsibility, for it is only by sharing experience that we can raise standards and improve judgement.

Rowland Mainstone has been most generous in his time in giving advice on the presentation of the section on the structural actions of historic buildings and in reading and correcting the text. He has also given permission to reproduce various diagrams from his classic book *Development of Structural Form* (Allen Lane, London, 1975) and has contributed Appendix I, so completing the structural section by looking at buildings as a 'whole', while my treatment deals with parts or elements and causes of decay of materials.

The content of this book has been considerably refined through further experience of lecturing at the International Centre for Conservation in Rome. I am grateful to Giorgio Torraca, Laura and Paolo Mora, Guglielmo De Angelis d'Ossat and Garry Thomson for their help and permission to use material and quote from their respective works.

I owe a debt to the Chairman and Council of ICCROM for allowing me to use the material in Part III which outlines the role of the conservation architect and which was prepared for lectures to the ICCROM Architectural Conservation Courses. In addition, much of the substance of the Introduction was taken out of a booklet entitled 'An Introduction to Conservation' which was prepared by me as Director of ICCROM for UNESCO.

I am very grateful to Azar Soheil Jokilehto for redrawing my original diagrams, to Cynthia Rockwell and Derek Linstrum for reading the text, to Alejandro

ix

Alva who provided Spanish terms in the Glossary, and to Keith Parker, Librarian of the Institute of Advanced Architectural Studies, at the University of York, for his help with both the Glossary and the Bibliography.

Special mention must be made of the help and stimulus I have received from James Marston Fitch, Professor Emeritus of Conservation Studies at the University of Columbia, New York City. He has pioneered conservation studies in the USA and shown their value in aesthetic education and given me help and encouragement over many years. Other individuals who have helped me with material are O.P. Agrawal, H. Akai, John Ashurst, W. Brown Morton III, Frederick Charles, Norman Davey, David Dean, Roberto di Stefano, Harry Fairhurst, Donald Insall, Bertrand Monnet, Wolfgang Preiss, 'Donnie' Seale, Marie Christie Uginet, Martin Weaver and Wilhelm Wolhert.

Institutions which have helped, besides the Deans and Chapters of St. Paul's Cathedral, York Minster and Norwich Cathedral, are:

The Department of the Environment (UK) including the Building Research Establishment, BRE, and the Princes Risborough Laboratory;

The Department of the Interior (USA);

The Fire Protection Association, FPA (UK);

The International Centre for the Study of the Preservation and the Restoration of Cultural Property, ICCROM;

The Royal Commission on Historic Monuments (UK);

The United Nations Disaster Relief Organisation, UNDRO;

The United Nations Educational, Scientific and Cultural Organisation, UNESCO.

Firms which have helped materially are:

Proprietors of *The Architects' Journal*;
Ove Arup and Partners;
Feilden and Mawson;
McGraw-Hill and Company;
Allen Lane and Penguin Books;
The Oxford University Press;
Shepherds Construction Group Ltd.

Photographs are acknowledged in detail and I am especially grateful to Ove Arup and Partners for providing the diagrams relating to York Minster.

Lastly my gratitude and thanks are due to those who have typed and retyped the text and who had the patience to decipher my handwriting, my secretaries Dulcie Asker of Feilden and Mawson and Elizabeth Ambrosi and Charlotte Acker of ICCROM, to Bob Pearson who has edited this production and to the staff of Butterworth-Heinemann

As usual, the author takes full responsibility for what is written. Mistakes there may be, but I hope they are not serious and that they will not mislead any practitioner of conservation of historic buildings.

The book, which has taken a long time to write, is dedicated to my wife for her patience, support, encouragement and sacrifices in the cause of conservation.

Note on metrication

The question of metrication raises some difficulties, partly because the metre, being related to the earth's diameter, is a geographical dimension, whereas the foot with all its historic variations is still a human measurement. However, as metrication is the order of the day, I have complied, but have added the Imperial dimensions in parentheses.

As the dimensions themselves are often only approximations, I have worked to the approximation of 300 mm to a foot rather than convert to the closer degree of accuracy of 304.8 mm; likewise, an inch generally is considered to be 25 mm not 25.4. The problem is really conversion of one's ability to visualize what the dimensions and stresses in one system mean in another.

1

Introduction to architectural conservation

What is an historic building?

Briefly, an historic building is one that gives us a sense of wonder and makes us want to know more about the people and culture that produced it. It has architectural, aesthetic, historic, documentary, archaeological, economic, social and even political and spiritual or symbolic values; but the first impact is always emotional, for it is a symbol of our cultural identity and continuity—a part of our heritage. If it has survived the hazards of 100 years of usefulness, it has a good claim to being called historic.

From the first act of its creation, through its long life to the present day, an historic building has artistic and human 'messages' which will be revealed by a study of its history. A complexity of ideas and of cultures may be said to encircle an historic building and be reflected in it. Any historical study of such a building should include the client who commissioned it, together with his objectives which led to the commissioning of the project and an assessment of the success of its realization; the study should also deal with the political, social and economic aspects of the period in which the structure was built and should give the chronological sequence of events in the life of the building. The names and characters of the actual creators should be recorded, if known, and the aesthetic principles and concepts of composition and proportion relating to the building should be analysed.

Its structural and material condition must also be studied: the different phases of construction of the building complex, later interventions, any internal or external peculiarities and the environmental context of the surroundings of the building are all relevant matters. If the site is in an historic area, archaeological

Figure 1.1 Merchants' houses, Stralsund, German Democratic Republic

Inventories of all historic buildings in each town are essential as a basis for their legal protection. Evaluation is generally based on dating historical, archaeological and townscape values. Without inventories it is not possible to plan conservation activities at a national level

Figure 1.2   Trastevere, Rome, Italy

*A sound structure has been neglected. The results are visible: a
system of regular inspections and conservation planning could
prevent this sad state of affairs*

inspection or excavation may be necessary, in which
case adequate time must be allowed for this activity
when planning a conservation programme.

Causes of decay

Of the causes of decay in an historic building, the most
uniform and universal is gravity, followed by the
actions of man and then by diverse climatic and
environmental effects—botanical, biological, chemical and entomological. Human causes nowadays
probably produce the greatest damage. Structural
actions resulting from gravity are dealt with in Part I,
Chapters 2–5, and the other causes in Part II, Chapters
7–11.

Only a small fraction of the objects and structures
created in the past survives the ravages of time. That
which does remain is our cultural patrimony. Cultural
property deteriorates. and is ultimately destroyed
through attack by natural and human agents acting
upon the various weaknesses inherent in the
component materials of the object or structure. One

aspect of this phenomenon was succinctly described
as early as 25 B.C. by the Roman architect and historian
Vitruvius, when considering the relative risks of building materials:

> 'I wish that walls of wattlework had not been
> invented. For, however advantageous they are in
> speed of erection and for increase of space, to that
> extent they are a public misfortune, because they
> are like torches ready for kindling. Therefore, it
> seems better to be at great expense by the cost of
> burnt brick than to be in danger by the incon-
> venience of the wattlework walls: for these also
> make cracks in the plaster covering owing to the
> arrangement of the uprights and the crosspieces.
> For when the plaster is applied, they take up the
> moisture and swell, then when they dry they
> contract, and so they are rendered thin, and break
> the solidity of the plaster.'

Consequently, when analysing the causes of
deterioration and loss in an historic building, the
following questions must be posed:

2

(1) What are the weaknesses and strengths inherent in the structural design and the component materials of the object?

(2) What are the possible natural agents of deterioration that could affect the component materials? How rapid is their action?

(3) What are the possible human agents of deterioration that could affect the component materials or structure? How much of their effect can be reduced at source.

Natural agents of deterioration and loss

Nature's most destructive forces are categorized as natural disasters, and include earthquakes, volcanic eruptions, hurricanes, floods, landslides, fires caused by lightning, and so forth. Throughout human history, they have had a spectacularly destructive effect on cultural property. A recent, archetypal example is the series of earthquakes that devastated the Friuli region of Italy in 1976, virtually obliterating cultural property within a 30 km (19 mile) radius of the epicentres.

The United Nations Disaster Relief Organization keeps a record of disastrous events, a sample of which, covering a period of two months, is given in *Table 1.1*.

After natural disasters, less drastic agents account for the normal and often prolonged attrition of cultural property. All these agents fall under the general heading of climate. Climate is the consequence of many factors, such as radiation (especially short-wave radiation), temperature, moisture in its many forms—vapour clouds, rain, ice, snow and groundwater—wind and sunshine. Together, these environmental elements make up the various climates of the world which, in turn, are modified by local conditions such as mountains, valleys at relative altitudes, proximity to bodies of water or cities, to create a great diversity of microclimates within the overall macroclimates.

In general, climatic data as recorded in the form of averages does not really correspond to the precise information needed by the conservation architect, who is more interested in the extreme hazards that will have to be withstood by the building over a long period of time. However, if questions are properly framed, answers that are relevant to the particular site of the building in question can be provided by an expert in applied climatology.

Human factors

Man-made causes of decay need careful assessment, as they are in general the by-product of the industrial productivity that brings us wealth and enables us to press the claims of conservation. They are serious and can only be reduced by forethought and international co-operation. Neglect and ignorance are possibly the major causes of destruction by man, coupled with vandalism and fires, which are largely dealt with in Chapter 16. It should be noted that the incidence of arson is increasing, putting historic buildings at even greater risk.

What is conservation?

Conservation is the action taken to prevent decay. It embraces all acts that prolong the life of our cultural and natural heritage, the object being to present to those who use and look at historic buildings with wonder the artistic and human messages that such buildings possess. The minimum effective action is always the best; if possible, the action should be reversible and not prejudice possible future interventions. The basis of historic building conservation is established by legislation through listing and scheduling buildings and ruins, through regular inspections and documentation, and through town planning and conservative action. This book deals only with inspections and those conservative actions which slow down the inevitable decay of historic buildings.

The scope of conservation of the built environment, which consists mainly of historic buildings, ranges from town planning to the preservation or consolidation of a crumbling artefact. This range of activity, with its interlocking facets, is shown later in *Figure 1.21*. The required skills cover a wide range, including those of the town planner, landscape architect, valuation surveyor/realtor, urban designer, conservation architect, engineers of several specializations, quantity surveyor, building contractor, a craftsman related to each material, archaeologist, art historian and antiquary, supported by the biologist, chemist, physicist, geologist and seismologist. To this incomplete list should be added the architectural conservator.

As the list shows, a great many disciplines are involved with building conservation, and workers in those areas should understand its principles and objectives because unless their concepts are correct, working together will be impossible and productive conservative action cannot result. For this reason, this introductory chapter will deal briefly with the principles and practice of conservation in terms suitable for all disciplines.

Values in conservation

Conservation must preserve and if possible enhance the messages and values of cultural property. These

Table 1.1   Some Natural Disasters, over a Two-Month Period (Courtesy: UN Disaster Relief Organization)

Date (in brackets if date of report)

(1.2.80)   Cyclone Dean swept across Australia with winds reaching up to 120 m.p.h. and damaging at least 50 buildings along the north-west coast. About 100 people were evacuated from their homes in Port Hedland. Violent thunderstorms occurred on the east coast near Sydney.

12.2.80   Earth tremor, measuring 4 on the 12-point Medvedev Scale, in the Kamchatka peninsula in the far east of the Soviet Union. No damage or casualties were reported.

(12.2.80)   Floods caused by heavy rain in the southern oil-producing province of Khuzestan in Iran. The floods claimed at least 250 lives and caused heavy damage to 75% of Khuzestan's villages.

14.2.80   Earth tremors in parts of Jammu and Kashmir State and in the Punjab in north-west India. The epicentre of the quake was reported about 750 km north of the capital near the border between China and India's remote and mountainous north-western Ladaka territory. It registered 6.5 on the Richter Scale. No damage or casualties were reported.

(17.2.80)   Flood waters swept through Phoenix, Arizona, USA and forced 10 000 people to leave their homes. About 100 houses were damaged in the floods.

(19.2.80)   Severe flooding caused by heavy rain in southern California, USA, left giant mudslides and debris in the area. More than 6000 persons were forced to flee as their homes were threatened. Nearly 100 000 persons in northern California were without electricity. At least 36 deaths have been attributed to the storms. Some 110 houses have been destroyed and another 14 390 damaged by landslides. Cost of damage has been estimated at more than $350 million.

22.2.80   Strong earthquake measuring 6.4 on the Richter Scale in central Tibet, China. The epicentre was located about 160 km north of the city of Lhasa. No damage or casualties were reported.

(23.2.80)   Severe seasonal rains caused widespread flooding in seven northern and central states of Brazil, killing about 50 people and leaving as many as 270 000 homeless. Heavily affected were the States of Maranhao and Para where the major Amazon Tributary Tocantins burst banks in several places, as at the State of Goias where 100 000 \people were left without shelter. Extensive damage was caused to crops, roads and communication systems. The government reported in late February that 2.5 billion cruzeiros had already been spent on road repairs alone.

(26.2.80)   Heavy rains brought fresh flooding to the southern oil-producing province of Khuzestan, Iran. At least 6 people were reported killed and hundreds of families made homeless by the renewed flooding.

27.2.80   Earthquake on Hokkaido Island in Japan. The tremor registered a maximum intensity of 3 on the Japanese Scale of 7. No damage or casualties were reported.

28.2.80   Several strong earth tremors in an area 110 km north-east of Rome, Italy. The tremors, which registered up to 7 on the 12-point Mercalli Scale, were also felt in the towns of Perugia, Rieti and Macerata as well as in north-east Rome. Slight damage to buildings was reported.

28.2.80   Earth tremor in the Greek province of Messinia in the south Peloponnisos, Greece. The tremor, which registered 3.5 points on the Richter Scale, damaged houses and schools.

7.3.80   An earthquake measuring 5 on the Richter Scale was felt on Vancouver Island off the coast of British Columbia, Canada. No damage or casualties were reported.

(9.3.80)   Heavy flooding in the southern provinces of Helmand, Kandahar and Nimroz in Afghanistan damaged or destroyed 7000 houses and rendered over 30 000 people homeless.

9.3.80   Earth tremor in eastern parts of Yugoslavia, measuring 6.5 on the Mercalli Scale. The epicentre was placed at 300 km south-east of Belgrade. There were no reports of damage or casualties.

(9.3.80)   Persistent drought in central Sri Lanka was reported to affect agricultural production and to ruin 150 000 acres of prime tea plantations. Water and electricity supplies were restricted by the government.

15.3.80   Heavy rains caused widespread flooding in north-western Argentina causing the deaths of 10 people, with 20 reported missing. Nearly 4000 people were evacuated after the San Lorenzo river overran its banks.

16.3.80   A volcanic eruption occurred in the Myvatn mountain region in northern Iceland. No damage or casualties were reported.

16.3.80   Earthquake on the island of Hokkaido, Japan. The tremor registered a maximum intensity of 3 on the Japanese Scale of 7. No damage or casualties were reported.

19.3.80   Medium-strength earthquake in the central Asian Republic of Kirghizia near Naryn, USSR. No damage or casualties were reported.

23.3.80   Medium-strength earthquake near the border between Afghanistan and the USSR. Its epicentre was located about 1120 km north-west of Delhi. No damage or casualties were reported.

24.3.80   Earthquake measuring 7 on the Richter Scale in the Aleutian Islands off the Alaska peninsula, USA. Its epicentre was estimated just south of Umnak Island.

28.3.80   Torrential rain and strong winds struck central and southern areas of Anatolia, Turkey, cutting road and rail traffic. A landslide in the village of Ayvazhaci killed at least 40 people, while an additional 30 villagers were reported missing. In Adana Province 12 000 houses were affected by floods.

Figure 1.3 Merchant's house, Stralsund, German Democratic Republic

Decay has gone so far that only the facade can be preserved and the interior has to be rebuilt. Taking the city as a whole, this may be justified. However, there is a danger of deception when only townscape values are considered

Figure 1.4 Merchants' houses, Stralsund, German Democratic Republic

Conservation work in progress. After a thorough study and re-evaluation it was found that these merchants' houses could be rehabilitated satisfactorily

values help systematically to set overall priorities in deciding proposed interventions, as well as to establish the extent and nature of the individual treatment. The assignment of priority values will inevitably reflect the cultural context of each historic building. For example, a small wooden domestic structure from the late eighteenth century in Australia would be considered a national landmark because it dates from the founding of the nation and because so little architecture has survived from that period. In Italy, on the other hand, with its thousands of ancient monuments, a comparable structure would have a relatively low priority in the overall conservation needs of the community.

The 'values' assigned to cultural property come under three major headings:

(1) *Emotional values*: (a) wonder; (b) identity; (c) continuity; (d) spiritual and symbolic.
(2) *Cultural values*: (a) documentary; (b) historic; (c) archaeological, age and scarcity; (d) aesthetic and symbolic; (e) architectural; (f) townscape, landscape and ecological; (g) technological and scientific.
(3) *Use values*: (a) functional; (b) economic; (c) social; (d) political and ethnic.

Having analysed these values they should be condensed into a statement of the significance of the cultural property.

The cost of conservation may have to be allocated partially to each of the above separate values in order to justify the total to the community. Whereas for movable objects the problem of values is generally more straightforward, in architectural conservation problems often arise because the utilization of the historic building, which is economically and functionally necessary, must also respect cultural values. Thus, conflicts can arise between cultural and economic values and even within each group, for example between archaeological and architectural values. Sound judgement, based upon wide cultural preparation and mature sensitivity, gives the ability to make correct value assessments.

Ethics of conservation

The following standard of ethics must be rigorously observed in conservation work:

(1) The condition of the building must be recorded before any intervention.
(2) Historic evidence must not be destroyed, falsified or removed.

(3) Any intervention must be the minimum necessary.
(4) Any intervention must be governed by unswerving respect for the aesthetic, historical and physical integrity of cultural property.
(5) All methods and materials used during treatment must be fully documented.

Any proposed interventions should (a) be reversible or repeatable, if technically possible, or (b) at least not prejudice a future intervention whenever this may become necessary; (c) not hinder the possibility of later access to all evidence incorporated in the object; (d) allow the maximum amount of existing material to be retained; (e) be harmonious in colour, tone, texture, form and scale, if additions are necessary, but should be less noticeable than original material, while at the same time being identifiable; (f) not be undertaken by conservator/restorers who are insufficiently trained or experienced, unless they obtain competent advice. However, it must be recognized that some problems are unique and have to be solved from first principles on a trial-and-error basis.

It should be noted that there are several fundamental differences between architectural and arts conservation, despite similarities of purpose and method. First, architectural work involves dealing with materials in an open and virtually uncontrollable environment—the external climate. Whereas the art conservator should be able to rely on good environmental control to minimize deterioration, the architectural conservator cannot; he must allow for the effects of time and weather. Secondly, the scale of architectural operations is much larger, and in many cases methods used by art conservators may be found impracticable due to the size and complexity of the architectural fabric. Thirdly, and again because of the size and complexity of architecture, a variety of people such as contractors, technicians and craftsmen are actually involved in the various conservation functions, whereas the art conservator may do most of the treatment himself. Therefore, understanding of objectives, communication and supervision are most important aspects of architectural conservation. Fourthly, there are those differences which are due to the fact that the architectural fabric has to function as a structure, resisting dead and live loadings, and must provide a suitable internal environment as well as be protected against certain hazards such as fire and vandalism. Finally, there are further differences between the practice of architectural conservation and the conservation of artistic and archaeological objects in museums, for the architectural conservation of a building also involves its site, setting and physical environment.

Figure 1.5 A street after conservation, Stralsund, German
Democratic Republic

Preparatory procedures for conservation

Inventories

At the national level, conservation procedures consist initially of making an inventory of all cultural property in the country. This is a major administrative task for the government, and involves establishing appropriate categories of cultural property and recording them as thoroughly, both graphically and descriptively, as possible. Computers and microfilm records are valuable aids. Legislation protects from demolition those historic buildings listed in inventories. The inventories also serve as a basis for allocating grants or providing special tax relief for those who must maintain historic buildings.

Initial inspections

A preliminary visual inspection and study of each building is necessary in order to know and define it as a 'whole'. The present condition of the building must be recorded methodically (see Chapter 13) and then whatever further studies are required can be reported. Documentation of these studies must be full

and conscientious, which means a diligent search of records and archives. In some countries, reliance may have to be placed on oral traditions, which should be recorded verbatim and included in the dossier created for each building.

When a country has a statistically significant number of reports, together with estimates given in recognized categories of urgency, it can assess the probable cost of its conservation policies and decide priorities in accordance with its budgetary provision. It can then plan its work-force in accordance with its needs and allocate adequate resources.

All historic buildings should be inspected regularly at five-year intervals, in order to establish maintenance plans. Such preventive maintenance should in most cases forestall the need for major interventions, and it has been proved that it reduces the cost of conservation of a nation's stock of historic buildings.

Continuing documentation

Complete recording is essential before, during and after any intervention. In all works of preservation, repair or excavation of cultural property there must

Figure 1.6   Doric temple, Silene, Sicily, Italy

Anastylosis can recreate the glories of the past, making the architectural values of space and mass more easily understood. Sometimes this is done at the expense of archaeological and documentary values. In this case the effect is spoiled by a plaster patch on one of the columns

Figure 1.7   Doric temple, Silene, Sicily, Italy

The column drums have been re-erected. Problems arise, however, as the stones have weathered differently while lying on the ground for centuries and it is this factor that gives the columns a rather strange appearance

always be precise documentation in the form of analytical and critical reports, illustrated with photographs and drawings. Every stage of the work of cleaning, consolidation, reassembly and integration, including all materials and techniques used, must be recorded. Reports on technical and formal features identified during the course of the work should be placed in the archives of a public institution and made available to research workers. Finally, if the intervention can in any way serve to broaden general knowledge, a report must be published. Often in large projects it may take several years to write a scholarly report, so a preliminary report or an annual series is desirable to keep the public informed and thus maintain popular support.

To ensure the maximum survival of cultural property, future conservators must know and understand what has occurred in the past. Consequently, documentation is essential because it must be remembered that the building or work of art will outlive the individuals who perform the interventions. Adequate budgetary provision must be made for documentation and this must be kept separate from that of the conservation works. Full documentation, including photographs before and after the intervention, is also useful if the conservation architect has to refute unjustified criticism.

Degrees of intervention

The minimum degree of intervention necessary and the techniques used depend upon the conditions of climate to which cultural property is likely to be subjected. Atmospheric pollution and traffic vibration must be considered, and earthquake and flood hazards should be assessed.

Interventions practically always involve some loss of a 'value' in cultural property, but are justified in order to preserve the objects for the future. Conservation involves making interventions at various scales and levels of intensity which are determined by the physical condition, causes of deterioration and anticipated future environment of the cultural property under treatment. Each case must be considered as a whole, and individually, taking all factors into account.

Always bearing in mind the final aim and the principles and rules of conservation, particularly that the minimum effective intervention is always the best, seven ascending degrees of intervention can be identified. In any major conservation project, several of these degrees may take place simultaneously in various parts of the 'whole'. The seven degrees are: (1) prevention of deterioration; (2) preservation of the existing state; (3) consolidation of the fabric;

(4) restoration; (5) rehabilitation; (6) reproduction; (7) reconstruction. These degrees of intervention are dealt with below.

Prevention of deterioration (or indirect conservation)

Prevention entails protecting cultural property by controlling its environment, thus preventing agents of decay and damage from becoming active. Neglect must also be prevented by sound maintenance procedures based on regular inspections.

Therefore, prevention includes control of internal humidity, temperature and light, as well as measures to prevent fire, arson, theft and vandalism, and to provide for cleaning and good overall housekeeping. In an industrial environment, prevention includes measures to reduce both atmospheric pollution and traffic vibrations. Ground subsidence must also be controlled; it is due to many causes, particularly abstraction of water.

In summary, regular inspections of cultural property are the basis of prevention of deterioration. Maintenance, cleaning schedules, good housekeeping and proper management also aid prevention. Such inspections are the first step in preventive maintenance and repair.

Preservation

Preservation deals directly with cultural property. Its object is to keep it in its existing state. Repairs must be carried out when necessary to prevent further decay. Damage and destruction caused by water in all its forms, by chemical agents and by all types of pests and micro-organisms must be stopped in order to preserve the structure.

Consolidation (or direct conservation)

Consolidation is the physical addition or application of adhesive or supportive materials into the actual fabric of cultural property, in order to ensure its continued durability or structural integrity. In the case of immovable cultural property, consolidation may for example entail the injection of adhesives to secure a detached mural painting to the wall and likewise grouting of the structure.

With historic buildings, when the strength of structural elements has been so reduced that it is no longer sufficient to meet future hazards, consolidation of the existing material may have to be carried out. However, the integrity of the structural system must be respected and its form preserved. No historical evidence should be destroyed. Only by first understanding how an historic building acts as a whole as a 'spatial environmental system' is it possible to introduce new techniques satisfactorily, or provide a suitable environment for objects of art, or make adjustments in favour of a new use.

The utilization of traditional skills and materials is of essential importance. However, where traditional methods are inadequate the conservation of cultural property may be achieved by the use of modern techniques which should be reversible, proven by experience, and applicable to the scale of the project and its climatic environment. This sensible approach to conservation uses appropriate technology.

With short-lived materials, including reeds, mud, rammed earth, unbaked bricks and wood, such materials and traditional skills should be used for the repair or restoration of worn or decayed parts. Preservation of the design is just as important a function of conservation as preservation of original materials. Finally, in many cases it is wise to buy time with temporary measures in the hope that some better technique will be evolved, especially if consolidation may prejudice future works of conservation.

Restoration

The object of restoration is to revive the original concept or legibility of the object. Restoration and re-integration of details and features occurs frequently and is based upon respect for original material, archaeological evidence, original design and authentic documents. Replacement of missing or decayed parts must integrate harmoniously with the whole, but must be distinguishable on close inspection from the original so that the restoration does not falsify archaeological or historical evidence. In a sense, the cleaning of buildings is also a form of restoration, and the replacement of missing decorative elements is another.

Contributions from all periods must be respected. Any later addition that can be considered as an 'historic document', rather than just a previous restoration, must be preserved. When a building includes superimposed work of different periods, the revealing of the underlying state can only be justified in exceptional circumstances. That is, when the part to be removed is widely agreed to be of little interest or when it is certain that the material brought to light will be of great historical or archaeological value; and when it is probable also that the state of preservation of the building is good enough to justify the action. These are difficult conditions to satisfy, and unfortunately they may be brushed aside by unscrupulous archaeological curiosity.

Restoration by anastylosis, using original material, is justified when supported by firm archaeological evidence and when it makes a ruin more comprehensible, allowing the spatial volumes to be visualized more easily. If taken too far, it can make an historic site look like a film set and devalue the message of the site. This and the problem of patina and lacunae are dealt with in Chapter 17.

Rehabilitation

The best way of preserving buildings as opposed to objects is to keep them in use—a practice which may involve what the French call '*mise en valeur*', or modernization with or without adaptive alteration. The original use is generally the best for conservation of the fabric, as it means fewer changes.

Adaptive use of buildings, such as utilizing a mediaeval convent in Venice to house a school and

Figure 1.9 Doric temple, Silene, Sicily, Italy

This plasterwork was probably unnecessary and detracts from the presentation of the temple. Certainly, Vitruvius' specification was not followed, for Portland cement was used with the inevitable resultant cracking

Figure 1.10 Temple of Zeus, Jerash, Jordan

Should the Temple of Zeus be subject to anastylosis? Most people know what a Roman temple using the Corinthian order should look like. The stones as they lie bear eloquent testimony to the force of the earthquake which destroyed the city in AD 794—a fact of historical significance

laboratory for stone conservation, or turning an eighteenth century barn into a domestic dwelling, is often the only way that historic and aesthetic values can be saved economically and historic buildings brought up to contemporary standards.

Reproduction

Reproduction entails copying an extant artefact, often in order to replace some missing or decayed parts, generally decorative, to maintain its aesthetic harmony. If valuable cultural property is being damaged irretrievably or is threatened by its environment, it may have to be moved to a more suitable environment and a reproduction substituted in order to maintain the unity of a site or building. For example, Michelangelo's 'David' was removed from the Piazza della Signoria, Florence, into a museum to protect it from the weather, and a good reproduction took its place. Similar substitutions have been undertaken for the sculpture of the cathedrals of Strasbourg and Wells.

Figure 1.11 Temple of Zeus, Jerash, Jordan

The fallen stones give archaeological evidence sufficient to make a model to demonstrate the original design

11

Reconstruction

Reconstruction of historic buildings and historic centres using new materials may be necessitated by disasters such as fire, earthquake or war. Reconstruction cannot have the patina of age. As in restoration, reconstruction must be based upon accurate documentation and evidence, never upon conjecture.

The moving of entire buildings to new sites is another form of reconstruction justified only by overriding national interest. Nevertheless, it entails the loss of essential cultural values and the generation of new environmental risks. The classic example is the temple complex of Abu Simbel (XIX Dynasty), Egypt, which was moved to prevent its inundation following the construction of the Aswan High Dam, but is now exposed to wind erosion.

Avoiding 'planning blight'

In the sphere of economics and town planning the demands of conflicting interests have to be resolved. 'Planning blight', an economic disease caused by lack of decision or by attempting too ambitious schemes, must be avoided. The lessons of conservation are that minimum interventions at key points are best for the community. For example, the work of the State Institute for Restoration of Towns and Objects in Prague shows a completely integrated approach to conservation from a town plan at 1/50 000 scale to a full-sized detail.

No proposed conservative action should be put into effect until it has been analysed and evaluated in the light of an objective clearly defined in advance. Possible contradictions in values must be resolved and the 'least bad' or minimum intervention decided upon; then the conservation architect can prepare his scheme for approval.

In all conservation of historic buildings, continuity of policy and consistency of artistic treatment is desirable; this is best obtained by nominating an architect who must be given overall responsibility for the project but who is also subject to multidisciplinary advice. His is the inescapable responsibility for making history or destroying it.

The conservation architect and his team of co-workers

The conservation or historical architect, in addition to his (or her) basic and practical experience as a general architect, must have a knowledge and understanding of early building technology and must be

Figure 1.12   Salerno Cathedral, Italy

Contrary to the Venice Charter, the baroque work has been unpicked to satisfy archaeological curiosity and expose early Christian arcading. How will the situation be resolved? Will the baroque be reinstated for the benefit of the whole or will the earlier period take precedence. It is vital to decide on a clear presentation policy in conservation

Figure 1.13   St Peter's Palace, Leningrad, USSR

The remains after enemy bombardment and before restoration work were daunting and grim. Cultural property must be fully documented to guard against disasters, thus making restoration possible

12

Figure 1.14   Palais de Rohan, Strasbourg, France
(Courtesy: Klein-Franc Photo Publicité and B. Monnet)
The palace in 1945 after the bombing of 11 August, 1944

able to identify the original fabric and later additions, and interpret his findings to a client. To execute any scheme he must co-ordinate the work of archaeologists, engineers, planners, landscape architects, contractors, suppliers, conservation craftsmen and others who might be involved in an historic building project.

The conservation architect is the generalist in the whole building conservation process. His work is outlined in Part III. He must have a good knowledge of all periods of architecture, combined with a thorough understanding of modern building practice; he must be able to preserve the artistic and historical value of the old structure, yet prepare schemes which are satisfactory in respect to modern requirements. This latter includes complying with relevant requirements laid down by codes of practice and building regulations, or obtaining waivers to any inapplicable building codes regulations where justified by reference to fundamental principles. He needs not only a knowledge of building technology but also an understanding of the pathology of buildings as evidenced by sinking foundations, crumbling walls and rotting timbers. This book is primarily written for just such a person.

Figure 1.15   Palais de Rohan, Strasbourg, France
(Courtesy: Photo Frantz and B. Monnet)
The synod chamber after reconstruction by Architect en Chef, Bertrand Monnet

Architectural conservators

The difficulty which the conservation architect has in finding, and communicating effectively to, those scientists who are able to appreciate his problems has led the American National Conservation Advisory Council to recommend the recognition of a greater degree of specialization in architectural conservation.

The person with these special responsibilities would be called an 'architectural conservator', and he should have a broad range of skills beyond those of either the conservation architect or arts conservator.

The architectural conservator must be trained in the new technology and in scientific laboratory methods now being applied to the conservation of artefacts in other fields; he must also be able to tap resources in such sub-specialities of chemistry as spectrographic analysis, radio-carbon dating and

13

Figure 1.16   Palais de Rohan, Strasbourg, France
(Courtesy: S. Norand and B. Monnet)

Aerial view of the palace after reconstruction following war damage. The building is used by the Council of Europe

Figure 1.17   Church, Stralsund, German Democratic Republic

This church has been turned into a maritime museum. The fabric is preserved and new spatial values created by insertion of a mezzanine floor. An interesting case of re-evaluation and adaptive use of an historic building, but purists might object

14

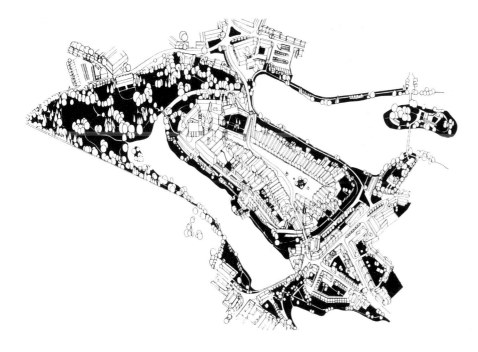

Figure 1.18 Telc, Czechoslovakia
(Courtesy: V. Uher and Statni Ustav pro Rekonstrukse Pamat-kovych mest a Objektj v Praze)

A typological and volumetric study of the town in axiono-metric projection

Figure 1.19 Central Square, Telc, Czechoslovakia
(Courtesy: V. Uher and Statni Ustav pro Rekonstrukse Pamatkovych mest a Objektj v Praze)

View looking south-east from the castle

Figure 1.20 Telc, Czechoslovakia
(Courtesy: V. Uher and Statni Ustav pro Rekonstrukse Pamatkovych mest a Objektj v Praze)

View looking north-west from causeway of castle and principal church

Figure 1.21 Structure of ICCROM's Architectural Conservation Course
(Courtesy: Arch. J. Jokilehto, ICCROM)

The course, held in Rome, is for architects, art historians, town planners, engineers and administrators who have had at least four years' professional experience and who wish to specialize in conservation. Within the overall structure, individual needs are met by variations of emphasis and allocation of time for research

HISTORIC BUILDING				HISTORIC CENTRES		
VISITS	PRACTICE	THEORY		PRACTICE	VISITS	
visits : history and concepts of conserv.	historic building : survey, historic research	concepts history and theory of conservation	rev.			JAN.
	recording	analysis historical-archaeol. study of building and environment, recording, photogrammetry	rev.			FEB.
practical-technical aspects	technical analysis	technology materials, humidity, climate	rev.			MAR.
	project for conserv.	conservation structures, presentation, adaptation maintenance	rev.			APR.
		towns analysis and planning in historic towns	rev.	historic centre: study of texture developm.	visits : conserv. of historic centres	MAY
		policy comparative aspects of legislation, inventory				JUNE

resistivity analysis. He should know how to use new archaeological techniques for analysing site evidence, computer technology for retrieval of recorded information and photogrammetry for producing accurate dimensional drawings and solving difficult problems of recording. Very few such men exist at present.

The role of conservation crafts

The scope of building craft skills in conservation ranges from the simple repair and maintenance of domestic properties to the most complicated work that can be imagined, for which the highest skills are necessary. The men to carry out the latter class of work should be classified as conservation craftsmen and have a status equal to that of other professionals engaged in conservation. The clock cannot be put back and the extreme diversification of eighteenth and nineteenth century crafts cannot be recreated artificially. However, a young but sufficiently experienced tradesman can acquire additional skills, and with artistic guidance, skilled application and the help of science he can repair and reproduce the craftsmanship of the past. The conservation craftsman therefore has to understand the history or technology of his craft and be able to analyse how historic work was set out and produced. Samples of past workmanship should be collected and used for reference, as is done in Amsterdam and at Torun, Poland.

It is to be hoped that more building contractors will specialize in repair and maintenance and that a new breed of conservation craftsmen, well versed in the history of the technology of their craft, will emerge to take a place with equal status and wages alongside the architect.*

Good workmanship

When the Parthenon was being built, the architect and sculptor (Ictinus and Calicrates), the free men, the freed men and the slaves all received the same wage of one drachma a day, and produced a masterpiece. Good workmanship thus depends upon proper pay for a fair day's work. Overtime and the bonusing of production have led to bad workmanship and should not be used to obtain increased output on historic buildings. Good workmanship comes from proper training, continuity of work and public appreciation and respect for the status of the craftsman. The sad situation in the building industry now, is that the more

Figure 1.22   Ethelbert Gateway, Norwich, England

The stone was so decayed that most of the evidence had disappeared. Research showed that an etching by J.S. Cotman, made in 1820, was a reliable basis for a reproduction by the sculptor

skilled the craftsman, the less money he earns because he is put on to the difficult, time-consuming tasks. The industry pays for quantity not quality, for muscle not skill.

Craftsmen are primarily responsible for the quality of workmanship. The ability to evaluate quality of workmanship depends upon experience obtained only from inspecting many buildings of different periods, but it is possible to generalize that a period when quality of materials was at a premium would tend to be a time of prosperity when building owners

---

*Operatives in the building industry in 1972 were earning as much as well-qualified architects, so this suggestion is not unreasonable, although it is likely to be resisted by vested interests.

17

Figure 1.23 South Portico, St Paul's Cathedral, London, England
(Courtesy: Feilden & Mawson)

Atmospheric pollution had destroyed the carving of the urns by dissolving over 20 mm (0.8 in) of the stone in half a century. Before it was too late a reproduction was made of Caius Cibber's early eighteenth century design. Here a master carver breathes life into new stone

were also prepared to pay for good work. However, generalizations are always dangerous and there could be pronounced regional variations within the same period. In England, I have found Romanesque and Early English workmanship to be generally better than Decorated Gothic, but quality improved in the late Middle Ages only to deteriorate in Tudor times and then gradually improve until the economic hardships imposed by the Napoleonic wars reduced standards. Some of the best workmanship was found in Victorian buildings, but since then there has been a gradual decline in standards, in spite of an increase in the standard of living.

To obtain good workmanship, materials and detailing must be suitable and skills must equal design. Possibly the highest qualities of workmanship were achieved in the Baroque period, when it seems that Gothic freedom and adventure were given a further lease of life by the designer-craftsmen. Compared with Continental architects and builders, the English have always been parsimonious with regard to materials, to save which they were prepared to go to great lengths. This attitude led to a smaller scale in English architecture, which can be seen in a study of the plan and sections of St Peter's, Rome, with walls

13 m (43 ft) thick and St Paul's, London, with walls of less than 3 m (10 ft). Designing to rather finer limits meant an ultimate sacrifice of durability.

It is interesting to note that of the part of the Ospizio di San Michele, Rome, which was built hurriedly and cheaply, a section fell down after about two centuries, whereas the rest has been consolidated at much less expense. In earthquake zones the quality of workmanship is often the difference between collapse and stability. Although workmanship is extremely difficult to assess, a study of all repairs carried out previously is indicative of quality. It can be said that any structure built with undue haste is liable to contain bad workmanship.

The context of inspecting historic buildings

In this book, great emphasis will be placed upon the initial inspection of the historic building. This has to embrace the whole problem as comprehensively and quickly as possible. Suggested norms for an experienced conservation architect are five hours sitework for a small historic building, ten hours for a more complicated one and between 20 and 40 hours for a difficult or large one, although York Minster took 2000 man-hours to inspect because of its architectural complexity, and St Paul's Cathedral about 1200 man-hours because of its size.

The causes of decay are so complex, and indeed two or three causes may be operating simultaneously, that it is usual for an architect to be unaware of all but the obvious ones when making his first inspection. This must not deter him—his role is to record facts and then seek the causes.

The work of survey, inspection and report should take account of the building in its town planning context. Planners can be of great assistance in preventing traffic vibration by diverting heavy vehicles; in preventing or reducing atmospheric pollution by correct siting of industries and power stations in relation to historic buildings; and in reducing fire hazard by considering access for fire-fighting vehicles.

How this book deals with the subject

Part I: Structural aspects of historic buildings (Chapters 2–6)

Gravity is both the force that keeps buildings standing and the major cause of their destruction. Structural actions and analysis of the failure of elements form the basis of this part of the book. Typical defects in various forms of structures are reviewed and examined in

Figure 1.24 South-west tower, St Paul's Cathedral, London, England
(Courtesy: Feilden & Mawson)

The cornices of St Paul's protect all the other masonry and so are the first line of defence against the effects of atmospheric pollution which is dissolved in rain water or condensation. After over 250 years many stones were defective and had to be replaced. A large stone has been lifted 50 m (164 ft) and is then carefully lowered into place, then grouted and pointed and protected with lead. Handling such heavy stones weighing up to a ton needs great skill, the prerogative of the mason, and also strong scaffolding

order to enable the architect to evaluate the structural condition of the historic building for which he is responsible.

In dealing with structural analysis, the value of R.J. Mainstone's outstanding work *The Development of Structural Form* must be recognized. This classic book is essential reading for architects, art historians and archaeologists. It makes the structural problems of historic buildings intelligible without the use of calculations. This statement may cause some wonder in certain quarters until it is remembered that the majority of major historic buildings were built long before mathematical analysis was developed by Poleni in 1742. The original builders had excellent correlation between hand and brain, and by using acute observation were able to analyse—if not exactly

quantify—the lines of thrust in buildings which depend more upon the form of the structure than on the strength of the rather weak (by modern standards) materials of which it was made.

To quote Donald Insall: 'Buildings are mortal.' It should be stressed that there must be a point in time when a building will collapse if maintenance is neglected and the building is not repaired. This point was reached less than 24 hours after the writer had inspected the north portion of the Ospizio di San Michele in Rome on 31 March, 1977. 'Mortality' applies in nature as well as in the works of man, for mountains erode, valleys fill in, the earth's surface is altered by earthquakes and the seas' levels change. The pyramids of Gizeh, as structures, have immense intrinsic strength, but even they have lost their outer

19

skin and are gradually eroding due to the action of climate. Luckily, historic buildings were almost all overdesigned and so have reserves of strength, but this overdesign was not consistent. Some parts will therefore be more highly stressed than others and cause strains to concentrate on one weak part, to the point of its collapse. Any study of the strength of a building must be at three levels and consider, first, the form of the whole structure; secondly, the structural elements, i.e. roofs and walls, foundations and the soil they rest upon; thirdly, the materials of which the component parts are made.

Before starting an investigation and certainly before undertaking any major intervention, the engineer and architect should have a clear idea of the objectives. What were the important characteristics of the building, which was it most desirable to conserve, and for what future use? Continued 'use', in the normal sense of the word, is always preferable to mere preservation, since it enables the building to continue to play a full role and this provides the best guarantee of continued attention and proper care. But there are also outstanding historic buildings or ruins which have an important future use as physical embodiments of past cultures or examples of supreme past achievements, without which we should be much poorer and which should be lovingly conserved for the real contribution they make to the fulness of our lives.

In making investigations it is all too easy for the professional to find a defect which may give laymen immediate alarm and concern, and for him to pronounce a verdict, without proper investigation, that the structure is unsafe or beyond repair. This attitude is common among those without experience of historic buildings, although they may be eminent in the field of conventional building, and does not take into account adequately the fact that the historic building has stood successfully for several centuries even though it may have quite serious deformations and defects. Whereas facts must be faced and structural faults recorded, the good points in the structure, however deformed, must be assessed and ingenuity used to find simple and elegant solutions which maximize the use of existing material and knit together the historic structure in such a way as to give it a further lease of life, while not prejudicing future interventions.

The best further safeguard for the future is to place the building under the continuous care of someone like a Dom Baumeister or a cathedral surveyor, preferably assisted by a permanent small staff of skilled craftsmen who learn to know the structure intimately and can measure its movements and monitor its structural health.

Whatever the objectives of its conservation, each historic building presents unique problems. It is an individual structure and its needs should be individually assessed, while keeping a proper sense of proportion about the justifiable depth of investigation. As has been said before, investigation of the needs should take into account all relevant facts, including not only the future use but also the environmental conditions, the foundation conditions and the past history. This last information could be very important in correctly interpreting apparent signs of distress. Usually, the present condition of the structure provides some clues to it, but documentary sources should also be consulted.

A qualitative structural assessment based upon visual inspection should precede and guide quantitative analyses which may otherwise be based on mistaken assumptions or misleadingly concentrate on the more obvious aspects of the problem to the neglect of the real total situation. Analyses should also start from first principles and not attempt to take short cuts by using rules from current codes of practice or other design procedures, since these are never truly applicable. Architects and engineers working on historic buildings need some qualitative intuitive understanding on which to build, and a basic vocabulary with which to formulate and communicate their insight. They should also be made fully aware of the need to have an adequate picture of the structural action as a whole before attempting detailed analysis of any part.

Where remedial interventions are considered to be necessary, they should respect, as far as possible, the character and integrity of the original structure. They should also, as far as possible, use materials similar to the original ones. Where different materials are substituted, their physical characteristics should harmonize with the original, particularly with regard to porosity and permeability, and care should be taken not to introduce elements of excessive strength or stiffness into a structure which will usually be less stiff and more accommodating to long-term movements than contemporary structures. The final choice of the approach to be adopted should be made only after a proper appraisal (consistent with the scale of operations and the resources available) of alternatives, with some eye to the future.

Part II: Causes of decay in materials and structure (Chapters 7–12)

Climatic causes of decay vary immensely the world over. The best techniques of conservation practice are required wherever climatic extremes are met. Natural disasters are here included with the problem of climate. Generally, it may be said that sufficient thought has not been given to flood and earthquake hazards as these affect historic buildings. Lack of maintenance strategies has led to earthquakes being blamed for much loss of life and destruction of cultural property which could have been avoided by preventive maintenance. Climate also dictates what botanical, biological and entomological causes of decay may occur and to a large extent the strength of their attacks. The chapters dealing with these causes are not meant to summarize or replace the extensive literature on these subjects, but rather to treat them from the point of view of the practising architect, highlighting some of the preventive measures that can be taken.

One comment arising from the study of the effect of climate on building design is that this phenomenon is absolutely fundamental. What could be more idiotic than putting an all-glass facade into a structure in the Persian Gulf (or anywhere else perhaps), showing a complete disregard for the climate and the lessons to be learned from the local buildings.

A chapter on the man-made causes of decay, which are complicated and widespread, discusses the problems of vibration from heavy traffic and industry, of water abstraction and of atmospheric pollution (Chapter 11).

Chapter 12, dealing with the internal environment of historic buildings, is the corollary to that on climate, as the primary purpose of buildings is to modify the harsh or enervating external climate in favour of man, thus enabling him to pursue his domestic activities and his work, social, spiritual and leisure aims. It is important to understand a building as a spatial environmental system. This chapter hopefully makes clear that there is a heat and moisture equation which must balance, and how if you alter one factor in the equation, you must also alter all the others.

Part III: The work of the conservation architect (Chapters 13–19)

Although this book considers all the causes of decay before dealing with inspections, in practice the architect generally has to inspect a building and then diagnose what is wrong and finally decide how to cure it. However, by following a logical plan it is possible to emphasize the wholeness of the building and the concept of its action as a structural environmental spatial system. The chapter on inspections should be particularly useful to archaeologists and conservator/restorers (Chapter 13).

Research, analysis and recording might be considered before an inspection is made, yet in practice until you have looked at the fabric in its totality you do not know what needs further study, what sort of analysis should be made and what depth is justified, nor do you know what recording is necessary. This chapter has therefore been placed after the one on inspections. The inspection should indicate what is necessary to be studied and used as the basis of obtaining authority and funding for the next stage of necessary investigations to be made in depth. For instance, in the case of York Minster, a soil mechanics investigation and structural analysis, together with exploration of the structure, were shown to be essential as a result of an inspection which had no preconceptions.

Inspections, followed by careful research, analysis and recording, are not an end in themselves. Action must follow. The first action should be to devise a strategic maintenance plan, so the chapter dealing with this important matter comes next. When the millennium comes, all historic buildings will have regular inspections and conservation will be based upon preventive action, which, involving as it does minimum intervention, is the highest form of conservation.

Some 9000 historic buildings in the charge of the Church of England, mostly mediaeval churches, have been cared for on this basis for 25 years and the amount of annual maintenance required has fallen dramatically, so it can be proved that organizing the conservation of historic buildings on a preventive maintenance basis saves money. Yet most owners and administrators fail to understand this and are reluctant to commission regular inspections and organize preventive maintenance, as they are unwilling to pay the fee for professional services, or in the case of the government, to employ sufficient staff.

Passive and active fire protection form Chapter 16 of the book. It is a question of forethought and good management to prevent damage by fires, as well as loss of life. Security is also becoming increasingly important as standards of public behaviour decline. Part of the philosophy is summed up by Murphy's law: if it can happen it will happen—so we must prevent the thief and vandal and avoid the danger of fire.

Next, a chapter on the presentation of historic buildings is included. Before any conservation action is undertaken, both the objective and the way the building is to be presented should be discussed and agreed. Difficult aesthetic and art historical questions and possible contradictions should be resolved before works are started. For example, will archaeological excavations threaten the stability of the structure? The values of patina and problems of dealing with lacunae and ruins also come under the subject of presentation and so are discussed in this chapter.

To complete this part, chapters on cost control of

conservation projects and rehabilitation of historic buildings are included. Much time and money is wasted and damage done to cultural buildings due to lack of agreed concepts of conservation, leading to expensive changes of mind due to lack of policy and of firm control in execution which must be delegated to one competent person after the policy has been decided by a multidisciplinary group of experienced experts. Conservation policy for an individual building will be based on inspection, further studies and the objective of the presentation, all subjects dealt with in previous chapters. It should not be made by one man, as the responsibility is too great, but for consistent artistic interpretation one man, like the conductor of an orchestra, must be in charge of the execution of the works.

Special techniques of repair and reconstruction of buildings form the final subject, with scaffolding, shoring, jacking, drilling, grouting, together with consolidation of stone, as topics. The young architect who can use these techniques is useful, but if he can get outside his professional strait-jacket and manage labour, order materials and use a theodolite, he would be invaluable in developing countries.

It is gratifying to find how useful and universal the principles of prestressing are; this is because most traditional materials, except wood, are weak in tension and by applying prestressing one can give old structures a new lease of life.

Summary

The conservation of historic buildings constitutes an inter professional discipline co-ordinating a range of aesthetic, historic, scientific and technical methods. Conservation is a rapidly developing field which, by its very nature, is a multidisciplinary activity with experts respecting one another's contribution and combining to form an effective team.

The modern principles which govern the organization and application of conservation interventions have taken centuries of philosophical, aesthetic and technical progress to articulate. The problem of conserving architecture and the fine and decorative arts is not simple. Even in a scientific age that has developed the technology of space travel and atomic power, the solution to local environmental problems and the prevention of decay still present a major challenge. Only through understanding the mechanisms of decay and deterioration can we increase conservation skills for prolonging the life of cultural property for future generations, but we must admit that decay is a law of Nature and we can only slow the process down.

Part I

STRUCTURAL ASPECTS OF HISTORIC BUILDINGS

2

Structural actions of historic buildings

Loadings

The initial state of all the internal actions in a structure was determined by its construction, whereas its subsequent behaviour depends upon external circumstances and its changed condition. A structure must, however, have the capacity to resist in an acceptable manner all the loads that it is likely to have to bear. Rapidly applied loads may have a much greater effect than the same load applied slowly, and when such loads are changed rapidly and are rhythmically repeated they can have even more damaging dynamic effects if their repetitions coincide with the resonance of the structure. The commonest dynamic load is wind, but earthquakes are essentially dynamic loads acting horizontally on all parts of the structure above ground as the result of vibratory displacements of the foundations. Traffic, while producing comparatively small dynamic loads, can have major long-term effects. Active loads such as the weight of people, furniture and goods, vehicles on a bridge or water against a dam have to be balanced by the resistance of the structure and these, together with the dead weight of the structure, have to be passed on, and balanced by, the opposed resistance of the soil below the foundations. Whether there is an adequate reserve margin of strength and stiffening in all the structural elements of an historic building and their interconnections to resist live and dead loadings is often a matter of judgement.

Under applied loads each element tends to give way to some extent and it is through this limited 'giving way' or deformation that the necessary resistance is developed. Moderate tensile loads are beneficial on tensile structures giving greater stiffness and stability. Excessive compressive loads may lead to buckling and loss of stability through the harmful bending actions they induce in slender structural elements. Chapter 2 of Mainstone's *The Development of Structural Form* amplifies these points. Changes in temperature and humidity or even the setting of cement can produce expansions or contractions which, if restrained, produce large active loads.

The internal actions or forces inside a structure are known as tension, compression, bending, torsion and shearing. A building must have the capacity to resist all of these forces simultaneously, as necessary, but to have this capacity depends in the first place on the geometry of the structure together with the strength and relative stiffnesses of the individual elements and their joints. Where the structure permits of only one pattern of equilibrium it is statically determinate, but if more than one pattern is possible then the structure is statically indeterminate and the loads will take the path through the stiffer routes and by-pass those parts that give way more readily.

Determinate and indeterminate structures

Ancient structures tended to be massive and indeterminate since they were built of relatively weak materials. With stronger materials and the application of mathematical analysis, modern structures have tended to become much lighter, and in the process of paring away materials such structures have tended to have less reserves of strength and to have lost good thermal and acoustical qualities.

Examples of determinate structures are trusses, three-hinge frames, portal frames and catenaries such as suspension cables. A determinate structure will collapse if even one element fails, for it lacks the ability to readjust itself.

An indeterminate structure has the possibilities of many readjustments within its form and can absorb

25

Figure 2.1 Ospizio di San Michele, Rome, Italy

This section collapsed less than 24 hours after it was declared unsafe by the author on 31 March, 1977. The basic cause was bad workmanship. The evidence of imminent collapse was a new bulge in the wall between two windows. The pattern of collapse tells much about the condition of the structure

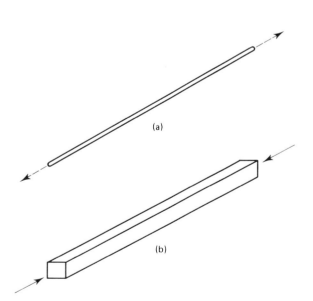

Figure 2.2 Types of loadings—(a) tension and (b) compression

Arrows indicate the direction of the applied force. Dotted lines indicate tension or pulling apart. Solid lines indicate compression or pushing together. Tension requires positive joints

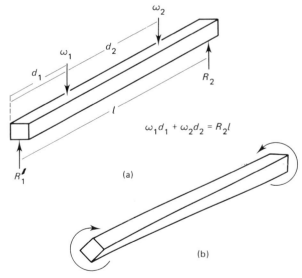

$$\omega_1 d_1 + \omega_2 d_2 = R_2 l$$

Figure 2.3 Types of loadings—(a) bending and (b) twisting

In bending, applied loads some distance from the end of a beam cause equal and opposite couples in their own plane. Twisting is caused by equal and opposite couples

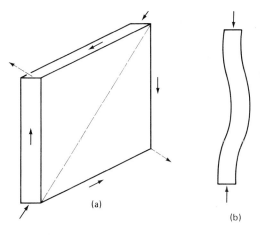

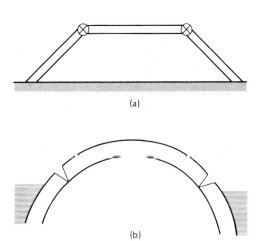

Figure 2.4   Types of loadings—(a) shear and (b) buckling
(Based on R.J. Mainstone)

In shear, one part tends to slip over the other along the shear line (shown dotted). Buckling is a sign of overloading in members that are not sufficiently stiff

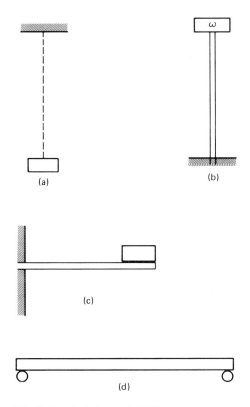

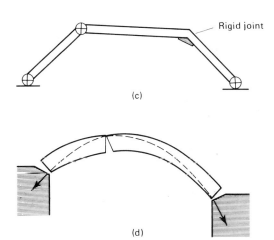

Figure 2.6   Examples of stable structures
(Based on R.J. Mainstone)

(a)   Two-hinge frame with ends fixed
(b)   Cracked arch with firm abutments and two fractures at quarter-span
(c)   A three-hinge frame
(d)   A deformed arch having three cracks with one abutment that has settled. Note that the line of thrust must go through the hinges

Figure 2.5   Determinate types of stability
(Based on R.J. Mainstone)

(a)   Suspension
(b)   End fixity
(c)   Cantilever
(d)   Beam on two supports

new loadings, settlements and distortions. In statically indeterminate structures, deformations lead to the establishment of one of many possible patterns of equilibrium. Further deformations reduce the number of choices left to the structure, which tends to become more and more nearly determinate in the process of time. Each structural form has its own characteristic faults, limitations and typical patterns of behaviour. The total deformation that an indeterminate structure can absorb is a matter of judgement which must depend upon consideration of analogous situations, while bearing in mind that analogies must not be pushed too far.

Calculation of stresses in historic buildings

The calculation of stresses in complex indeterminate structures is an extremely difficult task. The master builders of the Middle Ages and the architects of the Renaissance had only practical and empirical, not theoretical, knowledge of the forces involved in their buildings; but a cathedral which survives several hundreds of years is clearly the work of a good builder. The typical Romanesque and Renaissance structure is 'cavernous', i.e. a mass, as it were, hollowed out. Its aim was to disperse forces as much as possible. Walls were pierced to admit light only with caution, and vaulting and domes were designed so as to disperse rather than concentrate forces. The Gothic system conversely was to concentrate forces into frames of stone, and a cathedral was required to be as tall and light as possible. Viollet le Duc says that 'from the moment that the flying buttress was clearly expressed in the building the structure of the (Gothic) cathedral developed'. Isostatic diagrams help one to visualize stress distributions (see *Figures 2.7* and *2.8*).

Jacques Heyman (1966, 1969) and R. Mark (1972), who reviews Gaudet's propositions of 1902, have made interesting analyses of the forces in Gothic cathedrals showing how well the thrusts from the vaults were dealt with by flying buttresses. Mark has developed a method of photoelastic analysis based on scale models made of cast epoxyplastic plate 9 mm (0.3 in) thick and to a dimensional scale of 1:167. The models are subjected to loading in the same way as the original, but at an elevated temperature of 135 °C (275 °F); the stresses are then frozen and the model viewed in a polariscope. The pattern of stresses can be seen by lines of colour and the stresses may be calculated from the visible patterns and colours. Jacques Heyman in his paper 'The Stone Skeleton' deals with masonry arches, flying buttresses, vaults and domes. He considers that the stresses in Gothic structures are generally light and that failures generally occurred from other causes, often eccentric loads on foundations. Although Gothic structure is essentially one of transverse arched frames, longitudinal wall links have some effect. This was confirmed by war damage to the cathedrals of Rouen and Cologne, in which parts of the structures remained standing despite severe damage to buttresses and contra-forts, thus showing that when some flying buttresses are damaged the horizontal forces can be carried for a limited time elsewhere.

The outward horizontal stresses resisted by the flying buttresses may be as low as 10.30 kN/m² (1.5 lbf/in²) on single-arch buttresses and as high as 150 kN/m² (22 lbf/in²) on double-arch buttresses such as those at Notre Dame in Paris. The horizontal stress is caused by thrust from the roof and vault structures and by wind loading, which is variable. Flying buttresses have minimum and maximum horizontal loads imposed upon them, depending upon the direction and intensity of the wind, but function as long as the lines of thrust are within the masonry arch. A graphical method of analysis is shown in *Figure 2.9*.

Ove Arup and Partners used a shear panel convention to simulate the structure of the central tower of York Minster, and by this means were able to calculate the loads of the lines of thrust with the help of a computer (*Figure 2.10*). The lines of thrust showed eccentric loading on the foundations; this was one of the main causes of subsidence and associated danger to the superstructure. Likewise, calculations showed an eccentric line of thrust at the east end which had to be rectified by insertion of new foundations. The choir piers at York, which are of solid ashlar construction, were not rebuilt but only refaced after the fire of 1829; the central tower pier has an eleventh century rubble core with thirteenth century additions, all encased in a ring of rubble masonry, with a thin skin of fine ashlar executed in three or four phases in the fifteenth century and damaged by fire in 1829 and 1840. With such variables it is difficult to calculate the actual loadings on the masonry, for who can tell how much load is taken on the core with up to 70% mortar content and on the outer casing with about 3% mortar content? However, the average loadings are 3900 kN/m² (36 tonf/ft²) in these main piers. In the arcade piers of the nave and choir they are 4200 kN/m² (39 tonf/ft²) and in the piers under the western towers they are 6000 kN/m² (56 tonf/ft²). Similar loadings occur at Milan Cathedral. Salisbury is reported to have a loading of 4800 kN/m² (45 tonf/ft²) under the central tower and spire, whereas loads at Beauvais of 1300 kN/m² (12 tonf/ ft²) in the 6 m² (65 ft²) piers and at Norwich Cathedral of 1400 kN/m² (13 tonf/ft²) in the main tower pier are not quite so heavy. It may be helpful to keep in mind the figures for these loadings when making a visual inspection.

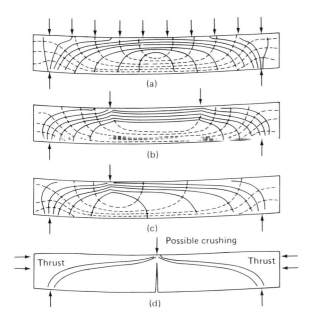

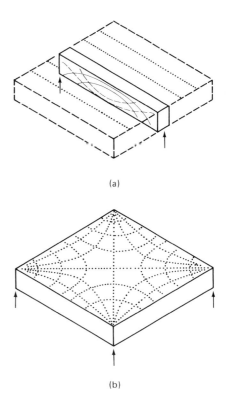

Figure 2.7 Isostatics of a beam
(Courtesy: R.J. Mainstone)

Isostatics are contour lines of tension (shown dotted) and compression (shown solid). The closeness of the contours indicates the intensity of stress. Where lines cross, shear occurs. It can be seen that tension is greatest in the bottom and compression in the top of the beam at mid-span. Shear is greatest at the ends.

(a) Uniformly distributed loading
(b) Two-point loads
(c) One-point load
(d) One-point load with crack

The occurrence of the cracks causes the beam to become an arch, only dealing with compressive stresses. Lateral thrusts are now required to retain it in position. Local crushing may occur

Figure 2.8 Isostatics of a slab
(Courtesy: R.J. Mainstone)

(a) A slab reinforced in one direction may be considered as a series of parallel beams
(b) A slab reinforced in two directions set on four supports. For simplicity, only tensile stresses are shown, but compressive stresses are equal and opposite. The stress pattern is remarkably like the pattern made by the ribs of a Gothic vault which, by using arched forms, removes the need for positive joints having tensile resistance but which generates outward thrusts

In such inspections the structural actions of all the elements should be visualized, but the structural action of the building must be understood as a whole. As an example, let us take an English Gothic cathedral. The structural elements of such a cathedral are clearly defined and consist of stone cross-frames, longitudinal arcades and walls, piers, arches, windows and doors, roofs and vaults, towers and foundations—all made up of the individual stones and timbers. Towers at crossings and at the ends of lines of arcades help to anchor these structures which are, however, subject to 'sway' or 'drift' in the joints of the masonry, mainly due to thermal movements or vibrations in the presence of a directional thrust. As the tower is heavier it will tend to sink, whereas the ends of the cruciform plan will move outwards and the wall and arcades will tend to spread sideways in the course of time.

In comparing examples of seventeenth century construction at St Paul's Cathedral, London, with Gothic York Minster (13–15th centuries), both buildings being similar in size and volume, one finds that the latter weighs about one-third of the former and that loadings in the piers are 8–12 times greater. In such highly stressed Gothic structures the lines of thrust must be carefully analysed, with geometry and scale taken into consideration.

Deformations

Records of the speed and sequence of the building operations should be studied for every major structure, so as to assess the effect of settlements and defects which arise during construction. The sequence used to be carefully worked out according to Viollet le Duc, in order to give a type of prestressing to buttresses.

It is important to differentiate between the initial deformations of a structure which may occur in up to 20 years from its completion and those that occur later. Considerable initial settlements usually occurred in arches using lime mortar when the centring

29

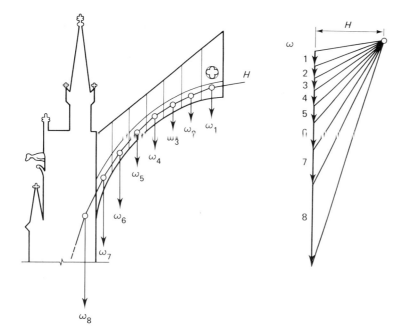

Figure 2.9 Graphical analysis of forces in a Gothic flying buttress
(Courtesy: Ove Arup & Partners)

The horizontal thrust must be known and the weights of each section calculated. The line of thrust can then be drawn from the diagram on the right. If the line comes outside the masonry, tension is indicated and this may lead to collapse

was stuck. Settlements of 50–100 mm (2–4 in) were normal during the construction of large buildings (like St Paul's Cathedral or the Capitol in Washington D.C.) and as much as 700 mm (28 in) was recorded for the piers of one of Perronet's large-span masonry bridges.

Deformations may not only result from taking up loads but from seasonal changes in temperature or internal heating, from changes in moisture content of materials and from differential settlements, movements of the ground or alterations to the structure that introduce a new pattern of equilibrium. There is continual movement in the cracks of an historic building which have a seasonal envelope. When movement is cumulative in one direction it is making a significant deformation. Accordingly, the more elastic materials are, the more likely they are to be compatible with the structure as a whole. This is one of the advantages that lime mortars and plasters have over modern cement mixes.

Cracking, crushing and yielding of materials can be looked upon as gross deformations with loss of stiffness in the structure or as modifications in the interconnections of the structural elements. In practice, if it were possible to inspect closely enough, most historic buildings will be found to have cracked and yielded in numerous places. Some cracks may not be permanent and may close if a load is removed. Much cracking is part of a continuing process of adjustment to continually varying loads and deformations due to thermal or moisture movements and wind. Although it is not harmful *per se*, the long-term consequences of such cracking may be the letting in of water, or if it becomes blocked with debris or dust shifted by vibrations the crack may get progressively wider.

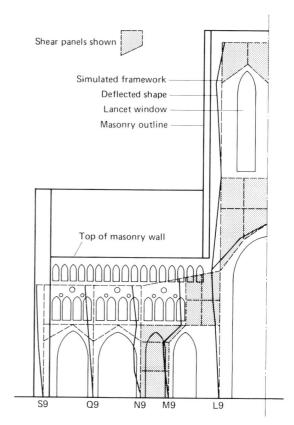

Figure 2.10 Shear panel computer analysis of York Minster's central tower
(Courtesy: Ove Arup & Partners)

Calculated deflections of the central tower and transept due to gravity loads acting on an uncracked simulated structure were found by computer analysis

In those structures made of brittle materials that are weak in tension, but much stronger in compression, and particularly in vaulted structures of masonry or concrete, visible patterns of cracking can be a revealing indication of the nature of internal action. Since cracks in masonry occur more or less at right-angles to the principal tensile stresses, these cracks indicate the direction of the principal compressions, which are parallel to the cracks. This is a form of structural analysis by the building itself.

Apart from the above question of observation, analysis and diagnosis of weaknesses, the question of above-ground interventions rests chiefly on the choice of materials suitable for consolidation or repair and the treatment of the cracks inevitably found in buildings constructed without preformed expansion or other movement joints. Thermal movements and movements due to changes in moisture, as well as the consequences of fire or the introduction of central heating, can all induce cracking. Because, even in the absence of extreme events, some cyclic movements must continue to take place, it is useless to attempt to eliminate all cracking. Necessary reinforcement should be designed simply to keep it under control.

The great merits of traditional elastic, relatively absorbent and easily renewed lime mortars for pointing and rendering should be emphasized. Portland cement mortars are, on the other hand, stiffer, almost impermeable and excessively strong, so that repairs tend to break away in large sections or subsequent weathering destroys the original, weaker, brick or stone rather than the pointing. It must be recognized, however, that climatic conditions vary greatly and that the role of an external wall as weather skin and environmental filter likewise varies. The correct choice of materials in a particular case can only be made in terms of the local conditions, considering the total function of the wall (which might, for instance, have an important fresco on its other face) and the existing construction and materials, together with the available materials and skills.

The correct choice of materials for structural consolidation is different. In any wall or pier it is desirable that the core should be as strong and stiff as the facings and should be well bonded to them. Except in the case of some solid brick walls, a few walls of solid ashlar masonry and most Roman concrete walls, this is rarely the case. Short of completely reconstructing such walls and piers with weak rubble cores and the like, grouting is the only available technique, possibly assisted by the introduction of a limited amount of reinforcement. Stronger mortars for this purpose are desirable, but Portland cement mortar again must be criticized on the grounds of excessive hardness, lack of elasticity and impermeability.

With uniform loading on ground that offers uniform support, a building should settle uniformly even if the ground loading is excessive by modern standards. In the case of an historic building, such settlement will usually have taken place long ago and now matters little. Even a linearly varying settlement, perhaps as a result of a continuous variation in the support conditions over the length or breadth, matters little if the resulting bodily tilt of the building is not excessive in itself or in relation to its height. Inclinations of 1% are quite common. Differential settlements of a non-linear kind, such as a greater settlement in the centre of a building, are the ones that matter most, since they can be absorbed only by weakening deformations of the superstructure. Observations of comparable structures may help in assessing how much differential settlement a building can accept, although it must be remembered that this tolerance is partly dependent on the original speed and sequence of construction. With a slow building programme in which construction is carried up fairly uniformly over the whole extent of the building, much initial settlement is accommodated without structural deformation, by built-in changes of level. In such cases, settlement histories over the centuries can, and should, be constructed, as has been done for the Leaning Tower of Pisa and for York Minster.

Usually, conditions below ground remain virtually unchanged through the centuries, whereas the structure above ground suffers a progressive loss of strength due to weathering and decay of materials and the disruptive effects of cyclic temperature changes, etc., interrupted from time to time by human interventions. This situation should not, however, be taken for granted. Water levels in particular may change as a result of drainage, pumping, obstruction of underground flows, or other interventions, and conditions may also be changed by adjacent works of other kinds. The effects of a change in the water table may be difficult to predict, but are usually undesirable. Preservation of the water table is therefore usually important. It was, for instance, reported that two-thirds of the present increase in the inclination of the Leaning Tower was due to water abstraction and that the earlier water table was now being reinstated by pumping in water. Local de-watering or pumping constitutes a similar danger, particularly if it leads to the removal of silt. An example can be quoted where running water under a building leached sand from beneath it and led to a settlement of 300 mm (12 in). Stopping the flow stabilized the situation.

Where differential settlement is leading to excessive deformation of the superstructure, the situation should be analysed in full in both its above-ground and below-ground aspects by architects, engineers and soil mechanic experts. The relative merits and costs of alternative schemes for strengthening the superstructure, underpinning it (i.e. carrying the foundation down to an existing firmer stratum), enlarging the foundations or improving the soil conditions should then be weighed against one another to select the best course of action, which should involve the minimum intervention and maximum retention of original material. Possible methods of improving the soil condition, each having the advantage of leaving the historic building untouched, include.

(1) Chemical stabilization by high-pressure injection (difficult in built-up areas).
(2) Weighting the surroundings to prevent adjacent uplift (difficult in built-up areas).
(3) Local water extraction to cause local shrinkage and thereby a corrective differential settlement.
(4) Drainage or de-watering.

Adoption of these methods calls, however, for thorough prior investigation with an assessment of the advantages and disadvantages. It is better to seek the 'least bad' solution rather than what appears the best. The least bad intervention is one that should be assessed in terms of least damage to the values of the historic structure and one that keeps most future options open. Cost efficiency and how easily the solution meets the requirements of statutory bodies are not prime considerations.

In all cases of possible hazard from ground movements, it is desirable to investigate the general geological background to locate and identify, for instance, a geological fault line or the presence of fine laminations in a clay soil. In earthquake zones such investigations are of the utmost importance. However, despite sophisticated laboratory tests of soils, the writer has found that often an important factor has been missed. Much also depends on careful and skilful control. Chemical stabilization, being irreversible, should be used with caution.

Three different possibilities exist in the way a building settles. (1) Equal settlement over the whole extent of the building, resulting in it sinking as a rigid body without rotation. Such settlements need not cause damage and if a building sinks evenly in fact it forms its own foundations by compressing the subsoil and so increasing bearing capacity. This is fairly normal with historic buildings and is accepted in the USSR with modern buildings where 80–100 mm (3.2–4 in) settlement is accepted. (2) Settlement that increases uniformly from one extremity to another, resulting in sinking and rotation of the whole fabric, as in the case of the Leaning Tower of Pisa. Rotation settlements may cause damage, especially when columns are tall and slender as in the case of Milan Cathedral. In new buildings cracks occur when rotation settlements

exceed 1/500 of the span, but 1/300 of the span is considered acceptable. In extreme cases rotation settlements can lead to overturning. (3) Non-uniform settlements which cause local deformations and eccentric loads on foundations by the sinking of those parts that are most heavily loaded or that stand on the weakest ground. Besides causing damage the deformations may cause dangerous eccentric loadings on the soil below the foundation. The larger the building, the more vulnerable it is to defects due to foundation settlements and failure due to unsatisfactory solutions of the static design and to deterioration of the materials, for the static and environmental stresses are both greater. On the other hand, smaller buildings are more liable to suffer from neglect, carelessness and changes to unsuitable uses. Luckily, most historic buildings have withstood the above-mentioned hazards, but it should be remembered that there have been many collapses and only the successful buildings are still standing.

Materials used in historic buildings

Let us consider the two main structural materials found in historic buildings—timber and masonry. Members of timber systems can resist tension as well as compression, and the joints can resist tension, but the strength of the total system is limited by the strength of the joints. The span is limited by the length of timber available. Known timber structural systems include, for walls, solid timber tree trunks set vertically or horizontally, post and lintel systems, box frames and cruck framing, and for roofs, simple beams, rafters and tie beams, trussed beams, arch braced beams, hammerbeam trusses and framed trusses.

Masonry structural systems include simple post and lintel systems, as for timber, but the commonest sort of masonry system is mass construction with pierced openings; stone skeleton frames were devised for sophisticated Gothic buildings with pointed arch and flying buttress, through which the lines of thrust were intended to flow within the physical limits of the masonry. In contrast to timber, the total strength depends more on the compressive strength of the materials rather than on the joints.

In the case of stone, its strength, quarrying facilities, lifting and transportation were also vital considerations. The longest stone beams known are in Fukien, China. They are 23 m (75 ft) long, are of granite and were used to build a multi-span bridge. Calculations show that the tensile strength of the stone is just sufficient to support this length. The length of wooden beams is limited by the length of available timbers.

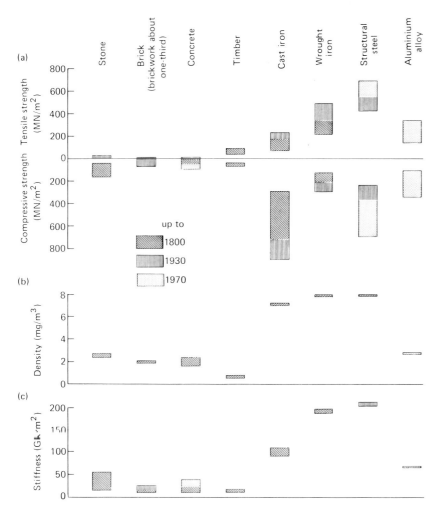

Figure 2.11 (a) Strength, (b) density and (c) stiffness of traditional and contemporary building materials compared (Courtesy: Allen Lane and Penguin Books)

Primitive openings in masonry walls were formed by large inclined stones set in an inverted vee, as in the Pyramid of Cheops or the Lion Gate at Mycenae. Arches may have developed out of the pseudo-arches found in ancient Greek polygonal walls at Delphi or out of the sloping construction of a drainage culvert at Babylon or the tomb of Menteumhet El Assraf at Thebes. In the bridge between Tiryns and Epidaurus, one of the oldest in the world, the arch effect may be accidental as the large keystone only spans the two cantilevered projecting lower courses. Pseudo-arches based on the cantilever principle were also used in the domed Tomb of Agamemnon at Mycenae and in the 'Trullo' dwellings of Apulia, as well as in similar huts in Provence.

The prototype of the domical structure in compression was in all probability the radial framework of bent reeds, saplings or curved timbers meeting at the apex and covered with turfs, thatch, skins or matted materials. Innocent describes such a construction built by charcoal burners in England in 1900, and similar vernacular buildings are found all over the world. Evidence of more or less conical domes of mud or mud brick have survived from the sixth or fifth millennium B.C. in Iraq. The use of stone in constructing domes followed that of the softer materials and by

1300 B.C. had reached monumental proportions with a span of 14.5 m (48 ft) in the Tomb of Agamemnon at Mycenae. These early domes were in fact pseudo-domes of conical shape as they were built without centring, with each ring of stone cantilevering inwards until capped by a large stone.

In the space of three centuries, Roman builders using pozzuolana cements achieved large arched spans—30 m (98 ft) was not unusual—that culminated in the Baths of Caracalla in A.D. 211. Often, as in the case of the Pont du Gard and Falerii Novi, arches were built of well-fitting stones without mortar. The largest surviving Roman bridge arches are those of the Pont St Martin near Aosta, which spans 35.5 m (117 ft). Such spans were not surpassed until the development of Portland cement and concrete with steel reinforcement in the latter half of the nineteenth century.

Three variations in arch construction were introduced by the Romans—first, the stepped pentagonal voussoirs which bonded into the masonry and spandrels alongside, secondly the flat-topped arch and thirdly joggled voussoirs. This joggling, which reached extreme elaboration in Ottoman architecture, facilitated construction and reduced the danger of collapse. The chain arch was a post-Roman development, conceived as an answer to building

33

small bridges on very poor foundations which were liable to tilt or spread. Examples are to be seen in Venice, but most are to be found on the Yangtze Delta of China where the type may have originated.

Like vaults, domes are generally built of brick or stone masonry. The earliest surviving concrete domes, dating from about 100 B.C., are in the frigidaria of the Public Bath in Pompeii, which had a conical form and span of only 6 m (20 ft). The so-called Temple of Mercury at Baia, which was really another bath, was built a century later and had a larger span of 21.5 m (71 ft). However, in the first and second centuries A.D. the development of the true dome was rapid, culminating in A.D. 128 in the Pantheon, which with its internal diameter of 43.3 m (142 ft) remained unequalled in size for 13 centuries and was not exceeded by more than a few centimetres for 19 centuries.

In the course of time, due to excessive consumption, as the supply of virgin wood was reduced, attempts were made to bolt and laminate timbers to form arches. The first major timber arches to be recorded were used in A.D. 104 by Apollodorus of Damascus in a bridge across the Danube, consisting of 11 spans of over 30 m (98 ft). They are illustrated in carved relief in Trajan's column.

Timber construction developed rapidly in Japan, where the reputedly oldest timber building, a pagoda dated A.D. 670, still stands in Nara which also possesses the largest timber building—the Toruji, dating from the thirteenth century which although reduced in size by a fire in the seventeenth century is still an immense structure.

The English hammerbeam roof, made of oak, was developed to span spaces without tie beams. It reached its supreme example in London's Westminster Hall (A.D. 1402), having a clear span of 20.5 m (67 ft) and length of 71.5 m (235 ft). Other noteworthy roofs include the Basilica Vicenza, span 20.5 m (67 ft), length 52 m (171 ft), using barrel vaults and steel ties, and the Hall of Justice in Rouen, span 17.2 m (56 ft), length 40.6 m (133 ft).

To replace timber and in search of fire-resisting construction, cast-iron beams and columns were introduced by Bage in 1796, followed by Boulton and Watt in 1799 and developed by Tredgold in the mid-nineteenth century.

Cast-iron arch forms initially followed timber: the Iron Bridge at Coalbrookdale (England) in 1777, with a span of 30 m (98 ft), was followed by Thomas Telford's bridges at Buildwas (England) and Craigellachie (Scotland). Eiffel developed wide-span steel trussed arch bridges for railway loadings, as at Garabait in Portugal. The Forth Bridge (Scotland), by Baker, was an outstanding achievement of its time, with three pairs of trussed cantilevers reaching out

207 m (679 ft) and carrying a central span of 106 m (348 ft) to give a total clear span of 520 m (1706 ft). In welded steel, the gateway arch at St Louis, Missouri, USA, built in 1966, is now a pre-eminent arch with its span of 192 m (630 ft).

When it was found, after several failures, that cast iron was weak in tension, a wrought iron substitute was used by Fairburn; subsequently, steel beams were developed in the later half of the nineteenth century and were exploited in steel-framed structures, which are beyond the scope of this book.

The structural capabilities of buildings clearly depend upon their materials, whose availability and characteristics determine the possibilities of span and height.

The primitive mud wall may stand up to three storeys, the rubble stone wall up to six or seven storeys. The stone arch may span 85 m (279 ft); the mass concrete arch 25 m (82 ft), the mass concrete or masonry dome 43.3 m (142 ft) (Pantheon); the Gothic stone skeleton and vault a span of 13 m (43 ft) springing to 40 m (131 ft) in height. The steel-framed skyscraper may reach 410 m (1345 ft); the reinforced concrete skyscraper 180 m (590 ft); the prestressed concrete dome can span 120 m (394 ft) and the steel suspension bridge 1020 m (3346 ft). With improvements in the technology of building, these figures will probably be exceeded; however, they are interesting in that the possible size of a structure can be compared with the materials of which it is made, so giving a basis of judgement. Nevertheless, the structural actions of a building depend upon its form.

All the main materials now in use are derived from the same basic materials that have been used for thousands of years—earth, rock, timber and metals—but have been improved in utilization and manufacture. Other new materials, such as plastics, synthetic resins and aluminium, lack stiffness in practice, so play a secondary role in construction, because for most structural purposes stiffness is as important as strength. In the context of historic buildings, reinforced concrete must be considered a new material.

If one compares the tensile and compressive strength, density and stiffness of the main structural materials used in historic buildings (stone, brick, mass concrete and timber) with cast iron and wrought iron, structural steel and aluminium alloy, striking differences are found. The historic materials except for timber are all very weak in tension, whereas the materials used in the nineteenth century and later, with the possible exception of cast iron, are strong in tension and exceptionally so in compression; even wrought iron, the weakest of them, exceeds the best stone in compressive strength. The comparative characteristics of 'new' and old materials are set out in *Figure 2.11*.

Although the strength of materials is of interest in extreme cases, generally it is not of major significance unless decay of the material affects the strength of a structural element; otherwise such decay is only of secondary importance. Most structural elements consist of one principal material. Historic buildings carry their loads by massive and stiff forms, differing from latter-day buildings which rely on relatively flexible structures having rigid joints and structural continuity and using both tension and compression equally.

Classification of historic structures in relation to structural actions

Although a classification scheme based on materials could be developed further, difficulties arise on account of the very different ways in which particular materials have been used. Further difficulties arise where, as often happens, several materials are used in a single building.

In Mainstone's classic study of the historical development of structural forms, mentioned in Chapter 1, classifications based primarily on the forms themselves were preferred. Elements were discussed first in several broad groups such as arches, vaults and domes; beams and slabs; trusses; vertical supports and foundations. Then different groups of complete buildings were considered, ranging from the simplest early huts to much more complex forms. These classifications were probably ideal for following the intricate pattern of interrelated developments of elements and complete buildings and, at the same time, gaining an insight into the essential characteristics of each form.

Where the historical pattern of development is of secondary interest in relation to the immediate problems of understanding particular structures and assessing their present state of health, a slightly modified approach may be adequate. In a paper written to introduce a symposium on Structures in Historic Buildings, held at ICCROM in 1977 and reproduced as Appendix I in this book, Mainstone offered his own suggestions, concentrating on the principal families of spanning elements. He emphasized, however, when presenting the paper, that each building must be considered as an individual, just as the doctor must consider each human patient as an individual if he is to care for him properly. Classifications and general understandings of the important characteristics and typical maladies of different structural families are a helpful basis for understanding the individual. But they should not be regarded as more than a starting point.

Chapters 3–6 look further at Mainstone's families of elements, although not in precisely the same sequence. Characteristic symptoms of structural distress are considered, together with some possible methods of strengthening or repair. Foundations are left to the end because the most accessible evidence of their condition is usually presented by the extent and nature of deformations and cracking of the superstructure. Although the approach is in terms of elements, it must also be emphasized that each structure must ultimately be considered as a whole before making a final assessment. Thus there is little value in considering the stability of, say, an arch, without considering its supports and the firmness of the ground on which they rest.

3
Structural elements I:
Beams, arches, vaults and domes

Beams

Post and lintel, column and beam and slabs made of beams side by side, resting on continuous walls, are the most elementary form of building construction in both timber and masonry. It is thought that, as in the development of the Greek Doric order, timber forms were generally carried on later in stone. Disregarding catenary forms of nomad tents, houses, temples, public halls and palaces were constructed this way until Roman times.

Just as a beam conceals within itself the action of an arch, so slabs contain the actions of shells and membranes. The directions of principal stresses, as shown earlier in *Figure 2.7*, of compression (thick lines) and tension (dotted lines) are known as isostatics. These give a picture of typical situations that will enable visible evidence to be understood and interpreted. A simply supported beam (free to rotate about the supports at its ends and to expand or contract longitudinally) is an element acting in bending, compression and in shear. In carrying any particular sets of loads, *a*, *b* and *c*, it is equivalent to a family of arches (compression) associated with an orthogonal family of catenaries (tension). These internal arches and catenaries adjust themselves within the beam to each change in the loads. When the beam cracks due to weakness in tension, as often happens with stone, the situation changes and the beam then acts mainly as an arch and produces outward thrusts. The beam may also fail in shear and for this reason, in the Near East and Italy, masonry flat arches were often built with joggled joints, to give greater earthquake resistance.

'The natural state of the masonry flat arch or lintel is the cracked state', according to Professor J. Heyman, who has shown that a lintel built of masonry cannot act properly until it has cracked. Moreover, in this condition it is safe provided the abutments can resist the lateral thrusts which the cracks generate. The pressures due to these thrusts are generally low compared with the crushing strength of stone, but they may be large enough to crush the soft decorative brick often used in English eighteenth century lintels.

The development of reinforced concrete and pre-stressed concrete beams was started by Pope in 1811 with a beam made of prestressed blocks reminiscent of the reinforced masonry in the Place de la Concorde and Pantheon in Paris, but the first to recognize the correct disposition of the tensile forces in a beam was Wilkinson, with his patent of 1854. This was further developed in 1897 by Hennebique and what was, in effect, a new material—reinforced concrete—was created. When cast *in situ*, reinforced concrete has the great advantage of obtaining structural continuity.

Decay and repair

Decay in timber columns usually occurs as a result of dampness and insect attack close to the ground. In oriental architecture the columns rest on a pad stone set raised above the general ground level. This prevents or at least reduces rising damp and termite attack. Decay in timber beams usually occurs where they are embedded and subject to fungal and insect attack. Penetrating rain also can cause decay and a beam may collapse as a result.

Cracks in stone columns and beams can be injected with epoxy resin and strengthened with dowels of stainless steel or bronze.

Steel columns or beams can have more material added *in situ* by riveting or welding, but satisfactory techniques of strengthening or repairing cast iron have not been found. The most hopeful field is that of plating using epoxy resin glues.

In the diagnosis and cure of defects in reinforced concrete, considerable difficulties occur—first in investigating the design, as the all important reinforcement is not visible, secondly in reinstating the

Figure 3.1   Transept arcade arch, York Minster, England
(Courtesy: Shepherd Construction Ltd, York)

*The thirteenth century arch has been severely damaged by the
settlement of the central tower. The top part had to be rebuilt, which
work revealed an earlier eleventh century window opening*

strength of lost parts, and thirdly in reinstating lost continuity. The structural conservation repair of historic skyscrapers will thus present problems the answers to which have not yet been found. Small cracks can be grouted with epoxy resins. Much the most difficult problem to deal with is the cure of rusting in the reinforcement, due either to cracks or to insufficient covering material and inadequate protection against the weather.

Arches

Arches must be considered in the context of the wall or arcade in which they are situated and of the thrust they exert on their abutments. Pointed and parabolic arches are special cases. The hinging effect is most relevant when the depth of the voussoirs is small in relation to the span. When voussoirs are deep in relation to span, arches are able to absorb deformations generally by slipping, as in the case of the Colosseum. In all cases the condition of the abutments is vital to arches. If these supports are sliding,

sinking or rotating, the stability of the arch itself is suspect; therefore, the abutments always need most careful consideration.

The sources of stress in arches come from the weight of the structure, dead loading and applied loads. In long-span masonry arches the dead load sometimes caused collapse when the shuttering was removed. Stresses can be increased by the settlement of an abutment.

Loads can be calculated by graphical means and then lines of thrust can be shown. Such diagrams are immensely helpful when investigating stresses in an arched construction (see *Figure 3.3*).

Assessment of strength of masonry arches

Assessing the condition and strength of masonry arches and vaults is one of the most difficult problems facing the architect responsible for an historic building. Calculations of their strength are rarely conclusive and, without the possibility of full-scale tests, experienced judgement must be the final arbiter. One

38

very important aid to assessing the condition of an arch is the full measuring of all movement, over a period of at least a year (much longer if possible), so that changes over all seasons can be studied. There are various ways in which the strength of an arch can be assessed by observation. The basic shape is of prime importance; parabolic and pointed arches are stronger than flat elliptical ones; arches with a good rise are stronger than flat ones and cause less thrust

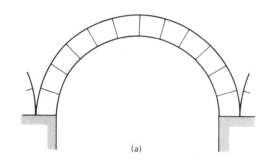

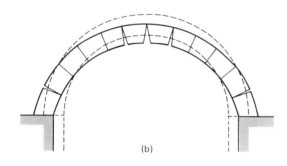

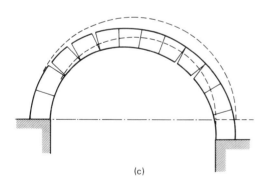

Figure 3.2 Deformation in arches
(Courtesy: Ove Arup & Partners)

(a) Intact arch
(b) Arch cracked by spreading abutments
(c) Arch cracked by differential settlement of one abutment

The voussoirs often compress the plastic lime mortar and are held in position by friction, so that the cracking does not constitute the formation of hinges. In practice, both actions are generally combined

on the abutments. As a rule of thumb, an arch is likely to be weak if its rise is less than a quarter of the span. The depth of the voussoirs is also important—the deeper, the stronger, as there will be a greater number of alternative lines of thrust available to meet various loadings. The flatter the arch, the more lateral thrust it produces; thus it depends for its strength more upon the firmness of its abutments, which should not be subject to movement and should be carefully inspected.

The nature and condition of the masonry, the thickness of the joints and condition of the mortar, the degree and direction of any deformation from the true line of the arch, and the width, length and position of any significant cracks must all be recorded.

Strength of bridge arches

Although they are not strictly historic buildings, ancient bridges have some special factors which apply, in addition to the above general comments on arches. The average depth of fill above the crown of the arch is important in distributing point loads, and good haunching at the abutments is essential for any bridge or arch. The impact of heavy vehicles is a frequent source of damage; this and the continued live loading to which all bridges are subject may give rise to longitudinal cracks running in the direction of the span near the edge of the arch, to bulging of the spandrels and to cracking of the wing walls. Longitudinal cracks may also be due to differential settlement of either abutment. Large cracks may indicate that the arch has broken up into narrower rings, each spanning independently, and this is a sign of danger. In some cases the insertion of pipes and other public services may have caused local damage which can only be discounted if the structure is built of good materials and workmanship, shown by good masonry set on its correct bed, or well-shaped, durable bricks in correct bonding with regular and narrow joints.

Cracks in arches

Arched architecture can absorb thermal movements and excessive loadings by forming local cracks in the arches which act as hinges. Three such hinges are theoretically permissible, but it must be remembered that with pointed arches the apex may act as a hinge, so only one hinge crack in each arc is safe. Thermal movements over long periods lead to 'drift' or the lengthening of the upper parts of walls caused by the sliding of the masonry in the arch's joints which tends to break up the mortar and weaken the abutments and spandrels.

Approximately tangential diagonal cracks near the sides of the arch springing, which spread up towards the apex of the arch, are generally due to subsidence of an abutment, and, if extensive, may indicate a dangerous state. Cracks in the spandrels near the quarter-points of the span indicate that the arch is acting as a hinged frame, but, other things being considered, do not indicate a dangerous state. Sometimes even if no settlement or cracking is visible the face of masonry in an arch or vault is seen to be bulging outwards. This usually indicates poor internal condition of the masonry—it may originally have been badly built with rubble, re-used stone or poor mortar, or it may have

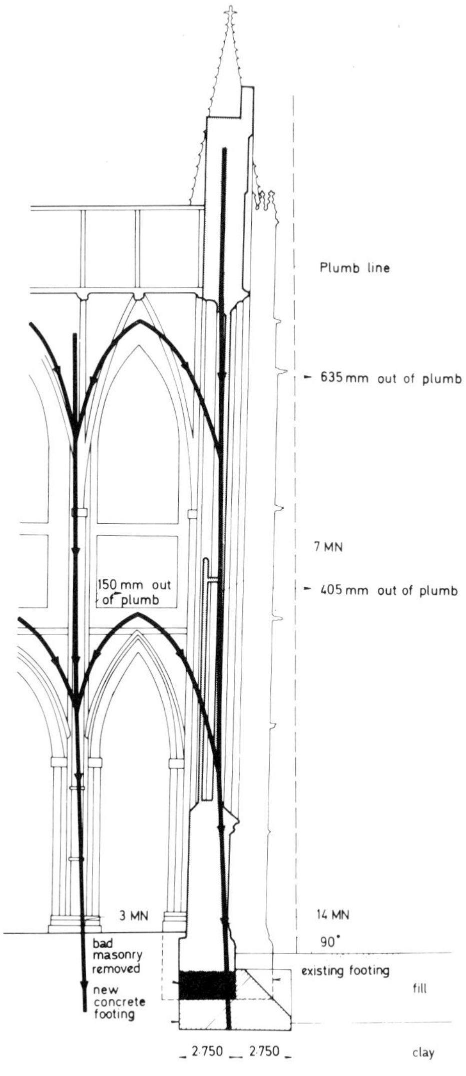

deteriorated owing to water penetration, etc. The soundness of the masonry can be confirmed by listening to the tapping of a hammer on the opposite side of the wall. Masonry and brickwork which are consistently wet or where damp often penetrates are likely to be weaker than similar dry areas.

Repair of arches

Repointing and grouting masonry in arches can, if applied to the maximum depth possible, greatly strengthen an arch. The repair of all types of arches may involve taking down the arch and rebuilding it, using a traditional falsework of timber and shoring with close-centred needles to carry the weights above the arch. On the other hand, if the arch is wide and the voussoirs are not of the full width it may be possible to rebuild half at a time or to take out defective stones or bricks and replace them individually. This has the advantage of not affecting the walling above to such an extent. Repair by rebuilding is rather drastic as it relieves compressive stresses, raising questions of prestressing the arch to avoid new deformations, which may require great ingenuity. Such prestressing can well be carried out with hydraulic jacks, as described in Chapter 20. Occasionally an arch can be freed by cutting out mortar joints and pushed back into position using hydraulic jacks.

Vaults

Vaults are usually constructed of stone or brick masonry, as these are good materials when used in compression, but other materials such as timber and plaster can be used. The ceilings of York Minster are an interesting example of a stone vault reproduced in laminated timber. Vaults such as Neumann used at Baroque Neresheim were constructed of tufa reinforced with iron tie bars. The complex cutting of stones with two curves to form vaults was avoided in Roman construction by the use of mass concrete. Later, brick ribs were introduced into the groin, as in the Baths of Diocletian where clear spans of up to 20 m (66 ft) were achieved. Such heavy construction demanded heavy centring, which was overcome by building the ribs first and then filling in the webs virtually freehand with a light curved centring. This procedure, as developed in Islam in the tenth century, had far-reaching consequences when adopted in Gothic buildings in the late twelfth and thirteenth centuries. Ribs also facilitated construction in three ways—first, they served as cover strips to the groins; secondly, they simplified setting out and along with the pointed arch gave freedom and flexibility in

Figure 3.3   Diagram of thrusts and movements—east end, York Minster, England
(Courtesy: Ove Arup & Partners)

The diagram shows the line of thrust dangerously close to the outside face of the wall and indicates eccentric loading on the foundations. New reinforced concrete foundations were designed to give concentric loading

Figure 3.4   Over Bridge,
Gloucester, England

*Because there were cracks at the
quarter-span and the bridge
sagged at its apex, where there
was also a horizontal crack, the
road authorities had signed a
contract to blow up this magnificent bridge of 45.5 m (150 ft)
built by William Telford. Due to
early settlement of the east
abutment the bridge had in fact
'hinged' at the quarter-spans.
Examination of the abutments
showed that they were still perfectly sound. The authorities
were persuaded to keep the
bridge as an ancient monument*

Figure 3.5   South face of tower,
Norwich Cathedral, England

*Due to aging, the c. AD. 1120
masonry of the tower has become rather decrepit. Repairs of
c.1870 had covered the defects
with rendering. A century later
the tower had to be consolidated
by grouting and refaced with
new stone which was bonded to
the interior with bronze cramps*

planning; and thirdly, they reduced the need for centring. After the stone facing had been placed, vaults were frequently thickened with a backing of brick or lime concrete, in which case the rib lost its structural function and in time might fall away from the vault. Loose ribs are met fairly frequently in Gothic construction. On the other hand, if thin, the vault itself might fall, leaving only the diagonal ribs and transverse arches standing. The care with which the masonry of vaults was designed is shown in *Figures 3.7* and *3.8*, taken from Viollet le Duc's book on construction.

Groined vaults form a naturally stiff shape and are, in effect, diagonal arches formed within the thickness of the vault and therefore the maximum compressive forces will occur at the springing of the arch. Cracks might therefore form parallel to the groins.

The ribs in pointed arch buildings are the decorative expression of a constructional element, in that the ribs initially formed a permanent shuttering for the vault. Most early Gothic vaults are generally quite thick, i.e. from 150 mm (6 in) to 450 mm (18 in), and may be considered as ribbed domes resting on four points called the *'tas de charge'*. The walls may move away from the vault and may leave a gap of 30 mm (1.2 in) or more. In time, ribs may drop away from the vault they are supposed to support, becoming a hazard should they fall, so in inspections great care must be taken to check that all ribs are safe. To be certain of this is difficult, and a detailed inspection from scaffolding may be necessary.

There are outward thrusts in high vaults with pointed arches. To counteract these forces, deep buttresses together with flying buttresses were developed, with decorated pinnacles. The effectiveness of this buttressing depended upon the depth of its projection and the top weight of pinnacles which could help maintain the line of outward thrust within the safe limits of the masonry. Buttressing was sometimes inadequate to counter the outward thrust from the vault and roof, so one often sees iron or steel ties that have been placed across the vault at the springing.

Thin, continuous barrel vaults resting on parallel walls or arcades may produce quite small thrusts which are well distributed and can be countered by the massive weight of the walling, which diverts the lines of thrust downwards.

The stresses on vaults covered by pitched roofs come mainly from their own weight and their inability to deform if their supports move. Ribs may form unstable mechanisms liable to collapse. Assessment of damage and analysis will therefore depend first upon correction of the causes of structural distress in the supports. When these have been dealt with, the vault itself can be looked at; ribs will have to be rebuilt together with damaged sections of the vault. It is important that ribs, when rebuilt to a correct shape, are prestressed by use of wedges or hydraulic jacks which can be removed later. Vaults can be consolidated with a penetrating grout. If the cracks are fine, an epoxy resin formulation is good, but if they are large, normal mortar grouts should be used in the vault first, and then regrouted with the epoxy resin. If such methods are not practicable, metal ties across the springing of the vault will have to be inserted, as was common in the past.

Domes

The technological achievement of Roman architecture represented by the dome opened up a new architectural era with the potential of large, unencumbered interior spaces, but the design was hampered by the necessary heavy construction, as the thickness of the walls of the dome was 1/10 or 1/15 of the radius. The great weight of early domes produced tension in the perimeter, which was indicated by circumferential cracks in the lower part such as occurred in the Pantheon and later in St Peter's, Rome. Lightness came only in the twentieth century, when with the use of materials like reinforced concrete a ratio between thickness and span of 1/200 was found to be practicable.

The dome of St Sophia (A.D. 532–537) in Istanbul, with its span of 31 m (102 ft) is one of the supreme examples of this structural form. Built on pendentives and flanked by two hemidomes, it gives a breathtaking sense of dematerialized floating space which is enhanced by the flat surface treatment of mosaics and marble. To resist tensile forces, the stones forming the cornice above the pendentives were cramped together with iron and, at the base of the dome, wooden bonding timbers were built into the brickwork.

Lightness in dome construction was obtained by divorcing the inner and outer shells. Such domes were developed by Islamic architects to produce fascinating external profiles with improved weather resistance provided by a durable and impervious surface of glazed tiles of intense colour, or of gilded copper tiles.

So as to minimize cracking of domes, efforts were made to reduce the weight of the structure by coffering and by using hollow pots to reduce the outer thrusts in the lower third of the dome. Tension rings of wood and stone were also inserted by Brunelleschi in the Dome in Florence and of wrought iron by Wren at St Paul's in London with the same objective. Ribbed domes, such as those of the Grunbadi in Kharka, the Library of Friday Mosque in Isphahan and San Lorenzo in Turin, are of particular architectural interest.

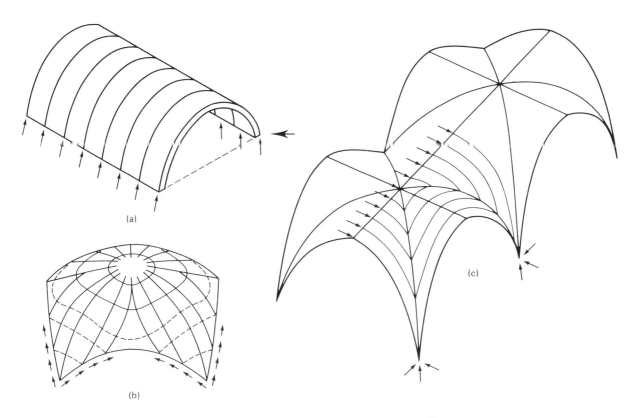

(a)

(b)

(c)

Figure 3.6 Vault forms
(Courtesy: R.J. Mainstone)

(a) Barrel vaults may be treated as a series of parallel arches. The outward thrusts are small if the spans are small and the vault thin in relation to thick outer walls. Ties in tension may link the walls together to resist this thrust

(b) Domical masonry vault—isostatics. The compressive forces are important, and meet together in the centre. Tensile forces are resisted by the outer walls or the next domical vault

(c) Quadripartite Gothic vault. The ridges are held in position by equal and opposite thrusts. All the compressive forces are brought down to the 'tas de charge'. The vault arches act in parallel to the side walls so cracks here do not matter

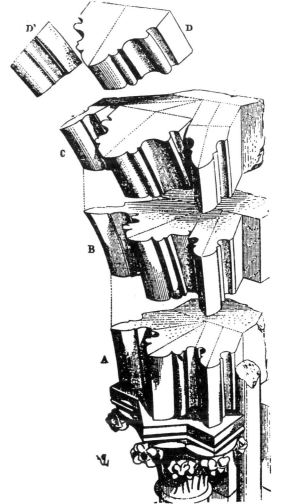

Figure 3.7 A 'tas de charge'
(After Viollet le Duc)

The setting out of such stones needs a master in solid geometry and was done full size on a tracing floor making templates for each stone. Note that stones A, B and C are bonded integrally into the outer wall

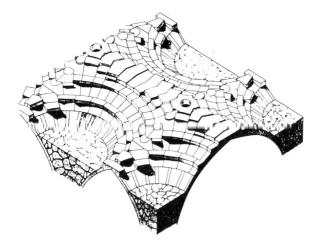

Figure 3.8   A Gothic vault from above
(After Viollet le Duc)
Note:
(1)   *the form is curved in two directions, so giving great stiffness*
(2)   *the heavy stones at the apex of the arches and in particular the central boss which key the structure together*
(3)   *the filling above the tas de charge*
(4)   *often the vault is thickened by a covering of mortar or bricks and mortar*

Some outstanding recent examples include the 'small' and 'large' sports palaces built by Nervi for the Rome Olympic Games of 1960. Of reinforced concrete precast voussoir construction, these domes are built to such fine limits that regular and careful maintenance will be the best way to ensure their preservation. Torroja with his Market Hall in Algeciras, Spain, Saarinen, Ammann and Whitney with the TWA terminal in New York and Utzon and Arup with the Sydney Opera House have also made a great contribution to the twentieth century art of covering large areas with the minimum of support.

Like arches and vaults, the dome depends upon the firmness of its supports, so causes of distress must be looked for there. The dome itself suffers from two

Figure 3.9   North choir aisle vault, York Minster, England

A general view of the vault adjacent to the north-east pier of the central tower. Severe defects, resulting from the settlement of the tower, can be seen in the ribs and panels

Figure 3.10   North nave aisle vault, York Minster, England
(Courtesy: Shepherd Building Group Ltd)

*Cosmetic repairs at intervals by generations of masons without
professional supervision had obscured vital evidence. The failure to
diagnose or record continuing settlements led to this critical
situation*

major causes of stress—first, tension in the lower part
where the angle subtended at the centre is greater
than 51° 08′ from the vertical, resulting in circumferential cracking; secondly, due to thermal movement, as the shape of the dome and the rest of the
building are different, leading to radial cracks.

Mainstone's diagrammatic plans of the superstructure of St Sophia analyse the principal compression
thrusts and show radial tensile cracking and the
location of shear failure. These all contributed to the

spreading of the supports which, within about 20
years of its completion, accentuated by an earthquake,
led to the partial collapse of the rather shallow dome,
which was completely rebuilt to a greater height.
Brunelleschi's masterpiece, the Dome of Santa Maria
del Fiori, Florence, has ribs and coffers which lighten
the structure of the linked shells. Wren's solution for
St Paul's in London relied upon an inner dome and a
cone which supports the cupola, together with a timber structure to form the outer dome.

Figure 3.11   North nave aisle vault, York Minster, England (Courtesy: Shepherd Building Group Ltd)

Recent cracking in the vault was caused by settlement of the north-west pier of the central tower. However, most of the cracks had been mortared over previously without diagnosis of their cause

Figure 3.12   Vault over choir of Naples Cathedral, Italy (Courtesy: R. di Stephano)

After wartime bomb damage, the roofs had to be reconstructed. An elegant arched ribbed dome in welded steel was devised to support the metal deck on which the roof tiles rest

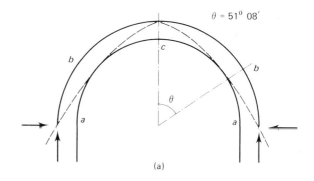

(a)

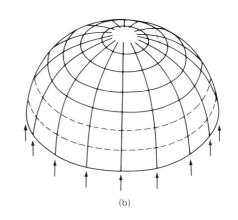

(b)

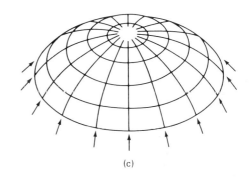

(c)

Repair of domes

Because domes may crack radially, repairs and strengthening have generally consisted of inserting chains to act in tension. For the 1925–31 restoration at St Paul's, the two drums of the dome were linked together with forty-eight 100 mm (4 in) diameter diagonal rods in tension and ninety-three 63 mm (2.5 in) diameter tie rods. Two additional steel chains were inserted to encircle the base of the drum, being respectively 132 m (433 ft) and 180 m (591 ft) long and weighing a total of 58.5 t (57.5 ton). The four quarter-domes had 100 mm (4 in) diameter ties and the eight piers were each reinforced with 36 mm × 30 mm (1.4 in × 1.2 in) oval deformed rods and had 91.5 t (90 ton) of Portland cement grout injected. In this way the structure was united and the cause of differential loading on the foundation removed.

Catenaries

Although these structures scarcely come within the scope of this book, a few random remarks may be of interest. The tensioned curve of a primitive nomad's tent was, of course, the prototype of the curved membrane structure. But this form had scarcely developed beyond the large circus tent until the mid-twentieth century when fabrics with high tensile strength were evolved from man-made fibres. In the USA, the saddle-shaped roof of the Raleigh arena with a span of 100 m (328 ft) by Norwikci and Severad, the Saarinen and Severad hockey rink at Yale University and the Dulles Airport building by Saarinen, Ammann and Whitney are all examples of reinforced concrete carried on suspension cables. Again, meticulous maintenance procedures are the key to their preservation.

Catenaries were developed in China from woven bamboo cables. The very early iron tie rod suspension bridges are also a type of catenary, the most notable being in Yunann which dates from A.D. 65 and has a span of 75 m (246 ft). All suspension bridges require continuous care and maintenance to ensure their stability, as the failure of one cable can cause disaster. Indeed, a long suspension bridge needs as much maintenance as a large cathedral. In some cases, suspension cables have had to be welded in places where weaknesses have developed.

In 1940, the collapse in the USA of the Tacoma Narrows suspension bridge, having a span of 850 m (2789 ft), led to a painstaking scientific inquiry into the causes of the failure, which was found to be due to vibration caused by high winds. Freeman Fox's Forth, Severn and Humber suspension bridges in England reflect developments to make the deck stiffer in order to increase resistance to such dynamic loading.

Figure 3.13 Spherical domes
(Courtesy: Allen Lane and Penguin Books)

(a) *Geometry of a hemispherical dome. Early domes were thick because the action of tension in the lower part ab below $\theta°$ was not fully appreciated. Tension rings were inserted in the lower parts*
(b) *The isostatic diagram shows the zone where tension occurs*
(c) *In flat domes with no part below $\theta°$ no tension occurs, but much greater thrusts are imposed on the abutments*

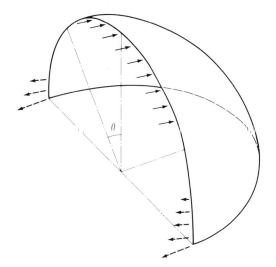

Figure 3.14 Actions of hemidomes

A half-dome may be considered exerting compressive pressure in the upper part and tension in the lower part when an element in the whole structure

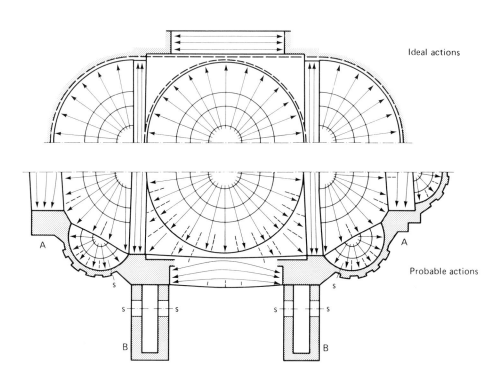

Ideal actions

Probable actions

Figure 3.15 St Sophia, Istanbul, Turkey: part plans of the superstructure
(Courtesy: Allen Lane and Penguin Books, and R.J. Mainstone)

Above—the dome and semidomes and main north arch shown with their outward thrusting actions contained, ideally, by cramped string-courses at the springing levels acting as continuous ties. Below— the probable actual behaviour with associated tensile cracking, shear failures and major deformations. Light continuous lines show the directions of the principal compressions (thrusts), heavy broken lines indicate ties, light broken lines indicate tensile cracking, and s—s denotes the approximate location of a shear failure. For simplicity, no account is taken of the window openings in the dome and semidomes, and the exedrae semidomes are omitted from the upper drawing, but the representation of the probable actual behaviour does take into account the progressive nature of the deformations as construction proceeded

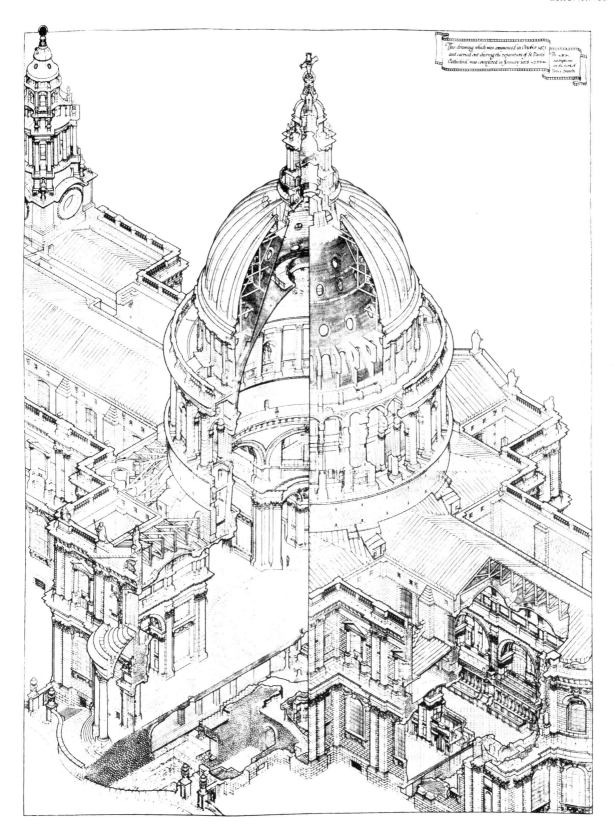

Figure 3.16   Isometric projection of St Paul's Cathedral, London, England
(Courtesy: The Dean and Chapter of St Paul's and Feilden and Mawson)

The double dome resolves internal and external aesthetic problems. The cone supports the 813 t (800 ton) cupola, the cross of which is 112 m (365 ft) above ground. Tensile thrusts are resisted by some five chains as well as the pillared buttressing round the drum. Two more chains of stainless steel were added in 1925

4

Structural elements II: Trusses and frames

Because trusses and frames require tensile strength for their function, masonry is excluded from this section which focuses on timber construction and its repair.

Development

What is reputed to be the oldest surviving timber roof truss, found in the church of St Catherine on Mount Sinai, dates from the sixth century. It is probable that the early Roman basilicas, such as St Peter's and St Paul's Outside the Walls, had trussed roofs of timber. The Pantheon anticipated structural development by some seventeen centuries by having a metal truss of bronze; unfortunately, it was melted down.

In Japan a timber pagoda at Nara, dated A.D. 670, is the oldest complete timber building in the world. The same city has a Buddhist temple, the Toruji, that is the largest in the world, which is a rebuild of an even bigger eighth century design. Both are framed structures using the tensile strength in timber in order to cantilever the wide roof overhangings that are characteristic of oriental architecture.

Early mediaeval roofs consisted of couples of rafters pinned together at the apex and having a short collar about one-third of the way down. These rafters were covered with longitudinal battens to which the roof covering was fixed. This type of construction gave no resistance either to the lateral spread of the rafters, subjected to bending movements and deformation, or to longitudinal tilting. Stability depended on three joints, one at the apex and two at the ends of the collar, so failure of any one of them tended to allow the foot of the rafter to push off the wall plate or move outwards on the supporting wall. It also induced considerable thrust outwards on this supporting wall.

In late mediaeval times the roof came to be built using principal rafters with purlins supporting common rafters. There might be two or even three purlins in each roof pitch. The principal might have arch-braced wall posts together with a collar which might also follow the curve of an arch with its soffit. Above the centre of the collar a king post might be inserted and often this king post was linked with arch bracing in the longitudinal direction. In addition, further arched wind bracing might be introduced into the panels formed by the principals and purlins in the same plane as the roof and rafters. This type of framed roof construction was extremely elegant and economical, and a fine example may be seen in St Clement's Church in Norwich, England.

Palladio's sixteenth century bridge over the river Cisman near Barrano, Italy, was an important achievement in truss design. Wren's truss for the Sheldonian Theatre, Oxford, was also a noteworthy example of the seventeenth century, and from the eighteenth century we have examples of scientific trusses such as at St Paul's and St Martin-in-the-Fields, London.

The American timber trusses and bridges from the first half of the nineteenth century, using magnificent timber from the white pine, made a contribution to the development of this form. Because of shortage of timber in Europe, wrought iron and steel replaced timber for large-span roof construction in the nineteenth century, early examples in England being Euston Station, London, in 1837, and Liverpool's Lime Street Station, in 1849, with a span of 46 m (151 ft). In London, in 1875, Liverpool Street Station by Fairburn and Hodgkinson is significant in that the principle of continuity is introduced into a multi-span steel-framed structure with arched trusses of graceful design, resting on tall cast-iron columns. This development led to portal frames that have truly rigid joints which are capable of execution by welded

51

construction in steel or glued construction in wood. Mies Van der Rohe's Crown Hall, built in 1956 at the Illinois Institute of Technology, with its clean detailing in welded steel, is likely to become an historic building.

Space frames—three-dimensional trusses with rigid joints—are a more recent development based upon sophisticated structural analysis and welding techniques.

Analysis and assessment

The development of effective triangulation in timber trusses was hampered by difficulties in jointing, as the joints themselves are generally the points where trusses fail. Wood used for trusses creeps as a result of the tensile stresses imposed by the structure and movements caused by variations of humidity. When subjected to bending stresses the longitudinal fibres may be stretched by tension and squashed by compression; if this process occurs repeatedly, the wood may deteriorate in a manner similar to fatigue in metal. Where subject to tension the timber may lengthen, and splits and clefts formed during seasoning may widen. Likewise, metal nails may loosen their hold and as time goes on the wood fibres contract and leave a void into which atmospheric damp penetrates and condensation occurs, causing corrosion of the nails. The English mediaeval practice of using wooden treenails and dowels avoided this possibility; when metal nails were used, the holes were frequently charred before driving the nails so as to reduce the corrosive effect of the acids in the wood upon the iron. Putting varnish or grease into screw holes, as is done in boatbuilding, is the best practice.

The shrinkage and compression of timber also leads to the loosening of wooden structural joints; the resulting play between them, due to movements induced by wind, may quickly cause the whole structure to become dangerous, especially with extra loadings caused by snow. Because joints offer ledges and cracks where beetles can lay their eggs, these vulnerable points are often attacked first and most intensively. Joints are also vulnerable as they trap water or condensation, thus starting the rot/beetle attack sequence. Pine buildings in Norway and Sweden, with ventilated joints designed to be self-draining so as to minimize this source of trouble, have proved to be remarkably durable.

Joints may fail in tension (e.g. tenons may pull out or dowel pins fail) or may fail owing to distortion of the structure and to having to withstand forces never envisaged by the designers. Failure in a joint may set up a chain reaction. Typical of this is the scissors-type truss, the thrust from the ends of which can force a

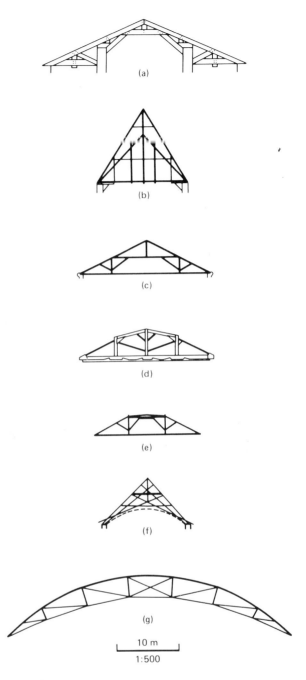

Figure 4.1   Roof trusses from the second to the nineteenth century
(After R.J. Mainstone)

(a) *Pantheon, Rome, Italy—second century*
(b) *Notre Dame, Paris—thirteenth century*
(c) *Theatro Olympico, Vicenza, Italy—sixteenth century*
(d) *Sheldonian Theatre, Oxford, England—seventeenth century*
(e) *Royal Hospital, Greenwich, England—eighteenth century*
(f) *Church at Steinbach, Federal German Republic—eighteenth century*
(g) *Lime Street Station, Liverpool, England—mid-nineteenth century*

Figure 4.2   Baguley Hall, Manchester, England
(Courtesy: W.J. Smith ATD, and DoE Ancient Monuments Dept)

The hall is an exceptional thirteenth century timber-framed structure of the greatest archaeological value. The joints in the framing were attacked by rot and insects so that it had to be held together by ties, several of whose anchorages show. In addition, the slate roof was in poor repair. Attempts were made to repair the timber in situ, but this was found to be impossible. It was decided to take the framing down, repair the joints and reconstruct the frames and roof

Figure 4.3   Baguley Hall, Manchester, England
(Courtesy: W.J. Smith ATD, and DoE Ancient Monuments Dept)

The thirteenth century interior 'screen wall' frame seems remarkably solid, yet behind this facade it has been ravaged by deathwatch beetle attack and the integrity of the structure is imperilled

Figure 4.4   Baguley Hall, Manchester, England

Roof timber repairs. A roof rafter having the minimum amount of new oak inserted in order to make good a tenon joint. Dismantling is necessary for this work, but by restoring the joints the structural integrity of the building is maintained

masonry wall outwards; this movement may be further aggravated by leaking gutters, leading to dry rot and beetle attack in the rafter ends which in turn allows further movement that breaks the joints higher up the truss.

The most common causes of failure in roof carpentry construction are poor structural design, poor quality or lightweight timbers, alterations made after the initial construction such as cutting through tie beams, loss of strength owing to aging of timber, breaking of joints, sagging and spread due to rotting of ends of beams, rafters and wall plates or movement of supporting masonry. Purlin joints are often found to be fractured.

To repair a timber-framed structure, first the structural system must be studied, for example to determine whether it is the early box-framed type of construction (possibly with jetties and exposed timbers) or the later balloon framing with hardwood or softwood studs. Posts, girders, summers, principal rafters and braces should all be traced and the timbers inspected to ensure that they are intact and the joints secure.

When the original frame has been discovered, it should be surveyed and drawn in every detail. Often it is necessary to strip out parts of the building in order to do this: wallpaper, plaster, brickwork, inserted floors, ceilings, partitions and fireplaces may have to be removed with caution, for what at first might

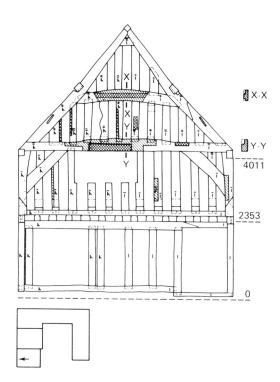

Figure 4.5   Chester House, Knowle, Warwickshire, England
(Courtesy: *Architects' Journal* and F.W. Charles)

Drawing to be read in conjunction with the timber repair schedule for Truss 1, opposite (Architect: F.W. Charles)

Timber repair schedule—Truss 1 (see Figure 4.5)
Dimensions are given gross, allowing for tenons and cutting to waste after checking dimensions on job. Mortices in members are not generally noted—refer to drawings. New timber only is given

Member		Description
Threshold	I	5 ft 6 in × 8 in × 3 in tenoned one end, morticed other
Sill beam	I-K	15 ft 0 in × 8 in × 8 in tenoned both ends
Main post	I	7 ft 6 in × 8 in × 13 in rebated top, 2 tenons, bottom tenon
Door post	I	7 ft 0 in × 8 in × 8 in tenoned both ends
Stud	I	6 ft 0 in × 9 in × 4 in tenoned both ends
Stud	I	6 ft 0 in × 9 in × 4 in tenoned both ends
Stud	K	6 ft 0 in × 8 in × 4 in tenoned both ends
Stud	K	6 ft 0 in × 8 in × 4 in tenoned both ends
Main post	K	7 ft 0 in × 8 in × 13 in as main post
Plate	I-K	Renew end 4 ft 6 in × 6 in × 6 in scarfed, morticed to post
Bressummer	Ī-K̄	19 ft 6 in × 6 in × 7 in tenoned both ends
Main post	Ī	Renew end 2 ft 6 in × 10 in × 6½ in scissor scarf, tenoned, patch 2 ft 6 in × 5 in × 3 in
Brace	Ī	as existing
Brace stud	Ī	Renew end 1 ft 9 in × 9 in × 3½ in tenoned
Brace (upper)	Ī	as existing
Brace stud	Ī	Renew end 1 ft 9 in × 9 in × 3½ in tenoned
Stud	Ī	Renew end 1 ft 9 in × 10 in × 3½ in tenoned
Stud	Ī	Renew end 1 ft 6 in × 9 in × 3½ in tenoned, patch 2 ft 3 in × 5 in × 3½ in
Stud	Ī	Renew end 1 ft 6 in × 9 in × 3½ in tenoned
Short stud	Ī	3 ft 0 in × 9 in × 3½ in tenoned
Short stud	K̄	Renew end 1 ft 6 in × 7 in × 3½ in tenoned
Short stud	K̄	Renew end 1 ft 6 in × 9 in × 3½ in tenoned
Stud	K̄	6 ft 6 in × 10 in × 3½ in tenoned both ends
Brace stud	K̄	Renew end 1 ft 6 in × 8 in × 3½ in tenoned, patch 3 ft 3 in × 2 in × 2 in
Brace stud	K̄	Renew end 1 ft 6 in × 8½ in × 3½ in tenoned
Brace (upper)	K̄	as existing
Brace	K̄	as existing
Main post	K̄	Renew end 2 ft 6 in × 10 in × 6½ in scissor scarf, tenoned
Tie-beam	Ī̄-K̄̄	Patch 9 ft 6 in × 1 ft 3 in × 7 in—see drawing, patch 1 ft 6 in × 5 in × 7 in
Principal rafter	Ī̄	Renew end 5 ft 6 in × 12 in × 6 in scarf, tenoned. Purlin blocked
Collar beam	Ī̄-ĪK̄̄	Patch 5 ft 9 in × 15 in × 4½ in
Struts— below collar		All as existing but allow for replacement of 50% tenons and: 1 new end 12 in × 8 in × 3½ in tenoned patches 1 ft 6 in × 5 in × 3½ in 2 ft 9 in × 3 in × 3½ in 2 ft 9 in × 3 in × 3½ in 2 ft 3 in × 3 in × 3½ in
Struts— above collar		3 ft 0 in × 10 in × 3½ in tenoned both ends, rest as existing
Yoke	Ī̄	as existing
Principal rafter	K̄̄	as existing

appear to be rubbish can be some unexpected original feature. The inspection may show severed tie beams, decay caused by leaking roofs and pipes, and fractured floors and walls without proper means of support except loose bricks or plaster lath. Shakes in old timber may not matter, but where there are large knots one may find indications of incipient breaking which must be repaired. Large shakes are often found in old oak beams. Inspection must decide whether these materially weaken the timber. These shakes can offer the female deathwatch beetle a convenient crevice in which to lay her eggs; they also allow moisture to penetrate and reach the heart of the wood. It used to be the custom to fill these shakes with putty mixed with hair, but such a filling has little ability to expand and contract with seasonal movement of the timber, and caulking with tar and hemp as is done on ships' decks has been suggested. The use of artificial rubber sealing compounds would appear to be more satisfactory, as these are adhesive yet flexible, although their colour may be a problem. Large shakes can also be filled with pieces of matching timber cut to shape and slipped into position and then 'gunned' with sealing compound.

F.W.B. Charles writes:

'The replacement of original members by new timber is clearly an even more exacting task than framing the original building. Not only must the dimensions be dead accurate but the new components must be inserted into an existing frame instead of assembled in a logical sequence of operations followed in the original construction which would allow slight adjustments to be made and the timbers fitted afterwards. The problem of shaped or curved timbers is even more difficult. In the original building the profile for instance of a carved brace determined the exact location of mortices cut into the receiving members. In a replacement the member must not only fit the mortices, but its form must be as grown, that is, in accordance with the natural grain rather than shaped by tools. It may also have to match a corresponding member which survives in the original structure. Since no two branches of a tree are ever exactly alike, this difficulty can be insuperable.

'In restoration work, compromise is often inevitable. Jointing new timber on to old where, say, an end of a beam has decayed, combines these problems with the additional one of forming an exact and secure joint. This calls for an entire vocabulary of joints for a purpose seldom met in the original construction. Yet the designs of these joints have all been acquired from actual examples. Even the most sophisticated scissor scarf joint indispensable in replacing main posts, was found in a Middle

Littleton tithe barn dated *circa* 1250. The difference between repair joints and construction joints is that modern powerful adhesives can now be used for the former to ensure the repaired member is as strong as the original. In construction joints the use of adhesives would of course defeat the object of timber framing in permitting the slight movement necessary to prevent fracture.

'The behaviour of new oak depends largely on its method of conversion. Boxed heart and cleft timbers are less liable to shake or warp than sawn timber. Cleaving is also the means of avoiding knots, at any rate on the important upper face or exposed surface. It seems that new timber converted in the traditional way will not suffer ill effects either when used as new components inserted into the existing framework or when jointed as a repair to an old timber.

'Conversion by bandsaw is a different matter. When the timber is wholly dry, shakes appear, and while there is no reason to believe they affect impermeability or stability, their ultimate extent and depth is unforeseeable. Knots produce radial shakes and become loose. Lastly, the timber contracts and warps to an appreciably greater extent than traditionally converted timber.

'It is best to accept the distortions of age as part of the maturity of the timber structure, for the distortion itself is not necessarily a sign of weakness. As an alternative to the repair of a broken joint, its strength can be restored by strapping with metal. Dowels like stirrups in a reinforced concrete beam can also be inserted so as to strengthen *in situ* cracked beams against shear. No artificial strains should be put on the timber work in an attempt to force it to do otherwise than it wishes. As warping stresses are very severe, once a frame has been taken apart by knocking out the pins and pulling the joints apart, it is by no means certain that it will go together again. Exposed timber members which have suffered from rot can be repaired by scarfing, and joints can be strapped or pinned and bolted using fish plates to transmit tension. If the feet of posts or crucks have rotted, these can be repaired by bolting on stone or concrete feet, but no attempt should be made to jack up or straighten the old timber structure. When fixing unseasoned new oak, it should be remembered that the tannic acid therein can destroy steel nails. Bronze fixings should be used if possible, or else galvanized steel.'

The repair of timber-framed structures can be attempted by *in situ* scarfing, but this is often clumsy and unacceptable. The structure can be consolidated as it is, by using fibreglass reinforcing rods and epoxy

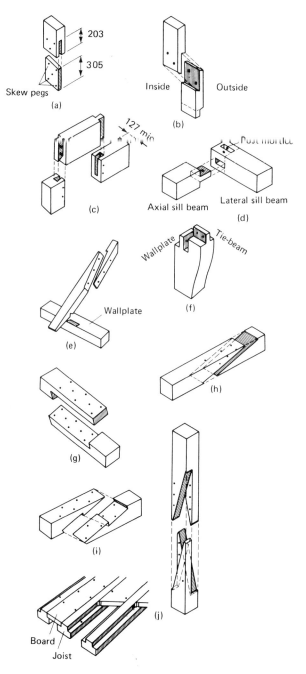

Figure 4.6 Chester House, Knowle, Warwickshire, England (Courtesy: *Architects' Journal* and F.W. Charles)

Timber carpentry joint details used by the architect in repair work:

(a) *Slip or fish tenon for studs, rods, etc.*
(b) *Repair joint for studs only*
(c) *Dovetailed tenon inset for collar or tie-beam*
(d) *Sill beam joint*
(e) *Face-splayed scarf for rafters*
(f) *Post head—wallplate and tie-beam joint*
(g) *Edge-halved scarf—vertical, horizontal or inclined member, minimum length: depth × 3*
(h) *Scarf for repairing horizontal members, minimum length: depth × 2*
(i) *Tabled scarf—beams and joists with both end fixed skew-pegged, minimum length: depth × 2.5*
(j) *Scissor scarf for repairing posts, minimum length: depth × 2.5*

Figure 4.7 Gable of house in Weimar, German Democratic Republic

Timber framing and various types of infill including brick and wattle and daub used in a typical mediaeval house

Figure 4.8 Three houses, Christianshaven, Copenhagen, Denmark
(Courtesy: Architects W. Wohlert and H. Laugberg and J. Fredstund)

Although condemned in 1960, these mid-eighteenth century timber-framed houses were economically conserved in 1975. Roofs had to be reconstructed and windows to a great extent renewed, and external plaster had to be removed and renewed

Figure 4.9 One of the three houses at Christianshaven, Copenhagen, Denmark
(Courtesy: Architects W. Wohlert and H. Laugberg and J. Fredstund)

Detail of timber framing and windows before conservation

Figure 4.10   The three houses at Christianshaven, Copenhagen, Denmark, after conservation
(Courtesy: Architects W. Wohlert and H. Laugberg and J. Fredstund)

After conservation, careful studies were made of the external colours

resins, but such work is chancy, messy and not necessarily fire resistant—and also ignores the original structural design whose integrity should be preserved. It is therefore generally necessary to dismantle a timber-framed building section by section, recording every action archaeologically; then each joint can be reconstituted with the minimum use of new material and reassembled according to the original design, but with no attempt to eliminate distortions caused by time. Dismantling and reassembling is practised in Japan, but distortions are eliminated, since the character of Japanese architecture, with its walls all of light sliding screens, demands regularity if they are to function. Inevitably there is some loss of material in the infill panels but the integrity of the design and function of the timber frame is conserved.

The repair of timber frames has two further aspects—first, rot at or near ground level due to rising damp and rain splash, and secondly, open joints and attack by wood-boring beetle throughout the frame. To avoid damp penetration into the timbers, the tenons on the posts should be cut to face upwards where possible and holes in the upper surface of horizontal members should be avoided or the joints should be designed to drain; rot and beetle attack generally starts as a result of moisture standing in these undrained joints. If the filling masonry is loose and the external plaster has been taken off, new sills may be inserted and posts can be repaired by splicing. Joints may be pulled together by irons; old oak dowels or treenails can be drilled out and renewed, and faulty timbers can be replaced using scarfed joints. Lastly, all sapwood and areas affected by beetle attack should be cut back and a durable preservative applied after any gluing.

5

Structural elements III: Walls, piers and columns

Walls, piers and columns all form part of the same system of enclosure of space and support of the roof. Stone and brick masonry are considered together as they are so similar, but mud brick has special problems of its own, so is studied in a separate section. Timber walls must not be forgotten, but here the problems are not so much structural as the decay of the material itself, which will be dealt with in the chapters on causes of decay, in Part II of the book.

Walls—different types of mass construction

Each geographical region and period in history has had its own characteristic way of building walls. Therefore, each type of wall has different preservation and repair problems dependent upon its construction and the strength of the primary and secondary materials; for example, unbaked brick laid in mud mortar, unbonded stone blocks, closely fitted polygonal masonry laid dry and random rubble in lime mortar will age differently from, say, bonded masonry laid in mortar or Roman mass concrete walls.

Ruins can often be informative about the nature of structural systems, as the collapse pattern of a wall may show how it ultimately failed and thus how a similar type of wall should be reconstituted and strengthened.

Figure 5.1 Split facing stone, St Paul's Cathedral, London, England
(Courtesy: Feilden & Mawson)

A detail of split facing stone on the west front of the cathedral (ground level). When under great pressure sedimentary stone will laminate if it is laid incorrectly, as in this case where the bed is parallel to the face

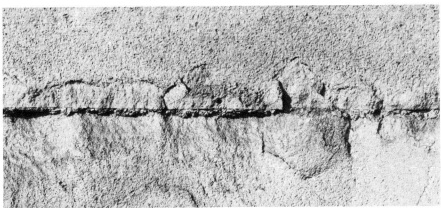

Figure 5.2 Spalled facing stone, St Paul's Cathedral, London, England
(Courtesy: Feilden & Mawson)

To get a very thin joint at the outer face, the ashlar from St Paul's was worked with a hollow bed. Unfortunately the mortar has not always set properly in the middle of the thick walls, and with compressive settlements excessive loads are thrown on the outer edge, causing spalling like this along the joint line

Most stone-faced mediaeval and Renaissance walls are filled with random stone rubble set in a mass of mortar between the two outer faces of stone ashlar or plaster. They were raised one course at a time and then filled with a sort of mass concrete. Such walls may appear to be more or less homogeneous but should the casing be defective the core will erode easily and may lead to runaway failure. For strength and durability they depend much upon the quality of the mortar which represents at least 30% of the volume.

To preserve the wall, its core must be protected against internal erosion by penetrating rain which can, over centuries, wash out large internal voids; hence the primary importance of pointing masonry joints for preventive maintenance. Then there is also another danger, for when lime is used in thick walls the lime may not carbonate and set properly in the centre of the wall.

Many thousands of town buildings, particularly in Europe, were built of ordinary masonry in a rough, almost careless way with the walls coated with plaster. The solidity of such structures depends much upon the binding capacity of lime mortar and the frequent use of wood and iron bands or chains to provide tensile strength. Dry rot and decay from beetle attack of these embedded timbers is a typical fault of such construction, except perhaps in drier continental situations such as central Europe or Spain, where buildings are still constructed this way.

The load-bearing wall is probably the commonest type of building construction element. Load-bearing walls of masonry were used in buildings ranging from the Palace of Versailles to the country villa or farmhouse, including churches and castles, mosques and monasteries. Such buildings may suffer damage because of thrust from defective roofs, but overall damage is more likely to result from defects in foundations and thermal stresses (the larger the building, the more vulnerable it is). Defects due to disintegration of walls when the binding material of lime or cement deteriorates, and defects due to moisture, decay and aging or rotting of wood reinforcements, are also inherent in this form of construction.

The importance of soft thick mortar joints in allowing small movements to take place without consequential damage may not be fully appreciated. It has been observed that many masonry structures can settle up to 100 mm (4 in) or more, depending upon the quality of the mortar and the thickness of the joints, without showing the movement by cracking, for the movement is absorbed by compression of the mortar. There may be a time lag of weeks or months between the actual movement and the showing of fresh cracks.

Thin mortar joints may cause cracking and spalling

of individual stones. This defect is very common in St Paul's Cathedral, London, where the joints are about 4 mm (0.2 in) in thickness on the face but wider behind; the effect is that when the wall is loaded and the lime mortar compresses, much greater stresses are thrown on to the face thus causing spalling. As thin mortar joints are surrounded by stone, the strength of the mortar is of less importance and the mortar is often overstressed, when it may break up into powder and tend to fall out of the joints.

Shear and tensile cracks are quite common in masonry walls, the former resulting most often from settlements and the latter from inherent design defects. Diagonal cracks indicate shear, generally resulting from unequal settlements. Local settlements may cause cracks soon after the building's erection, possibly due to faults in the ground such as an old tree, a midden or bog hole or well. Cracks may also be caused by the building having been initially put up over a 'pipe' (a hollow void) in chalk or in gravel subsoil or by a local patch of sand or other material under the foundations. In some cases, archaeological remains have contributed to the cracking pattern by giving the foundations unequal bearing capacities.

Compressive cracking consisting of close fine vertical cracks in an individual stone or brick is rare, as the walls and piers of most historic buildings are generally strong enough to resist this force. Sometimes, however, it occurs in the form of spalling along the outer edges of stones which have been bedded on too thin a mortar joint, or with a hollow bed, which throws all the weight on to the outside edges. Spalling may also occur when vertical lengths of stone— detached columns for example—are built alongside normal coursed masonry, because the compression of several mortar joints in the coursed masonry throws a greater loading on the long length of stone which has only one compressible joint. The fall of Beauvais Cathedral is attributed by Professor Heyman not to over-daring design but to slow shrinkage or compression in the mortar joints of the clerestory wall, which then caused the overstressing of the monolithic detached shafts whose failure in turn triggered off the whole collapse some 20 years after initial completion.

Walls faced with ashlar and filled with rubble become fissured in time and liable to damage from vibration. Also, if the joints in the external facing are fine and the blocks of stone are large there is a danger that the core will consolidate, leaving the skin to carry the loads in full with resulting pressure cracks, spalling and even bulging.

The low tensile resistance of masonry set in soft elastic lime mortar leads to a particular formation of cracks, as shown by records of structural movements in York Minster, indicating that it takes several months for movements and the readjustment of stresses in one part of a building to affect those in another. Due to the plastic nature of lime mortar, it would appear that tensile forces tend to concentrate slowly upon one course of stone which eventually cracks; then the mortar adjusts itself and the process is repeated and the next course above or below cracks. Thus a quite small horizontal tensile force can cause large cracks through a massive wall. For this reason masonry is suspect when it has to take any horizontal tensile force, unless all the stones are cramped together. The dead weight of the superimposed masonry generally cancels out any tendency for vertical tensile forces to occur from wind loading, except in light structures such as spires.

It has been said that the failure in timber systems is not so likely to be due to structural causes so much as to the decay of the material itself, particularly where it enters into or is close to the ground. This decay can lead to the failure of the masonry structural elements by causing new stresses to be imposed upon the remainder of the structure; for example, the rotting of embedded beams in foundations can cause cracking of the walls like any other defect in the foundations. The rotting of timber piles exposed to different conditions by the lowering of the water level is another example.

The effect of the decay of timber roofs on load-bearing walls below can be equally disastrous, particularly where the walls are pushed outwards. The rotting of one end of roof beams can cause multiple collapse, because the other end of the falling beam may lever sound masonry out of position. Likewise, if the walls themselves move because of foundation settlements, or for other reasons, they can have an equally adverse effect on the roof construction. In mixed structures, the wooden elements are liable to shrinkage in all dimensions and also are vulnerable to decay from fungi and insects. As has been said, the joints of the wooden elements are the weakest parts and if these fail there is a danger of thrusts developing on the walls, which they were not designed to resist.

The investigation of defects in walls and their appropriate repairs are topics dealt with after the next section, as are the particular problems associated with mud walls.

Piers and columns

Worn joints in masonry are caused by weathering, aging, vibration or excessive stresses. Their presence can be determined by a test to see how easily water penetrates through the masonry and joints. As symptoms of defects in piers and columns, worn joints may be followed by the spalling or splitting of individual stones, disintegration of the mortar and slight displacements which may indicate excessive local pressure as well as the uneven bedding of stones or consolidation of the core. Cracked stones are the

Figure 5.3 Lead joint under column, St Paul's Cathedral, London, England
(Courtesy: Feilden & Mawson)

Over two centuries of steady pressure has squeezed out the lead from this joint, below a west portico column, like cream from a bun. The lead has saved the stone from being split by unequal pressures

63

result of such uneven bedding or torsion and shear resulting from settlement or even vibration. If a visual inspection shows good reason, then cores must be taken to investigate more fully the cause of decay.

Bulges in piers, often accompanied by fine vertical cracks, are very difficult to detect. They indicate overloading and weak masonry which is buckling and may well be dangerous, so shoring may be necessary before any further investigation is made. Before considering any repairs, the loadings on the columns or piers should be approximately calculated. Before repairs can be carried out on columns and piers, temporary work consisting of strapping and cradling and shoring is necessary. A very sophisticated system of cradling has been developed for the repair of the piers in Milan Cathedral, which enables individual stones to be cut out and replaced, or whole sections of the pier to be removed and replaced. The inventor did not reveal the details of this process, but it must have involved prestressing.

After water tests have been made, the next step is to grout the masonry in a pier in order to consolidate it. The masonry is wetted and cracks are washed out. This preliminary washing generally indicates the size of voids to be met and the grout mix can be adjusted accordingly. Grouting should be carried out in stages from the ground upwards. When very fine cracks are met in a pier, epoxy resin grout can be used, combined with stainless steel dowel pins.

The problem of all cutting out and replacement repairs is that when the stone is taken out it is under pressure and the distribution of forces is altered. When the new stone is put back it cannot usually be prestressed and therefore some local readjustment of the stressing is bound to occur before the new stone will carry its load. If the mortar joints are fairly wide this generally happens without difficulty, but if the mortar joints are narrow and the stone brittle, then further cracking may result from the repair.

Piers of composite construction or those built at different times always present special problems because later works are rarely found to have bonded satisfactorily with earlier work. Furthermore, work of different periods often leads to the formation of a vertical joint which can get filled with dust, thus setting up a wedging action if there is any vibration.

The repair of the main piers of St Paul's Cathedral, in London, is an interesting case study. Cracking was due to eccentric loading and differential settlements which this loading induced in the foundation. The foundations of the piers were suspected of being overloaded in 1913, but it was not until the cracking of the main piers that a commission was set up to control the great restoration work of 1925–32. The piers were strengthened by the insertion of about 91.5 t (90 ton) of cement grouting and laced together with 32 mm

(1.25 in) diameter oval bars of deformed 'staybright' stainless steel. Earlier wrought iron tie bars inserted by the architect Robert Mylne in 1750 were replaced by 16 large stainless steel rods. The remedy can be said to have succeeded when, after almost 50 years, further settlements have ceased. It is now assumed that the foundation loadings have equalized themselves. In this case, a symptom was corrected rather than the cause, but the structure helped cure itself, possibly at the expense of future possibilities of conservation.

Investigation of defects in walls

Cracks in wall elevations may be of three types. Those, over the point of settlement, sloping toward the centre of gravity indicate a failure of the centre of the wall, and those opening outwards towards the extremities indicate settlement at the ends of the wall. Causes for such cracks should be investigated in the foundations. A further type of crack is vertical and may be the result of weak material, shrinkage or thermal movements. Vertical cracks, wider at the top, can mean that a wall is moving outwards or rotating on eccentrically loaded foundations.

Cracks may also result from the phasing of building work and therefore it is highly desirable to know the construction sequence of a building so as to assess the date of a crack and whether it is active or static. Cracks and settlements due to initial defects generally occur within the first 20 years of the building's life.

Walls suffer from the same general defects as piers and columns, but are less vulnerable to eccentric loads in the plane of the wall as these can easily be distributed along its length. Open joints due to thermal movement, aging and vibration damage are the most common defects. Spalling of stone is comparatively rare, particularly if the bed joints are reasonably thick, as is most usual in ancient construction of ordinary buildings. Cracked stones are due to local pressures or bad construction such as inadequate bonding or the junction of works executed at different periods. Bulges due to weak masonry or overloading are difficult to detect, although not uncommon. They can indicate that a wall is near collapse.

Bulges may occur in weakly bonded masonry buildings, particularly if they have been refaced with a different material. For example, a clay lump building may be faced with brick or a brick building refaced with stone, and bulges may occur when the facing becomes separated from the core or backing, due to disintegration of the building material or long-term vibration. Such bulging may be caused by the cumulative effect of thermal movements which causes the facing to expand, creep or drift while the core remains more static. Ultimately, quite large bulges and cracks will form behind the facing. Bulges up to 100 mm (4 in) occurred in the Norwich Cathedral spire, which is a 115 mm (4.5 in) brick structure faced with 75 mm (3 in) stone. In this case the bulges were aggravated by the ratchet action prompted by wind vibration of dust and mortar which fell into the vertical cracks and wedged them open. Thermal action caused additional movement and the dust gradually fell further down, thus splitting the structure vertically.

Walls may have other defects besides cracks. One obvious flaw is an outward inclination; buttresses were often added to arrest such a movement, but unless they were prestressed or built on rock, they were generally of no value until the ground had been compressed and the wall had moved a good deal further.

In Norfolk, England, it was the practice in the thirteenth century to build walls with an internal batter, and the appearance of these walls can, at first sight, be alarming; however, inspection followed by taking accurate measurements and plumbing the out side face will usually allay this alarm. In exceptional circumstances walls which have leant outwards may be pushed back into position, if this does not mean altering the design of the building. If this course is taken, the cause of the previous movement must be cured or compensated for in the repair works, for instance by putting in a new foundation concentric with the actual loads.

To carry out this rather drastic realignment procedure, the wall is cradled on both sides in a framework of timbers that provides horizontal strength and rigidity (steel joists with timber packing may be used for greater strength). The vertical and horizontal timbers should be bolted together through openings in the masonry of the wall and diagonal braces are necessary to keep all in position. When ready, a suitable cut is made at the base—as in felling a tree—so that the wall will rotate into the correct new position with the whole wall in its cradling being pulled over by winches. The west front of Beverley Minster, England, was reported to have been repaired by this method in the eighteenth century. If it is in poor condition, the wall should be consolidated with grouting and reinforcement before such a drastic treatment. A similar sort of cradling may be used to protect a building against mining subsidence, as the object of the cradling is to make the wall into a single rigid unit.

When working properly, buttresses exert a horizontal resistance to a wall moving outwards, their effectiveness depending upon the extent of their projection and their own weight which acts vertically to deflect the resultant line of thrust.

Voids in stone walls

Although voids are often found in the walls of historic buildings, it is reasonable to assume that the walls were originally solidly constructed. These voids may have been formed by the mortar decaying and falling as dust downwards and outwards through cracks or faulty joints, or alternatively the decayed mortar may have been dissolved by acid-laden rain water and leached away, forming micro-caverns similar to the macro-caverns at Cheddar and the Gouffre de Padirac. Evidence of this process has been found in the Norwich Cathedral tower and observed in the southwest tower of St Paul's Cathedral and in the tower of York Minster.

The size of voids is unpredictable, but 0.1–0.3 m³ (4–11 ft³) is not uncommon and the total may well amount to 5% of the volume of the structure. The initial crack and the subsequent void are both significant in terms of structural analysis.

Whereas cracks and slipping can be detected by visual observation, suitable methods of detecting the size or location of voids are problematic. Ultrasonic methods may be successful in some cases. As for all wall defects, simply tapping with a hammer and listening to the note can be helpful. Voids of 75–100 mm (3–4 in) diameter can be found with atomic isotopes, using plant weighing three-quarters of a ton. Ultrasonic detectors are much handier but unfortunately do not appear to be able to distinguish between cracks and mortar joints and so have limited usefulness. Thus, so far there seems to be no simple, efficient method of detecting voids except by drilling 25 mm (1 in) holes and testing with water.

The condition of masonry can be investigated by using a diamond drill to take cores say 75–100 mm (3–4 in) in diameter at not less than 75 mm (3 in) from the surfaces and in the centre of the wall. These cores should be inspected carefully, as how well the sections hold together indicates the condition of the mortar and stone. After taking the core, a lamp and mirror on a stem can be pushed down the hole and large cracks and voids can be seen with the aid of this apparatus, as it is rotated.

Water can be passed into the core hole through a sparge pipe. By limiting the outflow of water to groups of holes in the pipe, some indication of the pattern of fissuring can be obtained. Such a water test is very useful in determining the general quality of the masonry and should be used before major grouting work is proposed, but caution is advised because with masonry in very poor condition such treatment might lead to an unfortunate collapse.

General repair of walls

Walls can be repaired by cutting out the defective parts piece by piece and so renewing the wall, but if it is in very poor condition it is advantageous to grout it first. Grouting work cannot be guaranteed; all it can do is to consolidate work temporarily by filling voids. Grouting cannot renew worn-out materials. Indeed there is a danger that grouting may accentuate defects by filling vertical cracks with a hard material that does not bond to either face.

When repairing a very thick wall, it is often possible by rebuilding a section to carry out the repair a half-thickness at a time, but care must be taken to ensure that the two halves of repair are properly bonded or tied together. If this procedure is used, the wall need not be completely supported by needling and shoring, although any opening will need temporary struts. If a large area of wall has to be rebuilt, the new work should be prestressed after the mortar has hardened sufficiently by using flat-jacks to ensure that the new wall carries its share of the total load. It is sometimes advantageous to build a relieving arch above an arch that has to be repaired. Walls may have to be cradled with steel and timber bolted tight together wherever the opportunity presents itself, so as to make a rigid entity prior to structural works.

To prevent the crushing of the masonry by scaffolding, packing pieces should be of hardwood, although there is a danger of damaging old walls from raking and flying shores if the wedging is too tight. If needling is necessary, seek out old putlog holes. One advantage of tubular steel scaffolding is that it does not need putlog holes, but can be fixed to the face of the wall using stainless steel ties drilled into the masonry at inconspicuous spots. After serving its purpose, all shoring must be removed with great care.

Re-pointing masonry

Portland cement pointing should never be used for stone, as it is too hard, too rigid and too strong, and being too impervious it promotes frost damage. The strength and porosity of the mortar for stonework should be related to the strength of the stone itself. For instance, for stone with a crushing strength of 55 500 kN/m² (8000 lbf/in²) a mortar with a crushing strength of about one-third of the stone is ideal. Although the use of stone dust is often advocated by practical masons, this may have dangers: first, the fines must be sieved out, as otherwise the surface of the pointing is too much like putty; secondly, in the case of some stones the remaining coarse particles may decompose in time and thus spoil the mortar. On the whole, therefore, this practice is not to be encouraged

and reliance should be placed on getting the colour and texture of the sand right and adjusting the whiteness of the mortar by using white Portland cement if necessary. A sharp crystalline sand with a little sparkle is desirable. The basic mix is 1 part of cementacious material to 3 of sand, but in exposed positions the mix may be 1 to 2 or 2½. Ideally, the cementacious material should be a warm-coloured hydraulic lime, but as such a material is practically impossible to obtain nowadays, a premixed coloured lime cement mortar may be used, with 3–9 parts of hydrated lime to 1 part of cement by volume. The aesthetic aim with stone work is generally different from that with brick or flint, as the pointing should be as close in colour and texture to the stone as possible and should in no way interfere with the appearance of the stone. With brickwork, the final colour and texture of the mortar is even more important as up to 30% or 40% of the area of the wall is affected. In time the colour and texture of the sand will dominate.

Buttressing

Repair by inserting buttresses is often ineffective, for they may pull away from the wall they are supposed to support or, if well bonded, even pull the wall with them. New buttresses should thus be designed to exert a positive horizontal thrust and be built on prestressed soil. Faults in old buttresses can be rectified by using needles and flat-jacks resting on enlarged foundations. Inflation of these flat-jacks will prestress the buttress together with the foundation and so apply a horizontal force to the wall.

The addition of buttresses, however, alters the appearance of an old building and should not be undertaken until all other methods have been considered and rejected. The well-known inverted arches which strengthen the piers of the central tower at Wells Cathedral are fine examples of technical skill, but such virtuosity would be unnecessary today with new techniques available that enable repairs to be carried out in an invisible way. Buttressing of walls can be carried out using concealed cranked reinforced concrete columns, with horizontal pressure applied by jacking the underground toe to prestress the virgin soil. Visible ties to hold the tops of walls together are undesirable, and in some cases unthinkable, but if the ties are above a vault and not visible, there can be no objection on visual grounds. Ties of this sort can be anchored to a reinforced concrete ring beam in order to restrict outward thrusts from a roof or outward creep in a wall.

As an alternative to buttressing, where the vault crown comes above the line of the wall plate, a possible solution is to use 'A' frames of reinforced concrete. This was done in the re-roofing of the Norwich Cathedral nave and transepts where the fifteenth century vault rises well above the low twelfth century clerestory walls. These frames replaced defective timber scissor trusses.

Repair of fractures

Vertical fractures in masonry walls are repaired by working up from the bottom to the top and bonding both sides together. In brickwork, bonders may be inserted across cracks, but as bricks are weak in tensile strength, indented stainless steel wire reinforcement in the thickness of the joint can give the required resistance. If wall thickness allows, narrow precast concrete bonding beams can be cut in and faced within the thickness of a brick or stone wall. An example where this was found necessary was in a sixteenth century brick building with large mullioned windows, whose window sills were being pressed upwards because the walls flanking the windows were settling more than the lightly loaded sills. Reinforced concrete beams were let in below the window sills to equalize the loading on the ground and allow walls including windows to settle as a whole. Cracks in brickwork or flintwork can be repaired by large dovetailed stitches of reinforced concrete up to 1.5 m (5 ft) long cut into the wall and used to hold the two sides of the crack together; the dovetails give sufficient anchorage in sound flintwork, while the shrinkage of the concrete is a form of pre-stressing that helps to close the crack.

Forming openings in walls

It is generally much more expensive to cut holes in stone walls than in brick, because of the size of the blocks and the greater difficulty of needling and shoring stonework with large irregular coursing. With stone masonry the outer skin should, if possible, be snapped off in say 80 mm (3 in) thickness by using feathers, i.e. steel wedges. The surface can then be reinstated exactly using the original facing stones when the works are completed. The difficulty of cutting holes for needles can be overcome if a diamond coring drill is available, as this machine can cut a neat circular hole of 150 mm (6 in) or 250 mm (10 in) diameter through most types of wall without damage or vibration. Then a steel joist can be inserted as a needle, and concreted into position. After the concrete has set, struts with hydraulic or screw jacks can take the load of the wall via the needles; then the opening can be formed. In this way stress redistribution and settlement by compression of the shoring are avoided and structural disturbance is minimized.

Openings in flintwork are difficult to form, for

Figure 5.4 Barn gable, Oxnead Hall, Norfolk, England

The gable was leaning outwards and the central pier had settled somewhat after a builder had formed two large garage doors

there is a danger of local collapse, i.e. a run if the mortar is weak or the material is badly bonded. Sometimes one meets clay lump walls with brick facing; forming openings in this construction needs extra care, as the bearing capacity of clay lump is very low.

In repair work, too much cutting out of stone, particularly if the stones are large, should not be undertaken as this may well shake the whole wall and cause damage which will only show in the fabric many years later. Tools usually used in cutting holes are the hammer, chisel, crowbar, Kango electric hammer, and compressed-air drills and augers with a variety of bits.

If new openings have to be formed in a wall during alteration work and the wall is thick enough, the execution of the work in two halves using twin beams or arches can be both kinder to the old fabric and more economical in cost, because needling and shoring may be unnecessary. An alternative method is to insert, in a row, precast concrete blocks with pre-formed holes for reinforcement wires. When all the blocks have been inserted one by one the reinforcement is pulled through the holes, post-tensioned with hydraulic jacks and then grouted into position. In this way a beam is put into the thickness of a wall without major structural redistribution of the forces and the wall below the beam can be cut away safely without needling and shoring. Care must always be taken when cutting openings into old walls to ensure that the end bearing of the beams is sufficient, and if this is not the case a reinforced frame should be inserted, surrounding the whole area being cut out. Where there is also a danger of adding a concentrated load to a poor soil, an advantage of this method is that, by forming a complete four-sided frame, the load is spread much as before without the risk of altering the existing below-ground bearing.

As has been said, new work rarely bonds perfectly to old, and therefore a mechanical key or the use of non-rusting metal dowels may be necessary. The old work should always be well wetted to encourage adhesion, for new mortar will not adhere to dry and dusty surfaces. Provided they are not subject to damp conditions, special resin-based bonding agents can be used to improve the adhesion of new to old. All old material that can be re-used should be set aside and cleaned.

Concrete fill for restoration work is improved by using crushed brick in the aggregate and, following the old practice, mortars may also have ground brick together with sand added to the mix. The final pinning up of new work in an opening needs great care, and is usually done by driving in two pieces of slate to act as wedges; then any voids should be grouted. A cement-based expanding grout can be used if it is kept back from the surface some 75 mm (3 in) and the joint pointed with a lime mortar. Flat-jacks inflated by hydraulic pressure are a sophisticated way of dealing with this problem.

Repair of rubble walls

Rubble is irregular random masonry with an undressed face. Before being grouted rubble walls should have their cavities washed out from top to bottom. Pointing should be carried out round each stone with a flush joint and then finished with a dry brush so as to bring out the sandy texture. The primary object of pointing is to keep storm water from running into the building, but it will also contain the grout which is inserted as described elsewhere. Rubble walls are weak at their angles and, to counter this, corners are often built of dressed freestone. Because this dressed stone might have been imported and thus was expensive, quoins are often of inadequate size or are poorly bonded and therefore come

away from the wall. In this case, they must be tied back to the rest of the rubble walling by drilling in ties or dowels of non-rusting metal such as stainless steel or delta bronze.

The charm and interest of rubble masonry lies in the ability of the observer to detect each individual stone, but the aim is not a rustic effect. In earlier centuries, rubble walls were generally limewashed* or covered with very thin lime-rich plaster which amounted to not much more than a skin of whitewash. Modern plaster technique raises a difficulty in that it obscures the contours of the stones and is often applied too thickly to be received by the projecting quoins. Old plaster techniques can be successfully imitated by using very fine clean sand washed at least six times in distilled water and a 1 : 1 lime mix.

Figure 5.5 Barn gable, Oxnead Hall, Norfolk, England

To stabilize the gable it was reinforced with stainless steel wire in the horizontal joints and then re-pointed. Stranded steel cable would have been better than the wire as the mortar has more bond or adhesion. Such cable is available from yacht chandlers in 2 mm, 2.5 mm, 3 mm, 4.5 mm and 6 mm diameters. The gable was tied back at the same time into the side walls of the barn. The expense of rebuilding was avoided by this simple expedient

---

* See Ashurst, Vol. 3 'Mortars, Plasters and Renders' pp. 44–48

Repair of ashlar walls

Ashlar walls generally consist of one or two faces of squared, finely fitted stones with the interspace filled in with odd pieces of random rubble mixed in mortar. When the mortar sets it loses its moisture and decreases in volume. The thickness of the mortar joints in the facework decreases very little in comparison with the decrease in the large amount of mortar in the core which can shrink considerably; thus the internal core may subside leaving the upper part of the structure carried on two relatively thin faces. In construction using lime mortar, much depends on the speed of building, because the rate of hardening of the lime mortar is slow and the height of the lifts is consequently limited. If the building proceeds too quickly, the outer faces are likely to be overstressed and to bow outward, thus tearing away from the weak core. Indeed, Braun states that nearly all cases of failure in ashlar walls are due to this separation of the core from the face, and the problem of conservation is how to tie it back.

Grouting would do nothing but fill the vertical crack between the face under stress and the inner core, and although it might help stabilize the ashlar during the repair work it is not an adequate method of restoring the unity between the core and the face. Two methods for this can be used. The first is by the provision of binders going right through the wall. These should be inserted where there are already broken or decayed stones which will have to be replaced or where there are old putlog holes which can be filled in. A second method is by deep tying back, using rustproof cramps with dovetailed or fishtailed ends. These can be cut into areas of sound rubble and bonded to the stone face. Alternatively, long dowels can be embedded in epoxy resin glue anchors.

Rebuilding masonry walls

When any part of a masonry building has to be taken down for re-erection, a system should be devised for marking each stone as it is removed. For simple cases a marked elevational photograph would suffice, but for a whole building, courses should be numbered from the foundations upwards and stones numbered from left to right on each elevation and all openings lettered, with each of the stones forming the dressed surround numbered in association with the key letter, the drawings being used as an index. This process is similar to that used for the prefabrication of stones for a new building in ashlar masonry.

Taking down a large area of rubble wall presents special difficulties as it is virtually impossible to employ a code. In this case a reference grid of smallish squares can be marked out in a removable paint on the face of the wall, as has been done at Machu Pichu in Peru. What must be aimed at is to record the character of the wall face by both black and white and coloured photographs and, if possible, a sample of the old work should be left to guide those concerned with reconstruction. When repairs in stone work have to be concealed, the facing stones should be snapped out as mentioned earlier.

Repair of window mullions and tracery in stone

Mullions and tracery can be repaired by halving and gluing sections on to existing masonry. Epoxy resin glues are especially made for this purpose. Cusps and finials can be refixed by using stainless steel or bronze dowels and glue. Because these sections are very exposed to weathering, they should only be repaired in a durable stone. For mullions, it is sometimes necessary to use end bedding in order to obtain the necessary long, thin sections. Repair should always ensure that the upper surfaces are properly weathered, and for this purpose a mixture of epoxy resin and stone dust is useful.

Substitutes for stone in repair

Reconstituted synthetic stone was formerly made with white or coloured Portland cement and ground stone dust, latterly with resin binding agents instead of Portland cement. Unfortunately, synthetic stone on a large scale looks like synthetic stone and often weathers poorly and too uniformly, with surface cracking and crazing. Its life is limited and in nearly every case that the writer has examined it has failed one way or another after some 30 years. It is inexpensive, however, and in limited applications—for small-scale dentistry, weathering of concealed surfaces and making casts of decaying sculpture—it has valid uses. The problems to be overcome are the amount of cutting back and dovetailing required, as in dentistry; the matching of colour and texture; and the question of porosity, which must be equal to or slightly greater than that of the original material. Some architects, however, have more faith in reconstituted stone than the writer. Optimistic supporters in some recent experiments in the German Democratic Republic and Switzerland say it is more durable than natural stone, and they claim to have solved the porosity problem. The material is moulded on to a rustless armature which is pinned securely to its base.

Natural stone, when laminated, can be repaired by

69

pinning and grouting with resin inserted by a hypodermic needle.

In treatment of damage to London's Westminster Hall after a terrorist's bomb, flaking stone was consolidated with fine glass fibre pins pushed into an epoxy resin mortar which had been injected by a mastic gun. The surface was protected by a latex coating, which was later peeled off, and the joints were finished with lime mortar, after which any cracks were filled with fine resin grout inserted through a hypodermic needle. Loose plaster can also be consolidated by similar resin injections.

Repair of flint walls

Walls of knapped flint over six centuries old look in perfect condition today because flint itself, being pure silica, is almost indestructible except by fire. The weakness of a flint wall lies in its mortar and in the bond between flint and mortar backing and between the face and backing.

If the mortar of a flint wall is too hard, capillary cracks occur; if too soft, the mortar ultimately decays because of all the rain the impermeable flint diverts on to it. Flint walls should be lightly tested with a 2 kg (4 lb) hammer to see if the flints are well bedded and also to detect any of the possible bulges which are a common defect due to the lack of internal bonding. When rebuilding flint walls it is difficult to keep a true face, and shutter boards may have to be used and work carried out in 300 mm (12 in) lifts. Bricks or stones may be used as cross-binders in flint walls, and this mixture of materials can be utilized to give attractive decorative effects.

To obtain good adhesion—for flint is a material with no suction—it is good practice to dip the back of the flint into a bucket of mixed lime cement grout before placing it in position. The mortar should be pressed into the joints before the initial set and the work brushed over. After the initial set the wall should be lightly sprayed with water to expose the aggregate in the mortar.

Repair of brickwork

The most common defect in brickwork is the aging and decay of the pointing; secondly, individual bricks may have failed owing to frost action; thirdly, one often finds vertical cracks, particularly through the arches of windows and the walling above and below sills, as well as diagonal cracks. As always, the cause of the defect must be rectified before cosmetic repairs are undertaken. Brick walls are often rendered and the rendering may be cracked owing either to sul-

phates in the brick itself or to structural or thermal movements. Cracked impervious rendering can collect and conduct large quantities of rain water into the brickwork, trapping it and preventing evaporation. Before removing rendering it is wise to ask the question why the wall was not rainproof or whether the bricks were disintegrating generally under frost action. Brick was often hacked and keyed before being rendered and so after removal of rendering the exposed surface may not be satisfactory. A small test should be made before committing oneself to a course of action. Lime plaster renderings can be removed quite easily, but some lime will be left in the pores of the brickwork and will add to the patina of its age. Roman cement can be removed in great slabs, whereas cement rendering will, when prized off, generally pull away the face of the brickwork and leave a new face in a totally unsatisfactory condition.

Vertical cracks can be repaired by cutting in new matching brickwork or, if the coursing is out of alignment, can be made good with pieces of matching roof tile. If greater strength is required, special small precast concrete beams of the same depth as one course of brickwork can be cut in behind the outer face of the brickwork. Alternatively, 2.5 mm (0.1 in) diameter stranded stainless steel cable can be embedded in the brickwork at a depth of about 40 mm (1.6 in). This is a very simple, economical and effective way of reinforcing brickwork and can, if necessary, be used round a whole building to tie it together.

It is very important that new bricks should match the old in colour and texture, and that the old form of bonding and jointing should be followed. Equally important is the colour of the mortar, as well as the profile and texture of the pointing. For re-pointing, brickwork should be raked out to a minimum depth of about 20 mm (0.8 in) and the pointing inserted with a special trowel. Normally each brick should show and be given a slightly recessed or hollow joint, brushed to give texture while the mortar is still green. Smudgy edges to pointings are undesirable. The effectiveness of a brick wall against rain penetration and its durability depend upon the condition of its pointing.

The colour and texture of pointing have a major effect on the appearance of a brick wall, for pointing may cover 30–40% of the area. If it is too light in colour it gives a recently re-pointed wall a garish and stark appearance. Darker colours of mortar bring out the colour of the bricks, but the colour must not be cold, as in the grey produced by Portland cement. Earth colours can be used to reduce the whiteness of some limes. If a natural darkish buff-coloured hydraulic lime can be obtained, this is the best. In the long run, however, the colour of pointing will depend upon the sand used, and in the short run the sand will decide the texture of the mortar, so choice of a well-graded sharp gritty sand is important. This is not the easiest sand to use, so bricklayers may object unless they are convinced as to the importance of using a rather coarse sand, which when sprayed and washed down after the initial set will show good texture. The profile of the joint will also greatly affect the appearance of the building. With old bricks having slightly eroded contours the mortar should be slightly recessed and given a slightly concave section, using the trowel handle or a radiused piece of wood. This should be offered up as a sample before finally specifying which should be done, as the factors of colour and texture and profile all interrelate.

It is worse than useless to try to cover up decayed bricks with coloured cement. If a face of a wall must be renewed, it is best to tie the new brickwork back to the old as in cavity wall construction and then possibly grout the gap between the new and the old in order to prevent water seepage and frost action.

Repair of rubbed brick arches

Few brickyards still produce the soft, sandy bricks known as rubbing bricks that may be found in arches. Rubbed brick arches can be salvaged in restoration work by sawing through the joints, after first removing the window frames. It will be found that a spoiled or damaged voussoir can often be turned round and the new face rubbed to match the old. A weakened rubbed brick arch can be made safe by using the brickwork as a permanent shuttering for a reinforced concrete lintel. The brick should be bonded to the concrete using stainless steel lugs and the lintel can be cast *in situ* incorporating the lugs or, alternatively, the lugs can be fitted into a dovetailed slot in a precast lintel while the arch is being rebuilt.

Repair of half-timbered work

Brick panels in half-timbered work were often laid diagonally or in chevron pattern to ensure a tight joint between the brick and timber. Moisture movements in the timber cause cracking between the frame and whatever filling material is used, and wind and rain find it easy to penetrate these cracks. For this reason, in the eighteenth century it became the fashion to plaster over half-timbered work. A.R. Powys writes: 'It is a mistake to assume that the plaster should be removed and the building should be restored to its older form.' He points out that the plaster probably covers previous alterations, particularly changes in window design. If brickwork has to be renewed, a weather check in the mortar joint is essential to combat shrinkage and wind penetration.

Figure 5.6 The Holy Shrine of Al Abbas, Kerbala, Iraq

The tiles have been stripped off and the parapet removed. Distress in the brick arch is due to two causes: first, pumping of ground water which is removing silt, especially from the corners; secondly, the thermal expansion of the new reinforced concrete porch which expands and contracts quite violently each day with the extremes of temperature. Unfortunately there is no expansion joint between the concrete porch and the wall, so the weak brick arch suffers

71

Fortunately, with plaster-faced walls major repairs, even rebuilding, can be carried out in aesthetic harmony because the whole surface is generally repainted. This is quite different from repairs to weathered and textured masonry, where any alterations are almost impossible to conceal.

Disadvantages of Portland cement in repairs to historic buildings

Portland cement, in its various specifications, is a magnificent material for modern structures which require its strength and quick-setting qualities. It is useful in reinforced concrete, with suitable aggregates, to strengthen and consolidate the structure of an historic building, under professional guidance.

On the other hand, Portland cement is not designed for use in mortars or plaster on historic buildings, which do not require its specific good qualities, but which suffer from its defects and side effects on traditional materials. Its disadvantages are as follows:

(1) Its use is not reversible. To remove it damages all historic building materials, which cannot then be recycled.

(2) It is too strong in compression, adhesion and tension, so that it is not compatible with the weak materials of historic buildings. It is a paradox that such weak materials have the greatest durability.

(3) Because of its high strength it lacks elasticity and plasticity when compared with lime mortar, thus throwing greater mechanical stresses on adjacent materials and hastening their decay.

(4) It is impermeable and has low porosity, so it traps vapour as well as water and prevents evaporation. Consequently it is no good for curing damp walls. In fact, the reverse is true, for if used it only drives moisture upwards. When used as mortar its impermeability accelerates frost damage and increases internal condensation.

(5) It shrinks on setting, leaving cracks for water to enter, and because it is impermeable such water has difficulty in getting out. Therefore, it increases defects caused by moisture.

(6) It produces soluble salts on setting which may dissolve and damage porous materials and valuable decoration.

(7) It has high thermal conductivity and may create cold bridges when used for injections to consolidate walls.

(8) Its colour is 'cold' grey and rather dark. The texture is too often smooth and 'steely'. These characteristics are generally judged aesthetically incompatible with traditional materials.

Portland cement should *not* be used for mortars or plasters in historic buildings, but as a last resort a small proportion of Portland cement, preferably white cement, although this costs more, should be added to the lime, but not more than 10% of the volume of the lime should be added without expert advice.

The traditional methods of burning and slaking lime are best, but have been lost in many countries. Traditionally, lime mortars in the mix of 1 part lime to 3 parts of coarse sand were used. The sharper and more varied in size of its particles, the better the sand. Its colour determines the ultimate colour of the mortar. Its texture can be improved by scraping with a small trowel.

In thick walls and to accelerate setting, some pozzuolanic material should be added. Some countries like Italy and Germany have natural pozzuolana; in others, it is possible to crush broken brick and tile to obtain this material, which is added as part of the sand proportion to improve the setting characteristics of lime.

Because it is modern, efficiently marketed by advertising and is readily available, and because it is indispensable to the modern building industry, many people think that Portland cement is ideal, but to sum up—unless it is correctly used, Portland cement mortar is the enemy of historic buildings.

Mud walls

Mud in brick form, clay lump or adobe, or rammed earth as cob or pisé or khesht, is probably one of the oldest and most-used building materials in the world and is of particular importance in Africa, China, India, the Mediterranean region, Middle East and South America. The oldest mud bricks are about 8000 B.C., from Jericho. In dry desert conditions in Peru there are examples that have stood over three millennia, yet in humid conditions, structures may only last a decade.

Mud brick is used in domestic buildings of up to three storeys height and for mosques. Ancient Egyptian palaces were built of it, as were the defensive walls of cities. Needham quotes Chinese walls of over 20 m (66 ft) in thickness. Such thick walls would resist artillery fire better than any other material due to their shock-absorbing capacity and small tendency to splinter. Mud brick forts still exist in Arabia and Africa.

The merit of mud construction, particularly in hot arid climates, is that it is comfortable due to its high thermal capacity and gives insulation, being cool by day and warm by night. Mud also has low capillary attraction. Low cost and ready availability of materials and the small amount of energy used in construction

Figure 5.7   Modern mud wall near Kerbala, Iraq
The destruction of the base by evaporation and salt crystallization shows clearly

Figure 5.8   Mud plaster wall, Mosul, Iraq
Mud plaster showing the amount of chaff used as bonder

are also advantages which may convince builders that this material should not be despised. Even so, the ancients knew full well that unless maintained regularly a mud building could not be expected to last long. However, the material of an obsolete or a decayed building is readily recycled into a new building and perhaps improved by conservation techniques.

Mud brick is made up of clay silt and sand, the sand content generally being increased by addition so as to reduce shrinkage and cracking upon drying. Mud mortar was often used but the bricks were also laid dry. Fibrous material such as chopped straw or reed, even animal hair, is added to the wet mix. Blood and other additives may be used to strengthen the mix and although bacteria are thought to destroy the cellulose of the fibrous materials, it has been proved that stronger bricks are made this way. It is thought that tannins, proteins, sugars or the products of their decomposition can stabilize mud bricks; certainly ancient recipes contain many suggestions of this nature. Ropes and mats of reed were often used to increase the tensile resistance and a surface protection was always added—in its simplest form this was a clay or claylime plaster, but in ancient Iraq a baked-brick or terracotta surface was sometimes used.

Building in mud brick is a social activity in which the whole community can be involved. The material is readily available, but false economics and unreal land values coupled with the belief that it is a backward material led to its unwarranted rejection.

Decay of mud brick

Rain plays havoc with unprotected mud brick structures, especially if it comes in short torrential storms which cause rapid erosion and deep furrows, for running water will quickly widen any cracks and may cause part of the structure to collapse. Structures with reed layers are far more resistant. Rain splash or puddles at the lower level also erode the base of the wall, particularly if water is allowed to collect and soften the mud brick.

Mud buildings will decay unless the walls are protected by good roofs with overhanging eaves and are built upon damp-proof foundations raised above the surrounding ground, and the surfaces maintained in good condition with an annual coat of mud lime plaster, being followed by coating of a more weather-resistant material such as limewash or tar, which can easily be renewed without affecting the wall structure.

73

Maintenance and repair of mud brick

The capping of the wall and provision of rainwater drainage to sufficient channels or soakaways are the first priorities for preventive maintenance. The maintenance of mud brick walls has to be at least an annual procedure to make sure that the roof is sound or that the capping has no cracks and that rain water drains away from the base with ample-sized drains to deal with sudden exceptional storms.

A mud brick wall, providing it is capped, decays by a surface weathering process; probably rain reorientates the clay plates parallel to the surface of partially dissolved bricks, so increasing their resistance. In Iraq in the spring, climatic changes between 1400 hours (2.00 p.m.) and after sunset can be as large as ± 75% RH and ± 25 °C, and in the early morning condensation must take place. The surface of the bricks thus undergoes a daily cycle of swelling and contraction which may result in fine superficial cracks and detachment of the weathered layer, but this is a slow process compared with the action of rain or groundwater.

The bottom 100–300 mm (4–12 in) of a structure is also vulnerable because of the effect of the capillary rise of moisture carrying soluble sulphates, chlorides and carbonates, which on evaporation show white efflorescence, the crystallization disintegrating the surface inexorably. This action causes deep erosion of the base of the wall at a rate far more rapid than weathering of the surface. Mice and birds also cause damage, as well as the roots of plants, which are difficult to eradicate.

Materials for capping and repair of mud brick should meet the following requirements: (a) they should be fairly resistant to water; (b) they should not exhibit strength or thermal expansion much in excess of the mud brick walls; (c) they should not differ in colour, texture and porosity from the original material; (d) they should be inexpensive, as large quantities are usually needed.

A recommended procedure is as follows. A local

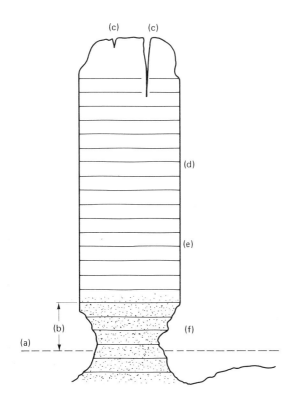

Figure 5.9   Decay of a typical unprotected mud brick wall

The factors causing decay are
(a)   Maximum level of rain water, mud dissolves
(b)   Zone of evaporation about 300 mm (12 in)
(c)   Rain erosion aggravated by cracks and furrows
(d)   Rain erosion of surface plaster
(e)   Condensation at dawn softens surface
(f)   Erosion by ground-water evaporation and formation of salt crystals

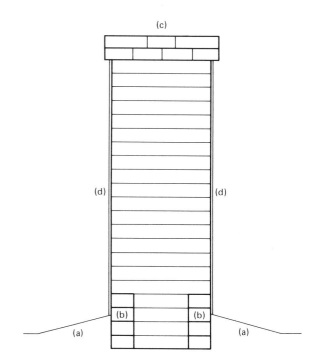

Figure 5.10   Repair of a mud brick wall

(a)   Ground is sloped to drain away from base
(b)   Erosion repaired with mud bricks
(c)   The wall is capped with two courses of 'improved' mud bricks incorporating some lime
(d)   The wall is given a weathercoat of mud plaster reinforced with fibres and containing some lime

clayey soil, as originally used for the manufacture of mud bricks, should be taken and mixed with abundant water and left covered with water to temper for at least a week. The wet soil is then mixed to form a slurry consisting of 8 parts of water to 1 part of sand and 1 part of Portland cement. Chopped straw is added to improve the mechanical properties of the mix, which is then set to dry in moulds resting on sand, which gives a rough texture. The bricks should have a wet-mat covering for about a week and be turned over after three days to ensure even drying. After a week they can be allowed to dry in the sun.

The tops of mud brick walls, if not roofed over, need special attention. A sloping rendering of mud cement mortar made like mud bricks but without the addition of straw is not very satisfactory as it cracks after setting, even if executed in two coats. However, mud cement mortar is useful for grouting of cracks in walls, because it is not subjected to rapid drying. A course of cement mud bricks oversailing by about 10 mm (0.4 in) and set so as to shed the rain, is a better form of capping. Unfortunately, cement mud bricks are slightly different in colour from those of simple mud.

Surface treatment of mud brick walls is best carried out by using ethyl silicate 40, which is the cheapest method available and which is applied by spraying with hand-operated plastic pulverizers of commercial type. The solution is diluted by an equal part of 96% commercial ethanol, no water being added as a sufficient amount is contained in the mud bricks for the action of hydrolysis. After being thoroughly mixed, the solution is left to stand for a short time until it heats up due to the chemical reaction. Two litres per square metre (3.5 pt/yd²) are required to form a weather-resistant layer of sufficient consistency. After some days the porosity of the mud brick course is regained and a second treatment is beneficial. The treatment is only effective on vertical surfaces or steep slopes, as on horizontal surfaces the thin crust is insufficient to resist the erosive action of heavy rain.

If the surface layer is partially detached, adhesion can be restored using polyvinyl acetate emulsions diluted with water and mixed with mud to form a liquid grout.

Mud brick walls can be repaired by removal of the defective lumps and insertion of new bricks of approximately the same size and strength, which are then plastered over and limewashed to match the old surface.

Repair of rammed earth

Rammed earth, known as cob or pisé or khesht, is more difficult to repair than mud brick as the material is homogeneous, and since the repair is wetter it shrinks, making it difficult to obtain a bond between old and new work. For this reason, the defective area should be cut out square and the dried mud bricks set in mud lime mortar used before applying a plaster coat and limewash.

Repair of wattle and daub

In Northern Europe, before bricks became common, mud in the form of wattle and daub was used as an infill in half-timbered work, being fixed to the sill and head of the space, and also for internal partitions. Sometimes the framing timbers were grooved to provide a check to wind and rain. The hazel sticks out of which the wattle was woven are generally attractive to wood-boring beetles and have often disintegrated completely. Repair, if it is necessary, can be done by copying the old methods. If no wind and water check has been formed in the oak frame, one can be planted on by screwing a tapered oak fillet to the sides of the frame. Brick infill in half-timbered work is generally evidence of later repairs.

Maintenance of archaeological excavations

Archaeological excavations present additional problems of maintenance: due to the lowering of the ground level, precautions must be taken to deal with rain which might destroy all the evidence being laboriously acquired. Exposure of previously buried walls subjects them to new static stresses as well as changes in temperature and moisture content and capillarity, which may be most serious due to dissolved salts having penetrated the mud brick. If roofs are put over old walls they may well impose too great loads. Once recording has been done, often the safest policy is to refill the archaeological site using sifted material from the excavation.

6

Structural elements IV: Foundations

The history and methods and materials of foundations are generally the same as the walls which they support, although in some cases new structures have been built upon old foundations.

Foundations are that part of a building which distributes the loads from roofs, floors and walls on to the earth below. This is generally done by a widening of the wall into a footing which bears on to the soil under the building; however, in many early buildings no such widening was practised. The major factor in the permanence of a building is the sufficiency of its foundations and if this is lacking there is no sense in spending large sums of money elsewhere on superficial restoration work.

Ground movement is not at all uncommon. Geologically it occurs continuously and in extreme cases causes earthquakes. It can be induced by man-made activities such as mining and underdrainage. Heavy rain can also induce landslides, while underground streams, especially in chalk and gravel, can cause potholes and caves under buildings. Conversely, blocked underground watercourses may cause the water table to rise. The absolute movements of a building—with the exception of earthquakes—are of less concern than differential or relative movements which may be caused by different types of ground under the building or uneven loading of different parts of the building.

The geology of the ground upon which a building stands and which carries all the dead and superimposed loads can have short and long-term effects. Ground movements must be considered normal for all buildings with long life, but for important historic buildings it is necessary to record these movements, as a time will come when preventive action must be taken. Abstraction of ground water is one of the principal reasons for ground movements, causing the shrinkage of clays and peats; mining subsidence is another cause of such movements. Tunnelling and drainage also cause ground changes. There are gradual geological movements in most countries which may affect the water table and underground drainage patterns. Excessive reliance upon septic tanks and local dispersal can cause a rise in the ground water under a city, whereas irrigation schemes such as at Mohenjodaro in the Indus Valley and the High Dam at Aswan can raise the water table over whole provinces causing acute problems of humidity, dampness and crystallization of salts.

Heavy buildings planted near an historic building can alter the ground stresses and cause movement, and their foundations may block underground water movement.

Ground failures do not always appear suddenly. The soil, particularly if of low permeability, may well creep even when below its actual shear resistance. The structure above accelerates the effect of ground failure as this induces eccentric loadings and turning movements. The rate of movement may die away with time as soil resistance builds up due to its compression, or alternatively it may accelerate towards collapse.

With an architecture of thrust and counterthrust, loads are concentrated on to piers and buttresses enabling the windows to be large, and this means that not only are differential settlements likely unless the original foundations took this into account, but also that they can within reason be accommodated. These settlements may be aggravated by inconsistencies of the bearing capacity of the soil under the foundations which turn straightforward overall settlement into differential settlement, causing distortion and cracking of the superstructure. Very high loadings, up to 800 kN/m² (7 tonf/ft²) have been applied to foundation soils, and loads of 4000 kN/m² (35 tonf/ft²) are not unusual in piers. The ultimate stress of the soil had in fact been reached under the central tower of York Minster before the 1967–72 restoration, so there was a danger of the soil shearing.

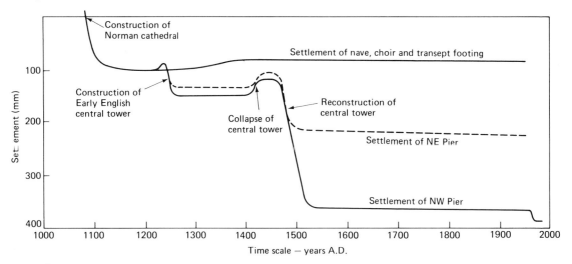

Figure 6.1 Hypothetical reconstruction of settlements since A.D. 1080, central tower, York Minster, England
(Courtesy: Ove Arup & Partners)

*Such a diagram combines history and soil mechanics and introduces the fourth dimension of time into
structural engineering. After being in unstable equilibrium for nearly four centuries, the foundations of
the central tower began to settle again due to lowering of a perched water table*

Investigation of foundations

The scientific study of ground carrying foundations
was started over two centuries ago by Coulomb and is
now a specialized study called soil mechanics, which
depends upon the nature of the soils defined by the
size of the particles and their geological origin. It
should be borne in mind that peat soils and fine-
grained plastic soils will compress and squeeze outwards and fine sand combined with water will run.

Before carrying out major foundation works it is
desirable to monitor any movements by establishing a
system of measurements related to an accurate and
reliable datum point, if this can be found not too far
away. Besides monitoring structural movements, it is
highly desirable to measure alterations in the level of
the water table. With sufficient time for measuring,
this movement can be estimated, according to
E. Schultze.* Deep ground water is another factor not
to be neglected. For example, abstraction of water
from the deeper layers of soil, as has occurred with
the underdrainage of London, which has sunk, like
Venice, a total of some 180 mm (7 in), causing water to
drain from the upper or perched water table through
fissures down to the lower water table. This situation,
combined with dynamic influences such as traffic
vibrations, deep construction and tunnelling, causes
settlements. It must be remembered that many buildings settle quite dramatically during construction,
the Leaning Tower of Pisa being the historic case—
corrections made during construction led to its
banana-shaped form.

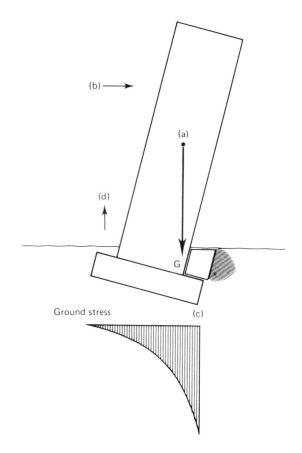

Figure 6.2   Extreme settlement of a tower

(a)   The weight acts through the centre of gravity
(b)   Wind forces add to the turning movement
*(c)   The pressure on the toe of the foundation increases rapidly as
the tower leans*
(d)   There is a danger of uplift

---

*In an unpublished paper given to a Symposium on Engineering
Interventions in Historic Buildings, organized by ICCROM in Rome.
Due acknowledgement is given for much of the material on founda-
tions.

The success of a building's foundations depends upon the nature of the soil on which it is built. As soils are infinitely variable, each problem of foundation failure must be individually examined. The nature of the soil* depends upon its grain structure and the geological way the soil was laid down; there are two general types—cohesive soils consisting of clays and silts composed of fine particles and non-cohesive soils consisting of sands and gravels composed of larger particles. With non-cohesive soils, eccentric loads can decrease the factor of safety very rapidly. The settlement of foundations can change the direction and relative magnitude of thrusts from roof and vaulting, setting up new stresses and thrusts in the fabric which the original scheme of counterbalancing of thrusts was not designed to meet.

Cracking and consequential damage are caused by differential settlements, which are largely due to unequal loading which can only be eliminated by enlarging those foundations that are overloaded. Ideally, in a building, all foundations should be subject to the same pressures, provided they are on ground which has the same load-bearing capacity. This was the objective in the restoration of York Minster.

If inspection reveals cracks and fractures that can be attributed to ground settlement, or if the structure is leaning, the probability is that stabilization of the foundations will be necessary. Such endangered structures are very sensitive, so great care is necessary in the execution of the work. The scheme for stabilization must be prepared after a full investigation; then the execution of the work must be considered together with what temporary works are needed. Often these latter considerations will modify the design proposals. Before finally choosing measures for stabilization, these should be the subject of *in situ* tests.

Defects in foundations may be indicated by a drop or sag in the line of the string course or plinth of a building that may be presumed to have been built horizontal, or in more extreme cases by cracks and even shattered stone. A.R. Powys writes that 'examination of suspected foundation trouble should be made, as much to prove that no work is required, as to discover what should be done'. The present writer's own experience endorses this advice.

First, the movements of the building should be measured and recorded. The inclination and deformation of the building should be studied for as long as possible. Inclinations are measured with plumb bobs,

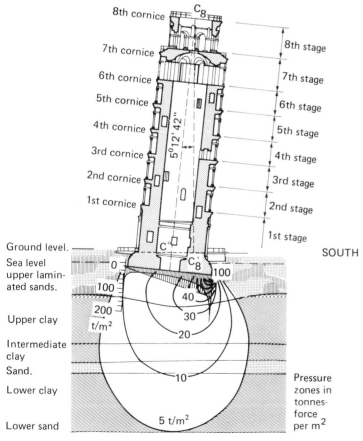

Figure 6.3 Leaning Tower of Pisa, Italy
(Courtesy: *Bollettino Ingegneri*)

Section showing pressure zones (in tonnes-force per m²) and levels of recent sands and clays which have been compressed by the weight of the tower which is approximately 12000 t (11810 ton). The inclination of the tower has been monitored accurately. Recently the tower was closed to tourists because of concern over the condition of its masonry. Ground water levels have been controlled with beneficial results. Currently (1992) there are proposals to maintain equilibrium by placing lead weights on the north side

*In Britain this information can be obtained from the Geological Survey.

optical plumb bobs, theodolites and inclinometers. Ground slopes should also be carefully recorded near leaning towers and walls. Ground water variations at different geological levels should be checked with piezometers.

All possible sources should be searched for plans and other relevant documents, and measured drawings should be made of the whole building recording all cracks and deformations. The possibility that the foundation walls may themselves have decayed due to the chemical action of salts in the ground should not be overlooked. If walls rest on wooden piles, these must also be checked, for often they have decayed due to alteration—past or present—in the level of the water table. Finally, the actual size and position of the foundations must be discovered, together with any archaeological hazards that may affect them.

Lowering of the water table is generally caused by pumping either for building works or for mining, in which case it will probably affect a wide area. Percolation into deep drains can also affect the water table.

A change in this level of the water table can alter the bearing capacity of the soil and may have other side effects, i.e. the raising of the water table may soften clay, or the lowering of the water table may cause drying and shrinkage of clay, or the washing away of fines out of gravel and ballast subsoils.

If the lowering has been rapid, considerable damage can be caused to an historic building (cf. Milan Cathedral). Prevention of this hazard is one of

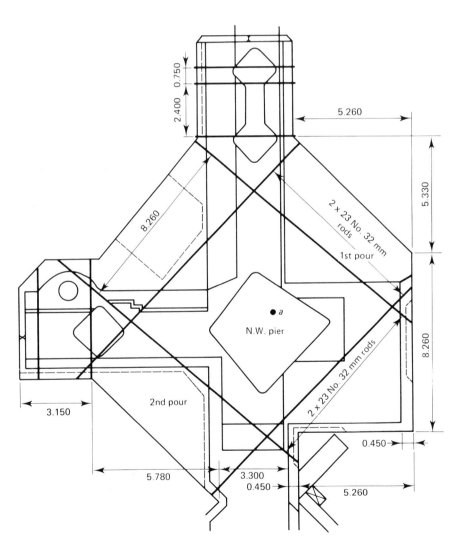

Figure 6.4   Central tower foundations, York Minster, England
(Courtesy: Ove Arup & Partners)

Plan of north-west pier foundations showing stainless steel post-tensioned layout. The project was to enlarge the area of foundations making them symmetrical about the line of thrust a, *so avoiding eccentric loads and dangerous pressures on the soil*

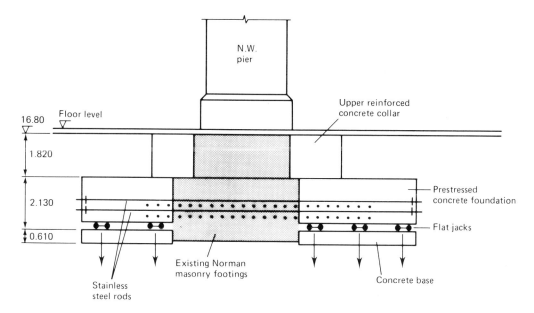

Figure 6.5 Central tower foundations, York Minster, England
(Courtesy: Ove Arup & Partners)

Section through north-west pier foundation. The existing masonry was contained with the new concrete. The flat-jacks were slowly inflated to prestress the soil and equalize loads carried by old and new work

the primary objectives of the St Paul's Cathedral Preservation Act of 1935, which gives the cathedral authorities the right to intervene if the upper ground water levels are threatened with change. Records show that the water level varies slightly with annual rainfall.

Raising of the water table occurs gradually in river valleys, particularly those that have silt-laden floods. Irrigation schemes such as in the Indus Valley affecting Mohenjodaro and the Nile affecting Cairo, have raised the ground water level considerably. Locally, increased sewage effluent from septic tanks can raise the water table under certain hydrological conditions, as at Kerbala in Iraq. If the water table land has been raised by some extrinsic cause this will show by dampness in cellars and increased capillarity and moisture content in walls. These are serious problems.

After the whole building, its site and setting, including adjacent buildings, have been inspected, then the soil and the underground environment must be studied. Simple methods of exploring foundations are in digging holes and/or measuring and probing with augers at an inclined angle. Soil can also be examined by taking cores with hand augers. General soil conditions can be obtained from government agencies. Detailed information is obtained by boring and retrieving cores for inspection and undisturbed samples for laboratory analysis including standard

soil mechanic tests such as triaxial tests for different types of soil. The object is to find the bearing capacity of the soil and to understand its characteristics based upon its stratification. The quality of the soil can be further explored and tested at great depth by driving heavy piles or pressure piles, which will indicate the load-bearing capacity of the soil.

Structural interventions to improve foundations

From inspection of the building and its environment and from the tests outlined above, it should be possible to make an assessment of the causes of structural damage, and for a specialist to produce calculations of the earth statics and to devise preliminary proposals for conservation of the structure through correcting faults in the foundations.

Methods of consolidation of foundations depend naturally on local conditions, and often several alternatives can and should be considered. The underground soil may be improved by chemical grouting, modern methods having been developed using boreholes 50 mm (2 in) diameter at 500 mm (20 in) centres involving pressures up to 200 atm to create piles with a bearing capacity of about 10.2 t (10 ton) each.

Figure 6.6 North-east pier foundation, central tower, York Minster, England (Courtesy: Shepherd Building Group Ltd)

As fresh cracks were found in the shaft of the north-east pier, this was explored first. Severe shear cracks were exposed and glass tell-tales were fixed - these breaking within six months indicated active settlement of the foundations, as suggested by freshness of the upper cracks. The lowest work is eleventh century followed by thirteenth century, and the upper work is fifteenth century. The eleventh century masons' technique of diagonal axe-cutting shows clearly

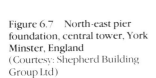

Figure 6.7 North-east pier foundation, central tower, York Minster, England (Courtesy: Shepherd Building Group Ltd)

Similar shear cracks were found on the west side. The strength of the horizontal strutting should be noted, with the screws and plates for applying pressure to contain the masonry. The polythene pipes are for injection of liquid grout

Figure 6.8   Investigation of
foundations, York Minster,
England
(Courtesy: Shepherd Building
Group Ltd)

*It was found that the Normans
had used a grillage of oak beams
to reinforce their foundations
and that by and large this grillage, a fragment of which can be
seen being held, had rotted away
leaving voids*

Figure 6.9   Investigation of
foundations, York Minster,
England
(Courtesy: Shepherd Building
Group Ltd)

*The photograph shows that the
voids were continuous and in
fact ran from below the high
altar nearly to the west end.
Under the central tower the
masonry had bent with the
settlement, but luckily none of
the voids had collapsed*

83

Overloaded earth pressures may be reduced by surface excavation, or uplift pressures may be balanced by a surcharge on the lightly loaded parts. If the soil is thick and compressible, adjustment of the ground water drainage will take a long time and is difficult to control. Depending upon the nature of the soil, adjustment can cause shrinkage, which might help a leaning wall or tower to return to a safer position; or conversely, with different soils, replenishment of the ground water, or at least mechanical control of its level, can assist in regaining or maintaining stability, as is practised in the case of York Minster. Only an experienced expert in soil mechanics can advise upon such esoteric matters.

Foundations can be improved by enlargement, or deepening, or the use of levers and anchorages and containment. Underpinning should be avoided in enlargement because of possible damage from local settlement during execution. The most elegant way to enlarge a foundation is to provide the increased area in reinforced concrete and then to needle through the wall and prestress the new foundation using flat hydraulic jacks. The classic way of deepening foundations is by underpinning, but more modern methods including pressure piles, vertical bored piles, root piles at an oblique angle and many other types of pile give better results and improve load-bearing capacity. When piling, it is imperative to choose a method that does not produce vibrations, so bored piles are essential.

Levers can be constructed so as to apply a back-turning moment and so reduce the effects of foundation failure on the opposite side. The moment can be applied by weights sliding inside a hollow caisson, or by a hydraulic jack or by tension anchorages fixed to piles. Tension rods which by prestressing can counteract the eccentric loads caused by foundation settlements require counterforts or anchorages sufficient to resist their tension. A suitable combination is a tension anchorage with micro-draw piles. Containment by simple sheet piling may be sufficient if the structure can withstand the vibration resulting from such a driving process.

Before projects are begun, field tests on the site should be carried out using the favoured methods of repair, all such tests being carefully monitored by measurements.

Temporary work relating to foundations

The question of whether temporary support is necessary must be carefully considered, bearing in mind that any works to foundations may cause further movements and induce increased danger until the works are finally completed. Schemes which are conceived in stages, so that results can be assessed step by step, have the advantage that they allow a minimum intervention to be practised. The same measuring procedures that were used for the initial assessment should be retained during the works and continued for some years afterwards in order to monitor the effectiveness of the work.

A temporary support always looks unsightly and creates its own foundation problems, particularly if the ground is poor. For such supports to be effective they should be set on hydraulic jacks which will ensure that the correct amount of support is applied. Such hydraulic jacks can also be used to provide an active back-turning moment to an inclined wall or tower. Temporary anchorages can be made using micro-pressure piles. Freezing of the ground may also provide temporary support but careful consideration must be given to the dangers of frost heave if this proposal is adopted. Schultze says that frost heave is generally not to be expected under existing foundations. Cradling of the whole structure comes within the scope of temporary works when dealing with foundations (it is also a technique used to prevent damage from mining subsidences). Besides cradling, elements can even be supported on cables in order to enable works to be carried out.

Lowering of the ground water level for a short time by local pumping is often sufficient but sometimes cofferdams or rings of well points are necessary. Such continuous pumping must be watched carefully, as lowering of the water table may induce active springs and quite violent water movement which is dangerous to the structure being repaired if any sand or silt is abstracted. In this case the work must be stopped immediately. Freezing the ground either wholly or into blocks can overcome these difficult conditions, which of course should have been foreseen by initial soil mechanic studies.

Excavation for foundation work must be properly planked and strutted and any underpinning must be needled and shored. Strutting can be done using screw-type props or the newer hydraulic props, which are safer as they can share loads equally and have less risk of individual failure. Timbers used for temporary structures, such as planking and strutting, should be treated with preservative as a precaution against wet or dry rot. Where loads are heavy and near the ultimate bearing capacity of the soil, and particularly if these loads are eccentric and on a clay subsoil, there may be a risk of some heave or uplift of the adjoining ground. This will place a restriction upon the area which can be opened up for foundation works at any one time. It may well be necessary to replace the weight of the soil excavated by an equal weight of sand in rot-proof sandbags. In an area that is

Figure 6.10   Archaeological sitework, York Minster, England
(Courtesy: Shepherd Building Group Ltd)

*The photograph shows the archaeologists at work. One is taking levels and another is holding a
measuring rod, while the third is recording the measurements and sketching on a drawing. The
remains of a post-Roman building on the Roman alignment at the west end are being recorded. In the
distance three labourers are assisting an archaeologist in an exploratory dig. On the left is part of the
main foundation of the south-west tower and the collar above had been inserted previously. Continuity
rods project outwards to bond the next piece of concrete firmly to the existing concrete, and the grooves
in the reinforcement are also to assist in securing a good joint. The necessary strutting has been left in
position and the concrete poured*

critical, it is wise not to expose more than say one-sixteenth of the total, but this will depend upon the circumstances.

Repair of foundations

If it is decided to enlarge the existing footings, these new foundations can be bonded to the old ones, using post-tensioned reinforcement. When new foundations are added to the old, it is likely that the new parts will not take up loadings until further settlements have taken place, but this problem can be overcome by the use of compression pads and inflatable flat-jacks. The latter can be used to depress a compression pad into the earth, and if the pressure is controlled carefully the exact load on the new foundation can be calculated and the stresses can be equalized with those on the old. Such a process must be carried out slowly by stages, with smaller increments as the pressure increases. If the pressure is applied too quickly, there is danger of punching shear and not giving sufficient time for the subsoil to adjust itself to the new loadings. After prestressing, the jack space is filled with grout to give a permanent connection with the new compression pad; the jack can usually be salvaged for re-use.

The most traditional method of repair to foundations is underpinning, i.e. the removal of defective footings and their replacement by new and enlarged ones. In this method, short lengths of walling are cut out and propped up while the larger foundations are inserted. The phasing of such work must be arranged extremely carefully, bearing in mind the problem of shift of load from one part of the structure to another during the course of the work. Underpinning should also include the use of flat-jacks in order to prestress the loading. A device known as the Pynford stool is most helpful for underpinning. This consists of an upper and lower steel plate of approximately 30–50 mm (1.2–2 in) thickness supported on tubular legs of approximately 800 mm (31 in) length. Each of these is capable of carrying loads of up to 102 t (100 ton) and they can be cut into position and grouted and wedged through the masonry, above and below, using an expanding grout to make sure the joint is tight. The wall above can thus be carried temporarily while new foundations can be inserted by being cast into position with the reinforcement passing through the four-legged stool. The success of underpinning depends however on the strength of the masonry above and if this is not sound, difficulties might occur. When underpinning foundations, the opportunity to insert a damp-proof course should be taken whenever possible.

Figure 6.11   Archaeological finds, York Minster, England
(Courtesy: Royal Commission on Historical Monuments, England)

A Roman column of the Headquarters Basilica lying where it finally fell, before the Norman York Minster was built. Also, a Norseman's tombstone. Interesting archaeological stratification shows. Sufficient evidence was obtained to shed a little new light on the Dark Ages in Britain

Figure 6.12   Tower, Bautzen, German Democratic Republic
(Courtesy: Ing. W. Preiss)

The tower was underpinned by W. Preiss of Dresden and the sequence of the operation was carefully worked out in 14 stages. The inclination of the tower was recorded and had increased by 21 mm (0.8 in) in three years. During the works this rate was somewhat exceeded, but on completion there was evidence of less inclination and a cessation of movement

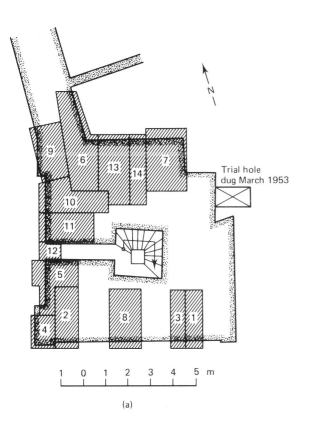

Figure 6.13 Tower foundations, Bautzen, German Democratic Republic
(Courtesy: Ing. W. Preiss)

(a)   Plan showing sequence of underpinning
(b)   Record of movement of tower from May 1950 to October 1954

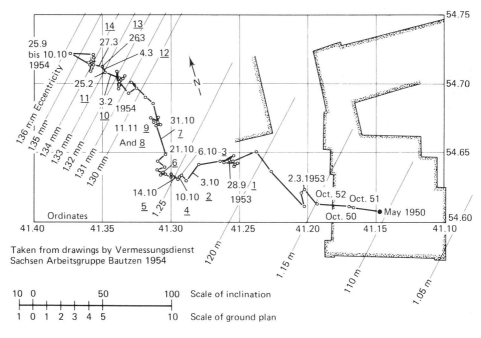

(a)

(b)

Figure 6.14 Underpinning work, east end, York Minster, England
(Courtesy: Shepherd Building Group Ltd)

New foundations under the east wall were required, so it had to be underpinned in stages of 1.2 m (4 ft). This shows the heavy grouting used to enable the work to be done

Figure 6.15 Underpinning work, east end, York Minster, England
(Courtesy: Shepherd Building Group Ltd)

The blocks are keyed together. The new foundations were inserted in a careful programme so as to control the settlements, which in this case were beneficial as they reduced previous distortions. The precious stained glass above and in the side walls was protected by cutting out the perimeter joints so as to allow for some movement

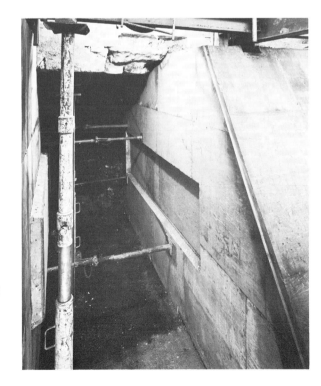

Part II

CAUSES OF DECAY IN MATERIALS AND STRUCTURE

Gravity causes buildings to fall down
External Causes of Decay. The *sun* produces *light* with *ultraviolet* and *heat radiation*

Climatic causes	*Biological and botanical causes*	*Natural disasters*
Seasonal temperature changes	Animals	Tectonics
Daily temperature changes	Birds	Earthquakes
Precipitation of rain and snow	Insects	Tidal waves
Ice and frost	Trees and plants	Floods
Ground water and moisture in soil dust	Fungi, moulds, lichens	Landslides
	Bacteria	Avalanches
		Volcanic eruptions
		Exceptional winds
		Wild fire

Internal Causes of Decay (Note: the building modifies and protects)
(Courtesy: Plenderleith, H.J. and Werner, A.E.A., 1971)

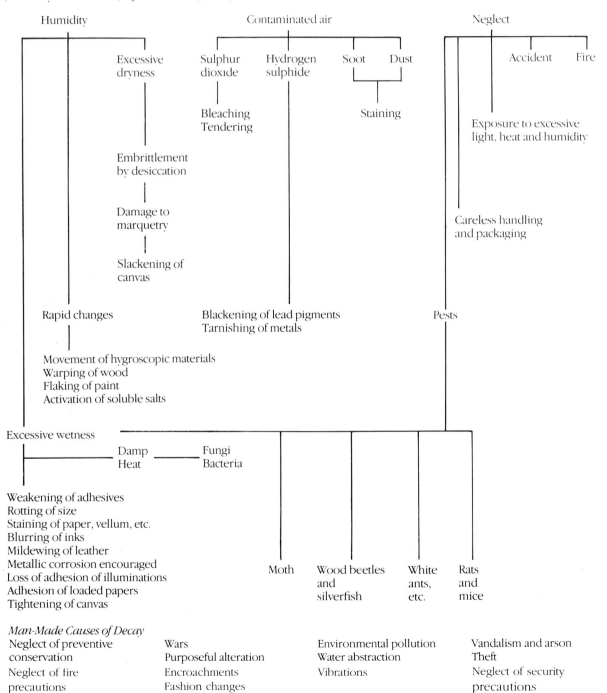

Man-Made Causes of Decay

Neglect of preventive conservation	Wars	Environmental pollution	Vandalism and arson
	Purposeful alteration	Water abstraction	Theft
Neglect of fire precautions	Encroachments	Vibrations	Neglect of security precautions
	Fashion changes		

7

Climatic causes of decay

Introduction

Previous chapters have dealt with the effect of gravity, one of the principal causes of structural decay. This chapter deals mainly with geographical causes, i.e. with climate and its side effects. Earthquakes are given a separate chapter.

Climate, in all its aspects, is one of the fundamental causes of the decay of buildings, through failure of their materials which in turn affects the structure. To give a simple example, mud brick or adobe may last thousands of years in extremely dry, arid desert conditions such as found in North Peru or Nubia, but less than a decade in the hot, humid climate of southern Nigeria. The resistance of building materials to climatic agents of decay decreases with their exposure and age. Even in temperate zones, solar radiation is found to be more destructive than frost. Water, in all its forms, is the agent that promotes chemical actions and gradual deterioration of building materials and actively damages buildings when heavy rainfall overflows gutters and rivers rise in flood.

Whereas the macroclimate of the world has been classified according to the growth of different types of vegetation or annual rainfall, this information is only of indirect value to the architect examining an historic building. The active components of macroclimate that affect a building particularly are radiation from the sun, seasonal temperature changes, rainfall, particularly storms which may cause flooding on both a micro or macro scale, wind and the transportation of ground moisture.

The siting of a building and the soil it stands on affect its microclimate which can modify the macroclimate considerably and so increase climatic hazards. For example, the ruined Villa Jovis on the island of Capri, built by the Emperor Tiberius *c.* A.D. 70, stands on a promontory rising about 300 m (1000 ft) from the Tyrrhenian Sea, exposed to the winds and salt spray as well as being liable to attract lightning strikes in an area noted for its thunderstorms. It has been shown that cities modify the macroclimate, being warmer in winter and also much more liable to heavy concentrations of atmospheric pollution. Other examples of microclimatic effects are frost ponds, shading by hills or mountains, and the ameliorating effects of water on temperature extremes, as well as that of the moisture content of the soil.

The architectural form and structure of a building will influence the microclimate of its parts. Indigenous or vernacular architecture shows how buildings were used as 'spatial environmental systems' to modify the external climate, one example being the wind towers and water-cooling chambers used in Iran and the Gulf States. Courtyards with water and fountains modify a hot, arid climate by providing shade and evaporation, as do trees when growing around a building. Particularly in hot humid climates, air circulation is important both for comfort and prevention of fungal attacks on organic material which often precedes insect attack, and in such cases one finds that the vernacular architecture of the country responds to its climate by having light, open structures with roof shapes designed to encourage air movement. If an historic building is to be used as a museum, both the external and internal climate will need careful consideration and the architect has a responsibility for defining and assessing the climatic factors which will affect the exhibits.

Solar radiation

Solar radiation is the prime cause of climatic conditions, and its wavelengths range from the ultraviolet (0.2 μm), through the narrow band of visible spectrum of light (0.4–0.9 μm) to up to infrared (8 μm),

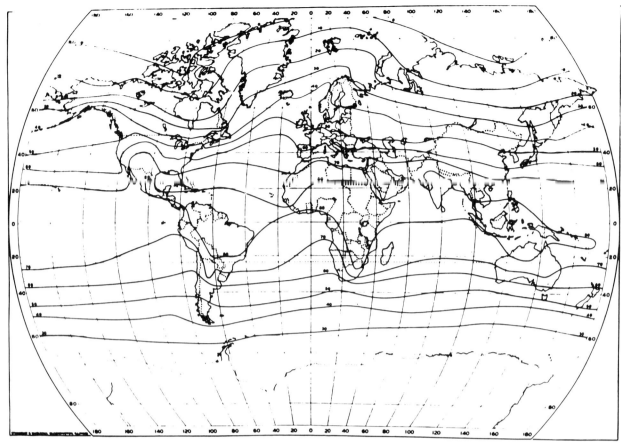

Figure 7.1   Mean annual temperature—world
(Courtesy: McGraw-Hill Book Co.; from Koeppe, C.E. and De Long,
G.C., *Weather and Climate*, 1958)

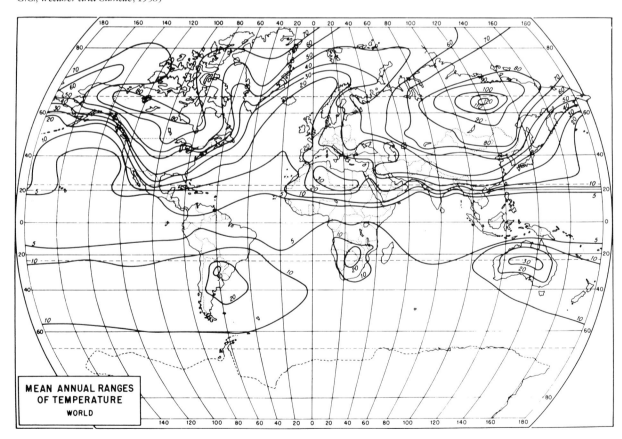

MEAN ANNUAL RANGES
OF TEMPERATURE
WORLD

Figure 7.2   World temperature ranges
(Courtesy: McGraw-Hill Book Co.; from Koeppe, C.E. and De Long,
G.C., *Weather and Climate*, 1958)

Figure 7.3   Holy Shrine of Al
Hussein, Kerbala, Iraq

*Thermal cracking in new
cement mortar rendering
around base of dome due to
large daily changes in temperature and use of an inflexible
material*

Figure 7.4   Palazzo at Fianello, Lazio, Italy

*Note the destructive effect of ultraviolet light and other climatic
elements upon untreated wood*

which has the greatest energy input.* All terrestrial
radiation is long wave, from 4 μm to 50 μm approx.
Different materials vary in their ability to absorb different wavelengths and only absorb a percentage of
the radiant energy falling upon them. This percentage
is known as absorptivity and varies from nought for a
perfect reflector to one for a perfect absorber. The
term 'albedo' is used by climatologists to define the
percentage of incoming solar radiation that is reflected from a surface. Materials that absorb well at
short wavelength are not necessarily good emitters at
longer wavelengths. Short wavelengths pass through
glass which, however, does not transmit the returning
long-wave radiation—a feature which is called solar
gain.

Ozone, water vapour clouds and dust restrict the
amount of solar radiation which is receivable by
between 30% and 60%. Maps showing mean daily
solar radiation averages for different months of the
year are available but these show radiation falling on
the ground, not on the vertical walls of a building, so
are not really relevant. Radiation can be measured by
a climatologist using a radiometer.

Light, especially the ultraviolet component, is a
destructive agent, particularly to organic materials

*1 μm = 1 micron = 0.001 mm; 25 μm = 0.001 in = 1 mil.

such as wood, textiles and pigments, and causes fading, embrittlement and loss of substance. Unprotected wood can erode at the rate of 5–6 mm (1/4 in) per century due to the combined attack of ultraviolet light and rapid moisture exchange.

Temperature and thermal expansion

The cause of air temperature change is almost entirely the heating effect of the sun by day through both short- and long-wave radiation and the loss of this heat by long-wave radiation and convection at night. Building materials are heated by solar radiation in three ways: by direct solar gain from external radiation; by indirect internal solar gain through windows—the 'greenhouse effect'; and by indirect heating via the external air whose ambient temperature is raised by the sun. The shaded part of a building stays relatively cool and immobile, being mainly affected by the seasonal average temperatures.

All building materials expand when heated and contract again when cooled, this expansion and contraction being called thermal movement which is a major cause of decay in buildings. The colour and reflectivity of the material alters the radiant heat input,

which is the main factor inducing temperature increase. Dark, matt materials, for example, absorb more heat than other materials. The extent of thermal movement depends upon the temperature range resulting from the heat input and modified by the thermal capacity of the structure, the thickness, conductivity and coefficient of expansion of the material (*Table 7.1*). Building materials with high absorptivity may reach temperatures much higher than that of the ambient air. Thermal movement is reduced by the restraints the structure can impose.

The ranges of change in climatic temperatures vary considerably, being narrow in a humid tropical rainy equatorial climate, moderate in a maritime cool summer climate, wide in continental steppe and polar tundra conditions and extreme in arid desert climates, where daily and seasonal variations are at their greatest. The range of thermal movements tends to vary correspondingly and, bearing in mind that a building of low thermal mass is most sensitive to daily variations, it is not surprising to note that in hot desert climates the traditional permanent buildings are all of heavy construction, having a high thermal mass to compensate for the daily temperature changes.

A study of temperature ranges of stone surfaces shows that they reach temperatures much hotter than

Table 7.1 Thermal Expansion Coefficients of Materials used in Buildings (unit m/m°C) (By courtesy of ICCROM)

Material	Coefficient		
Concrete	10×10^{-6}		
Concrete with gravel	$9 \div 12 \times 10^{-6}$		
Concrete with expanded clay	$7 \div 9 \times 10^{-6}$		
Cement mortar	$10 \div 11 \times 10^{-6}$		
Lime mortar	$8 \div 10 \times 10^{-6}$		
Limestone	7×10^{-6}		
Brick	5×10^{-6}		
Granite	8×10^{-6}		
Glass (10% alkali)	4.8×10^{-6}		
Iron	11.5×10^{-6}		
Steel	$10 \div 14 \times 10^{-6}$		
Copper	16.8×10^{-6}		
Aluminium	23.8×10^{-6}		
Lead	29.4×10^{-6}		
Pine, along fibres	5.4×10^{-6}	across fibres	34.1×10^{-6}
Oak, along fibres	3.4×10^{-6}	across fibres	28.4×10^{-6}
Fir		across fibres	58.4×10^{-6}
Wood laminates	$10 \div 40 \times 10^{-6}$		
Polyester resins	$100 \div 150 \times 10^{-6}$		
Glass–polyester laminates	$35 \div 45 \times 10^{-6}$		
Epoxy resins	60×10^{-6}		
Epoxy with silica filler (1 : 5)	20×10^{-6}		
Acrylic resins	$70 \div 80 \times 10^{-6}$		
PVC	$70 \div 80 \times 10^{-6}$		
Nylon 66	$70 \div 100 \times 10^{-6}$		

the atmosphere. Readings taken on these surfaces show: (a) Borobudur (Indonesia), from 25 to 45 °C in 4 h (5 °C/h); (b) Abu Simbel (Egyptian Nubia), from 15 to 41 °C in less than 8 h (3.25 °C/h); (c) Persepolis (Iran), from 2 to 34 °C in 6 h with a maximum rise of 16 °C in half an hour. It takes time for heat to penetrate, and at a depth of 50 mm (2 in) or so the temperature of the stone is close to the average. However, a repeatedly heated and cooled skin cannot resist indefinitely. At Persepolis the limestone reliefs have lost their sharp outlines only 30 or 40 years after being uncovered from the soil that preserved them for two and a half millennia.

The stresses induced in building materials by temperature changes are dependent on the following five factors:

(1) The magnitude of absolute dimensional change in the material, which is the product of its dimensions multiplied by the coefficient of expansion and temperature differential and the effects of changes in relative humidity.
(2) The elasticity of the material.
(3) The capacity of the material to creep or flow under load.

(4) The degree of restraint to the movement of the material by its connection to other elements of the structure.
(5) The change in moisture content by evaporation.

The amount of solar heat gain in a structure is determined by the angle of incidence of the radiation to the receiving surface and by the thermal properties of the receiving surface (some surfaces are reflective or are made so by being painted white, whereas others are absorbent). Heat gain is modified by evaporation of moisture in porous masonry and also by the effect of exposure to wind. As well as affecting the temperature of the material and internal air volume, solar gain can affect the internal temperature of the building by radiation through windows (unexpectedly, in the months of March and September, solar heat gain through windows can be greater in Scotland than in the Sahara).

Although thermal mass and conductivity must be taken into account, temperature differentials can be set up between various building elements of differing absorption and with different angles of incidence; for instance, between a lead roof which is subject to heat gain and has a much higher coefficient of expansion,

Figure 7.5   Seventeenth century monastery wall, Suzdal, USSR
Frost has destroyed poorly burnt or otherwise defective bricks

95

and a stone wall which, having great thermal mass and being light in colour and therefore less absorbent of heat and at a more obtuse angle to the sun's radiation, is little affected. Although traditional lead roofs are well designed to absorb comparatively large movements, the fatigue caused by repeated movements is the main reason for their decay.

Thermal movements

Depending upon the nature and elasticity and plasticity of the mortar (hard cement mortar aggravates thermal movement decay because of its lack of resilience), thermal movements in masonry are not generally acute unless the building is longer than 30–50 m (100–160 ft). Since the upper portions of a building are not shaded by its surroundings and are further away from the earth with its almost infinite thermal mass, they are liable to be subjected to greater solar gain and therefore to expand and contract more. The usual sign of thermal movement in a building as a whole is cracking of the upper portions or the loosening of the stones in their joints. As expansion of masonry is not necessarily followed by equal contraction, small annual thermal movements can build up to a considerable extension over a period of years. This is called creep or drift. For example, the north and south arcaded walls of the choir of York Minster are restrained at the west by the central tower, whereas the east wall, being without restraint and having foundations already eccentrically loaded, has moved a total of 626 mm (25 in) in a temperate climate under the influences of annual thermal movements of 1–2 mm (0.04–0.08 in) during some 550 years.

Let us consider thermal movements under three sections: (a) the movement of a block of stone set in a wall; (b) the movement of the wall itself; (c) the movement of a building as a whole.

Thermal movement of a block of stone set in a wall

Considering a notional block of stone set in the external face of the wall, the structural forces which are applied to the five embedded sides should be for practical purposes constant, as wind loads and variation in live floor loads have little effect on massive construction. Foundation settlements may occur which would vary these forces, but these are dealt with elsewhere. Here we will consider only those thermal movements due to heat gain by day and loss by night on the sixth exposed face of the block.

Heat is transmitted through the stone by the process of conduction, but there is a considerable time

lag in the flow due to the thermal mass, low conductivity and moisture content of the stone. This means that a steady state is never achieved within the block of stone. In temperate, humid climates, such as that of England, the heat gain:loss equation is modified by evaporation of moisture in the pores of the stone which tends to damp down the heat gain or loss which would otherwise occur owing to daily temperature fluctuations. Depending upon the season, there will be an inward or outward flow of heat through the stone. In late spring, summer and early autumn there is a net gain, whereas in late autumn, winter and early spring there is a net heat loss. Temperature differential across the block of stone is likely to be greatest in the early afternoon of a hot day, but because of the time lag the temperature gradient will not necessarily be in a straight line.

In England, however, even assuming the most extreme conditions, the stresses within the stone due to temperature differential are unlikely to cause cracking of sound building stone. If the restraint is greater than the stresses engendered by thermal movement, the stone will not move. If the bedding of the stone is imperfect, causing the outer edges to be exposed to higher stresses, the edges may spall or crack at the arrises, especially if the joints are thin in relation to the dimensions of the stone, and more especially if the stone is large and heavily loaded. (In some mediaeval buildings one will find that up to 30–40% of the wall area is in fact mortar; at St Paul's Cathedral, in the outer facing of ashlar some 225–450 mm (9–18 in) thick, this proportion is reduced to the order of 3% of the wall area.) Cracking may be aggravated if the stone is shaped so as to produce a fine narrow joint on the outside face, while behind the face it rests on a deeper mortar bed, for even without thermal movements such a construction throws a greater load on the outside edges. There is a great deal of such spalling in the horizontal joints of the lower pilasters of St Paul's.

Thermal movement of a wall

The second aspect of study should be thermal movements in the wall of a large, heavy, stone structure. The outer and inner faces are generally of ashlar blocks, but the core is often of rubble material all being set in a lime mortar which is weak in relation to the strength of the stone. Each type of masonry will have different physical characteristics, for as the core has a greater proportion of soft mortar it is more compressible than the outer faces. A masonry wall can absorb stresses to a remarkable degree, first by compressing the mortar, secondly by absorbing internal strains, thirdly by friction between the blocks

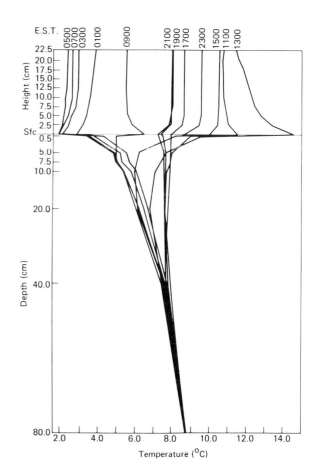

Figure 7.6   Profiles of air and soil temperatures at Seabrook, N.J., USA
(Courtesy: McGraw-Hill Book Co.; from Mather, J.R., *Climatology: Fundamentals and Applications*, 1974)

of stone, and finally by the plastic nature of lime mortar.

Thermal movement of a whole building

As it takes a great deal of heat to raise the temperature of a heavy building with thick walls by even 1°C, so it takes time for the heat to flow through the stone and mortar. There is a tendency for the outer face to be heated up before the core can respond and long before the inner face is affected. This time lag would affect the theoretical temperature gradient. Generally, conditions at the inner face are for practical purposes nearly constant and almost dimensionally stable, whereas the outer face will expand and contract. In a continuously heated building where winter and summer internal temperatures are almost the same, movements in the inner face of a wall will be minimal.

The degree of lateral restraint depends largely on the plan of the building's cross-walls, buttresses, etc., along with the effect of the thermal mass of the ground, the strength of end walls and their super-imposed weights, and the friction between the blocks of stone set in mortar. If walls are firmly restrained at their extremities to cross-walls and to the remainder

of the structure, they will tend to bow outwards in summer and curve inwards in winter as the outer face lengthens or shortens. As mentioned previously, the nearer one gets to the top of the building, the more it is affected by temperature changes, and these changes will be more acutely felt because there is less restraint at higher levels.

Stresses set up by thermal expansion in a typical limestone with a crushing strength of 21 000 kN/m² (200 tonf/ft²) are about 330 kN/m² (48 lbf/in²) per °C. In the worst conditions likely to be met in England, with the average daily air temperatures varying between 2 °C (35.6 °F) in winter and 16 °C (60.8 °F) in summer, the theoretical effect of temperature changes would be to induce a local maximum stress of about 4000 kN/m² (580 lbf/in²) which is much less than the compressive strength of any building stone. In the vertical plane no movement would occur until the upward thrust due to the thermal expansion exceeded the downward thrust due to self-weight. For example, in a wall loaded at 1600 kN/m² (232 lbf/in²) no vertical movement would occur until a 5.5 °C (41.9 °F) temperature had occurred across the whole sectional area. Even a large daily temperature change would be acceptable because, since only a small thickness of wall would be affected, the stresses could be

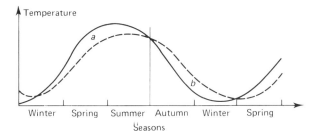

Figure 7.7 Hypothetical comparison of average air temperature and surface temperature of a thick masonry wall

The heavy line shows average seasonal air temperature; the dotted line shows the surface temperature of the walls of a heavy historic building with large thermal mass. In spring and summer the heavy fabric of an historic building is liable to be colder than the air temperature which is increasing, as shown by the time lag ab which amounts to two or three months. Condensation is probable. In autumn and winter the fabric is liable to be warmer than the average air temperature, so condensation risks are reduced. The heavier the construction, the greater the area of ab and the longer the time lag

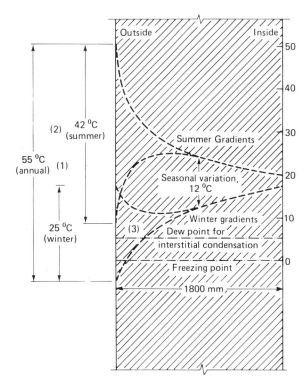

Figure 7.8 Theoretical temperature changes in a thick masonry wall

(1) *Temperatures may range through 55°C (99°F) or more on the surface, falling below freezing on cold winter nights. This wide variation should be compared with a 12°C (22°F) seasonal variation in the centre of the wall and 2°C (3.6°F) in the interior, which probably receives some heating in winter*

(2) *Daily variations of the surface temperature will be greater in summer, say 42°C (76°F), compared with winter, say 25°C (45°F)*

(3) *The dewpoint for interstitial condensation is near the outer surface and this may freeze in the outer layers*

absorbed within the stone and mortar. In arid continental climates, stone structures have withstood a diurnal range of as much as 45 °C (113 °F).

Whereas rapid daily temperature fluctuations tend not to penetrate more than a few centimetres, seasonal temperature movements create more noticeable effects because the centre of the wall core warms up and the whole building tends to expand. However, as with daily temperature changes, upward movement tends to be reduced by the compressive forces of dead weight, and horizontal movement is thus restrained. The expansion of the core of the wall has less effect because of the large proportion of soft mortar, and there is in any case a lower range of temperature movement in this region. Difference of movement between the outer face and the inner core may cause vertical cracks to occur like the ones noted in the west front of the Capitol in Washington, D.C.

Thermal cracks in a building are not likely to show in its horizontal joints, although there may be some crushing in the mortar joints. Movement in the horizontal plane will show by a tendency for vertical cracks to form if mortar is compressed beyond its limits or if the wall does not return to its original position. In such a case, the ends of the wall having expanded outwards, more so near the top of the structure when the seasonal contraction occurs, vertical cracks tend to open as there is no tensile force to close them. The mortar turns to powder as it is crushed, and when contraction occurs the fine particles tend to fall and fill the lower part of the crack. In addition, dust and grit from the atmosphere may also become lodged in the open crack, forming a new bearing surface for next season's expansion; cracks thus tend to widen gradually by the process called drift or sway, which has been noted by many observers.

Expansion of other materials

The above discussion of thermal movements in a building has dealt with stone masonry, as this illustrates the problems most clearly. Brick and stone rubble or mass concrete structures such as Roman walls and vaults react in the same way as stone, but if they have a larger proportion of soft mortar in the joints they are rather more accommodating.

The importance of the mortar cannot be overemphasized. One can compare a long boundary wall laid with lime mortar that shows no expansion problems, with a short wall built with Portland cement mortar that needs to have expansion joints every 10 m (33 ft). In mass concrete and stone rubble construction, the percentage of mortar to stone can vary from 30% to 70%, in brick construction from 10% to 40%

and in stone from 1% to 30%. Where the percentage of mortar is small the joints are most liable to show thermal distress. Often the external wall is plastered, and if this plaster has the same characteristics as the soft mortar then thermal movement will cause only fine hairline cracks. As mud, brick and adobe are relatively weak, with low thermal expansion and conductivity, they also have very few thermal movement problems.

Wood moves markedly and fairly quickly with changes in the relative humidity of the air and these movements are far greater than thermal movements. Because of its nature, wood is generally used in a framed structure which is able to absorb both thermal and humidity movements.

The action of moisture*

The presence of water in any of its various forms causes or accelerates the decay of most building materials. The access of water to porous masonry materials may be caused by rain. Water reaches a masonry surface when the rain hits the surface directly; it may also reach the surface indirectly, falling somewhere else on the building and gaining access through a more complicated path. The latter case often produces the worst damage, because the rain water picks up soluble materials along its path, and destructive crystallization processes occur when the water evaporates. Faulty disposal of rain water is the most frequent cause of deterioration in ancient masonry.

Water also penetrates porous masonry materials through capillary action; suction is exerted by capillaries. The height of the capillary rise of water in porous masonry materials depends mainly on the pore size (the smaller the size, the higher the rise) and the rate of evaporation from the external surface (as evaporation increases, the rise is reduced). The capillary rise increases with time, as soluble salts are carried by water into the masonry and become concentrated there when the water that carries them evaporates from the side surfaces of the wall. The increased concentration of soluble salts causes in turn another force of attraction for water, since it must diffuse from low salinity to high salinity regions. The result is that an equilibrium is never reached, and the capillary rise of water increases with the structure's age. Old thick masonry sometimes shows capillary rises as high as 8–10 m (26–33 ft), 4–5 m (13–16 ft) being common. Sometimes the water drawn up by capillary action into the masonry is rain water that has

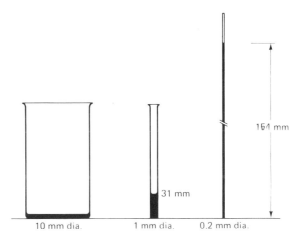

Figure 7.9   Capillarity
(Based on G. and I. Massari)

Capillarity increases as the size of the passage decreases. It can reach heights of 8–10 m (26–33 ft) above ground. Porous building materials are a network of capillaries of varying diameter which draw water sideways as well as vertically

been discharged near the base of a wall by a faulty gutter system.

Finally, water can gain access to masonry materials directly through the air, either by condensation or by the deposition of aerosols, such as mist, fog or salt spray. Condensation occurs when the air is damp and the masonry surface is colder than the dewpoint of the air. Condensation occurs on the coldest surface available; therefore, 'cold' materials, i.e. materials with high density and high thermal conductivity, are most affected by it. Metals and compact types of stone are examples of such cold materials; concrete is colder than brick and lime mortars.

Condensation water is far more dangerous than rain water because it sweeps a large volume of air in front of the cold surface (the Stefan effect), cleaning it completely of all suspended dirt or gaseous pollutants. Liquid solutions containing free sulphuric acid then form on masonry surfaces in polluted atmospheres, and particles of carbon black, iron oxides, calcium sulphate and other substances are deposited.

Aerosols are liquid or solid particles suspended in gases—in this case, air. Liquid droplets formed around sodium chloride crystals, spread in the air by sea spray, can travel long distances over land, becoming progressively more acidic as they meet city atmospheres or gases originating in swampy areas. Aerosols hit surfaces that are particularly exposed to air currents and discharge their particles on them. They are also attracted by cold surfaces, where they produce effects similar to those of condensation, even if the temperature on the surface does not drop below

*This section is by G. Torraca, Deputy Director of ICCROM.

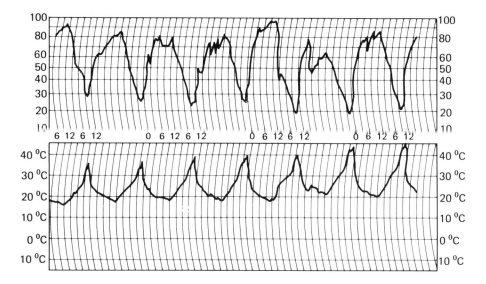

Figure 7.10   Thermohygrograph readings at Cloche, Iraq, Spring 1968
(Courtesy: G. Torraca, Mesopotamia, 1968)

The readings show how relative humidity changes ± 75% with temperature ± 25°C between a hot noon and cool night with constant absolute moisture in the air. Even in desert conditions it is possible for condensation to occur in the early hours of the morning

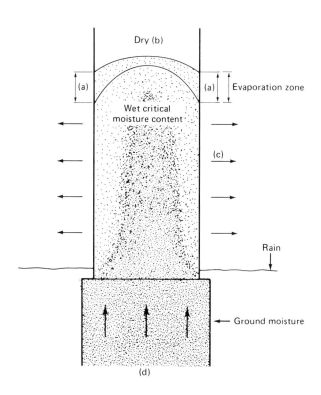

Figure 7.11   Excess moisture in a wall

(a)   *Difference between summer and winter evaporation zones. Decay due to crystallization within the surface is critical*

(b)   *Stone or brick are accepted as dry if their moisture content is 3% of the volume or 5% of the weight. For tuff, 3% by volume and 8% by weight is considered dry*

(c)   *Constant evaporation from the surface only*

(d)   *Moisture is supplied from the water table or excessively moist soils*

the dewpoint. Thus, seaside buildings are obviously exposed to aerosols.

It is often not easy to decide by which mechanisms water has gained access to a masonry material. Condensation, in particular, is often not sufficiently considered, the 'humidity' it produces being attributed to rising damp when it appears in the lower register of walls or to the penetration of rain when it appears in ceilings and vaults. The consequences of misjudgement are often ruinous. As a general rule, in the case of cold, compact, low-porosity materials, it would be wise to suspect condensation first, while the reverse attitude might be taken for more porous materials. Accurate temperature/relative humidity surveys should be made as often as possible.

A characteristic feature of water distribution inside hard porous masonry materials is the existence of a critical water content that depends on the type of porosity and the nature of the material. Above the critical content, water can move freely in the liquid state inside the porous body, whereas below the critical value, water is held inside pores and can be removed only by evaporation. It is often difficult to dry a masonry structure because the critical water content may be quite high. For instance, in walls containing hygroscopic soluble salts, as in Venice, the critical water content can be as high as 18%, according to some authors.

Walls appear wet up to a certain height in a structure where the water content is at the critical value. Above this point, walls appear dry, and the water content drops sharply to a low level.

Precipitation of moisture

Atmospheric moisture may occur in vapour or gas form, known as humidity, water in minute droplet form or as ice crystals, known as fog or clouds, or as liquid precipitation known as drizzle, rain, sleet, snow, soft hail (graupel), snow grains, hail, rime, glaze and dew.

Humidity is measured by hair hygrometers, psychrometers or lithium chloride meters, which give a more rapid and complete response to changes in humidity than human hair. Moisture precipitation is measured by means of a rain gauge. A rainfall of 10 000 mm (400 in) over 12 months in the tropics may be far less of a problem than exceptional downpours such as 31.2 mm (1.23 in) in 1 minute at Unionville, USA, on 4 July, 1956 or 126 mm (4.96 in) in 8 minutes at Fusseh, Bavaria, on 25 May, 1920. Rainfall average intensity decreases rapidly with its duration, the greatest amount recorded for a year being 26 461 mm (1042.6 in) in 1860–61 at Cherrapunji, India.

Rainfall data is generally presented in terms of annual or monthly averages. For most localities in Europe, 80% of the total rainfall is due to intensities of precipitation below 50 mm/h (2 in/h). However, the point rainfall intensities in which we are interested for the design of rainwater disposal systems that will be unlikely to flood, are much larger than averages. Heavy rainfalls are generally concentrated in duration and locality and if they are time averaged they can be considerably underestimated. Data for individual countries (*Table 7.2*) shows variations of over 100% for different places, indicating that national design standards should be taken with caution.

Using a graph of the cumulative distribution of rainfall intensity (*Figure 7.13*), it will be seen that the rate of 75 mm/h roughly corresponds to the 10^{-3} percentage of time (5 min) and gives the following corresponding values (which should be doubled for design purposes):

Curve 1. Tyrrhenian Coast of Italy (Genoa, Rome, Naples) and Adriatic Coast of Greece ... 230 mm/h

Curve 2. Central Italy, South Continental Europe ... 165 mm/h

Curve 3. North Continental Europe ... 100 mm/h

Curve 4. Scandinavian Countries, UK, Ireland ... 70 mm/h

Curve 5. Norway, North Scandinavian Countries ... 35 mm/h

The data is related to instantaneous values used for high-frequency radio transmissions which are affected by rain. For architectural conservation, further research is necessary. The information gained from the high-frequency radio research is, however,

Figure 7.12   Aventino, Rome, Italy

A garden wall shows clearly the effect of rising capillary moisture and the evaporation zone where crystallization of ground salts destroys the plaster and brickwork

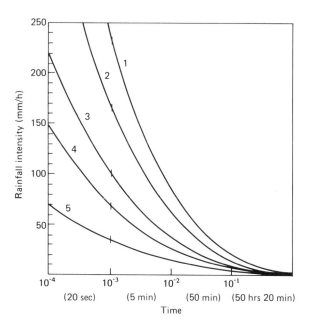

Figure 7.13   Cumulative distribution of rainfall intensity (Courtesy: Fedi, F., 1979)

Percent of time a given rainfall is exceeded in one year, e.g. 75 mm/h (3 in/h) is exceeded 5 minutes each year in the UK

Table 7.2 Meteorological Stations for Rainfall Intensity Measurements (Courtesy: Fedi, F., 1979)

| Country | Locality | Period | Years | Rain gauges | | | | | P_0* (%) | H† (mm) | |
				No.	Type	Area funnel (cm²)	Sensitivity	Int. time (sec)		Meas.	Estim.
Finland	Helsinki	76–77	1	1	C	730	5 mm/h	15	2.1	260	—
Sweden	Stockholm	54–63	10	1	TB	750	0.2 mm	60	3.5	—	757
Norway	Arendal	67–75	7	1	TB	750	0.2 mm	60	3.5	647	—
	Gardermoen	67–73	6	1	TB	750	0.2 mm	60	2.5	406	—
	Opstveit	68–75	8	1	TB	750	0.2 mm	50	6.8	1364	—
	Kjeller	75–76	2	1	TB	750	0.2 mm	60	2.9	338	—
	Trondheim	67–75	9	1	TB	750	0.2 mm	60	4.7	564	—
	Halden	74–75	2	1	TB	750	0.2 mm	60	3.5	489	—
U.K.	Slough	70–74	5	1	DC	150	5 mm/h	10	4.3	—	700
	Mendlesham	73–75	3	3	DC	150	5 mm/h	10	3.5	—	338
Ireland	Cork	70–75	6	1	S	648	0.2 mm	600	7.0	—	1145
Germany, F.R.	Darmstadt	75–76	2	10	DC	225	7 mm/h	10	3.0	—	485
Netherlands	Leidschendam	72–74	2	6	DC	284	7 mm/h	10	3.0	—	740
Belgium	Louvain La-Neuve	70–75	5	1	TB	1000	0.05 mm	60	3.5	—	970
France	Paris	65–76	12	1	S	313	0.2 mm	60	5.0	646	—
	Dijon	72–76	5	1	S	313	0.2 mm	60	5.0	—	796
Switzerland	Bern	74–75	2	8	TB	200	0.1 mm	60	4.0	960	—
	Jungfrau	74–75	2	4	TB	200	0.1 mm	60	4.0	1133	—
	Valais	74–75	2	5	TB	200	0.1 mm	60	2.0	596	—
Austria	Graz	75–77	1	1	TB	200	0.1 mm/h	360/R	3.2	—	493
Portugal	Lisbon	75–77	3	1	S	200	0.2 mm	300	4.0	—	950
Italy	Genoa	77–78	1	1	TB-C	1000	0.2 mm/h	720/R	6.4	1603	1602
	Milan	67–70	2	10	TB	1000	0.2 mm	60	3.0	–	1190
	Udine	76–77	1	1	TB-C	1000	0.2 mm/h	720/R	6.5	1575	1594
	Rome	75–77	2	1	TB-C	730	0.27 mm/h	986/R	3.1	1143	1125
	Bologna	76–77	1	1	TB-C	1000	0.2 mm/h	720/R	3.0	631	628
	Fucino	75–77	2	1	TB-C	730	0.27 mm/h	986/R	4.8	1386	1328
	Bari	76–77	1	1	TB-C	1000	0.2 mm/h	720/R	2.2	520	498
Greece	Kefellinia	74–75	1	1	C-S	730	5 mm/h	15	0.8	752	—
	Kerkyra	74–75	1	1	C-S	730	5 mm/h	15	3.1	734	—
	Aliartos	74–75	1	1	C-S	730	5 mm/h	15	0.67	522	—
	Milos	74–75	1	1	C-S	730	5 mm/h	15	0.82	374	—
	Hios	74–75	1	1	C-S	730	5 mm/h	15	0.32	543	—
	Athens	74–75	1	1	C-S	730	5 mm/h	15	1.6	264	—
	Hiraklion	74–75	1	1	C-S	730	5 mm/h	15	0.62	398	—
	Mikra	74–75	1	1	C-S	730	5 mm/h	15	1.7	421	—
	Kalamata	74–75	1	1	C-S	730	5 mm/h	15	0.29	640	—

*P_0 is the average percentage of time in which rainfall exceeds 0.2 mm/h.
†H is the actual or estimated annual rainfall (in mm).

Table 7.3 Recommended Parameters for the Design of Windows Exposed to Rain

| Exposure pressure measured in water gauge (w.g.) | Windows watertight at: | | Leakage not excessive at: | |
	Normal bldgs.	Historic bldgs.	Normal bldgs.	Historic bldgs.
Normal exposure	4 mm w.g. (0.16 in)	6 mm w.g. (0.24 in)	16 mm w.g. (0.63 in)	24 mm w.g. (0.95 in)
Moderately severe exposure	16 mm w.g. (0.63 in)	24 mm w.g. (0.95 in)	30 mm w.g. (1.18 in)	45 mm w.g. (1.77 in)
Severe exposure	30 mm w.g. (1.18 in)	45 mm w.g. (1.77 in)	60 mm w.g. (2.36 in)	90 mm w.g. (3.54 in)

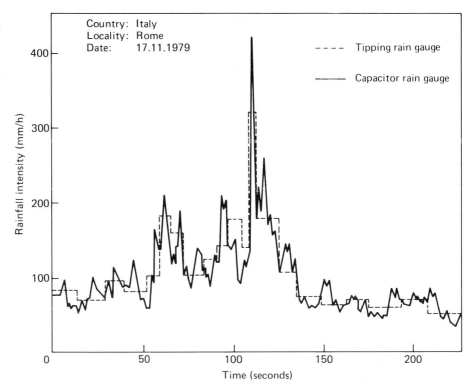

Figure 7.14   Example of time behaviour of rainfall intensity, Rome, Italy (Courtesy: Fedi, F., 1979)

100 mm/h (4 in/h) is exceeded for about 80 sec on this chart with a peak of 400 mm/h (16 in/h) for a short time

helpful in establishing a picture of point rainfall and the profile of a storm, as shown in *Figure 7.14*.

In such a storm, with gutters and down-pipes running full bore at a design level of 75 mm/h (3 in/h), it is clear that flooding would be liable to occur for about 100 seconds, sufficient to cause serious trouble below parapet or valley gutters.

Rainfall records are the basis of rational design, but records of averages need interpretation. In the UK the rainfall probabilities can be predicted for any given site by a computer program. The Metereological Office, London Road, Bracknell, Berkshire, England, will supply rainfall probabilities for a given map grid reference, but the lesson of these figures is that rainwater disposal systems must be generously designed and should always have overflows to take care of exceptional downpours.

Backed up by high wind pressures, rain in exceptional circumstances can surmount checks of 75–100 mm (3–4 in) in height. Wind exposure also affects window design. *Table 7.3* gives some recommended design parameters; it will be noted that 50% higher standards are recommended for historic buildings because over a longer period of time they may have to withstand more severe conditions.

Both the rate of rain falling in a short period and the direction in which it is driven are of crucial importance in the maintenance and preservation of a building. In Britain, exposure to driven rain is least severe in the East Midlands, London and the south-east; most driven rain comes from the south-west in the western half of the UK and from the direction of the coast

elsewhere. The ability of rainwater disposal systems to deal with the worst possible storms of short duration is vital. The short-term rate of run-off varies with the slope and friction of different roofing materials, being greatest for sheet metals.

Rain can penetrate to the interior of a building and cause various kinds of decay. Absorbent surfaces such as brick provide a very satisfactory answer to the 'damp dripping' British climate, but it should be remembered that the absorption capacity is limited and after 2–3 days of heavy driving rain a solid wall 350 mm (14 in) thick, which is usually satisfactory, will become saturated and may well show signs of rain penetration. The absorption capacity of stone is much less, for most types are nearly waterproof. Once the surface of stone or brick is saturated, large amounts of water will stream down tall vertical surfaces and, as mentioned previously, wind pressure will force this through cracks or even through the material itself if it is sufficiently porous. Rain penetration can cause internal decay in stone walls forming large internal voids, some of which may require 250 l (55 gal) or more of filling material such as grout. Voids totalling about one-twentieth of a wall's volume can be formed after five centuries or more.

The absorption capacity of a building material is an important consideration. A permeable or absorbent material must not be jointed or pointed with a more dense or impermeable mortar or else rain water will be trapped in the pores of the material and when there is a frost will cause severe damage. In warm weather, a thin porous wall wetted by rain may be so

Figure 7.15   St Paul's Cathedral, London, England
(Courtesy: Feilden & Mawson)

Weatherproofing faults have allowed severe recrystallization to occur on the inner stone lining of the south-west tower. The pointing of stone or brick masonry to prevent penetration of moisture is an elementary but most important action in preventive maintenance. The ladder is viewed from below

Figure 7.16   St Paul's Cathedral, London, England
(Courtesy: Feilden & Mawson)

A general view of the northern-most chamber under the west steps. Acid water penetration has dissolved stone which has re-crystallized

much cooled by rapid drying conditions as to induce internal condensation if the internal air is humid.

Hard, impermeable materials throw greater strain on their joints and require harder mortars. Taking glazed terracotta or flintwork as an example: although the material is almost indestructible by rain or frost it requires more frequent repointing than brick, and to counter this erosion a somewhat harder mortar is permissible, but it must not be completely impermeable, for an impervious mortar such as Portland cement is liable to small cracks which will induce the inward movement of rain water by capillary attraction.

Dissolved salts

The composition of salts and their action by evaporation are as follows:

(1) The salts that are potentially the most dangerous to the rendering and to the painted surface of a wall are the *sulphates of sodium, potassium, magnesium and calcium,* because according to where they crystallize they cause serious disintegration owing to the failure of cohesion of the materials. Calcium sulphate can form a white veil over the surface or it can be crystallized within the rendering by the sulphation of calcium carbonate to which a polluted atmosphere contributes.

(2) The *nitrates of sodium, potassium and calcium* are soluble salts which normally give rise to thick efflorescences easy to eliminate and of which the disintegrating action is inferior to that of the sulphates.

(3) *Calcium carbonate* is a main component in construction in the form of limestone. Calcium carbonate has not by itself a disintegrating effect once it has crystallized, but it forms incrustations that are very hard and intractable.

(4) *Sodium chloride* is normally a surface deposit, having been transported by sea air, and in itself does not cause disintegration. However, it is able by a process of hydration and dehydration to promote the disintegration of surfaces by its action on other salts that may be present under the effect of varying temperatures.

(5) *Silica* contained in certain rocks, in clays and in cements is in a form that can be transported very slowly towards the surface by infiltrating water. A long-term effect is the formation of white incrustations of silicon dioxide (opal) or of silicate mixed with other substances, notably calcium carbonate.

Figure 7.17   Presbytery parapet, Norwich Cathedral, England
Fourteenth century masonry in an exposed position was badly eroded. It was patched with Portland cement which accelerated the decay. Freezing expansion has opened up cracks

Frost and snow

The relative coldness of a climate is measured in degree days, i.e. the number of days when the temperature falls below 18 °C (64.4 °F), multiplied by the degrees drop below that temperature. There is considerable variation in this figure throughout Britain — from 800 in the south to approximately 2000 in the far north. But it is not extreme cold that causes damage to buildings so much as frost changes—the actual process of freezing and resultant expansion of ice and subsequent contraction on thawing, which may occur in the British climate on average between 1.5 and 2 times per day in winter. In the case of foundations which may be affected by frost heave, the number of frost changes is rapidly reduced by increasing the depth of the foundations. The following information, based on data from Potsdam, illustrates this point. Although it represents a colder continental climate than Britain's, it is one with fewer actual frost changes.

Depth in ground mm (in)	Number of frost changes per year
0 (0)	119
20 (0.8)	78
50 (1.97)	47
100 (3.94)	24
500 (19.7)	3.5
1000 (39.4)	0.3

Figure 7.18 Presbytery parapet, Norwich Cathedral, England

The stone is crumbling due to freezing expansion. Again, patching with Portland cement mortar has accelerated decay. The design and shape of the mouldings is now in danger of being lost. The masonry was reproduced using the traditional techniques

Figure 7.19 North cloister arcade, Norwich Cathedral, England

Frost damage in winter of 1962–63. Some stones with poorer frost resistance were disintegrated by severe freezing

Figure 7.20 No. 7 Warehouse, Hull, England

Neglect of rainwater downpipes led to saturated brickwork and thus consequential frost damage. The surface of the brick was disintegrated

Figure 7.21 No. 7 Warehouse, Hull, England

After years of neglect the rainwater downpipes became blocked and then cracked due to freezing; they then flooded the walls behind them, saturating the brickwork, which in turn was damaged by frost

Foundations should be deep enough to avoid frost heave or expansion which can cause the subsoil to move with consequent damage. This depth also depends on the type of soil; in the UK it is taken as 455 mm (18 in) on sands and gravels and 910 mm (3 ft) on clays. In Sweden the minimum is 1500 mm (5 ft). The use of salt on roads has side effects in polluting ground water and causing water mains to be frozen at depths greater than 910 mm (3 ft), as happened in 1963 in Britain.

Ground temperatures also vary between summer and winter. At a depth of 1 mm (0.04 in) below ground, the variation at Potsdam can be between 20 °C (68 °F) in July and 1 °C (33.8 °F) in February; at 12 m (39.4 ft) depth there is much less variation, temperatures being 10 °C (50 °F) in February, and actually coldest in August at 9 °C (48.2 °F).

Freezing damages porous building materials such as brick and stone, particularly if they are saturated with water. The resistance of these materials depends upon the size of the pores and their hydrophilic or hydrophobic structure. If ice forms in the pores having a good structure it can expand on freezing without damage. In prolonged frost, however, ice may actually build up inside the material because of condensation of water vapour. Acceptable frost resistance is specified in British and other national standards.

Snow falls in flakes and lies in thick blankets on roofs and over the ground. Driven snow can attach itself to near vertical faces and be blown in through ventilators and other openings and, having penetrated, can cause stains on ceilings and floors when it melts. There are many types of snow, the Finnish language having nine words to express them. Snow is a good insulator and reflector of heat, and in the hands of the Eskimo it is a sophisticated building material. If snow lasts during the winter, traditional design, such as the Swiss chalet, takes account of this and uses it for insulation; but in countries where snow is more occasional, steep pitches on roofs are used to shed snow quickly before it can build up a heavy load. In England no allowance is made for snow loads on pitched roofs, but an allowance for 1.5 kN/m² (30 lbf/ft²) is necessary for flat roofs.

Melting snow on a steeply sloping roof can form mini-avalanches which descend from the eaves, tearing down gutters if present and breaking conservatory or other glass windows below. To prevent this, snow boards are sometimes provided at the eaves. If there are parapets or valley gutters, melting snow can cause blockages, with melted water rising above the level of the waterproofing and so causing flooding. Packed snow often has to be removed by hand, although in sophisticated installations embedded electrical heating can be used. For hand operations, a wooden shovel is recommended in order to avoid damage to the roof covering. Duckboards reduce the hazard of flooding blockage in gutters and make roof maintenance easier. Snowboards and duckboards should be strongly constructed of impregnated softwood, western red cedar or durable hardwood (timbers like oak should not be used on lead roofs as they may cause acid attack).

Wind

Wind is the result of different atmospheric pressures in the weather system. Direction, speed, gustiness and frequency of calms are important characteristics of wind. Wind speeds vary at different heights and cause turbulence. Most published data on wind involves a considerable amount of averaging which reduces the usefulness of such data when considering historic buildings. Wind-roses give a general picture of wind conditions in a locality. Those given by Mather for the Delaware Valley in 1965 show how variable a quantity wind is from place to place (*Figure 7.23*).

Clearly the structure must be strong enough to resist wind pressures; it must also be able to resist the associated suction on the lee side. It might well be assumed that because an historic building has succeeded in resisting all probable strengths of winds during its lifetime, it will be strong enough to resist all future wind forces, but this does not always follow, as the structure may have deteriorated and there is always the possibility of an exceptional wind. Forces generated by wind can cause buildings such as bell-towers to sway. The 99 m (325 ft) high Norwich Cathedral spire has been found to move about ± 76 mm (3 in) to and fro in a high wind. A sway of even 0.10 mm (1/250 in) can be noticeable, for man with his cave-dweller ancestry is very conscious of sway and quakes. It is theoretically possible for wind pressure to cause tension in a windward face of a tall, thin structure. This becomes an actuality in tall, relatively light structures such as spires, where the uplift can exceed the dead weight of the structure. In Norwich Cathedral this effect was countered by a vertical tie bar. It is said that Leonardo da Vinci recommended a pendulum, i.e. a tie bar tensioned by a heavy weight, to prevent uplift by such tension forces, and Wren appears to have used a similar idea in his repairs to the spire of Salisbury Cathedral.

Most coastal areas may expect winds of up to 97 km/h (60 m.p.h.) mean, with 162 km/h (100 m.p.h.) gusts. In Britain these will be exceeded in Cornwall, Wales and the west coast of Scotland, but will be somewhat less in the south-east. The Building Research Station suggests that the wind speed should be modified by a design factor for building life; for an historic building, where risks cannot be taken and a

Figure 7.22   The Cathedral Close, Norwich, England

Bad frost damage had occurred to the base of a garden wall in combination with rising moisture. Variegated ivy was planted to protect the wall against frost, thus rendering repairs unnecessary

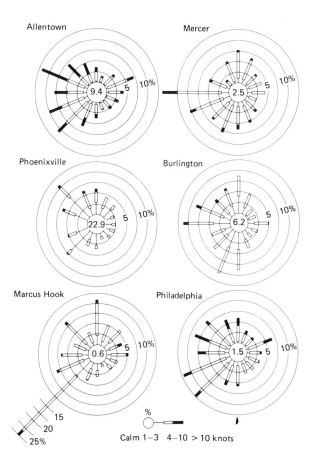

Figure 7.23   Annual wind roses at selected stations in the Delaware Valley, USA, for 1965

(Courtesy: McGraw-Hill Book Co.; from Mather, J.R., *Climatology: Fundamentals and Applications*, 1974)

Figure 7.24   Spire, Norwich Cathedral, England

The W.N.W. buttress showing stone decay and multiple cracking and some previous repairs. The damage was caused by wind vibration and sway that got progressively greater as the structure deteriorated

design life of 200 years is not excessive, it is recommended that this factor should be at least 1.5 on the recommended design wind speed for the locality. Tornadoes with their centrifugal vacuum effects are touched upon in the section on natural disasters later in this chapter.

Because roof coverings such as tiles and even lead sheets can be lifted by lee-side suction, their fixing should be carefully considered and detailed; loosely fixed slates can often be heard to 'chatter' in a high wind. (With prevailing westerly winds, the lee suction eddy from a church tower normally falls on the nave roof and it is common for tiles to be lifted in this area; extra nailing is the obvious remedy here.)

Wind exacerbates the general external erosion of most building materials. If a small piece of hard grit gets into a surface pocket, gusts can rotate it at high speeds and thus drill quite a large hole in soft stone. After the reconstruction of the Temple of Abu Simbel in Egypt, a violent windstorm driving little stones lifted from the ground in front of the temple severely damaged the face of one of the figures on the facade.

Rapid evaporation by wind causes salt crystallization to take place within the wall rather than on the surface. This breaks up the material of the wall and causes cavitation, which intensifies evaporation and further crystallization—a phenomenon called cavernous decay in stone. The eroding action of wind combined with sand or dust can ultimately destroy massive buildings. Wind-borne sea salts and rain can have similar effects, as may be seen at the megalithic temple of Hagar Quin, Malta, which was built of globigerina limestone.

Indeed, the most serious effects of wind pressure are found in conjunction with rain. When combined with heavy rain, wind causes serious internal decay after the surface reaches saturation point and the rain, driven by wind pressure, penetrates cracks, fissures and porous materials. Wind will also blow rain sideways, a point often neglected in detailing, leading to unsightly streaks which occur where vertical upstands and joints check the sideways movement of the rain water and thus cause concentration of the flow downwards.

Particulates, smoke, dust and sand particles

Particulates or aerosols are solid particles that remain suspended in the air. Particles that settle in still air are dust, sand or grit. Smoke is the result of incomplete combustion of fuels.

The diameter of particulates is measured in microns (abbreviated μm) which are one thousandth of a millimetre or one millionth of a metre. Particulates larger than 15–20 μm settle near their source of

Figure 7.25 Spire, Norwich Cathedral, England

The N.N.E. angle buttress with poorly bonded stone, repaired in at least four different periods, but the crack and bulge which are due to wind vibration were serious

Figure 7.26 Spire, Norwich Cathedral, England

Note the decay of nineteenth century 'plastic' repairs. At the N.N.E. angle is a broken wrought iron strap of an eighteenth century repair, but the fine crack to its left is more ominous. It is caused by wind vibration and is repeated on each of the eight sides, heralding the failure of the structure

Figure 7.27   Spire, Norwich Cathedral, England

Major repairs to tower and spire, west face. An inspection in 1961 showed that urgent work was needed to prevent the spire from collapsing. It was consolidated with grout and strengthened with reinforced concrete rings and stitches. A great deal of the brick lining had to be renewed and about one-quarter of the external stone was replaced. The spire was reinforced with stainless steel in the horizontal joints. Work on the spire took two years and was completed in 1963. In 1976 it withstood a 170 km/h (105 m.p.h.) gale

Figure 7.28   Holy Shrine of Al Hussein, Kerbala, Iraq

Vertical cracking at the base of the thirteenth century minaret between the minaret and main body, due to wind sway and differential settlement of two completely different structures. It is a sort of natural expansion joint and so should only be filled with soft material

origin in still air, but winds can transport particles of 100 µm to even 10 000 µm in size, depending on their speeds. In cities, particulates arise largely from fuels burning in power stations and from vehicles, so there is generally a lot of sooty tarry material in them. They are usually acidic from absorbed sulphur dioxide and often contain traces of metals such as iron, which can cause deterioration. This effect is noticeable on some copper roofs in Melbourne—on buildings adjacent to trams, whose brake blocks of cast iron give off dust which accelerates the corrosion of the roofs.

The particles of matter that are transported by winds at normal speeds range from about 100 µm to 10 mm. The minute particulates, which form a thin smoke or haze, do not fall at all, due to their inherent susceptibility to collisions with molecules of air and water and the very feeble pull of gravity. Small particles are carried considerable distances before they fall to the ground; otherwise, their rate of fall increases with the square of the logarithm of their size.

When the wind at ground level is sufficiently strong to dislodge and propel stationary particles into the air they may be lifted to a height of about 1500 m (5000 ft) or more, according to Kendrew, forming a dust storm. Larger particles (sand) have a bounding movement, with an average height of just over 1 m (3.3 ft), impinging at an angle between 10 and 16 degrees. If the ground surface is hard (pebbles or rocks), the sand grains may bounce to greater heights; on the other hand if the surface consists of loose grains of similar size, the vertical displacement is lessened by dissipation of frictional energy which may dislodge more grains of sand, so producing a surface cloud of sand with no increase in height.

A light breeze causes the slow and almost imperceptible movement of sand grains and it is by this means that vast quantities of material are moved over a period of time, such as the dunes of sand in deserts which can engulf a settlement or oasis.

On the lee side of a building or wall there is a low pressure zone which also occurs along the other sides to lesser extent. It is noteworthy that the traditional central courtyard of not more than 6–7 m (19–23 ft) gives the best protection against dust driven by wind from any direction. Perimeter courtyards of the same width give variable protection depending on the direction of the wind.

Historic buildings may be threatened by sand movement and wind-blown sand and pebbles. Local information should be obtained and traditional precautions reviewed before any possible intervention into microclimate control. For museums, dust is a major nuisance and should be reduced and eliminated by filtered air supply, keeping a positive pressure inside the building and an air lock at the door. In

Figure 7.30   North-west tower, St Paul's Cathedral, London, England
(Courtesy: Feilden & Mawson)

A comparison between the moulded base of the column or the outer face of the building and inner face shows the enormous wear suffered by even a hard limestone from wind erosion and pollution

Figure 7.29   Furness Abbey, Lancashire, England
An example of combined action of wind erosion and rising dampness. The wind causes evaporation and the crystallization of salts within the pores of the stone which breaks down the surface progressively

Figure 7.31   Carved ornament, St Paul's Cathedral, London, England
(Courtesy: Feilden & Mawson)

The central acorn feature was fractured and eroded by wind and pollution. Note the reduction of size in comparison with the replacement which is shown in two stages: the rough work prepared by the mason for the carver, and the process of carving

order that the filters may be correctly designed, the size of the particulates in the atmosphere must be measured and graded.

Dust disfigures the exterior and interior of historic buildings. In Stockholm it may be remarked that the colour of the plaster finish of buildings appears rather dark. Holmström (verbal communication) states that research has shown that this is due to the black dust from motor tyres and asphalt roads settling on the rough rendered surfaces of the buildings, and suggests that a smooth finish to the plaster would reduce this effect. In St Paul's Cathedral, the dust was analysed and at least half of the material was human detritus—or a by-product of the millions of tourists who visit the cathedral. At York Minster, dust was 5–6 mm (0.2–0.24 in) deep on upper surfaces and generally obscured defects which became apparent when the interior was cleaned and washed down. Dust makes the architect's work of inspecting historic buildings both dirty and more difficult.

Figure 7.32 Dust deposit, Cairo Museum, Cairo, Egypt

Dust is one of the most difficult environmental hazards to combat as it gets into all unsealed spaces. Here it lies thickly on a roof light

Figure 7.33   Church, Scarperia, Italy

Damage by landslip. This Renaissance church was built on a geological fault. It is also vulnerable to earthquakes

Figure 7.34   Church, Scarperia, Italy

Details of cracking. Repairs always fail if the cause is not diagnosed: in this case a geological fault leading to a landslip

Figure 7.35   Church, Scarperia, Italy
Details of internal cracking due to the landslip

Figure 7.36   Record of flood levels, Ferrara, Italy
In the eighteenth century, flooding of the River Po up to first-floor level was usual. A record was kept on the Ducal Palace

Natural disasters

Besides earthquakes, which are dealt with in Chapter 8, the main list of violent, unforeseen and calamitous natural disasters which may affect historic buildings includes seismic sea waves (tsunamis), tidal waves, landslides and landslips and phenomena related to land movements and disruption, volcanic eruptions and gaseous exhalations, spontaneous combustion, cyclones, hurricanes, tornadoes, whirlwinds, water spouts, typhoons, floods, avalanches and snowslips, and even unexpected frost, for if this occurs only at infrequent intervals it can be all the more damaging for being unexpected.

An interesting example of a natural disaster is the Sun Temple at Chauvim Huamtar in Peru, initiated in 1600 B.C. and covered by a landslip of liquid mud in A.D. 1540. Only now is the temple being excavated and consolidated. A case of land movement due to a geological fault is that of the Iron Bridge, in England, at the village of the same name, which was being crushed by a closing of the river Severn's banks. Insertion of a massive concrete strut under the river bed has prevented this. At Scarperia, in northern Tuscany, the mediaeval castle and a Renaissance church are badly cracked due to landslipping along a geological fault.

Tornadoes consist of whirlwinds which move rapidly and have the power to lift roofs off buildings and throw cars about. At the centre of this whirlwind is a sudden vacuum which causes buildings to expand outwards from their own internal air pressure. With the light timber construction of domestic and farm buildings in the USA, a tornado causes a building to disintegrate; the safest areas are central halls or bathrooms, which generally remain intact.

Floods

Floods have been recorded over a long time in many countries, and certain levels can be predicted to occur at intervals of 10, 50, 100, 200 and even 1000 years. The Nile is the classic case of recording, as the prosperity of Egypt depended upon the height of the flood—that is, until the Aswan High Dam was built. Unfortunately one may not have to wait a hundred years for a 100-year flood, as it may come tomorrow. Besides tragic loss of life, floods mainly affect historic buildings, but if they submerge a city great harm will be done to furniture, books, carpets and tapestries. When the Arno predictably flooded Florence in 1966 it was found that heating oil floating on the flood waters added materially to the damage. In the case of sea flooding, which may occur when high winds add their impetus to high tides, the salt water damages the building fabric and might lead to permanent damp-ness—such is the threat to Venice, which was also badly flooded at the same time as Florence.

After such major disasters, massive first aid is needed. Streets must be cleared, rubble removed and bodies recovered. Then conservators must be mobi-lized to save cultural property of all types from further damage by over hasty or wrong treatment. The Inter-national Centre for the Study of the Preservation and Restoration of Cultural Property (ICCROM), in Rome, has the task of mobilizing and co-ordinating help when it is needed.

The lesson one should learn from records of past floods is to put vulnerable cultural property, such as books, manuscripts, archives, water colours, oil paint-ings, and wooden objects and all ethnographical and organic material, above any conceivable flood level. If this is not possible, then precautions must be taken by providing pumps and drainage sumps, together with material ready for blocking up vulnerable openings such as basement windows. Polythene, sandbags and even bricks and cement should be kept in reserve. Burst pipes also cause internal flooding of buildings, so no pipework should be allowed through storage areas for such cultural property.

Lightning

Perhaps the most frequent of natural causes of violent damage is lightning, which is the natural means of equalizing the electrical potentials of the earth and the atmosphere. When, in certain atmospheric con-ditions, the potential difference builds up sufficiently, a high-voltage discharge will take place involving currents of up to 160 000 amps for a few milliseconds. The discharge is usually in the form of a double flash, with 60% of the total energy dissipated in a flash from atmosphere to earth and 40% in the reverse direction.

Lightning has a tendency to strike the tops of tall objects (buildings and trees) standing up above the general ground level. When there is substantial elec-trical resistance in the path between the point of striking and the mass of the earth, damage will generally be caused. This is because, by Ohm's law, energy will be dissipated in a resistance when current flows through it. When the current is of the magnitude involved in a lightning discharge, the total energy can be many thousand megawatts; this is nearly all dis-sipated as heat, with the result that any moisture pre-sent is flashed into steam with explosive force. This steam is what splits trees, shatters stones and causes most of the damage. The nature of the damage is quite unpredictable; it is basically as if a high-explosive detonating fuse were running through a structure, the degree of disruption depending on variables such as

differences in resistance and moisture content in materials in different parts of a building.

Lightning can cause damage in other ways, most seriously by setting fire to timbers, by melting and cracking metal objects and by causing overloading of electrical wiring and devices through inductive ef-fects. It can cause damage by indirect means, such as when displaced tower masonry falls through a lower roof, and it can cause objects to be thrown about and damaged by magnetic effects.

If a lightning discharge, instead of passing suddenly at random through the fabric of a building, can be confined to low-resistance conductors passing directly to earth, these ill-effects can be avoided; the principle of lightning protection is to provide such a conductor. A conductor also allows ground potential to move upwards and so neutralize the threat of a strike.

Whether an historic building should be fitted with a lightning conductor or not depends on the following factors:

(1) The cultural and economic values of the building and its contents.
(2) The size and height of the building.
(3) The location and surroundings of the building.
(4) The record of previous lightning strikes on the building.
(5) The general assessment of risk in the geographi-cal location of the building.
(6) Whether the lightning conductor can be main-tained regularly.

There are belts of country and even individual sites where lightning strikes are more frequent than else-where, and if a domestic building has a record of two or three strikes in 10 years a conductor is definitely required. Information to help evaluate the risk is contained in BS 6651:1985. This new code greatly increased the requirements for lightning protection with more downtapes all to be bonded together at parapet level and ground level. As architects are not necessarily informed when new codes are promul-gated they should ensure that the specialist instructed, test the lightning protection installation and draw his attention to any deficiencies. Whether or not there is a conductor, insurance cover against lightning damage can be obtained without difficulty.

A tower with a flat top and parapet should have a ring conductor around the top with four terminal spikes, as well as a single terminal if there is a tall central flagpole which can carry the terminal. If there is a metal roof and no parapet, a single terminal will suffice, provided it is bonded to the roof. There should be two down tapes.

Figure 7.37   Lightning conductors, St Peter's, Rome, Italy

This massive building with walls 13 m (43 ft) thick and superbly built with good travertine, need only fear earthquakes and lightning. The ball is bronze gilded and well protected against strikes

Very few churches are entirely protected by a terminal on top of the tower. It is, however, rare for lightning to strike churches anywhere else but on top of the tower, so unless the nave or chancel is very long or high or exceptionally valuable it is a justifiable risk to let the tower conductor suffice. In domestic buildings, chimneys are especially vulnerable, as a column of hot smoke especially during the summer months is much more conductive than the surrounding air and doubles the effective height of the chimney as far as lightning is concerned. A single terminal on the chimney top will give the necessary protection.

In addition to the code of practice mentioned above, which covers the installation of a conductor system in great detail, there are certain points which apply particularly to historic buildings. Routes for tape conductors, for instance, can have distinct aesthetic implications and must be planned carefully in conjunction with a specialist or consultant—but the architect must have final approval.

The main down-lead must go by the most direct route possible and avoid all sharp bends, particularly loops such as might be needed around a cornice. It is better to drill through a cornice and line the hole with a lead or plastic sleeve. Otherwise lightning can leap across a loop by the shortest path, at best punching a hole through a cornice on the way, at worst shattering a length of stone that is difficult to repair.

When a tape has to pass from interior to exterior it should do so through a hole of at least 150 mm (6 in) diameter, sloping downwards to keep out rain and wired to keep out birds. Metal roofs, structural steelwork, bells and metal bell frames should be connected to the conductor system; so too should minor metal items (flashings, gutters, etc.) if they are close to the down-lead or bonding tape and form a possible alternative route to earth. Gas and water

115

pipes, electric conduit, metal sheathing and earth continuity conductors should be connected to the main down-lead if possible.

The point in an installation most vulnerable to neglect is the connection between down-lead and earth terminal. If possible, this should be contained in a small chamber with a removable cover, so that it is easy to inspect and repair. Earth terminals are usually sectional copper rods with the capability of extension when necessary to improve earthing.

It is the moisture in the ground which provides the conductive path for lightning strikes, as the minerals making up the soil—silica, alumina, lime, etc.—are poor conductors in themselves. In summer, sandy soils sometimes become so dry that resistance to earth is very high just when the conductor system is most needed. When this happens, matters can be improved by putting rock salt in the terminal box or in the soil and watering the ground with a hose. If there is a high resistance to earth from the terminal, the conductor will still operate—although less effectively than normally—but there will be a risk of great disturbance of the ground and possible damage to the foundations.

Where protection is necessary and has been installed, it is essential to maintain the original electrical performance. If joint continuity is lacking, for example, the conductor can be more of a liability than an asset, as the lightning discharge might leave the conductor halfway down and possibly cause more damage than if it had struck directly. A contract should be arranged with a specialist firm to service the system at one-year to, at the most, five-year intervals; some valuable high-risk buildings need annual inspection. All connections on tapes and elevation rods should be remade every 20 years, however difficult access to them may be (as on a tall spire). After a lightning strike has taken place, it is wise to have the installation checked.

Insurance against disasters

Insurance of historic buildings against fire and natural hazards poses difficult problems, particularly as much of the fabric and contents is irreplaceable. Full documentation is an essential element of disaster preparedness. Record drawings of the building should be made although this is rarely the case. The standard should be that required by the United States Historic Architectural Building Survey.

In the case of the contents, including furniture and fittings, there should be a complete inventory with record photographs and measured details with further details of acquisition and cost to substantiate a possible insurance claim. It is interesting to note that the value of the contents of a historic building may be several times that of the fabric. All these records should be duplicated and kept in a safe place in fire-proof cabinets.

Full insurance cover of historic buildings is expensive, but the insurers will insist on uplift for inflation and unless agreed otherwise will reduce the claim by the percentage shortfall in cover. With large buildings which are unlikely to be completely destroyed by a disaster such as fire, insurance can be for the largest single event, if the building is properly compartmented.

After a disaster questions about insurance will be asked immediately. Was the property properly insured? Early contact with the insurance company is essential and a loss adjuster will be appointed to act for them. The loss adjuster will review whether the full value was insured. If not, the value of the claim will be reduced in proportion to the percentage shortfall. Preparation and evaluation of insurance claims is time consuming and the cost of this time is a legitimate part of the claim. If all the supporting documentation is available it will be a triumph of disaster planning. Full insurance claims, however, should not be made until reports have been obtained from all concerned, including police and fire brigade if involved, and a meeting held under the chairmanship of a responsible person to establish all the facts of a case. Frivolous or badly framed claims only waste time and lead to increased premiums. Detailed estimates of damage should be obtained to substantiate the claim.

8

Historic buildings in seismic zones

Introduction

Earthquakes—the shifting of the earth's crust—can result in devastating destruction. While there is a growing body of knowledge about the nature of earthquakes, we cannot predict with confidence either their precise time of arrival or their intensity. We can predict only that they will eventually happen.

Even with our present knowledge of technology we can do nothing to reduce either the frequency or the intensity of earthquakes. The only thing we can do is to take precautions to mitigate potential devastation. Beyond the obvious need to protect human life, we must also take responsibility for protecting historic buildings and monuments. Already we have suffered major losses of important structures.

Earthquakes are different from other disasters in their capacity to destroy almost instantaneously without warning, causing extensive, often irreparable damage to cultural property. Preparing for and responding to earthquakes involves local, provincial (state), and national (or federal) organizations.

Earthquake preparedness must incorporate planning for contingencies common to most other types of disasters—especially fire, flood and looting. By planning ahead vital time can be saved after the disaster has struck. Fortunately the conservation of cultural property utilizes different skills, techniques and materials from those required to reconstruct modern buildings. As a result, conserving our cultural heritage does not necessarily compete with other recovery operations for scarce resources in the post-disaster situation.

Improvement of the seismic resistance of historic buildings should be integrated into a regular maintenance programme, based on periodic inspections by specially trained architects and engineers. Administrators in seismic zones should ensure that these inspections are carried out and that a full inventory with detailed documentation is prepared before the next earthquake. Disaster preparedness has to combat the natural inclination of the people to say, 'It won't happen here,' or 'not in my lifetime'. The only responsible policy is to work consistently and effectively to plan for the eventuality of an earthquake.

In seismic zones, the strengthening of valuable cultural property should be included in the general programme of preventive maintenance and, when economically possible, in conjunction with other major building repairs such as renewal of roofs or strengthening of walls and foundations.

Well maintained historic buildings have a relatively high degree of earthquake resistance. Bearing in mind that earthquakes and the reaction of historic structures to an earthquake are both unpredictable, the most profitable field of study is the analysis of previous earthquake damage in the locality. These case studies can provide the basis for future

Figure 8.1 Quasr el Bint, Jordan

This remarkable second century AD building was given tensile reinforcement against earthquakes by insertion of lacing bands of timber—most of which eventually rotted. However, it proved effective in preserving the outer walls while the roof collapsed

117

Table 8.1 Modified Mercalli Intensity Scale (Courtesy: Editor, *Consulting Engineer*, May 1978)

Num-ber	Descriptive term	Effects	Acceleration (cm/s²)
I	Imperceptible	Not felt. Registered only by seismographs	<1
II	Very slight	Felt in upper storeys solely by persons at rest	1–2
III	Slight	Felt indoors. Vibrations like those caused by light trucks passing by	2–5
IV	Moderate	Hanging objects swing. Vibrations like those caused by heavy trucks or a jolt such as that occasioned by a heavy object striking the wall. Parked cars are set in seesaw motion. Windows, doors and crockery rattle	5–10
V	Fairly strong	Felt outdoors. Sleeping persons wakened. Small objects not anchored are displaced or overturned. Doors open and close. Shutters and pictures are set in motion. Pendulum clocks stop and start or change their speed	10–20
VI	Strong	Walking is made difficult. Windows, crockery and glass break. Knick-knacks, books, etc., fall off shelves; pictures fall from the walls. Furniture moves or is overturned. Cracks in weak plaster and materials of construction type D. Small bells ring (church, school)	20–50
VII	Very strong	Noticed by car drivers and passengers. Furniture breaks. Material of construction type D sustains serious damage. In some cases, cracks in material of construction type C. Weak chimneys break at roof level. Plaster, loose bricks, stones, tiles, shelves collapse. Waves created on ponds	50–100
VIII	Destructive	Steering of cars made difficult. Very heavy damage to materials of construction type D and some damage to materials of type C. Partial collapse. Some damage to materials of type B. Stucco breaks away. Chimney, monuments, towers and raised tanks collapse. Loose panel walls thrown out. Branches torn from trees. Changes in flow or temperature of springs. Changes in water level of wells. Cracks in moist ground and on steep slopes	100–200
IX	Highly destructive	General panic. Material of construction type D completely destroyed. Serious damage to material of type C, and frequent collapse. Serious damage also sustained by material of type B. Frame structures lifted from their foundations, or they collapse. Load-bearing members of reinforced concrete structures are cracked. Pipes laid below ground burst. Large cracks in the ground. In alluvial areas, water, sand and mud ejected	200–500
X	Extremely destructive	Most masonry and wooden structures destroyed. Reinforced steel buildings and bridges seriously damaged, some of them destroyed. Severe damage to dams, dikes and weirs. Large landslides. Water hurled onto the banks of canals, rivers and lakes. Rails bent	500–1000 (≈1 g)

Construction method A:
Good workmanship, mortar and design; reinforced, especially laterally, and bound together using steel, concrete, etc.; designed to resist lateral forces.

Construction method B:
Good workmanship and mortar; reinforced but not designed to resist strong lateral forces

Construction method C:
Ordinary workmanship and mortar; no extreme weaknesses such as failing to tie in at corners, but neither reinforced nor designed to resist horizontal forces

Construction method D:
Weak materials such as adobe; poor mortar, low standards of workmanship; horizontally weak.

MM 1956	MSK 1964	RF 1883	JMA 1951
I	II	II	
II			I
III	III	III	
IV	IV	IV	II
V	V	V	III
VI		VI	IV
	VI	VII	
VII			
	VII	VIII	V
VIII		IX	
IX	VIII		
	IX	IX	VI
X	X		
XI	XI	X	
			VII
XII	XII		

Table 8.1 *continued*

XI	Disaster	All structures collapse. Even large, well-constructed bridges are destroyed or severely damaged. Only a few buildings remain standing. Rails greatly bent and thrown out of position. Underground wires and pipes break apart	1–2 g
XII	Major disaster	Large-scale changes in the structure of the ground. Overground and subterranean streams and rivers changed in many ways. Waterfalls are created, lakes are dammed up or burst their banks. Rivers alter their courses.	> 2 g

Intensity scales:
MM 1956 Modified Mercalli
MSK 1964 Medvedev–Sponheuer–Karnik
RF   1883 Rossi–Forel
JMA 1951 Japan Meteorological Agency

applications of strengthening measures as part of a general programme of building maintenance.

Nature of earthquakes

The surface of the earth consists of about twenty independent tectonic plates floating on a softer inner layer. These plates are in continuous motion relative to each other because of currents in the internal liquid core of the earth. Thus, elastic energy accumulates along the edges of the plates, and is eventually released with a sudden movement, which causes brief, strong vibrations in the ground—an earthquake. The place in the earth's crust where this energy release occurs is the focus, or hypocentre. The vibrations propagate very quickly in all directions, but generally become weaker with distance.

Very often a major earthquake is preceded by some foreshocks and is nearly always followed by aftershocks, some of which can be of comparable strength. The intepretation of foreshocks is difficult and thus they are seldom useful in predicting a major earthquake. Aftershocks can be very dangerous, as they will react upon already damaged structures.

Magnitude and intensity

The magnitude of an earthquake is expressed in degrees on the Richter scale. It indicates the absolute strength or energy release of the earthquake and is calculated on the basis of recordings of the earthquake by accelerometers or seismographs in different locations.

While magnitude characterizes the earthquake itself, intensity indicates the effects of the earthquake in a determined place. Intensity is most often expressed in degrees (I to XII) on the Modified Mercalli Scale, which classifies the observable

damage to buildings and installations caused by the shaking ground. Damage caused by an earthquake of a given magnitude and the intensity with which the earthquake is felt in a determined place, depends on many factors: the distance from the epicentre, the main direction, frequency, content, type of seismic waves, the local ground conditions, the condition of the buildings affected (i.e. whether

Figure 8.2   Church of San Francisco, Antigua, Guatemala (Courtesy: Architect D. del Cid)

This church was damaged at the end of the eighteenth century in a great earthquake and left in a ruined state. It suffered further damage in the great earthquake of 1976

they have been well maintained and the quality of workmanship on previous repairs), their form and design, etc.

Maximum ground acceleration is used to indicate intensity, but it is only one of the important factors determining intensity; it is a directly measurable value that can be used easily in calculations. It is expressed as a fraction of g the gravity acceleration.

It is not surprising that the unfavourable ground conditions of the Friuli, Italy, earthquake (6.4 Richter) produced a result (Modified Mercalli IX and X) as devastating as the 1976 Guatemala earthquake of 7.6 Richter, one of the most severe ever recorded, with forty times the energy input of Friuli. In Friuli the second major shock followed a whole series of minor tremors and caused great havoc to buildings already weakened.

Another significant example is the 1985 Mexico earthquake, with a magnitude of 8.1 and an epicentre in the Pacific Ocean. In Zihuatanejo, on the coast, less than 100 kilometres from the epicentre, the earthquake registered an intensity of VII on the Modified Mercalli Scale, but an intensity of IX in some parts of Mexico City, about 400 kilometres from the epicentre. This was due partly to the focusing effect in the wave propagation and partly to the geological structure of the valley of Mexico City. Because of local variations in ground conditions, the intensity in Mexico City varied between VI and IX.

The secondary effects of earthquakes, such as landslips (landslides), road fractures, bridge failures, floods, and ground movements with changes of underground water levels and flow, can be devastating. The first effect is to disrupt communications and make rescue difficult. In addition, an earthquake site is generally held in a pall of dust.

Knowing the risk

Inhabitants of seismic zones must realize that they live between two earthquakes. Barclay G. Jones, observes that, even after administrators recognize the problem and take steps, their policies and preparations must continually be updated and re-evaluated. 'Institutions and public bodies must face the problem and establish policies', to protect the cultural heritage.

Complete safety is unobtainable, so the issue is how much safety is feasible to achieve, or conversely how much danger is tolerable. Three concepts are involved in assessing dangers:

Hazard: The probability that a disastrous event of given intensity will occur in a particular place.

Vulnerability: The degree of loss that will be sustained by an element from an earthquake of given intensity.

Risk: The probable loss, combining the hazards of location and the vulnerability of buildings and their contents. Risk can be removed, transferred, shared, accepted or accommodated.

A major earthquake may affect several administrative zones, provinces, or even countries. It is necessary to make not only a hazard assessment of a country, but also very specific and technical assessments of individual sites containing valuable cultural property.

Seismicity

The mean interval between two earthquakes of a certain intensity at a certain place is called the return period of earthquakes with that intensity at that place. Return periods are of limited use for prediction, especially when the place is subject to earthquakes from various independent foci, but they provide valuable statistical information. The return periods of earthquakes of various intensities enable the risks to be assessed. In the ancient capital of Pagan in Burma, the acceleration is estimated at $0.2g$ with a return period of 100 years, but in 500 years the estimate increases to $0.6g$. A large and recent earthquake indicates less probability of recurrence; thus, the hazard is lower, but increases with time.

In all estimates of acceleration and return periods, there is a large element of doubt. For safety reasons, the seismologist may overestimate and this may lead to unnecessary interventions in historic buildings. At present, it is thought wiser not to evaluate intensities with return periods greater than one hundred years when designing strengthening measures for historic buildings, as this will avoid excessive interventions that may not last the specified return period. It is better to devise schemes that do not prejudice future interventions and can be strengthened if desired. Maximum accelerations should be given for specific sites so that alternative courses of action can be studied and compared

Seismic zones

Seismic zones correspond mainly to the edges of the tectonic plates that support the continents and oceans. Seismic maps are available in every country and are periodically updated, although, as Pierre Pichard explains, 'These maps are not as a rule, distributed widely enough and in most cases are unknown, for example, to those responsible for monuments.' However, these maps are invaluable in establishing a clear picture of the most threatened sites.

It is therefore recommended that national and internal organizations responsible for the cultural heritage co-operate with scientific and government authorities, to develop seismic maps that pinpoint historic monuments, cities and quarters, archaeological sites, and significant museums and libraries. This will provide a clear picture of the most valuable sites and the priorities to be observed.

Building vulnerability

The vulnerability of cultural property, both buildings and objects, varies widely. This vulnerability derives from differing characteristics of each particular earthquake, the soil upon which the structure rests, and the characteristics of the structure itself: foundations, intrinsic faults due to design form, lack of bonding, poor workmanship, and extrinsic faults due to lack of maintenance and decay.

Vulnerability reduction plans must be devised and instituted. The structure of vulnerability reduction plans is consistent: inventory, recording and documentation, risk assessment, protection, emergency procedures, and restorative processes.

Vulnerability studies should be made for earthquakes of different intensities, and the effects of different degrees of proposed intervention should be assessed. Different types of earthquakes will have different impacts on each individual historic structure, but computer models can help assess potential damage from each. These studies will show the most likely scenario and the range of variation from the median.

Most national or state codes for new buildings are determined by the estimated thresholds of tolerable risk. Unfortunately, it is rarely possible to do this for historic buildings, especially the large number of rural vernacular buildings or traditional dwellings in historic centres.

The actions needed to prepare seismic safety plans for historic buildings are:

(1) Estimate seismic hazards in terms of the expected occurrence of earthquakes of various intensities and their return period.
(2) Estimate seismic risk (loss of life, material damage, functional loss, building degradation).
(3) Identify structural systems and models for analysis for historic properties. Prepare record drawings and seismic survey forms.

(4) Evaluate structural responses to earthquakes of various intensities.
(5) Determine type and degree of damage for different predicted seismic intensities.
(6) Develop alternative upgrading (strengthening) methods and estimate costs, applying conservation ethics to determine the minimum intervention necessary.
(7) Develop plan schedules and give approximate estimates of cost of alternative schemes for different return periods.
(8) Prepare a management plan for a chosen scheme. Obtain budget allocations based on accurate estimates. Execute desirable works to increase seismic resistance.

Examination of earthquake damage shows that the direction of the waves has a considerable effect on the resistance of the building. The following is an imagined scenario of earthquake damage. First, roof tiles begin to slip and fall, weak timber joints break and the roof timbers batter the walls. Then cracks form in the corners of the walls and where stresses concentrate around door and window openings and in vaults and arches. The centre portion of the vault or arch may slip downwards wedging the structure apart. The roof falls in and portions of the vaults and domes fall. Pinnacles and towers rotate, shift and fall causing damage, and facades slip apart. The structure disintegrates into large lumps if well built, and rubble if badly built. With simple vernacular buildings the front walls fall out into the street and the roofs and floors crush the occupants.

The basic causes of damage are relative ground displacements and inertia loads that result from ground accelerations. The factors affecting the seismic performance of a historic building are its mass, stiffness, periods of vibration (all of which affect the loading), damping capacity or the ability to absorb energy, stability margins, structural geometry, structural continuities and distributions of mass and resistance. Historic buildings usually lack the ductility and structural continuity which can be designed into new buildings. The compatibility of the various structural elements and the availability of alternative structural actions, when some elements fail, are important considerations.

Lastly, there is the general condition of the structure—has it been well maintained and carefully repaired in the past? Earthquakes seek out the hidden weaknesses in a building, so are often blamed for what was a faulty repair, bad workmanship or lack of preventive maintenance.

According to the Mercalli grading, most historic buildings come within the lower strength classification being stiff structures made of brittle material.

Figure 8.3   Friuli, Italy
(Courtesy: Architect G. Tampone)
Earthquake damage

However, Mercalli quite rightly lays great emphasis on the quality of workmanship. Perhaps he is unduly critical of adobe, which, if mixed with long straw or tough grass, can achieve remarkable strength and toughness.

Strengthening of historic buildings

For simplicity we should consider two main classes of historic buildings:

(1) The sophisticated (for its time) with high quality workmanship and materials.
(2) The vernacular which has evolved using materials available locally which meets climatic conditions as efficiently as possible.

In vernacular architecture improvements are possible using modern materials to increase tensile resistance and bonding, but a blind use of reinforced concrete can be disastrous, so the nature of the building needs understanding. The typical weaknesses of South European vernacular buildings are found in the construction of the door and window openings and in the tying of the roof structure and floors into the walls; however these weaknesses can

be rectified. Much can be learned from typical failure patterns in previous earthquakes, which will show various degrees of damage.

Sophisticated buildings are much more complex so it is impossible to generalize as each is an individual. Strangely the original construction rarely includes anti-seismic elements except metal cramps in masonry and ties across arches openings and wide span vaults. Their vulnerability depends on three main factors:

(1) Foundations. Is the soil homogeneous? What is its nature and likely seismic performance? Is there ground water?
(2) Intrinsic faults due to form, design and lack of bonding.
(3) Extrinsic faults due to lack of maintenance and decay (especially at the ends of embedded timbers).

A historic building may have already survived several earthquakes. This shows its resistance but it may also have been weakened.

The historic building can only be understood through a study of its history, including sequence of construction, details of previous repairs and restorations and former earthquakes. Lack of

Figure 8.4   Friuli, Italy
(Courtesy: Architect G. Tampone)

Earthquake damage

maintenance, injudicious alterations and continual erosion of its resistance by the combined causes of decay, including pollution and vibration, will also have caused weakening by cumulative effects. These can only be countered by regular inspections and a maintenance and repair strategy. The maintenance strategy should aim at a gradual upgrading of the earthquake resistance of the building, in which way economic results will be obtained gradually providing that building owners recognize seismic risks.

The shock waves of earthquakes are various and the seismic responses of historic buildings are infinitely variable. Seismic codes and standardized procedures will not take into account the nature of a specific historic building. Some of the so-called strengthening measures imposed incur damage and reduce the value in historic buildings. The upgrading of seismic resistance needs understanding of the nature of historic buildings and the ability to make difficult judgments. Such buildings are generally stiff but built of weak materials; it is vital that all means of strengthening should be compatible.

The role of the architect in seismic zones

After having researched the seismic history of the building and having studied the relevant codes and seismological maps, the conservation architect has an important role in initiating action to save historic buildings.

In a specific case, the first step is to make a condition survey of the condition of the historic building, noting all the visible defects and classifying the urgency of corrective actions. The causes of decay should be diagnosed. The second step is to define its significance and identify the values that give it this significance so that all the specialists involved at a later stage may understand and respect the authenticity of the fabric.

The greatest danger to historic buildings comes from engineers who are unaware of their unique values and apply the Codes literally, or who are unwilling to accept responsibility for making judgments. It can be said with some justice, that many a historic building has the options of being destroyed by the Codes or by the next earthquake.

123

Figure 8.5   Ospedelletto di Germona, Friuli, Italy
(Courtesy: C. Silver)

*Private house with fresco on the facade. Attempts to save this
structure were abandoned due to the severe earthquake damage.
Collapse was judged to be imminent and conditions too dangerous
to permit detachment of this fresco, which was a nineteenth century
copy of a seventeenth century original. The house was demolished*

As the vast number of vernacular buildings are
unlikely to be studied individually, the conservation
architect may be involved in drafting practical
guidelines for their strengthening so that builders
and owners do not destroy the authenticity of their
buildings.

Site investigation

The geology of the site greatly affects the risk, as was
shown in the 1987 earthquake which destroyed ten-
storey modern buildings in Mexico City and left
historic buildings scarcely damaged as their vibration
mode did not coincide with that of the earthquake.

The engineer will be jointly involved in research
into the geology of the site, as this will affect the risk
by several degrees. Microzoning will indicate local
faults that increase the risk and geological strata that
may either decrease or increase the risk. The level of
the ground water should be investigated as it may

Figure 8.6   S. Stefano, Antegna, Friuli, Italy
(Courtesy: C. Silver)

*Nineteenth century plaster hides the fine Lombard (c. A.D. 700)
bas-reliefs and the frescoes. The keystone of the arch of the presbytery
has been temporarily propped to prevent immediate collapse*

induce liquefaction. The foundations should be inspected and the ground probed if necessary.

In addition to the direction of the shock wave, the predominant frequency of these waves and the natural frequency of the building and ground are vital questions. The stiffness of the building in relation to the properties of the subsoil should be assessed by a seismic engineer. The whole building may vibrate at a certain frequency due to its form and stiffness, and if there is dynamic resonance the structural damage will be much greater. Cracking and other disruption of the structure may accidentally increase or decrease this resonance. In a severe earthquake, badly bonded elements act like battering rams oscillating in different modes. It has been observed that a masonry building can survive a few shocks of great intensity, but that vibration of long duration is damaging. In general stiff buildings suffer less if the ground is soft and flexible, less if sited on hard rock, but soft ground with sedimentary layers at depths down to two or three hundred feet can amplify the shock. Sloping strata and variegated soils such as peat or clay, should be identified as these increase the vulnerability.

Shock waves can be focused by the terrain and tend to concentrate in ridges. In order to assess the risk more accurately than is possible in a generalized code, it is desirable for the engineer to establish the seismic spectrum of the historic building.

Structural investigation

The form of the building will affect its resistance to seismic shocks; in descending order circular, octagonal or square plans have good resistance, whereas a long building, or one with projecting wings, is more vulnerable. Elements which have different modes of vibration are also vulnerable. In assessing the seismic performance of a building the elements likely to dissociate themselves should be identified; these include chimneys, gables, balconies, roof structures and towers.

During an earthquake, stresses will tend to concentrate wherever structure changes, as at openings, and where materials with different characteristics are introduced. Corners are vulnerable because stresses come from two directions. Previous repairs and the introduction of incompatible materials in strengthening programmes, often result in damage.

One of the great difficulties faced by engineers is to assess the strength of brick or stone masonry set in lime mortar. Cores should be taken from masonry walls to ascertain the quality of the mortar and to estimate its strength. The mortar itself, may with time, have lost its cohesion or have become as strong as Portland cement mortar. Cracks and fissures will indicate loss of strength.

The structural system must be examined at three levels; as a whole, as elements and as individual materials, to decide upon its action. The quality of the original workmanship is a material factor in the assessment of which the historic evidence is useful.

A change of use in a historic building can have serious implications from a seismic point of view, especially if the dead weight is increased by furniture, office equipment, files and books. A use that is sympathetic to the building and its authenticity must be chosen.

A full investigation of the condition of the historic building, should involve archaeologists, historians, geotechnicians, materials scientists besides architects and engineers. The key experts should make joint inspections in order to discuss the problems *in situ* and to use the evidence available in the fabric of the building itself.

Strengthening timber buildings

Provided their joints are sound, and the timbers are not attacked by fungi, timber buildings are considered to have good earthquake resistance. Unfortunately they are vulnerable to fires, which are often a by-product of an earthquake. If strengthening is necessary, elements can be strapped together and the structure bolted to its foundations. Walls and roofs can be given additional strength by the addition of plywood linings. Plaster and wattle-and-daub panels in timber framing can be strengthened with galvanized expanded metal reinforcement nailed to the framing on both sides.

Strengthening masonry buildings

Possible methods of strengthening masonry walls against seismic force loading are:

(1) Drilling and grouting in vertical steel reinforcement down the full height of the wall.
(2) Thickening the existing walls on the inside with sprayed concrete.
(3) Thickening the existing walls with cast-in-situ reinforced concrete.
(4) Cutting away a layer of existing brickwork and replacing with cast-in-situ reinforced concrete.
(5) Base isolation.

Thickening walls with sprayed or cast concrete is not recommended. However, if internal walls are

Figure 8.7   S. Stefano, Antegna, Friuli, Italy
(Courtesy: C. Silver)

The interior of this small church contains important cycles of superimposed frescoes dating from the twelfth, fourteenth and fifteenth centuries under nineteenth century plaster. The altar in the presbytery was found to be constructed from important Lombard bas-reliefs, also covered by nineteenth century plaster. Friuli has the highest level of rainfall in Italy. Therefore, the church has been covered with plastic sheeting to protect the cultural property inside. The proppings of wood proved insufficient; thus two steel cables were locked about the exterior walls

Figure 8.8   S. Stefano, Antegna, Friuli, Italy
(Courtesy: C. Silver)

Presbytery from outside. Note plastic-sheet waterproofing and two steel cables that encircle the exterior walls

plastered and of thick enough brickwork a layer of which can be cut away, it is possible to insert reinforced concrete to replace the brickwork and then make good the plasterwork to the original design.

Although it involves specialist skills and equipment drilling and grouting methods are to be preferred, in spite of their greater expense, because the addition of reinforcement does not seriously affect the disposition of weights and is compatible with the existing structural system.

Base isolation has been applied to historic buildings, the most notable example being the City and County Building in Salt Lake City, Utah. Although the insertion of base isolators reduces the need for strengthening the historic fabric with consequent reduced loss of original material, it is difficult to install unless there is a basement and a gap of as much as 300 mm (12in) all round the building to isolate it from the ground which will move during an earthquake.

Vernacular masonry buildings

Examination of earthquake damage shows that bonding of walls together at corners is vital, together with the tying of floors and roofs to walls. The insertion of tensile reinforcement with some degree of prestressing to bond elements together, gives the masonry of historic buildings greater earthquake resistance. Experiments have shown that adobe or mud brick with diagonal prestressed cables anchored at top and bottom, have much greater resistance to dynamic forces. In existing adobe buildings, reinforcement, in the form of diagonal galvanized steel wires, might be added under the layer of mud plaster (stucco) that is normally renewed and anchored with small elements of reinforced concrete at top and bottom.

For simple two storey masonry houses built of lime mortar, Kolaric recommends reinforcement in both directions with 16 mm (0.6 in) steel ties fixed to the floor joists and anchored with 150 mm by 150 mm (6 × 6 in) plates, 5 mm (0.2 in) thick, which are recessed into external walls and then covered with plaster. Similar strengthening should be done at roof level where the anchoring of wall plates and tying together of roof timbers should be given special attention, as earthquake damage often starts at this point. The falling of heavy roof tiles and collapse of roof and floor timbers are, perhaps, amongst the major causes of loss of life, generally preceding or promoting the collapse of walls. The roof structure should incorporate diagonal ties which

can be used to strut gable walls. Tiles should be fixed with screws in holes drilled at the head.

A ring beam (bond beam) of reinforced concrete under the wall plate is an obvious improvement to the earthquake resistance of a masonry building; such a ring beam should be anchored securely to the walls, tied across the vaults and extended round the base of the domes. The mix of reinforced concrete should have strength characteristics similar to those of the masonry, so should consist of weak aggregates and mixes.

Considerable strengthening of masonry buildings can be obtained by grouting procedures of all types using hydraulic limes. In special cases the use of expensive polyester and epoxy resin grouts will be more than justified. Such grouts can be used following the normal injections, thus exploiting their penetrating power to fill fissures and fine cracks and avoiding the necessity of filling large voids with expensive materials. They are especially valuable as they increase the tensile strength of masonry and consolidate friable lime mortar, which weakness was reported to be one of the principal reasons for the collapse of many historic buildings in the Montenegro earthquake in April 1979. Rough masonry walls that are plastered can be strengthened in the way suggested for mud brick or by applying galvanized steel mesh on to both faces and tying both faces together at about 1 m (3.3 ft) centres, and then replastering.

Figure 8.9 Tuscania, Lazio, Italy

Emergency shoring after an earthquake is vital, as often the greater damage is caused by a second shock two or three months later. In this case, after some years the shoring has rotted where in contact with the ground. It often takes 10 years to rectify earthquake damage, so shoring should be rot-proof

Cross walls and partitions must be securely attached to the main walls. Lintels over doors and windows should extend at least 400 mm (16 in) beyond the opening to give added protection. If doors and windows are so placed as to cause a weakness in the wall, long reinforced concrete ties may have to be inserted in a concealed way, to disperse the concentration of dynamic stress which occurs at the corners.

Tall chimneys cause a hazard as they will have a different mode of vibration from the main building and are likely to collapse first, so causing damage and perhaps weakening a vital part of the structure. They should be strengthened, if possible, by vertical drilling and the insertion of prestressed ties or, if in poor condition, by being rebuilt at the same time inserting vertical reinforcement anchored securely to the mass of the wall below.

Earthquake shocks are transmitted to a building through its foundation. If the foundations fail the results will be totally disastrous, so foundations should always be investigated. If a building rests on a sloping stratum or variegated soils, such as peat and clay, special measures will be necessary, such as piling of varying depth to support the whole building on the same stratum, which must be sound itself and not liable to liquefaction when an earthquake occurs. The pile caps must be linked with horizontal beams and secured to the existing structure carefully. In other cases it may be sufficient to unify the foundations with ground beams around the perimeter.

To prevent mechanical plant from sliding, overturning and jamming during an earthquake, from 20 mm to 40 mm (0.8 in to 1.6 in) clearances may be necessary. There must be flexibility in the connections with pipes and wires and their fixings must be strong enough to withstand three dimensional movements. Electric mercury switches are dangerous, because vibration may activate them, and heating boilers with fire-brick linings are also liable to damage. Water and electric supplies to hospitals and fire-fighting services need special protection and should be examined by specialists. Also sculpture and landscape ornaments will need special fixings to prevent them from being thrown about during an earthquake.

Administrative procedures

The responsible engineer should present two or three practical alternatives to the multidisciplinary team for their review. The compatibility of the proposals with the historic fabric together with an estimate for their effectiveness must be considered. If this can be tested so much the better. Finally the 'least bad' solution should be chosen after assessing how it affects the values in the historic building and its significance. The questions of whether the intervention is the minimum necessary and whether the scheme prejudices future interventions should be answered.

When disaster strikes

The following actions are envisaged:

(1) Fight fires and prevent looting works of art. Prevent water damage from rupture of water supply pipes or fire-fighting.
(2) Protect as much cultural property as possible. Label and transport all movable cultural property to previously designated warehouses, fumigate and give first aid.
(3) Obtain the co-operation of the local civil and military authorities as soon as possible.
(4) Organize a quick inspection of damage and coordinate the work of conservators, architects and engineers. Grade damage to buildings.
(5) Set up multidisciplinary conservation teams and allocate labour to repairs, giving priority to immediate protection against the weather.
(6) Seek international aid through disaster relief agencies, requesting special equipment needed.

Emergency action

Following an earthquake, there is great human shock. Obviously, priority must be given to saving life and evacuating casualties. Fires have to be fought and looting prevented. People must be fed and given shelter. In the emergency situation after a major disaster, normal administrative channels may not be working and responsibilities may be taken over by relief organizations, the military or civil defence. These organizations have communications networks and other resources that may operate independently, bypassing existing institutional procedures. Disaster relief agencies and cultural property authorities do not yet have a tradition of co-operation. Thus, special guidelines for rescue actions in and around historic properties need to be incorporated into the plans of existing disaster relief agencies.

The emergency plan for an institution should be compatible with the overall recovery operation.

Specialized personnel, after attending to family and personal needs, should report to their institution to assist in recovery activities. These may include inspecting and assessing damage, securing objects from further damage from aftershocks, collecting broken fragments, protecting against water damage, dealing with flooding from broken water pipes, moving precious objects in the event of approaching fires, etc.

Immediate action is necessary to protect valuable movable property, which should be labelled, taken to a previously designated safe place, and protected from looting. Shelters should be erected over historic buildings, especially those with valuable contents.

Part of the shock syndrome is to assist in the destruction of what is left, arson is common, and wanton destruction of historic buildings that could have been saved is surprisingly frequent. In some countries, conservation organizations have enlisted the co-operation of military officers to organize security and fire-fighting measures. Earthquake protection could easily be added to these duties in seismic zones.

Emergency inspections

Following an earthquake, quick inspection of the damage is essential. Dangerous elements must be made safe. Historic buildings should have already been marked with the Hague Convention symbol. A system of documentation was developed for use in rescue operations following the Montenegro earthquake. Internationally recognized colour codes were superimposed on large scale maps to show categories of damage. Standard forms will enable all the information to be coded and analyzed efficiently. This system is provided below:

Usable—Green:
  Grade 1—slight superficial damage, virtually intact.
  Grade 2—superficial damage, non-structural.
  Grade 3—superficial, light structural damage.
Temporarily usable—Yellow:
  Grade 1—structural damage, e.g. roofs and ceilings.
  Grade 2—serious structural damage to walls etc.
Unusable—Red:
  Grade 1—severe structural damage, unsafe but capable of repair.
  Grade 2—partial collapse, eg. roofs, floors etc.
  Grade 3—total collapse, requiring reconstruction of walls, etc.

Emergency protection

After an earthquake temporary protection is vital. First aid will have to be given to buildings and objects. There may be a delay of months or years, hence the importance of temporary measures.

The safety of working conditions will need constant monitoring. Helmets and dust masks should always be worn. If perishable foods are left too long in markets or cold stores, severe health hazards arise due to decomposition, so much so that gas masks and protective clothing become necessary. Rats and other vermin increase and make the difficult work of cleaning much harder. A similar but more unpleasant risk occurs when it is the local custom to bury the dead in tombs above ground, for these disintegrate in an earthquake, scattering their decaying contents.

It is essential that experts in architectural conservation be involved, to prevent unnecessary demolition of cultural property and unthinking removal of archaeological material. They must have the authority and means to make historic buildings safe by temporary strengthening and shoring.

Architects with sound engineering judgment and wide cultural knowledge are necessary for this work. Also, military engineers should receive special training for earthquake duties. Particular emphasis must be given to structural first aid.

Glossary of earthquake terms*

Focus. The point within the earth's crust at which first rupture is estimated to have occurred. Earth masses have long boundaries along which relative movement occurs. Also the disturbance of the ground at or near the surface may be more severe away from the point immediately over the focus. The focus is typically about 20–30 km below the earth's surface.

Hypocentre. An alternative word for focus.

Epicentre. The point on the earth's surface immediately above the focus.

Epicentral distance. The distance from an observation station to the epicentre.

Hypocentral distance. The distance from an observation station to the focus.

Tsunami. A tidal wave occurring as a result of a sub-ocean earthquake. The velocity of a tsunami is related

---

*This glossary is reproduced by courtesy of the Editor of the *Consulting Engineer* (May 1978).

to the depth of the water by the formula $V = \sqrt{(Dg)}$, where V is the velocity and D is the depth. A typical period for such waves is 1 h and for a depth of say 5.6 km the velocity would be 800 km/h. The wave length therefore is about 800 km. At sea, the tsunami is almost unnoticed and its presence is only noted when it reaches a landmass.

Seiches. A disturbance within a closed body of water.

Mode. A shape of oscillation which can be generated in a given system of members and masses. Generally there are as many modes as there are degrees of freedom of the masses in the system. In any given mode the masses achieve the same proportion of their maximum displacement at the same time.

Normal mode. The first, or fundamental, mode in which greater displacements are observed further from the fixed base.

Modal response. The motion of all the masses in a system at any instant can be expressed as the sum of the individually factored modes. On a time basis, the factors applied to each mode vary so that the total response is continually changing. Mathematical examination of structures involves the assessment of response of systems, mode by mode, and the motion of system in a given mode is called a 'modal response'.

Period. The time taken for a system to move from the mean position and return but travelling in the same direction, i.e. in passing through the mean position twice. The fundamental period is that of the normal mode.

Critical damping. Damping can be applied to a system to slow down or reduce the amount of oscillation which takes place. Generally this is assumed to be proportional to the velocities of the masses and is referred to as viscous damping. Starting from zero this damping can be gradually increased until the masses return to the mean position at rest, having made one oscillation. The minimum amount of damping required to achieve this is the critical damping.

Damping. Any building system has some degree of damping. It is difficult to estimate damping due to the elastic performance of the structure taking into account joint slippage and damage to non-structural components, but whatever it is, it is normally expressed as a percentage of critical damping. It varies from 1% to about 10%.

Participation factor. At any given instant the contribution of a given mode to the total response can be assessed. The proportion of contribution of a single mode is called the participation factor of that mode.

Base shear. When a system is vibrating laterally in response to a chaotic disturbance a lateral force at the base of varying magnitude is required amongst other forces to maintain equilibrium. The probable maximum value of this force in response to a design disturbance is called the base shear. Certain codes obtain this directly and indicate means of distributing it throughout a system in order to obtain a seismic design loading pattern. By model analysis the base shear is only relevant to the base and probable loadings at other positions are obtained directly.

Spectrum. In seismic terms a spectrum is a relationship between the responses of systems in the form of acceleration, velocity and displacement and the period for various values of damping.

Response spectrum. A family of curves of spectra in response to a given ground disturbance. A large number of response spectra may be combined to give a design spectrum.

Fourier spectrum. A ground motion trace of time against acceleration, velocity or displacement can be broken down into a Fourier series of functions of period or frequency. A replot of these responses against period for a given disturbance is called a Fourier spectrum for that particular disturbance.

Strong motion accelerograph. This is a device designed to measure the absolute acceleration/time relationship of the ground on which the device is founded. The various properties of the device are a compromise to obtain, as faithfully as possible, the ground motion in spite of the variation of period of the ground vibrations.

Seismometer. This is a device designed to measure the effect of a ground disturbance on a particular structural system of given period and damping.

Seismograph. This is the normal seismological instrument of great sensitivity designed to determine the timing and nature of ground motion at points on the earth remote from the station. It is not capable of measuring actual site ground motion.

9

Botanical, biological and microbiological causes of decay

This chapter includes information on plants, bacteria lichens, algae and mosses and fungi; because of the damage they cause, fungi are given fuller treatment.

Botanical causes of decay

Ivy, creepers and other forms of plant life can cause damage if allowed to grow freely. Ivy drives a bullet-headed root into crumbling masonry and causes disintegration. Fresh ivy tendrils can, when forcibly removed, pull off a weak surface of brickwork or plaster, so the plant should be cut and killed and then left several weeks until it has lost its adhesive strength. On the other hand, the rather familiar sight of a boundary wall covered with ivy should be studied carefully because the ivy may in fact be holding up the wall, and if it is removed the wall itself may fall to pieces. On buildings proper, rather than garden walls, ivy must be kept in check to prevent its growth getting out of control. When it is cut, the stem should be treated with a strong weedkiller so as to poison the roots and prevent its sprouting again.

Stonecrop and wallflowers are pleasant, but they usually indicate decay and poor maintenance. Indeed the presence of growth often indicates that the pointing has perished, in which case it should be renewed as soon as feasible, incorporating a toxic agent in the mortar if plant growth is a constant nuisance.

Some kinds of wall-climbing plants do not damage masonry directly but must none the less be kept away from the eaves and gutters to avoid blockages. These include *Ampelopsis veitchii*, a form of Boston ivy with small ovate or trifoliated leaves, which is often incorrectly referred to as Virginia creeper; *Hydrangea petiolaris*, a climbing hydrangea; and *Hedera canariensis*, Canary Island ivy. The last is evergreen and can be grown over underburnt brickwork that is decaying due to frost as a form of protection.

The architect may well come into conflict with a client who is a keen gardener and puts the life of his plants before the maintenance of his building—or the architect may himself think the building looks better covered up. In such cases it is good practice to insert galvanized vine eyes and use stainless steel straining wires. Alternatively, the plants can be grown on frames; an advantage of this is that when superficial maintenance of the wall is required the frame can be unfixed and the plants bent forward intact on the frames.

The roots of trees and bushes can cause blockages and local ground dampness by finding their way into rainwater drains. In extreme cases, when rainwater drains are broken by roots, the leaking water can cause sandy types of soil to wash away from below foundations. Conversely in clay soils there is the well-known fact that trees, particularly poplars, can damage foundations by excessive withdrawal of ground moisture in summer, resulting in ground shrinkage and foundation movement with subsequent cracking of walls and partitions. Trees and plant growths can overwhelm historic buildings and sites in the tropics, where constant maintenance is required to hold them back.

Biological and microbiological causes of decay

Bacteria and lichens can cause the decay of building materials by producing acids which react chemically with the structural material. Examples of this are sulphate-producing bacteria which grow on stone, and lichens and mosses which produce acids that attack lead and also low-silica glass. Algae, moss and lichens all grow on brick and stone masonry and build up humus in which larger and more damaging plants can grow. There is an added risk from dampness and

Figure 9.1   A ruined temple at Sukothai, Thailand

Unrestricted plant growth poses great problems to archaeologists and conservators. Taking into account the climatic conditions, which favour rampant plant growth, in practice this ruined temple can only be dismantled and reconstructed

clogging of pores if the material is not adequately frost resistant.

Some micro-organisms develop rapidly if the air has a relative humidity of over 65%, and they spread quickly if there is light. They may take the form of spotty staining of varied colour. A durable cure can only be effected if the source of dampness is located and eliminated. After removal there is some surface loss in the form of tiny holes which may at first be almost invisible.

There are a great many varieties of algae; those that occur on most stone, brick or concrete surfaces are usually green, red or brown powders or filaments which may or may not be slimy according to moisture conditions. They derive their energy largely from sunlight, but need liquid water for survival.

Lichens are a combination of certain algae and fungi which can reproduce on moist external surfaces. The grey-orange and blue-green lichens seen on limestones in country districts may seem very attractive, but heavy growths of lichen and algae can hasten the decay of stone by the production of oxalic acids. They also slow down the drying-out process after rain, thus making frost damage more likely. They are a major problem for conservation in the tropics.

Mosses need a rough, moist surface on which soil and dirt can collect; once established they tend to hold moisture in the supporting surface of masonry or wood.

Toxic washes are used to kill algae, lichens and mosses. Incipient lichen and algae can be softened and removed by wiping with diluted ammonia, while heavier growths can be killed by spraying with formalin. Large areas of masonry can be sprayed with a solution of 25 g/l (4 oz/gal) of water of zinc silicofluoride or sodium pentachlorphenate or various branded solutions. Horticultural tar wash will also remove lichens and mosses, and as far as can be seen does not seem to discolour the background material more than temporarily. After the growth has died and shrivelled, it can be safely brushed away or carefully scraped off. Plants growing in joints or pockets of masonry can be killed by spraying with an appropriate gardener's weedkiller. It is important to kill the roots and remove any humus which may encourage future growths, and any pockets should be filled with mortar.

Fungi

Fungi, mildew, moulds and yeasts do not require sunlight for growth; they depend upon organic material such as plant life for their energy. Moulds normally appear as spots or patches that may spread to form a grey-green, black or brown furry layer on the surface. Any fungus has several basic requirements for propagation and growth: adequate water and oxygen supply, suitable temperature, a congenial substratum on which to grow, the space for growth, and finally of course the source of infection. If any of these requirements is inadequate, growth cannot take place. Water is a by-product of fungal growth; thus, if fungus has established itself in a piece of wood and the rate of drying is less than the rate at which water is produced by the breakdown of the wood substance, the attack will go on indefinitely with consequential decay. This fact emphasizes the importance of air movement and ventilation.

Certain minute fungi that attack wood can do immense and irreparable damage in a short time, and the softening effect of this decay or rot can encourage subsequent beetle attack. It is important to note, however, that fungal attack only occurs in well-seasoned wood if damp conditions prevail, i.e. if the moisture content of the wood rises above 20%. Thus, continuous heating and good air circulation, together with elimination of the entry of rain and moisture, prevent timber decay.

Detection of fungal decay in wood

The inspector should arm himself with a handy torch with a strong beam, a penknife and magnifying glass, and wear overalls or old clothes. He requires a knowledge of the construction of historic buildings.

Advanced stages of fungal decay are easily recognized because the structure of the wood is damaged, either crumbling or broken up into shrunken distorted cubes of lignin in extreme cases or with a bowing inwards and outwards parallel to the grain or waviness and blistering effect. The colour may be changed with a brownish or whitish discoloration, depending on the type of fungus, and this may show through paintwork, the brown colours coming from fungi that destroy cellulose and whitish flecks on a darker background from those that destroy lignin. In extreme cases the fruiting body is found in the middle of a whitish mass of hyphae. It may be sterilized immediately to prevent the spread of spores, but its location as the centre of the attack is valuable evidence in planning eradication.

When inspecting historic buildings it is important to look into corners and poorly ventilated cellars to check for fungal attack. Beams and joinery should be tapped with a penknife and if they give a dull or hollow ring, the point of the blade should be driven into the wood in several places to see if it has become relatively soft. Any timber that is embedded in masonry may have too high a moisture content and is therefore vulnerable to both fungal and beetle attack. Where appropriate, a further test is possible in long-grained soft woods by inserting the blade and prising up a splinter; a long splinter can never be prised up from decaying wood.

A musty smell may indicate extreme fungal attack, but in the author's experience this has been found to be an unreliable guide.

'Dry rot' fungus

The most serious form of rot in Britain is *Serpula lacrymans*, generally known as 'dry rot' because it can manufacture and carry its own moisture and thus attack dry wood as it moves away from its birthplace. It does not seem so serious elsewhere, either because of cold winters or lack of humidity in the climate. This fungus grows from a spore or propagates itself from fine hairlike roots or strands called hyphae, which may unite to form a snowy-white growth. When well established this growth can produce pencil-thick strands called rhizomorphs which extend to 10 m (33 ft) or even 20 m (66 ft) distance, and then it will grow a fruiting body producing yet more millions of spores. Hyphae strands can probe through damp brick and stone, following the mortar joints, or move behind plaster until they find more wood upon which to feed. They particularly like unventilated voids such as linings to walls, and embedded timbers such as wood lintels. Attack is slowed down, although not prevented, by low temperatures; also, high temperatures of 42 °C (108 °F) or over will effectively sterilize the fungus.

As millions of spores are produced by a fruiting body, amounting to 800 or 900 million per hour in tropical conditions, the air must always contain some, so the possibility of infection must be considered likely anywhere. The correct approach to the prevention of dry rot is to avoid conditions favourable to the growth of the spore by keeping the moisture content below 20%.

The cellulose in wood is the food source that supports the growth of the fungus, and so cutting off the source of supply is vital. Chairs, old books left in a damp basement or even carpenter's shavings swept carelessly into a heating duct, can become causes of dry rot. Blocked gutters and rainwater down-pipes are perhaps the most frequent causes as they provide the essential moisture for the fungus spore to grow. Blocked under-floor ventilators and impervious floor coverings, which reduce ventilation and so raise the moisture content of the wood, are other frequent causes of attack.

Control of dry rot

The eradication of dry rot is not work for amateurs, who may inadvertently destroy valuable evidence as to the source and the extent of the attack. It must be done by skilled specialists if the building owner is to be assured that a further outbreak will not occur. The total cost of rectification of dry rot damage to floors, joinery, plaster and decoration is often several times the cost of actual eradication of the fungus.

In every case, the cause and starting point of the outbreak must be identified and then the extent of the attack must be investigated to its limits.

Traditionally, when the extent had been established, affected wood throughout and beyond the affected area had to be removed. This was painful, especially to the owner of the building and even more so when valuable historic joinery was destroyed. In ordinary cases it was thought adequate to go 600 mm (2 ft) beyond the last trace of hyphae but to be additionally sure in historic buildings 910 mm (3 ft) was recommended. All hyphae must be killed or removed as otherwise the attack will be renewed with increased intensity.

Eradication of all the dry rot hyphae requires meticulous care. Sterilization by chemicals has replaced attempts by blow lamp to heat the stone or brick masonry until it is too hot to touch. It always seemed doubtful that the heat would reach sufficient depth, and the time required was considerable. In addition, the fire risk to cultural property was not negligible.

However there is an alternative approach which consists of controlling the environment making it unfavourable to the *Serpula lacrymans*. The attack can be inhibited with a spray of fungicide and, if ventilation can be increased and the cause has been removed, the dry rot will die in due course. Regular supervision is needed if this method is used.

'Wet rot' fungi

Wet rots are much less serious than dry rot as they do not carry their moisture with them, so their range is localized. The most common form, cellar fungus (*Coniophora cerebella*), requires a moisture content of 25% before it will attack wood; it has fine dark-brownish strands and a green, leathery fruiting body and produces masses of white hyphae. *Pooria vaillantii* has spreading string-like strands. *Phellinus megaloporus*, which is hardly ever found in modern buildings, occurs in historic buildings as it attacks hardwoods such as oak and chestnut where these are wet. Although wet rots are treated with the same chemicals as dry rot, the extent of the area requiring treatment is usually local and the hyphae are not dangerous. It is not necessary to go beyond the affected area with sterilization.

Osmophilic fungi

In Japan from the 1950s onwards synthetic resins have been used to consolidate wooden sculpture. Mori and

Arai report that a fungal growth was noticed some 15 years after parts had been treated with large amounts of resin. Examination showed that these were osmophilic fungi feeding on a layer of sugar which was a by-product of an action between the insect frass and the resin, drawn to the surface by capillary action.

Wood-staining fungi

Wood-staining fungi grow on the surface of wood and so produce stains. They do not affect structural strength, but can cause painted surfaces to flake off.

Fungicides

Irrigation of the wall with fungicidal solutions from reservoirs into holes drilled at spacings, depending on the porosity of the wall and flow characteristics of the fungicide, is an effective method of sterilization. Care should be taken to ensure that the salts thus introduced into the wall are not hygroscopic and do not aggravate capillarity. Irrigation is particularly useful to impose a preventive *cordon sanitaire* between an outbreak and valuable woodwork as yet unaffected. Such irrigation also protects timbers embedded in a wall, which are most likely to be attacked because of lack of ventilation and high moisture content.

There are many powerful proprietary chemical products dealing with dry rot, most in a suitable white spirit vehicle. The following chemicals can be used:

(1) Sodium pentachloride in the strength of 50 g/l (8 oz/gal) of water.
(2) Mercuric chloride or corrosive sublimate in the strength of 1 part to 1000 parts of water or methylated spirits (very effective, but highly poisonous, and needing great care in handling).
(3) Magnesium silicofluoride in the strength of 100 g/l (16 oz/gal) of water or sodium fluoride in the saturated solution in water, i.e. about 37.5 g/l (6 oz/gal) of water.

In damp cellars, the insertion of thin water-soluble rods of commercial preservative can be used as a preventive measure to sterilize the walls, exploiting the capillary effect of rising damp. Brushing or spraying all timbers with preservative may also prevent a dry rot attack or stop it spreading rapidly. Wall plates and embedded timbers can be drilled and infiltrated along their grain to avoid rot and beetle attack.

10

Insects and other pests as causes of decay

Insects

Organic materials such as wood are all vulnerable to insect attack. Insects cause a great amount of damage by weakening structural timbers and in many parts of the world they are a more likely threat to woodwork than fungi. The situation is becoming more complicated due to the fact that eggs and larvae of tropical pests may be imported with tropical woods. It is important that the architect be able to distinguish among different types of beetle attack, so that he can make an accurate assessment of the probable extent of damage. He is referred to the technical literature relating to the insects common in his own country, for without a detailed knowledge of the biology of the different groups of insects, effective measures for prevention of attack and repair cannot be taken. Eradication is much simplified by the fact that the different species nearly all respond to the same chemical treatment.

Identification of insects

A summary of the diagnostic details of damage by wood-boring insects and marine borers is given in the 'Remarks' column of *Table 10.1*. Identification roughly follows this procedure: what type of wood?—what size flight exit hole?—what sort of bore dust (called frass) is showing?—what sort of damage has occurred? Piles of bore dust and fresh clean-looking flight exit holes are usually symptoms of continuing activity. Live beetles may be found in the flight season when they emerge to mate and lay eggs. Larvae are rarely found on inspection, unless the affected wood is opened up to explore the extent of damage.

Incidence of beetle attack in the UK*

In the United Kingdom, about 80% of the reported attacks are by the woodworm of the common furni-

ture beetle (*Anobium punctatum*). About 5–8% of attacks are by the deathwatch beetle (*Xestobium rufovillosum*, about 4–5% by wood-boring weevils (*Euophryum confine and Pentarthrum huttoni*), about 2% by powder post beetle (*Lyctus*) and about 0.5% by the house longhorn beetle (*Hylotrupes bajulus*). The incidence of woodworm attack is longhorn beetle (*Hylotrupes bajulus*—see Technical Note No. 39). The incidence of woodworm attack is highest in the south-western counties. The deathwatch beetle, not found much in Scotland or Northern Ireland, is most prevalent in the south and south-western counties of Britain where rainfall is highest. Wood-boring weevils do not occur in Scotland and are most common in the London area. The house longhorn beetle is most common in Surrey and Hampshire but is occasionally found elsewhere; outbreaks must be reported to the Ministry of Agriculture in order that its spread may be stopped.

It is suspected that the incidence of woodworm attack is increasing and thus the number of predators on this species is also tending to increase. The predators are important, particularly the Clerid *Korynetes caeruleus* which is also a predator on the deathwatch beetle. It is thus possible that the increase in woodworm may be indirectly causing a slight decrease in the deathwatch beetle.

Woodworm can spread by flying; they attack only sapwood in oak but will also attack the heartwood in many other timbers, both hardwood and softwood. A large proportion of woodworm attack is found in roof spaces. If the attack is active, the flight holes are clean, sharp-edged and cream in colour. In inactive areas, the holes will be dirty and greyish in colour. As larvae have been found in apparently inactive areas, any places that have been affected should be treated.

*See BRE Digest 307:1986 *Damage by wood boring insects,*
BRE Digest 327:1987 *Insecticidal treatments against wood boring insects,*
BRE Digest 371:1992 *Remedial wood preservatives: use them safely* and
BRE Report 98:1987 *Recognising wood rot and insect damage in buildings*

Table 10.1 Summary of Diagnostic Characters of Damage caused by the Commoner Wood-boring Insects and Marine Borers (From Bletchly, 1967, by courtesy of HMSO)

Type of timber attacked (sapwood and heartwood— exceptions given under Remarks) S = softwood H = hardwood	Flight holes	Tunnels	Bore dust (frass)	Type of insect or marine borer	Remarks
H, S	Absent	Sometimes enlarged into chambers. (Separated by septa of wood in case of damp wood termites)	Cemented mixture of bore dust and wood chewings in mud	Subterranean termites	Tunnels connected to soil through mud galleries. Tunnel walls muddy. (Compare carpenter ant)
H, S	Absent	Sometimes enlarged into cavities	Ovoid pellets with 6 longitudinal ridges	Dry wood termites	Bore dust resembles small poppy seeds
Chiefly S	Absent	Separated by septa of wood	Large wet pellets	Damp wood termites	In damp wood
H, S	Circular $^1/_{32}$ to $^1/_4$ in diam.)	Circular. Diam. (similar to flight holes) sometimes variable in same piece of wood. Walls unstained or slightly so	Sometimes absent from parts of tunnels	Lymexylid ambrosia beetles	Active only in green timber. Compare Platypodidae and Scolytidae
H	Almost circular (about $^3/_{16}$ in diam.)	Oval	Longhorn type	Clytinid longhorn beetles	Little feeding under bark before penetrating into sapwood
S	Perfectly circular ($^1/_8$ to $^3/_4$ in diam.)	Circular. Diam. as for flight holes. Surrounding wood sometimes partly decayed	Very tightly packed	Siricid wood-wasps	Live larvae present in green and recently seasoned wood. (Tunnels appear oval in section if cut obliquely)
H, S	Oval (size depending on species)	Oval, separate and scattered	Mixture of coarse pellets and chips	Forest longhorn and Buprestid beetles	Feed under bark before penetrating into sapwood. Active attack in trees, logs and sawn timber whilst green. Attack by some species continues in seasoned wood. Compare house longhorn beetle
S	Oval (about $^3/_8 \times ^3/_{16}$ in diam.)	Oval, tunnels coalesce leading to breakdown of walls. 'Ripple' marks on walls	Similar to some other longhorns. Sausage-shaped pellets	House longhorn beetle (*Hylotrupes bajulus*)	Serious structural damage in undecayed sapwood of seasoned softwoods. Characterized by a thin superficial skin of wood concealing internal disintegration
H, S	Oval	Oval enlarged into cavities	Damp agglomeration of coarse pellets and shavings	Wharf-borer (*Nacerdes melanura*)	In damp decayed sleepers, poles, built-in timbers and harbour timbers
Mostly in beech, elm, maple and sycamore	Circular ($^1/_{16}$ in diam.)	Circular $^1/_{16}$ in diam. numerous	Fine very densely packed powder	*Ptilinus pectinicornis*	Active in seasoned wood. (Compare *Lyctus* powder post beetles)

(Left margin bracket label: Tunnels with bore dust)

136

Table 10.1 *continued*

Tunnels with bore dust					
H containing starch	Circular ($\frac{1}{16}$ in diam.)	Circular $\frac{1}{16}$ in diam. numerous	Copious fine loosely packed powder	*Lyctus* powder post beetles	Active in partly and fully seasoned wood. Confined to sapwood in timbers where the heartwood is distinguishable. Wood disintegrated beneath superficial skin in severe cases. Compare house longhorn beetle
Mainly H containing starch	Circular (up to $\frac{1}{4}$ in diam.)	As flight holes. Usually larger than *Lyctus*	As *Lyctus*	Bostrychid powder post beetles	See *Lyctus*. Mainly in tropical timbers. Unseasoned wood also attacked. Confined to sapwood in timbers where the heartwood is distinguishable.
S	Circular ($\frac{1}{16}$ in diam.)	As flight holes	Mostly brown (with a few white) bun-shaped pellets	*Ernobius mollis*	In timber yards and recently built houses. Often confused with *Anobium* but attack limited to bark and adjacent sapwood
Mostly H	Circular ($\frac{1}{8}$ in diam.)	As flight holes	Larger bun-shaped pellets (easily visible to naked eye)	Deathwatch beetle (*Xestobium rufovillosum*)	Common in old buildings especially in oak. Damage sometimes internal in large timbers and disintegration often severe
H, S (rare in most tropical H)	Circular ($\frac{1}{16}$ in diam.)	As flight holes; convoluted shape. Numerous	Small ellipsoidal pellets	Common furniture beetle (*Anobium punctatum*)	In wood usually more than 5 years old. Birch plywood very susceptible
H, S	Irregularly oval to slit-shaped with jagged edges	Circular (about $\frac{1}{16}$ in diam.). Mainly straight—compare *Anobium*	Similar to but smaller than *Anobium*	Wood-boring weevils, *Euophryum* and *Pentarthrum*	In damp and decayed wood. Sometimes with *Anobium*
Tunnels without bore dust					
Chiefly imported S	Absent or irregular	Partly concentric with the annual rings sometimes forming large cavities	—	Carpenter bees (*Camponotus* spp.)	Resembles termite damage but gallery walls are clean
H, S	Absent	Rapidly enlarge from minute size on surface up to 1 in diam. within. Chalky lining often present	—	Shipworm (*Teredo* spp.)	Floated timber, harbour fixtures and boats attacked in salt water
H, S	Absent	Honeycomb of small diam. ($\frac{1}{20}$ in) short ($\frac{1}{8}$ in) surface tunnels	—	Gribble (*Limnoria* spp.)	As for *Teredo*. Vertical timbers become eroded near water line to form a 'waist'
H, S	Circular ($\frac{1}{50}$ to $\frac{1}{8}$ in diam.)	Frequently across the grain. Diam. similar to entry holes. Walls darkly stained	—	Ambrosia beetles (Platypodidae & Scolytidae)	Wood surrounding tunnels sometimes also stained. Active only in green timber where bore dust ejected through bore holes made by adults. Compare Lymexylidae

Figure 10.1   Boreholes of the common furniture and death-watch beetles
(Courtesy: Department of the Environment, Building Research Establishment)

The boreholes of the common furniture beetle, Anobium punctatum, *are about 1.5 mm (0.06 in) in diameter, while those of the deathwatch beetle,* Xestobium rufovillosum, *are about 3 mm (0.12 in) in diameter. However, in the tropics each species may be larger*

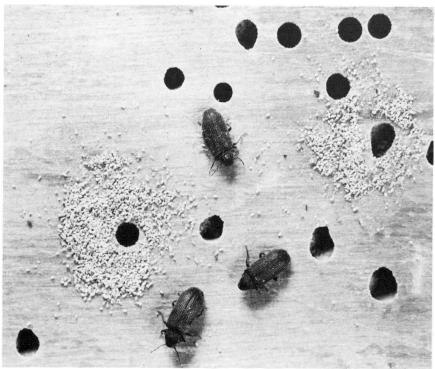

Figure 10.2   Boreholes, frass and adults of the common furniture beetle
(Courtesy: Department of the Environment, Building Research Establishment)

Boreholes, frass pellets and adults of the common furniture beetle, Anobium punctatum, *are visible. This insect has worldwide distribution*

Figure 10.3   The deathwatch beetle
(Courtesy: Department of the Environment, Building Research Establishment)

The deathwatch beetle, Xestobium rufovillosum, *is limited in its habitat. It is extremely difficult to eradicate from oak in mediaeval buildings*

138

Figure 10.4   Deathwatch beetle attack in central tower roof beams, York Minster, England
(Courtesy: Shepherd Building Group Ltd)

Deathwatch beetle, Xestobium rufovillosum, *attack in the main beams of the central tower roof had continued for centuries. The cast-iron bracket on the right is part of the 1831 repairs by Smirke. The friable timber is structurally unsound, but modern techniques might have been used to fumigate and kill the beetle and then vacuum impregnate the beam with a suitable epoxy resin formulation. These techniques were not, however, known in 1967. The beam proved to be structurally unsound after extensive exploration by drilling and had to be replaced*

Figure 10.5   Powder post beetle, Lyctus
(Courtesy: Department of the Environment, Building Research Establishment)

'Lyctus' forms circular holes 1.5 mm (0.06 in) in diameter, with copious fine powdered frass

139

Figure 10.6 Boreholes of the powder post beetle, Lyctus
(Courtesy: Department of the Environment, Building Research Establishment)

This beetle confines its activities to sapwood of hardwoods where sugar content is high, so is unlikely to cause structural damage

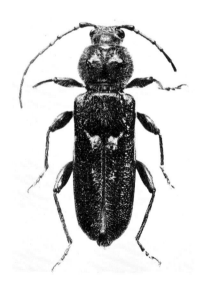

Figure 10.7 The house longhorn beetle
(Courtesy: Department of the Environment, Building Research Establishment)

The house longhorn beetle, Hylotrupes bajulus, is rare in Britain except in the south, but more common in warmer temperate climates

Figure 10.8 Balcony of house in Trudos Mountains, Cyprus

The destruction of structural timber at joints is by the house longhorn beetle, Hylotrupes bajulus in all probability. Note the crushing of the affected timber

Deathwatch beetle

In England the deathwatch beetle is one of the major enemies of historic buildings, as its favourite food is oak, the principal structural timber of old buildings, and it is extremely difficult to eradicate. Areas affected by rot or dampness are generally those in which an attack is first established. Because the attack can only be detected by the holes formed by the emerging beetle, it may be quite well established before even being noticed. New holes are clean, sharp-edged and clear of dust and dirt. Piles of frass may be found ejected from active holes. Old holes have crumbled edges and are dark and dirty.

After emerging from her hole in the spring the female mates and soon lays some 400 eggs, choosing cracks and crevices where the wood has been softened by rain or damp. The small larvae burrow into the wood, where in order to mature they must obtain sufficient food by boring. This process takes some time. In recently felled oak, five years may be long enough, but 10 or 20 years might be needed in hard, dry timber. The larvae bore up and down the grain of the oak in runs of about 1 m (3.3 ft) and each larva must travel some 14 m (46 ft) in all, making a series of runs parallel to the grain. Each external exit hole therefore represents a considerable amount of internal damage. The deathwatch beetle, once having emerged, crawls around searching for its mate and emitting a sound which is believed to be its mating signal; also, it may glide a short distance to other timbers and so initiate a new attack.

Control of deathwatch beetle

Eradication of the deathwatch beetle may take over 20 years of constant attention, particularly if the attack is in hard timbers. Eradication by means of timber preservative applied by brush or spray has been tried, but it cannot reach the larvae that are causing destruction. Furthermore, manufacturers' preservatives have a disappointingly short toxic life when applied externally. Drilling holes at 250 mm (10 in) intervals and filling them with liquid preservative is useful for protecting embedded timbers and vital areas such as beam bearings, but in hardwood the lateral spread of preservative is poor, as can be shown by using dyed preservative in a sample and cutting long sections and cross-sections to inspect penetration.

The strength of a beetle attack can be greatly reduced by burning smoke bombs to deposit insecticide upon the exposed faces of the timber when the beetles emerge to mate, between the end of March and the beginning of June. Provided the space can be enclosed for at least a day, the smoke method has been found reasonably effective. Furthermore, the cost of setting off a few canisters containing Lithane or Dieldrin every spring is low compared with that of erecting scaffolding up to a roof, cleaning down and applying a liquid preservative. Dieldrin is more persistent but is toxic. Lithane is also named Gamexene and is sold in a water-soluble solution. A series of annual smoke treatments over 10 years is recommended.

G.R. Coleman recommends a deathwatch beetle count before treatment throughout one emergence period, and states that the adult beetles, at the temperatures of an unheated church, will drop to the floor rather than fly and then not crawl far. This being so, the beetles can be sought out and collected once weekly and by recording their numbers and positions, the intensity and location of the attack can be assessed (*Figure 10.9*). The volunteer collectors need a torch, an artist's camel-hair brush and a card to collect the specimens and a receptacle to store them, together with a knee pad for comfort. It will be necessary to look under carpets and loose items of furniture. The location of each find should be marked on a ground plan and the numbers logged each week.

Smoke treatment is most effective in closed roof spaces or buildings such as churches. The instructions and precautions on the canister labels should be thoroughly read and followed. Windows, doors and other gaps should be sealed and all loose furnishing removed. Decorative items which cannot be moved should be covered, but in the case of 'secco' or tempera wall paintings, smoke treatment must not be used. All doors must be locked and notices posted to say that toxic insecticidal smoke is being used. The police should be notified and, because of a possible false alarm when smoke is seen coming out at the eaves, the fire brigade should also be warned. The building must be vacated for 24 hours before re-entry and cleaning. Before cleaning, the number and location of dead beetles should be recorded by the volunteers, as described above, but they and the cleaners should wear old clothes, use rubber gloves and have simple face masks to prevent inhalation of particles of toxic smoke. The volunteers' clothing should be washed and all waste sealed in plastic bags.

After treatment, information can be obtained from entomological examination of a sample of the dead insects, giving the proportions of unmated females, mated females which have not laid their eggs and mated females which have done so. If the annual total number of beetles killed goes continuously down then one can assume that the war of attrition is being won.

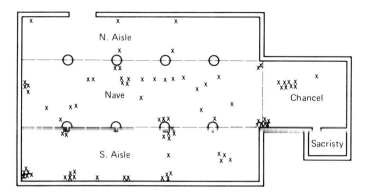

Figure 10.9   Deathwatch beetle count in a church, Norfolk, England
(Courtesy: G.R. Coleman)

Diagram shows an example of a completed ground plan after beetle collections (crosses indicate the positions of beetles collected from the floor). Following is an example of a completed table after weekly collections, and indicates heavy infestation:

Week ending	3 Apr.	10 Apr.	17 Apr.	24 Apr.	1 May	8 May	15 May	22 May	29 May	5 June	Total
Area:											
Nave	2	6	52	61	109	110	21	18	2	0	381
Chancel	0	0	6	21	20	10	11	2	1	1	72
N. aisle	0	1	0	1	3	4	0	1	0	0	10
S. aisle	8	2	29	45	82	65	68	10	12	0	321
	10	9	87	128	214	189	100	31	15	1	784

Carpenter bees

Generally the attack is on exposed timber and can be noticed as soon as it starts, because the buzzing of the bees is very noisy. The attack may continue for generations in the same timber and cause complete destruction.

The bees bore out large tunnels 30–40 mm (1.2–1.6 in) in diameter and up to 240 mm (9.5 in) in length, in which they construct a series of cross-partitions made of wood dust and saliva to form cells. An egg is laid in each cell and provided with food in the form of pollen or bee-bread; the larva hatches and feeds on this and after about three weeks pupates in the cell and after another three weeks emerges by gnawing its way out of the wood. With such a brief life cycle severe damage can occur in a short time.

Control of carpenter bees

To prevent initial attack or reinfestation, timbers should be either painted or coated with creosote, which must be renewed annually in tropical situations. A thick coat of limewash applied twice a year also prevents attack.

Timber already subject to attack may be treated by injecting the borer holes with a proprietary preservative or paradichlorobenzene in kerosene oil (paraffin) at the rate of 0.2–0.3 kg/l (2–3 lb/gal) and plugging the holes with wood.

Tropical insects

In many parts of the tropics, termites are commonly thought to be the main insect enemy but, apart from costal areas, if a building has been properly designed, constructed and reasonably maintained, the greater damage is reported to be inflicted by wood-boring beetles mentioned above. Furthermore, when certain tropical hardwoods are used structurally, or where sapwood is included in the hardwoods used for joinery and flooring, the risk of attack by powder post beetles is more likely than by termites. Whereas softwoods (both indigenous and exotic) may be attacked by the longhorn beetle *Oemidagahani* spp., powder post beetles of the families Lyctidae and Bostrychidae attack seasoned hardwoods only, reducing the sapwood to a fine flour-like powder. Although the damage is limited to the sapwood, the beetles may emerge through the adjacent hardwood. Most hardwoods containing starch are attacked and those with large pores such as antiaris and iroko are more liable to infestation. The attack is usually initiated in the timberyard and may be difficult to detect in the early stages.

In tropical conditions, the life cycle of these insects is completed very quickly. It is quite common for beetles to emerge and then reinfect the wood, causing serious structural damage to a building within a few years or less. Their presence is readily recognizable from the fine flour-like frass, along with round tunnels and holes of 1–5 mm (0.04–0.2 in) in diameter, depending on the beetle concerned. Through the agency of imported woods, many tropical pests have now to be combated in temperate zones, for example *Lyctus africanus*.

Termites

General

Termites are dangerous and voracious, and will attack wood, fibres or keratin materials and destroy almost anything, including synthetic material, that is not too hard, repellent or toxic. They have even been reported as attacking electrical insulation and plastic water pipes buried underground. Remarkable differences exist between the 2000 species, which should be identified by entomologists. As many as 50–100 species may co-exist in a tropical area; indeed 147 species have been found in Guatemala, whereas only one or two will be found in an area like southern France, Italy and central Europe. They are social insects and live in colonies with hundreds or thousands of individuals divided into large groups of workers and soldiers, which do not reproduce, and a few, often only a pair known as the king and queen,

which are reproductive and populate the colony. The queen lays as many as 4000 eggs in a day.

The species of termite that attack timber will be from one of two main groups—ground termites and drywood termites. Naturally resistant timbers tend to be gnawed by termites, but the soft non-resistant species may be completely hollowed out, except for an outside skin of wood, by drywood termites. Ground termites like to eat the soft spring and summer growth, leaving the late wood half-eaten, so they tend to form galleries of concentric circles around the annual rings in the cross-sections of wood, working along the grain and leaving thin paper-like pieces of wood as divisions. Contrary to popular statements, no timber is immune to ground termite attack, although the range of resistance of different timbers is appreciable: exposed to conditions of equal intensity of attack one timber may last less than five years and another over 100 years, with other timbers having a service life falling between these extremes. It has been found that the natural resistance of hardwoods decreases with age and after 100 or 200 years such tropical woods as jacaranda in Brazil lose this inherent resistance. Moreover, resistance to fungal decay is not necessarily an indication of resistance to ground termite attack. Such natural decay-resistant timber as heartwood oak does not show up well if exposed to termite attack.

It is said that termites are distributed in the tropical and temperate zones of the world within an isotherm of annual average 10 °C (50 °F), but H. Mori and H. Arai of Japan have found them in Hokkaido where the annual average is 7 °C (44.6 °F).

The termites given in *Table 10.2* are of importance to architectural conservationists.

Table 10.2 Some Important Wood-eating Termites

Family	Genus	Climate
	Ground termites	
Rhinotermitidae	Heterotermes	Tropics
	Reticulitermes	Subtropical and temperate zones; northern hemisphere
	Coptotermes	Tropical rainforest
	Schedorhinotermes	Tropics
Termitidae	Microcerotermes	Tropical rainforest
	Macrotermes Odomtotermes Microtermes }	Tropics
	Masutitermes	Tropical rainforest
	Drywood termites	
Mastotermitidae	Mastotermes	Warm
Kalotermitidae	Incisitermes Cryptotermes }	Humid coastal areas

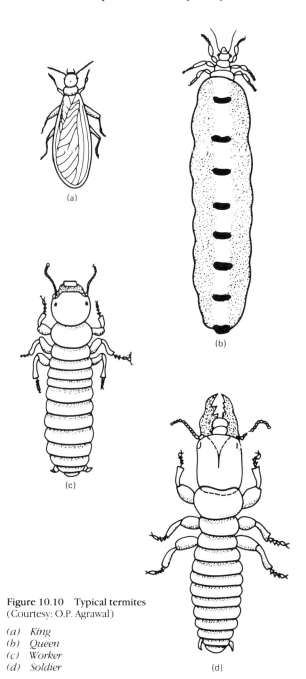

Figure 10.10   Typical termites
(Courtesy: O.P. Agrawal)

(a)   King
(b)   Queen
(c)   Worker
(d)   Soldier

Figure 10.11   Holy Shrine of Al Hussein, Kerbala, Iraq

Embedded wood has been attacked by termites. Other defects shown are sulphate attack in cement rendering (now cracking off) and ground salt crystallization due to transport by capillary action of rising damp

Ground termites

Ground termites live in large colonies in the earth, depending upon a source of moisture or water and the retention of an unbroken covered earthway from the soil to their sources of food; and these earthways or tubes are the most obvious signs of infestation. Ground termites do not make tunnels in timber; they tend to feed in restricted zones that become packed with mud as the attack progresses.

Excluding 'damp wood' termites which are not found in buildings, two main types of ground-dwelling wood-eating termites are of concern and these are differentiated by the way they digest the cellulose in the wood. Using a simplified classification, as there is in fact a great deal of variation in the food habits of termites which is not yet fully understood, the two types may be distinguished as follows. The first cultivates a fungus comb which is continually breaking down and being renewed. The comb is a sponge-like body made of chewed wood and built to fit the chambers of the nest. Each species has a characteristic type of fungus comb in its nest. The second type does not make a fungus comb and these species probably have protozoa in their gut which digest cellulose. How some termites digest wood is unknown, as they have neither protozoa nor fungus comb.

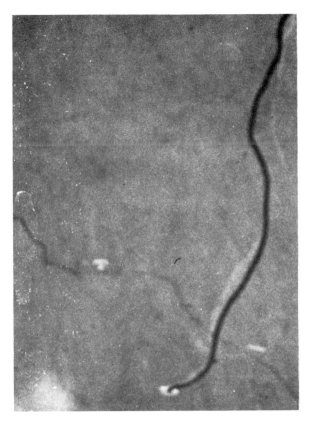

Figure 10.12 Holy Shrine of Al Hussein, Kerbala, Iraq

A termite track runs across brickwork in the minaret and penetrates a thick brick wall crossing a structural crack. The trail leads back to the ground some 20 m (66 ft) below. Insecticidal dust can be introduced to such tunnels

Ground termites will die if denied access to their underground home, which has a controlled environment. The nest is typically about 600 mm (2 ft) in diameter, is made of extremely strong cemented faeces and is almost watertight. With a moist warm atmosphere there is virtual climate control. Inside, the nest has a large number of cells with a sponge-like appearance. The cell for the queen is in the centre and is thick walled.

Control of ground termites
Effective control of ground termites is secured by proper design and construction of buildings with barriers provided not less than 200 mm (8 in) above ground level in all walls. Such termite shields should be of 0.46 mm (0.018 in) (26 s.w.g.) copper sheet acting also as a damp-proof course under severe tropical conditions, and in less severe conditions 0.50 mm (0.020 in) (24 s.w.g.) galvanized steel, or zinc sheet not less than 0.60 mm (0.024 in) may be used with the conventional bitumen damp-proof course below it. The shields, which must be continuous irrespective of changes in level, should extend outward 50 mm (2 in) and then downwards at an angle of 135° for another 50 mm. Joints in the sheet material

should be double-locked and sealed by soldering or brazing. Any holes cut for anchorage bolts should be sealed with a hot-poured pitch-based sealing compound. With solid floors it is necessary to provide an impervious floor all over the site. At least 150 mm (6 in) of concrete laid on a base unlikely to settle or crack and extending under all walls is recommended.

It is desirable to poison the whole area of the excavation and hardcore beneath the building and, using a stronger dosage, fill trenches around the footing with poisoned soil. Dieldrin, aldrin and chlordane have been found suitable, but it is advisable to seek the advice of forest entomologists before deciding upon a poisoning technique. Gaps must be sealed with poisoned mortar or a coal tar pitch-base sealing compound. Woody or other debris containing cellulose will attract ground termites (and incidentally induce dry rot); care should therefore be taken to ensure that none drops into foundation trenches or is left under subfloors.

Where these barriers cannot be provided, for example with timber such as railway sleepers, fence posts and poles placed in contact with the ground, the choice is between naturally resistant timbers and the less resistant ones adequately treated with wood preservatives.

In existing buildings a precaution against ground termites is for foundations to be exposed and the earth poisoned as it is replaced. In the bottom of this trench and elsewhere, holes can be drilled at 300 mm (12 in) centres and poisoned. Any soil at the foot of the cross-walls should also be poisoned so as to prevent termites climbing up the walls. Soil poisoning is only the first line of defence against ground termite attack and may become ineffective after some years. Chemical control by introducing white arsenic powder into the runways is effective in keeping down the termite population, but it is a palliative and not a curative measure in spite of claims to the contrary.

Where termites are a threat, at least two rigorous inspections should be carried out each year, one at the beginning and the other at the end of the rainy season (it is interesting to note that colonial Williamsburg, USA, has one man engaged full time in termite prevention). If damage due to ground termites is found, their contact with the soil and moisture must be cut off, all soil runways from bricks or other parts of the structure must be cleaned off and the subsoil poisoned by drilling holes at 300 mm (12 in) intervals and infiltrating appropriate chemicals. Any cracks and crevices in masonry, brickwork or concrete and pipe runs where termites might gain access should be poisoned and sealed. Any untreated and unprotected timber which may temporarily join the building to the ground and through which termites could gain access must be removed.

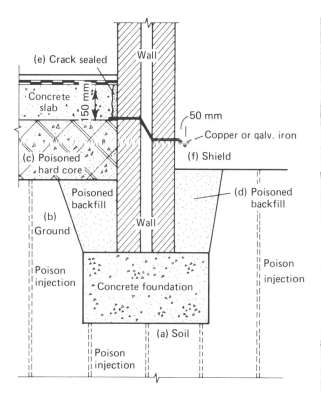

Figure 10.13 Precautions against subterranean termites

(a) *Soil poisoned under foundations*
(b) *Holes at 300 mm (12 in) poisoned*
(c) *Hardcore poisoned*
(d) *Poisoned backfill*
(e) *Coal tar or poisoned mortar seal in crack*
(f) *Metal termite shield protects 50 mm (2 in)*

Figure 10.14 Chapel in monastery of San Francisco, Lima, Peru

Active termite attack in an altar piece. Cleaners should be instructed to report such events to the architects in charge of the fabric

Drywood termites

Drywood termites, which are indigenous to Asia, South America and the Caribbean and have now become established in certain coastal regions of Africa, live in small colonies feeding on seasoned wood. They require no access to the soil. They invariably feed just below the surface of the wood, and in most timbers attack is more or less confined to the sapwood; they produce granular dust, appreciably coarser than that of furniture beetles, which showers out when the sound skin of the wood left on the surface of an attacked piece of timber is broken. The feeding termites also push out granular dust through their exit holes, the mounds of dust often being the only evidence of attack in progress, although their presence may also be indicated by heaps of excreta pellets, resembling small, light-coloured seeds, appearing below infested timber. Flight holes

resemble those of some furniture beetles.

The name 'white ant' which is applied to drywood termites is not strictly correct since these creatures, although insects, are not closely related to ants. Many of their habits are, however, similar to those of ants proper, with whom they compete and are therefore in enmity.

Drywood termites are all known to have protozoa in their gut as otherwise they cannot directly digest the cellulose in wood. They live on seasoned wood and are therefore an important pest. They live in completely self-contained colonies and only leave the wood to swarm and form a new colony, so external evidence of their presence is only the small hard pellets which they excrete. Their activities may continue unsuspected until the timber is virtually destroyed. The colonies are much smaller than the ground termites, so the process of destruction is slower. The next colony is started when a reproductive

146

pair, on entering a building, lodge in a crack or a crevice in something made of wood.

Feeding habits of drywood termites

When taking measures for control of termites, a knowledge of their feeding habits is necessary. They have systems of mutual feeding with saliva, with regurgitated partly digested food and with ejected faeces, which may be repeatedly eaten until there is no nutrition left. They also eat the cast skins and dead bodies of other members of the colony and sickly individuals may be killed and eaten by the soldiers. Because of these habits, contact poisons carried into the colony by a few individuals are spread rapidly and kill many more termites than the quantity warrants. Poisons in the wood which kill the protozoa ultimately cause the death by starvation of the termites which rely on this system of digestion.

Control of drywood termites

Drywood termites can be more troublesome than ground termites because of the difficulties of control of these air-borne pests. Precautions for rendering buildings safe from ground termites are ineffective against drywood termites; indeed, no economic methods exist to prevent drywood termite activity. The pest cannot be positively eliminated from building timbers and other indoor woodwork by screening buildings with fine metal gauze which, of course, is extremely expensive and usually impractical. Still, reasonable precautions can be adopted that will minimize the risk of drywood termite attack, with dependence on curative measures when attack occurs. Ordinary painting of wooden surfaces is recommended as an effective method of denying drywood termites entry into such timber, and where this is practical the course should be adopted, e.g. for joinery. Planing has been suggested, but this is not an economical measure for carcassing timber. It seems probable that the total exclusion of sapwood may appreciably delay drywood termite attack.

Finding evidence of drywood termite attack is difficult, even though they can be heard gnawing timbers at night. A thorough inspection by tapping the wooden members to find hollows is one laborious method of detection; another is to keep a close look out for frass or pellets of faeces when they fall from an opening.

Fumigation is a useful method of eradication, but it involves covering a whole building with a tent, as is done in the USA and Japan. Sheets with an overlap of at least 150 mm (6 in) are fastened together with strong clips to form the tent, which is held to the ground by long bags filled with sand. If necessary, sealing tapes are used.

Before tent fumigation, all food must be removed and pets and humans must be evacuated. Several emission points are used so that the gas is evenly distributed. The fumigant generally used must be stable. Sulphuric fluoride, being colourless, odourless, almost insoluble in water and only slightly soluble in some organic solvents, is favoured. It should be introduced slowly at the rate of 0.5 kg (1.1 lb) per 28 m³ (1000 ft³) and left for 24 hours to kill the termites. Other fumigants commonly used against drywood termites are methyl bromide and acrylonitrile. Fumigation must be carried out by properly trained men. After eradication of the termites by fumigation, unpainted wood should be brush-treated with preservative to reduce the risk of reinfestation.

The extent of the structural damage caused by drywood termites is apt to be misjudged; at first sight it appears devastating, but closer inspection usually reveals the destruction to be less severe than was thought. In furniture, panelling and high-class joinery, even a small amount of damage may be serious because the appearance is spoiled, but in carcassing timbers it is necessary for the damage to be sufficiently serious to weaken the structure before alarm need arise. In practice, drywood termite attack is localized. Some wooden members may be attacked while adjacent ones are quite free. Moreover, it is usually only parts of such members that are infested and then often only to a depth of about 13 mm (0.5 in). If the infested zone is removed and the remainder of the timber is liberally dressed with an oil-solvent wood preservative or even a volatile toxic substance like orthodichlorobenzene, attack will often cease and the reduced member is usually strong enough to continue carrying the load required of it.

Marine borers

Marine borers fall into two distinct groups: the molluscan borers *Teredo*, *Bankia* and *Martesia*, which are related to oysters and clams, and crustacean borers *Limnoria* and *Sphaeroma*, which are related to lobsters and crabs. They cannot live out of contact with sea water for more than a short time. The larva of the molluscan borer enters the wood by making a tiny hole on the outside and then tunnels along the grain, gradually enlarging these tunnels as it grows and emerges. Crustacean borers work more slowly, usually at the waterline, and destroy the timber from outside, the effect being as if the timber were eroded.

Marine borers attack wood and no timber is immune, although some naturally durable species offer resistance for a time. The attack leads to rapid destruction even of wood previously treated with preservatives, unless the amount for protection used is double that for fungi and termites.

Control of marine borers

One method of preventing marine borer attack is to dry the wood for a few days each month; alternatively, the regular application of creosote or copper–chrome–arsenic preservatives, details of which are given in Appendix III, is recommended. For vacuum impregnation before timber is used, loadings should be high, about 350 kg/m³ (22 lb/ft³) of creosote or 24–35 kg/m³ (1.5–2.2 lb/ft³) of the salts of the above preservatives.

Inspections for insect decay

The non-specialist who lives close to and cares for an historic building should be instructed in the differences between fungal and insect attack and be able to take samples of insects for specialist identification. Several samples should be put into a small bottle containing alcohol or methylated spirits and sent in a tin, to prevent breakage, to the architect or other person responsible for regular inspections of the building. Samples of bore dust and typical damage are valuable aids to identification and should be supplied.

The specialist, architect or surveyor should make a detailed inspection, using his knowledge of the relevant points in design and maintenance of buildings, including drainage and damp-proof courses and the need for ventilation. He should have a general knowledge of timber so as to distinguish between commoner types of hardwoods and softwoods and be able to differentiate between sapwood and heartwood. He must also know the habits of wood-boring insects, as this helps him to seek out the most likely areas of infestation. Identification of the different types of wood-boring insects and some knowledge of other insects found in flight holes or in crevices in wood, such as clothes moths or carpet beetles, which cause little or no damage to wood is an important part of his skill, which includes an assessment of the present state of activity and the probable extent of damage and risk of further spread of attack. He must propose remedial measures, the most appropriate method of preventive treatment and structural repairs if these are necessary.

Flight holes about 1 mm (0.04 in) in diameter in hardwoods may be due to *Lyctus*, *Anobium* or *Ambrosia* beetles which have a world-wide distribution. In tropical areas, the holes may be larger, even 2–3 mm (0.08–0.12 in). *Lyctus* is usually active in freshly seasoned hardwoods, whereas *Anobium* attack is normally slight in buildings, at least in temperate climates, less than 10 years old.

In softwood, flight holes of similar size probably indicate *Anobium ernobius* or *Ambrosia* beetles. Where difficulty is experienced in making accurate identification, samples should be taken and specialist advice sought.

Piles of bore dust (frass) and fresh clean-looking flight exit holes are the usual symptoms of continued activity. Live beetles may be found in the flight season when they emerge to mate and lay eggs. Dead beetles, usually furniture beetles, are often to be found under roof lights or windows and deathwatch beetles drop on to the floor below the infested timbers, so giving a valuable indication of the position and, by their numbers, the extent of the attack. This circumstance can be exploited by using fumigants in the flight season. The cleaning staff of any building should be alerted to collect dead beetles, noting the place they are found, and to report the occurrence of any frass. The presence of predators or adult parasites is also indicative of continuing wood-boring activity. A beetle containing moist internal organs indicates that it has recently emerged.

In historic buildings, wood-boring activity may sometimes have ceased, thus rendering remedial treatment redundant but giving the architect the difficult task of assessing the strength of the remaining elements. It is unfortunate that both fungal and insect attack occur frequently at structurally important points such as the ends of beams, where the wood may obtain moisture from the wall and be insufficiently ventilated and softened by fungal attack, or in joints where crevices exist convenient for egg laying.

Special attention should be given to wall plates where these lie under gutters which may be defective or flood occasionally. Lack of damp-proof courses at ground level, and in parapet walls and under window sills, gives rise to conditions favourable to beetle attack. Sapwood, which generally ages to a lighter colour than heartwood, is always most susceptible to beetle attack, so particular attention should be paid to the edges of boards and structural timbers.

Attack by the furniture beetle, deathwatch beetle and wood-boring weevil is more likely to occur where the wood has been wetted or subjected to dampness. In roof spaces, furniture beetle infestation may be found round the water tank due to wetting by condensation and may also be found in the communication hatch, dormer windows and ventilators for the same reason.

All wooden articles in storage, especially in roofs where they may be forgotten for years and particularly if they are made of birch, plywood or wickerwood, should be carefully examined before storage and treated with preservative, as they may introduce infestation into structural timbers. During an inspection they should be carefully examined.

A powerful easily aimed torch with a strong beam is essential for inspecting buildings for beetle and fungus attack. With this aid, the freshness of the flight exit holes can be judged and by angling the beam acutely the slight blistering effect, which is evidence of the house longhorn beetle, is revealed. Tapping the timber with a penknife, or for heavier members a light hammer, will indicate the general condition. Badly affected timbers have a hollow sound or dull resonance, while sound timbers ring true. The penknife can also be used to prod into the timber and comparisons of penetration for the same force are indicative of condition. The penknife and a small artist's paintbrush are of value in extracting samples of frass from bore holes, and a magnifying glass should be carried to examine this dust. Test tubes, previously filled with alcohol and corked, should be taken for collecting beetles or larvae for subsequent inspection in a laboratory by an entomologist, but matchboxes filled with cottonwool can also be used as temporary substitutes.

Termiticides and insecticides

Commercial termiticides are heptachlor, aldrin, dieldrin and chlordane, all of which are poisonous and dangerous to use. Creosote, sodium arsenite, DDT, gamma benzene hexachloride, pentachlorophenol, sodium pentachlorophenate, copper naphthenate and chromated copper arsenate are also used. Details of their chemistry are given in Appendix III.

Chemical preservative treatment against insects

A preservative is a substance which is applied to protect cultural property from attack by pests, whereas a pesticide is used to eradicate an active attack by pests, some only having a very short life. The ideal pesticide does not exist, but a given product should meet as many of the following requirements as possible:

It should: (a) be cheap; (b) be safe to user, i.e. be of low toxicity rating; (c) be effective in killing insect adults, larvae and eggs; (d) be fast working and easy to apply; (e) be able to retain its killing power.

It should not: (a) leave or form dangerous residues; (b) break down or lose its effectiveness in storage; (c) be absorbed by and build up in animal or plant tissue; (d) injure non-target animals or plants; (e) corrode or damage building materials or equipment.

For most people, protection by treatment means the economical preservative treatment of wood to prevent insect attack and fungal decay, but also under this heading should be considered soil poisoning and the surface treatments such as paint, varnish and textured finishes which have already been mentioned. In addition to their decorative purposes, these surface treatments play an important part in protecting wood from both weather and insect attack. Experience has shown that protective treatments are often used in the wrong place, with the wood in an inappropriate state, or used in the wrong way. The wood must have a sufficiently low moisture content to receive the treatment and have a suitable pore structure to accept the vehicle for the chemicals proposed.

Assessment of the possible treatment should be made from both the technical and aesthetic points of view. An analysis of the proposed treatment should be obtained and attached to the documentation of the historic building; failing this, a sample should be kept.

The supplier or manufacturer of the protective medium should be asked the following questions:

(1) How long will the protective effects last and will it be simple to renew or supplement the treatment during the life of the building?
(2) Can the treatment be properly carried out if local resources of trained men and facilities are limited?
(3) Is the treatment offered appropriate to the wood to be used and its probable moisture content at the time of treatment?
(4) Is the protective medium or the method of application hazardous to man, animals or birds and if so is there an acceptable alternative?
(5) Does the protective medium have a bad smell and if so how long will it persist?
(6) Will the treatment have damaging effects on other materials, e.g. paintings on wood, gesso work, electrical insulation or fixing nails of different metals, e.g. copper or Duralumin?
(7) Will other materials or the environment have a damaging effect on the treatment?
(8) After using the treatment is it possible to apply other coatings, e.g. paint, without serious difficulty?
(9) May or should the protective medium be coloured and if so will the colour be fast (note that the colour may be useful as a means of checking that treatment has been carried out and its depth of penetration)?

Martin Weaver points out that practically every pesticide is either toxic to man or can cause harmful effects. Toxicity tests are carried out in laboratories on animals such as rats and the lethal dose is recorded, when 50% of a group die, as LD_{50} and expressed in milligrams of chemical per kilogram of animal bodyweight. A LD_{50} less than 50 mg/kg is very toxic, 50–500 moderately toxic and 500–5000 slightly toxic. Normal aspirin has a LD_{50} of 1375. Toxic poison may also be released on evaporation of the vehicle in which the pesticide or preservative is dissolved, such as methanol or methylhydrate.

Sodium pentachlorophenol (PCP) has a LD_{50} of 50 and is extremely toxic itself, but it also contains small quantities of dioxin, the horrible poison released in the Seveso, Italy, disaster in 1976, and this has to be limited to 0.1 mg/kg of pesticide. Orthophenylphenol (OPP) with a LD_{50} of 2480 is much to be preferred and is available in two forms, named Dowcide A (water soluble) and Dowcide I (organic solvent), which both act as insecticides and fungicides with low risks to operators, occupants and ground-water contamination.

Most chemicals that are effective against termites, such as Chlordane, must only be applied by licensed specialists. The local medical officer can advise on municipal or provincial and state legislation regarding use of pesticides, as can the Forestry Department or Ministry of Agriculture.

Application of insecticides

In historic buildings it is generally impossible or very difficult to apply insecticides using vacuum or pressurized techniques. Oil-based preservatives and insecticides mostly need dry wood for their application to be effective, and it must be remembered that the solvents used give off fumes which are toxic and may be dangerous in high concentrations. These factors limit the effective application of insecticides and preservatives. Among the practicable techniques, brushing may be assumed to have 2–4 mm (0.08–0.16 in) penetration. Emulsions are less liable to produce toxic hazards and fire risks. Infiltration, by drilling staggered holes and filling them until saturation is achieved along the grain, is effective in softwoods but tests should be made for hardwoods. Impregnation at high pressure by guns fitted on to plastic nozzles is a pressurized type of infiltration but needs smaller holes and has advantages.

Liquid insecticides are mostly organic solvent-type preparations containing contact insecticides and stomach poisons. In addition to eradicant action, these preparations give some protection against reinfection. Emulsion-type paste insecticides show promise for treating large-dimensioned timbers by virtue of the amount that can be applied and their good penetrating powers.

Thoroughness of application is most important. First, all disintegrated wood must be cut away and all dust and dirt should be cleaned up with an industrial vacuum cleaner. Cracks, splits and holes for plumbing and electrical wiring should receive special attention. Low-pressure spray application, working up and down the timber and flooding the surface with about 1 l to each 3–4 m² (1 gal to each 150–200 ft²) of surface area, is the most convenient method of treatment and is necessary where access to timber is difficult, such as undersides of floors, ends of rafters and wall plates. Flight holes in large timbers may be injected, or specially drilled holes may be repeatedly flooded with preservative. Application by brush is an alternative to spraying for small areas; the liquid should be flowed on freely, not rubbed in.

Brush applications of wood preservatives are not fully effective unless repeated at frequent intervals, in tropical conditions as often as 6–12 months. Vacuum impregnation processes are in a different category; with adequate absorption of suitable preservatives, wood can even be made to outlast its mechanical life. Where new timber is being prepared for building purposes it must be soaked in preservative or given repeated brush coatings, each coat being applied before the previous one is dry. No cutting or boring should take place after treatment unless the exposed surface is re-treated. Structural timbers already built into the structure should receive two or more flowing brush coats, care being taken to soak the preservative into the end grain of beams or posts, since it is here that the attack generally begins.

For timber in contact with the ground in tropical conditions, the following preservative treatments are recommended:

(1) Pressure creosoting in accordance with BS 913:1972.
(2) Pressure impregnation with a water-borne copper–chrome–arsenic preservative in accordance with BS 4072:1966.
(3) Hot and cold open-tank process using creosote or preservative, as described in FPRL Technical Note No. 42.

For timber protected from the weather and not in ground contact an additional treatment is recommended:

(4) Timberizing diffusion impregnation of green timber with disodium octaborate tetrahydrate, as described in FPRL Technical Note No. 41 (this treatment is not considered effective against termites).

It is important for both vacuum pressure and hot and cold tank processes of timber impregnation that the wood be at a moisture content of less than 25%. Brushing or dipping with preservative is of doubtful value in the tropics, any protection afforded being literally only skin deep.

There are toxic hazards in the application of preservatives that are poisonous to human beings, and protective clothing must be worn. Goggles or visors and dust or fume face-masks should be used, and respirators will be necessary if work is in confined spaces which cannot be ventilated properly. Hands must be washed before eating or smoking. Great care must be taken not to contaminate water tanks, as anything greater than $1\mu g$ (10^{-6} g) per litre of water may require the whole water system to be replaced due to contamination, some water authorities even insisting on more stringent standards. Naked lights and unprotected bulbs must be prohibited; the fire and explosion risk is reduced if an emulsion-type preservative is used. There is a risk of staining plaster, and bitumen bonding may be dissolved by the organic solvents in the insecticides. Aqueous solutions of preservative, which may *cause* damage by making the timber swell, are less desirable. It is always wise to test samples of new preservative solutions for their staining effect before use. Some preservatives damage plastics used in electrical insulation or elsewhere.

Damage by animals and birds

The danger of pest-borne infection inside an historic building depends on three factors: its location, its use and its construction. Risks are high in food stores, food preparation areas and restaurants; medium in farm buildings and buildings with multiple occupancy such as flats, terraces, schools and institutions; and generally low where one owner is responsible and careful with regard to hygiene and care is taken to dispose of waste regularly and not let it accumulate. Location close to docks or some other use liable to encourage pests, including farm buildings and high density building, increases the risk, as does demolition and redevelopment. Unfortunately, the construction of historic buildings often enabled pests to establish themselves. Preventive measures must rely on controlling the internal environment. Mice can squeeze through holes about 6 mm (0.24 in) in diameter when young and young rats through a hole of 9 mm (0.35 in). Mice are excellent climbers and rats can burrow to depths of 750 mm (30 in) and will dig long distances horizontally, especially if the soil is loose, along the course of buried pipes or cables. Rats have even been known to dive through intercepting traps and the water seal of a W.C. pan. Pigeons can be kept out by reducing gaps to 40 mm (1.6 in) and for sparrows to 20 mm (0.8 in). Generally,

all glazing must be kept in good order to prevent ingress and detailing construction of roofs, close fitting external windows and doors, sealing round pipes and ducts with compartmentation and trunking of services should be given priority. Self-closers for doors and metal sheathing at the base of doors may also be considered.

Animals, including man, can damage buildings by urinating and defecating. Dogs can cause the decay of brickwork at street level and cats are said to damage zinc roofing or galvanized surfaces. Rats cause damage by building nests, which provide a likely spot for the start of a fire, and by gnawing at electric wires, for which they have a strange predilection. Old-fashioned 'combined' rainwater and soil systems give rats many opportunities for climbing up untrapped rainwater pipes and entering a roof space via a gutter. Their entry is best prevented by trapped gullies, balloons over vent pipes and properly protected air bricks. In Ghana, mice are serious agents of destruction in houses built of unbaked earth.

Birds, in particular pigeons and to a lesser extent starlings and jackdaws, can damage and disfigure buildings. Their droppings can block roof rainwater outlets and can cause grass and other vegetation to grow in gutters and in re-entrants on sloping roofs, and the bodies of dead pigeons frequently block drain outlets and downpipes. Jackdaws and pigeons like nesting in stairs and turrets of historic buildings, and it is necessary to wage constant warfare to keep them out.

As the excrement of birds, bats and insects is both alkaline and acid, it promotes decay of the surface, particularly of stained glass and wall paintings from which the dark deposits are difficult to remove. If birds win entry they build up so much mess and rubbish that it is a major task to get rid of it—and so unpleasant that workmen have refused to tackle the job owing to the lice and filth that have to be faced. The dirt birds introduce leads to infestation by beetles, particularly the longhorn beetle.

Roosting and nesting birds can be prevented by netting or spikes; sticky bird repellents can be applied to masonry, but there is a danger of staining the stone. High-voltage wires have been tried but these are difficult to maintain in practice, for when a sitting bird receives a shock it rises and instinctively defecates, often on to the wires, thus tending to create a short-circuit, so that the device itself is found to need too much maintenance. A simpler method which often works is the fixing of black nylon thread about 25 mm (1 in) above sills and landing edges. Glass sheets fixed above cornices are also reported to be effective.

Prevention of damage by animals and birds needs vigilance and routines of regular inspection if it is to be effective.

11

Man-made causes of decay

Introduction

Man-made causes of decay are complicated and have widespread implications in the conservation of historic buildings. So little has been done to prevent this type of decay that the present chapter can provide few answers to the questions it raises, because the problems are immense, involving economics and industrialization. What can be said is that unless the causes of decay of cultural property are properly analysed and the effects of each harmful agent to some extent quantified, there is a danger that the wrong priorities will be applied to protective measures. Much more measurement and evaluation of the effect of man-made causes of decay is needed. To obtain an approximate measure, comparative studies should be made of the rates of decay in different environments. The American practice of having Environmental Impact Statements is a step in the right direction. If decay were measured on significant buildings internationally, we could use them as laboratories of experience.

Industrial production, together with electricity generation, is the main cause of atmospheric pollution as well as the heavy traffic that causes vibration damage. However, several major industries already have conservation officers and are able to consider the effects of their proposals at the planning stage instead of bearing the cost of correcting mistakes at a later date. The American Environmental Protection Agency has helped in the development of this responsible trend, and it is hoped that in future every industry will have conservation advice available to top management.

Damage by vibration

In dealing with the effects of vibration on historic buildings, it is apparent that little research has been

Figure 11.1   Bankside Power Station from St Paul's Cathedral (Courtesy: Feilden & Mawson)

Electricity generating stations produce about one-quarter of the atmospheric pollution in Britain. Bankside Power Station, built shortly after World War II, has undoubtedly caused damage to St Paul's Cathedral and should never have been sited so close to a national monument. Expensive plant was installed to reduce the emissions of sulphur dioxide and it is claimed that 98% has been eliminated. As the generating station is now obsolescent, it is to be hoped that it will be demolished. The post-Wren statuary by Thomas Bird (fl. 1710) in the foreground has suffered severe damage and should be moved inside before it becomes meaningless

153

Figure 11.2   St Paul's Cathedral, south portico

Cracking and splitting of the masonry is caused by the compaction of the rubber core due to vibration throwing greater loads on the outer casing of ashlar. A traffic count showed sufficient vehicle units to halve the life of St Paul's Cathedral. The City of London co-operated by keeping the road surface smooth and now heavy vehicles have been banned, an important factor in preventive conservation

done and practically none of it has been financed by those interested in historic buildings. Noise and acoustic consultants are oriented towards the problems of new buildings rather than to existing ones, to the prevention of damage by initial design, rather than the limitation of damage by restricting the causes. Further, it is very difficult to measure vibration, which, although small, may be sufficient to cause long-term damage in an historic building in poor condition. Such a programme would require intensive instrumentation to cover all the permutations of a massive indeterminate structure, and no such programme has yet been financed or initiated. Positive proof of damage resulting from a given incident is almost impossible to obtain, as it is very difficult to distinguish between damage from vibration and the inevitable aging of a building. In the event, vibration pollution probably accelerates the aging process in proportion to its intensity. It is wise to remember that damage caused by vibration is generally irreversible and in practical terms irreparable.

It is extremely difficult to get any certain proof of

what damage may or may not have occurred due to vibration. Ground-transmitted traffic vibration, particularly that from heavy diesel vehicles, is becoming more regarded as a serious problem, although both the airborne and ground-transmitted energy inputs are small. Damage from pile-driving vibration is certainly common.

The practical difficulties of measurement to the required high degrees of accuracy over a sufficiently long period are very considerable, taking into account variable weather and temperature changes due to the annual cycle of seasons. Standards of permissible vibration input have been prepared which specify for well-built new buildings how much input can be received without noticeable damage occurring. To allow for the conditions of historic buildings, the German DIN standards have reduced the permissible input to one-fifth of that allowed for modern buildings. These standards, it should be remembered, are aimed only at short-term identifiable damage, and ignore the long-term cumulative effect of vibration; the writer therefore believes that the permissible input should be reduced to one-hundredth for historic buildings.

Whereas the threat of vibration from supersonic commercial aircraft may not materialize, vibration caused by heavy vehicles is very much a fact and a matter for immediate public concern. A vehicle travelling along a road generates vibrations in adjacent buildings in two ways. First, the variations in the contact forces between the wheels of the vehicle and the road surface generate oscillatory stress waves in the road structure which are transmitted through the ground to adjacent buildings. These stresses increase in proportion to the cube of the axle weight of the vehicle, so a 10 t (9.8 ton) axle load is one thousand times more damaging than a 1 t (0.98 ton) axle load. Secondly, pressure waves arising from the size, shape and speed of the vehicle, much like a bow wave, are transmitted directly through the air, together with pressure fluctuations mainly due to the engine exhaust, and the other mechanical noises produced by the vehicle. A noise of 100 dB gives an equivalent pressure of 2 N/m^2 (0.00029 lbf/in^2). The vehicle's wheel-suspension system, the dynamic axle loads and the stiffness of the chassis are all important factors in inducing vibrations. As axle loads are increasing in magnitude and heavy vehicles are not using greater numbers of axles, vibration problems are now becoming more widespread. In time, the cumulative effect of the damage they are causing will become more apparent.

In the short term, lath and plaster ceilings are particularly vulnerable to vibration. The key to the plaster and the condition of the lath should be carefully examined before any exposure to exceptional vibra-

154

Figure 11.3 St Paul's Cathedral, column in south portico

The compaction and uneven settlement induced by heavy traffic caused this column shaft to split near the base

tion such as piling. Wall panelling is also vulnerable as loose material may wedge behind the panelling and force it outwards. In Rome, valuable frescoes have become detached from walls due to traffic vibration. Vibrations may well initiate cracks in materials already subjected to temperature and humidity changes and settlements, and it is suspected they contribute to the fatigue of building materials. In extreme cases, instantaneous damage might be inflicted on fragile glass, loose plaster mosaics or pieces of stone, as well as insecurely attached features such as memorial plaques.

It is known that vibration can cause loss of foundation strength by affecting the subsoil. In some non-cohesive soils, such as sands, the long-term effect of vibrations is to increase the soil density by causing compaction. In some cohesive soils, such as silts, the effect can be destructive in terms of bearing capacity, and may even reduce load-bearing silt to a fluid. Therefore the problem is two-fold: first, possible loss of foundation strength; secondly, loss of structural strength in the superstructure. The architect must consult an expert if there is sufficient circumstantial evidence to make investigation in depth worth while, but must warn the owner of the building that such investigation involves sophisticated instrumentation and will probably be a long and expensive operation.

Measuring vibrations

The academic scientific approach to the problem of vibration pollution is that if you are going to ban causes of vibration that may damage historic buildings, such as traffic, piling or the sonic boom, you must state the level or amplitude of vibration that should not be exceeded. This might be done by extrapolating data from long-term fatigue tests, the fatigue concept being based upon possible resonances in the individual structural members of the building when the waveform of the disturbing vibration contains these resonant frequencies. This approach was adopted by the Royal Aircraft Establishment at Farnborough, England, in its attempt to assess the damage that the supersonic aircraft Concorde might cause to historic buildings. The attempt was praiseworthy but did not take into account sufficiently the nature of historic buildings, in that they are of such great variety of construction and condition as to defy, for practical purposes, purely scientific analysis. If such an analysis were possible, it would probably cost unreasonably large sums of money.

Vibration from road vehicles

Studies to date have been mainly concentrated on the vibrations generated by vehicle wheels acting on the road surface. Irregularities in the road surface of about 20 mm (0.8 in) in amplitude can cause peak particle velocities in the ground of 5 mm/s (0.2 in/sec). At this level it is assessed that minor, so-called 'architectural', damage may occur in houses of normal construction, but at half this level, i.e. 2.5 mm/s (0.1 in/sec), it is reported that vibrations become intrusive and annoying to the occupants. The frequencies of these annoying vibrations lie within the range 1–45 Hz, those above 15 Hz being audible but those below that figure also being capable of inflicting damage.

An English expert has written that there is agreement between German researchers, upon whose work the British Research Establishment's work is based, and Hungarian researchers, that no damage of any kind should occur to structures in a reasonably good state of repair at velocities below 2.5 mm/s (0.1 in/sec) applied to the foundations of the structure. This level lies in the upper limit of the easily noticeable classification in the Reiher Meister Scale of Human Perception.

The Institute of Building Materials and Structure in Holland suggests a velocity limit of ± 2 mm/s (0.08 in/sec) for the onset of plaster cracking and ± 5 mm/s (0.2 in/sec) for structural damage, while the German

155

Figure 11.4 St Paul's Cathedral, base of south-west tower

The internal condition of the masonry can be judged from this core sample. The outer ashlar is backed by rubble set in lime mortar which has broken up and become severely fissured. Traffic vibration causes and accelerates this type of internal decay, which can only be rectified by grouting with epoxy resins

DIN 4150 proposes a limit of 10 mm/s (0.4 in/sec) for residential buildings in good condition and 2 mm/s (0.08 in/sec) for historic buildings—a factor of only 5 in favour of historic buildings.

It must be emphasized, however, that these figures are for buildings of normal and sound construction and do not take into account long-term effects of fatigue and accelerated aging. If a structure is highly stressed for any reason, e.g. settlement, shrinkage, thermal stresses, these limits cannot be applied directly but may be used as the eventual reference point which is necessary for any assessment of the problem to be made.

Studies of the effects of vibration on new buildings were reported in 1971 by L. Kapsa of the Research Institute for Building and Architecture of Czechoslovakia. Extensive field tests were carried out and tables were produced giving the reduction of expected life in well-constructed dwellings subjected to various traffic densities. Traffic densities were measured by the number of vehicles per hour, vehicles of over 5 t (4.9 ton) each counting as 1 unit and lighter goods vehicles as 0.4 unit. Trams on tracks with poor foundation (i.e. rails with sleepers only) count as 1.5 unit. *Table 11.1* is set out with a 'decrease-of-life' factor which for certain favourable criteria is reduced; for example, by one for a bituminous road surface, by two if the buildings are of new brick, by three for a concrete road surface and by four for a steel- or concrete-framed structure.

Certain layout criteria increase the decrease-of-life factor: if the buildings have a footpath less than 1.5 m (5 ft) wide or if the frontage interval is greater than 8 m (26 ft), there is an increase of one; if the traffic speed is more than 20 km/h (12.5 m.p.h.) and if there is no footpath, there is an increase of two. The above criteria are added or subtracted from the decrease-of-life factors given in *Table 11.1* for traffic.

Table 11.1 Life Reduction of Houses due to Traffic

Vehicle flow units (per 24 hours)	Decrease-of-life factor	Life reduction (%)
up to 260	1	0
260–600	2	4.0
600–960	3	7.5
960–1540	4	10.0
1540–2660	5	15.0
2660–3440	6	20.0
3440–4660	7	25.0
4660–7440	8	35.0
7440 and above	9	50.0

The above summary of the effects of vibration is highly simplified but at least enough work has been done to prove that traffic vibration reduces the life of well-built modern houses. Although the results given here are not directly applicable to historic buildings, they clearly suggest that there is a serious risk of reducing the life of such buildings through subjecting them to severe traffic vibration. When applied to St Paul's Cathedral, these figures gave a life reduction of over 50% before the City of London banned heavy traffic. In practice, the maintenance of a smooth road surface, as well as a reduction of axle loads, is of great importance in alleviating the effects of traffic vibration.

M.E. House of the Wolfson Unit for Noise and Vibration Control, at the Institute of Sound and Vibration Research, Southampton University, England, has listed several areas where further investigation is required with regard to traffic vibration:

(1) A statistical survey of the road force inputs for a variety of locations, road construction and states

of repair would enable better forecasts to be made of long-term exposure of buildings to vibration.

(2) The propagation of waves (in particular Rayleigh waves) in a range of soils and substrata commonly encountered needs to be studied, with particular reference to frequency dispersion and damping.

(3) Much more experimental work is needed to determine the relationships between stresses in building elements and controlled ground inputs with known frequency distribution.

(4) Studies of age susceptibility would be valuable in buildings of similar construction, some of which have been subjected to higher than normal vibration levels over a long period and whose vibration history can be estimated with some reliability (e.g. near railway lines).

(5) It would be helpful to have tests on typical building elements to relate 'failure' stresses in relevant principal modes of vibration to commonly measured vibration parameters.

Vibration from pile driving

Vibration damage from pile driving may be the most common cause and source of danger to an historic building, particularly if it has poor foundations, cracked walls and spreading roofs. Bored piles generally give rise to very little trouble, driven piles may cause some damage, dependent on subsoil conditions, whereas piles with expanded *in situ* bulb bases are particularly liable to cause damage. Ground shock waves from the latter are unpredictable in their action, but can be strong enough to crack 300mm (12 in) of reinforced concrete.

An example is the church of St John, at Ousegate in York, England, which was in poor condition and rested upon an almost fluid river silt. When conventional driven piling was used for a new building next door, it was soon apparent that damage was being caused to the church. The floor heaved, cracks were opened and closed, and plaster was loosened and damaged by cracking. Complaints were made, and injunctions were threatened but could not be pressed home. A payment for the identifiable damage was negotiated, but concealed damage had undoubtedly occurred which might take years to be revealed in its full extent and could never be put right, nor could the real cost be quantified and claimed.

The argument might be advanced that rebuilding of city centre sites is a thing that must be anticipated and an historic building must in the nature of things expect this treatment. It was clear, however, that in the case of St John's, Ousegate, the wrong sort of pile had been specified. Soon afterwards, a nearby site was developed with another large building and the architect in charge of St John's, being forewarned, immediately wrote warning the developer's architects of the dangers to the church fabric. A meeting was arranged, rotary bored piles were agreed upon, and no difficulties or vibrations were experienced under exactly the same subsoil conditions. This example shows that prior negotiation is desirable, and that reasonable requests for a choice of pile that will not cause vibration should be met.

To protect historic buildings against damage from piling, recognized good practice should be for a 'stop clause' to be written into all piling subcontracts for all adjacent historic buildings. If this is done, the piling may be stopped immediately without incurrence of extra costs due to disturbance of the building contract; so that when a genuine complaint is made by the owner of the historic building, it can be met. As the cost of the delay will fall on the piling contractors the very existence of this 'stop clause' will make him more careful when advising on the choice of a pile, which, taking subsoil conditions into account, would not cause vibration damage to adjacent buildings.

The emphasis should be on prevention rather than cure of damage, for the cure is costly, doubtful and frequently impossible. Local authorities with their role of protecting the public interest could insert an appropriate clause in any planning approval to give nearby historic buildings adequate protection. Precedents for this type of protection exist in the St Paul's Preservation Act drawn up in London in 1935. The criteria for the decision can only be determined by qualified professional judgement, unhampered by commercial pressures.

Methods of protecting historic buildings from vibration

One method of protecting historic buildings from ground-borne vibrations has been suggested by the Building Research Establishment, England, in their publications; this is the insertion of vertical curtains of thixotropic grout in trenches to insulate the foundations of the building from vibration. The trench, however, would have to be at least equal in depth to one-third of the wavelength of the vibration concerned, and for low frequencies, dependent on the velocity of the wave propagation in the soil, this depth could easily exceed 5 m (16 ft). Before proposing such methods of insulation it would, of course, be necessary to carry out a thorough site investigation using soil mechanics techniques. Such a solution might be applied to the Colosseum in Rome, which at the time of writing is the centre of a large traffic roundabout and has been partially closed to the

157

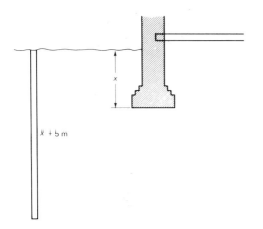

Figure 11.5 A thixotropic curtain

public on grounds of safety because pieces of stone are reported to have fallen from it.

The frescoes in the Villa Farnesina in Rome have been successfully protected from vehicle vibration damage by mounting the heavily trafficked road outside upon absorbent rubber pads.

The removal of the source of vibration is of course the best policy, as in industrial plants where the vibration is eliminated by proper mountings and insulating pads. In the case of traffic, town planning measures should be initiated to remove traffic from areas where there are important or large numbers of historic buildings. At the very least, road surfaces near historic buildings should be carefully maintained, heavy vehicles banned and vehicle speeds restricted.

Because historic buildings were built long before the increase in the vibration environment, whether airborne or earth-transmitted, the onus of proof should be on the people whose project might cause vibration damage to show that this is not the case, taking full account of the fact that an historic building is old, probably decrepit and full of latent defects. This is not just a debating point, as the facts are that vibration damage is irreversible and generally incapable of repair, except by rebuilding. In practical terms or for insurance purposes it is virtually impossible to assess the quantum of the damage resulting from a known incident, e.g. a seismographic survey for oil using explosive charges, let alone an unknown or unidentifiable incident, such as a passing supersonic plane trailing a sonic bang in a path 80 km (50 mile) wide.

It is impossible for the owner of an historic building to maintain a constant vibration watch and inspect his charge each time a suspected incident occurs—the cost would be phenomenal, the results at most impossible to prove and the culprits unidentifiable. When a severe vibration incident damages an historic

building, it may be likened to someone scratching the surface of an 'old master'. There is no real repair—it will never be the same. Because positive proof is unobtainable, it is therefore essential that local and central government should be persuaded to act in a civilized way and take steps to protect historic buildings from traffic vibration.

Water abstraction

As with pollution and vibration, water abstraction can have macro- as well as micro-effects. At the macro level, water abstraction for industrial purposes has caused Venice to sink and thus become more vulnerable to damaging sea floods. London has also sunk about 200 mm (8 in) because of underdrainage; the flood wall along the tidal Thames Embankment has had to be raised to meet the threat of flooding caused by high tides and a barrage has been built. The long-term effects of water abstraction have not yet been fully studied, but it appears that large, heavy buildings may sink relatively more than light structures, and if such buildings have differential loadings on their foundations, differential settlements may well be induced.

Both St Paul's Cathedral and York Minster stand on perched water tables which are liable to have their levels changed unless carefully controlled. In both cases, regular measurements are maintained. The St Paul's Preservation Act gives authority to protect the perched water level by control over the design of underground works within a rather small 'prescribed' area. Studies show that the cathedral would be particularly vulnerable to a rapid change in the water table. In the case of York Minster, cracking and downward movement of the main piers coincided more or less with a lowering of the perched water table, which might also have upset the load-bearing capacity of overstressed clay soil. Milan Cathedral suffered severely from ground-water abstraction and has had major repairs to cracked piers and superstructure due to differential settlements of about 25 mm (1 in) in its length and 9 mm (0.35 in) in its width.

The invention of the Newcomen pumping engine in 1746 enabled mining technology to be developed, with consequential enlargement of its scope and increase in underground water abstraction; at the same time, the area of mining subsidence was greatly enlarged. Such subsidence is likely to affect historic buildings, particularly large long ones.

Alteration of the water table has several possible effects, depending upon the characteristics of the load-bearing soil and the building. First, as the water table is lowered the surcharge on the subsoil is altered. Secondly, the load-bearing characteristics of

Figure 11.6   Mavis Bank, Midlothian, Scotland

Mining subsidence caused these severe settlements which led to the house being abandoned, so making it vulnerable to vandalism and finally fire. Yet it is not beyond redemption

the soil itself may change, and both will cause differential movements. In addition, if a building is set upon wooden piles the lowering of the water table may expose these and cause them to rot. Many buildings constructed on piles in mining areas such as the Ruhr have suffered in this way. In flat waterlogged areas, the changes in underdrainage due to mining are liable to be extremely difficult to deal with.

Soft-ground tunnelling, being liable to upset the water table, may therefore be of vital interest to the owners of historic buildings with shallow foundations. Such tunnelling is likely to increase in towns and cities in the future, particularly for large-diameter sewers and underground railways. Sewers, in particular, may have only a small surface cover and may have to be driven between the piles supporting buildings above.

Some new building works may raise underground water table levels. For instance, if solid foundation walls are constructed to such a depth and in such a position that they dam an underground water flow, this would cause lowering of the water table downstream and raising of levels upstream, with resulting difficulties in disposal of water to soakaways and increase of rising damp. As there is in general no legal protection of ground water under a building, the matter should be watched carefully if new buildings, sewerage or roadworks are proposed in the vicinity of an historic building. Underground water levels can also be affected locally by the bursting or leakage of sewers and drains and defective rainwater pipes. It is therefore of importance to record ground-water levels near historic buildings. The instrument designed for this purpose is a piezometer.

The flooding of the Holy Shrines in Kerbala, Iraq, was caused by the raising of the water table through

the modernization of the sanitation arrangements by an introduction of water-borne drainage to soak-aways. Unfortunately, the town lies in a depression, so the water table came up. In the case of the Holy Shrine of Al Abbas, a ring main was installed round the shrine and pumping instituted, but this was too vigorous and abstracted silt from under the foundations causing the four corners of the building to subside and the brickwork to crack. There are two possible cures: first, provision of a thixotropic curtain to isolate the shrine, although this depends on finding an impervious layer of soil; secondly, installation of sewers to drain and

Figure 11.7   Mavis Bank, Midlothian, Scotland

A detail of damage caused by mining subsidence, neglect and fire

159

Figure 11.8   St Paul's Cathedral
(Courtesy: Feilden & Mawson)

A good example of the build-up of soot that occurred on London's architectural heritage before the Clean Air Act. This type of pollution is a piece of social history relating to the pea-soup fogs of Victorian London, but its effect was to damage the fabric and distort its architectural values

remove the cause of the water table level being so uncomfortably high. Mohendjaro, in Pakistan, is also threatened by a major rise in the water table caused by improved irrigation, and this may be one of the causes of the recent increase in the level of the water table under the historic city of Cairo.

Atmospheric pollution

Atmospheric pollution is the by-product of industrial and commercial activities, heating and traffic. The effects of industrial pollution are international; it is believed, for instance, that British aerial effluents affect the whole of Scandinavia.

The most meaningful statistic is the amount of SO_2 produced per person. East European countries are the worst offenders as their controls are flouted by industry, however there is considerable room for improvement in the UK. The Chernobyl disaster in 1987 introduced a new dimension of pollution by atomic radiation which spread into Lapland and western areas of UK rendering meat from livestock grazing on contaminated vegetation a severe health hazard. Pollution control is an important factor in preventing damage to our cultural heritage.

The reduction of such effluent is an expensive matter, and its control should be international so that consistent standards are applied world wide. The greatest part of the pollution of the atmosphere arises from the burning of fuel in boilers, furnaces, domestic fires and in internal combustion engines. There are three normal categories of pollutant; first,

particulates, grit and dust, emittted mostly from industrial chimneys; second, smoke or finely divided solids, which coagulate to form soot; third, gases, the two most important of these being carbon dioxide (CO_2) and sulphur dioxide (SO_2).

In zones polluted by industry, which in effect include much of North America, Europe and Japan, rain is more strongly acid than natural rain which has a pH value of 5.6 due to dissolved carbon dioxide. Town rain may be as acid as pH 4 and is often pH 4.6. The acid strength of PH 4 is 25 times greater than pH 5.6, because sulphuric acid, although in much lower concentration, is very much more powerful than dissolved carbon dioxide.

Pollution is worse in anticyclonic weather when there are clear skies and low winds. A temperature inversion can aggravate the situation seriously, when the usual condition of the air getting cooler with height is upset by warm air acting as a lid and preventing the pollutant gases from rising and dispersing, so that their concentration rises.

Measuring pollution

Pollutants are measured in micrograms (millionths of a gram) per cubic metre of air, which is abbreviated as $\mu g/m^3$. To convert $\mu g/m^3$ to parts per million the molecular weight of the gas must be known.

It has been observed that the rain washed parts of alkaline stone, i.e. limestone and marbles and some sandstones, are the worst affected since the sulphate formed is continually washed away exposing a fresh

160

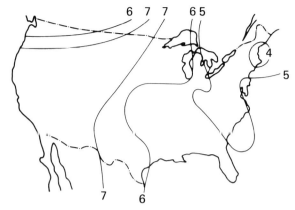

Figure 11.9 The acidity of rain falling in the USA in 1966

pH 7 is neutral, while below this figure rain is acid. One digit down on this scale represents a ten-fold increase in acidity; thus pH 4 is 10 times as acid as pH 5 and 100 times more acid than pH 6. Damage to limestone masonry also increases with ascending intensity according to the amount of pollution

surface to attack; and that sheltered parts are protected to a much greater extent, but blackened with a coating of soot and sulphate. On Saint Paul's, London, the whole surface is attacked by sulphates to a depth of about 3 mm (0.12 ins). After rain, the gutters show how much decomposed stone has been washed away. The extreme pollution has increased the corrosive attack on the embedded iron cramps, so causing further damage to the stone.

Portland stone is noted for its resistance to pollution, yet at St Paul's, erosion on exposed parapets and copings was about 30 mm (1.2 in) in 250 years as compared with 7 – 10 mm (0.3 – 0.4 in) of less resistant stone on provincial cathedrals. The maximum erosion noted was about 22 mm (0.9 in) in 45 years on the sculptured vases of the south portico gates. Examination of decay shows that the greatest effect occurs on cold, damp misty days when full office heating supplements the normal industrial emissions. Levels of pollution occur well above average on such days, while in contrast, when there is a fresh wind with rain, the SO_2 is either blown away or diluted.

In Britain smoke emission fell remarkably between 1951 and 1968, in spite of a 10% increase in population and 17% increase in annual gross energy consumption, and a continuing downward trend is forecast. It is clear that smoke emission is highest where domestic coal consumption is highest, for at least 85% of smoke appears to arise from domestic open fires burning coal. It follows that the modernization of domestic heating should be pressed forward energetically, especially in the north of England, where smoke and sulphur dioxide are still at high levels.

The Clean Air Act 1956 was one of Britain's first measures against atmospheric pollution. It has had beneficial effects in reducing grit, soot and gaseous pollution at ground level by making the use of smokeless fuel obligatory in certain zones, by controlling the emission of black smoke and by insisting that new chimneys be of greater height so as to disperse the products of combustion over a wider area. The Act does not have any jurisdiction over the emission of sulphur dioxide. Prior to the Act, soot deposits built up to a great thickness, indeed as much as 125 mm (5 in) was recorded on Saint Paul's Cathedral. The success of the Act means that it is now worthwhile to clean the exterior of buildings in urban centres. It has been pointed out that when smoke has been removed from the air more of the sun's heat reaches the surface of the earth to warm it up with respect to the air and so sets up turbulence, which by preventing stagnation of the air, prevents the building up of high concentrations of pollutants.

Wet and dry deposition of pollutants in buildings

Clifford Price, formerly of English Heritage, in *Industrial co-operation in the study of pollution effects* (1989), writes: 'Gaseous pollutants can find their way on to a surface of a building by two main routes; by dissolving in the rain that falls on to the building, or by reacting directly with the building itself. The first route is known as "wet deposition",

Figure 11.10 St Paul's Cathedral, parapets
(Courtesy: Feilden & Mawson)

Originally the joints were filled with lead, but severe erosion has worn the stone away leaving the joints standing proud about 25–30 mm (1–1.2 in) after 250 years of severe exposure

Figure 11.11 St Paul's Cathedral, cornices
(Courtesy: Feilden & Mawson)

*The projecting cornices protect the ashlar walls, but acid-laden
rain finds out any weakness of detail, especially where condensation and rain water drips. The projecting cyma recta top
moulding and fascia is badly eroded and grooved by rain water*

Figure 11.12 St Paul's Cathedral, detail of middle cornice
(Courtesy: Feilden & Mawson)

*The top moulding shows how the rain water has collected and run
down the fascia forming deep grooves about 30 mm (1.2 in) deep.
The surface of the stone has also been destroyed by sulphate attack
to a depth of at least 5 mm (0.2 in). The total erosion may be of the
order of 50 mm (2 in)*

and the second as "dry deposition". (The term "dry deposition" can be misleading, for pollutants will not react with a completely dry surface.) The distinction between wet and dry deposition is important. Wet deposition takes place when it is raining or snowing, whereas dry deposition takes place almost continuously. Wet deposition brings in pollutants from high up in the atmosphere (and so from distant sources), whereas dry deposition brings in pollutants from local sources as well. Theoretical calculations suggest that dry deposition accounts for much of the calcium sulphate (see below) that is found in sheltered limestone surfaces in polluted urban environments, though this does not necessarily mean that dry deposition is the dominant means of decay.

'Since calcium carbonate is soluble in acid, it follows that the pollutants described above will inevitably attack limestone buildings and monuments. Even unpolluted rain or air may have some effect, for the carbonic acid resulting from naturally occurring carbon dioxide is capable of dissolving calcium carbonate. However, chemical attack may only be the first and lesser form of attack, for the chemical reaction between the calcium carbonate and the pollutant can produce salts that can continue the decay indefinitely. Sulphur dioxide and sulphur trioxide, for example, lead to the formation of calcium sulphate. Calcium sulphate is not very soluble and is not readily washed out of the stone except in very exposed conditions. However, it is soluble enough that it can partially dissolve and then recrystallize as the stone wets and dries, and the pressures generated by crystal growth are enough to weaken and break down stone and mortar. There is still the possibility that episodes of rain of exceptionally high acidity may contribute directly to the dissolution of stonework, but we can discount the notion of buildings fizzing away gently every time it rains. Research supports the hypothesis that stone deterioration is enhanced by the pick-up of sulphur dioxide *between* showers of rain, whilst not being affected by the acidity of the rain itself.'

Carbon dioxide

Carbon dioxide occurs naturally, being given off by all living organisms as a product of respiration, as well as being a product of artificial combustion of fuel; when combined with rain water it produces carbonic acid. It must be appreciated that there is much more carbon dioxide in the world's atmosphere than there is sulphur dioxide, even the worst smog might have a concentration of 600 000 $\mu g/m^3$ of carbon dioxide and 1000 $\mu g/m^3$ of sulphur

Figure 11.13   St Paul's Cathedral, south-west tower cornice (Courtesy: Feilden & Mawson)

The important function of the cornices in protecting the walls below having been analysed during the inspection of the whole fabric, it was decided that these had to be restored to their original profiles, using the Wren drawings. The first priority was the western tower, where new stones were prepared and lifted into position. Some weighed nearly a tonne. The photo shows an experienced fixer mason at work, pointing-up a joint after grouting a large curved stone into position. The lead will be refixed with a projecting drip, in order to throw rain water clear of the stonework to prevent decay

dioxide. The amount of dissolved undissociated carbon dioxide is fairly constant over the whole of Britain at about 0.7 mg/l, but the amount of dissociated carbon dioxide may vary widely from place to place.

Carbon dioxide is capable of dissolving limestones made of calcium carbonate by converting into calcium bicarbonate, $Ca(HCO_3)$, which is water soluble. Acid rain penetrating limestone buildings due to poor pointing can dissolve the stone. Very little is known about the actual mechanisms of stone decay and whether some pollutants act as catalysts to others. This is a field where research, based on standard testing procedures, is much needed.

Sulphur dioxide

Sulphur dioxide occurs as a man-made by-product, although quite significant amounts occur by natural

163

Table 11.2 National Ambient Air Quality Standards (From the *Tenth Annual Report on Environmental Quality,* by courtesy of the US Environmental Protection Agency)

Pollutant	Averaging time	Primary standard levels	Secondary standard levels
Particulate matter	Annual (geometric mean)	75 µg/m³	60 µg/m³
	24 hours	260 µg/m³	150 µg/m³
Sulphur oxides	Annual (arithmetic mean)	80 µg/m³ (0.03 p.p.m.)	—
	24 hours†	365 µg/m³ (0.14 p.p.m.)	—
	3 hours†	—	1300 µg/m³ (0.5 p.p.m.)
Carbon monoxide	8 hours†	10 mg/m³ (9 p.p.m.)	10 mg/m³ (9 p.p.m.)
	1 hour†	40 mg/m³ (35 p.p.m.)	40 mg/m³ (35 p.p.m.)
Nitrogen dioxide	Annual (arithmetic mean)	100 µg/m³ (0.05 p.p.m.)	100 µg/m³ (0.05 p.p.m.)
Ozone	1 hour†	235 µg/m³ (0.12 p.p.m.)	235 µg/m³ (0.12 p.p.m.)
Hydrocarbons (non-methane)*	3 hours (6 to 9 a.m.)	160 µg/m³ (0.24 p.p.m.)	160 µg/m³ (0.24 p.p.m.)

*A non-health related standard used as a guide for ozone control.
†Not to be exceeded more than once per year.

means. It is produced in proportion to the sulphur content of a fuel as it is burnt. The amount of sulphur in oil varies typically from 0.75%*, for light oil to 3.5% for heavy oil, and in coal from 1.5% to 2.3%, although the effective emission from coal burning is lower, as about half the sulphur is retained in the ash. The sulphur content of natural gas is negligible. The density of emission of sulphur dioxide and of other major man-made air pollutants varies widely according to the locality, but it is generally highest in the centres of large cities, with maxima on cold misty days.

The concentration of sulphur dioxide in the air now has no correlation with the domestic consumption of coal, as it is the product mainly of large scale users as well as diesel-engined vehicles. In Britain the emission of sulphur dioxide reached a maximum in 1963 and had declined slightly since then because of the increasing use of natural gas and nuclear energy and the reduction of sulphur content in oil fuels.

*This refers to oil from North African fields. Oil from other producing areas has a higher sulphur content. (Table 2, *Shell and BP Industrial fuels,* 5th edition Jan 1970).

Ozone

Ozone is created in the upper atmosphere by the action of ultraviolet radiation on oxygen and diffuses down to ground level, giving a natural background of 40-80 µg/m³. The activities of man can considerably augment this background amount, which may itself be damaging, to around 500 µg/m³ in industrial zones. The series of chemical reactions which result in man-made ozone start with nitrogen oxides from automobile exhausts activated by sunlight breaking up nitrogen dioxide in a complicated chain of reactions resulting in the formation of ozone and the notorious peroxy acyl nitrate (PAN).

Thomson points out that in an industrial city observation shows the following pattern:

'1. Traffic increases in the morning before the sun is high, causing nitrous oxide (NO) and hydrocarbons to build up in the atmosphere.

2. Sunlight as it gets stronger, sets the cycle going. Ozone remains low so long as it is being used up in attack on NO and hydrocarbons.

3. The final stage occurs after nitrogen dioxide (NO_2) has taken over from NO as the predominant nitrogen oxide. The NO supply is reduced as the gases diffuse over the city. Now the concentration

of NO_2 in turn falls as it takes part in the formation of ozone and PAN. Since ozone has less NO to attack its concentration rises.

'Thus the chief final pollutants are ozone and PAN, which characteristically build up to a maximum shortly after midday. PAN is troublesome to all living things, both animal and plant, but probably of minor importance to antiquities. Ozone, as we have seen, is a potent antiquities poison.'

Ozone, as an intensely active oxidizing agent, causes metals to corrode rapidly. This is the probable cause of the rusting of embedded iron cramps in St Paul's Cathedral, London, which in the past years have begun to corrode and, by the resultant expansion, cracking and spalling the ashlar masonry. Exposed iron ties on St Giles's Cathedral, Edinburgh, have wasted to 40% of their sectional area in the past 50 years. The danger of ozone attack on the metal cramps in the Taj Mahal, India, due to the increase in pollution, may be serious.

Carbon monoxide and nitrogen dioxide

Carbon monoxide from motor vehicles is also a serious pollutant. Southern California had the worst short-term exposures to nitrogen dioxide at levels above 500 $\mu g/m^3$, Los Angeles in particular being 36 times worse than other parts of USA with 72 days above this level.

Chlorides

There have been no definitive calculations of chloride emissions in the UK, but it is estimated that by far the largest source is coal burning (240 kt in 1983), followed by manufacture of chlorine (15 kt) and refuse incinerators (over 5 kt). Chlorides can activate electrochemical actions between two different metals. Chlorides can be extracted from stone by using poultice techniques as they are easily soluble.

Other pollutants

The following hazardous pollutants were listed in 1971 in the USA: asbestos, beryllium, mercury. Since then vinylchloride and polyvinylchloride, benzene, arsenic and coke oven emissions have been added to the list.

Other aggressive acids are produced by industry; they are generally diluted rapidly. It is only in the immediate neighbourhood of their point of propagation that they call for special protective measures,

but they increase the erosive effect of rainwater over a much larger area.

Bacterial decay

It has now been confirmed that bacteria produce sulphur dioxide which augments that in the atmosphere and so increases the overall decay of sensitive stones.

Effects of atmospheric pollutants on building materials

Stone

Building stones have a wide range of durability as pollutants affect the calcium component of stones; limestones and calcareous sandstones suffer most. Natural weathering by rain, wind and frost is accelerated by pollution, in addition the expansion of salts within the pore structure as they crystallize and hydrate causes damage. The pore size distribution, mechanical properties and chemical composition of stones all influence their resistance.

The dissolution and recrystallization of calcium sulphate within the stone is termed 'memory effect' because of the likelihood that some of the sulphate might have been deposited in the past. Due to this effect, even if levels of pollution have dropped, stone decay may continue unabated.

The rate of decay may depend on catalysts. Particulates, i.e. smoke and soot, contain carbon, silicon, sulphur, aluminium, calcium and vanadium from oil-fired plants, and car exhausts contain many trace elements. NO_2 can enhance SO_2 pick up without producing any nitrates which can be detected.

There is really no satisfactory means of long-term protection of stone on the scale of buildings, nor is there any cheap method of preserving stone. Conservators of sculpture and similar decorative features have the choice of techniques based on lime for limestones or impregnation of sandstones with silane based preservatives, which need close control in their application. Lime treatments rely on a shelter coat which will need renewal at regular intervals.

Wood

The problems caused by atmospheric pollution are small compared by those caused by water, humidity and sunlight. Wood is protected by paints, oils, waxes and resin impregnation none of which is greatly affected by pollution.

Bricks, roofing tiles, terracotta

If bricks, roofing tiles and terracotta are resistant to frost they are unlikely to be affected by pollution.

Burnt clay products such as bricks, tiles and well made terracotta are rarely affected by the crystallization of soluble salts, so are generally sulphate resistant, but common fletton bricks, which contain considerable amounts of sulphates and have a bad pore structure, are a notable exception and should not be used on historic buildings. Good sand/lime bricks are also rarely affected, although poor quality ones suffer badly.

Mortars, renderings, cement, concrete

Lime mortars are affected by pollution as well as rain, wind and frost. The lime is gradually eaten away, exposing the aggregate. Lime mortars in foundations may be damaged by polluted ground water. Renderings tend to fail by cracks admitting rain which may cause sulphate attack in the substrate. Portland cement is attacked by pollutants, leading to an increase in volume and consequent disruption of mortars and masonry. Concrete may erode due to the action of weather and pollutants. The alkaline protective quality may deteriorate causing reinforcing steel to rust. Anti-carbonation treatments include limewash, two pack polyurethene epoxy formulations, bitumen, acrylics and chlorinated rubbers.

Glass

Modern glass contains a high level of sodium and silicon, while mediaeval glass has a high level of potassium with lower levels of sodium and silicon so is less durable in polluted atmospheres.

Modern glass is affected by surface leaching which increases its durability. Regular washing is necessary to remove soiling.

It has been suggested that mediaeval glass should be protected from both water and SO_2 by coating but there is concern that such coatings would be penetrated by water vapour.

Externally mounted double glazing, with ventilation of the inner space, is considered the best way to protect important window glass; alternatively the historic glass may be refixed behind new glazing sharing the internal environment (isothermal glazing).

Ferrous metals

The resistance of plain carbon steel in open exposure to the atmosphere is poor. Corrosion is primarily due to oxygen and moisture but is accelerated by SO_2, particulates and chlorides. Additions of copper, nickel and chromium reduce the corrosion susceptibility of steels.

Painting is the commonest form of protection. Painting may fail through several different mechanisms and these may act in combination. The direct effect of pollution on the paint vehicle or pigments can lead to cracking, blistering or thinning of the paint film. Degradation of the substrate can damage or detach the paint film.

Rusting of iron and steel in polluted atmospheres produces corrosive salts. Corrosion products are recycled causing further corrosion and they must be removed from pits and crevices. Abrasive, grit blasting or acid pickling are possible treatments; if the corrosion is serious wire brushing is inadequate, and thorough cleaning to remove the whole of the corrosive product before any restorative treatment is essential. Exposed metal should be given a protective coat immediately after cleaning. Repainting components before they have become heavily corroded is advisable. Zinc rich paints and patent products which combine with rust have their uses.

Non-ferrous metals

Layers of oxide produced on non-ferrous metals in dry conditions usually have a considerable effect in protecting the underlying metal. However, relative humidity, condensation and rain water can produce corrosive conditions. Rates of corrosion depend on the time the metal is wetted or during which the critical relative humidity is exceeded. Particulates can initiate localized corrosion and increase the agressiveness of SO_2. Copper, lead, aluminium, nickel and tin and their alloys are all resistant to corrosion in polluted atmospheres. Zinc and cadmium corrode slowly.

Zinc

In rural areas zinc sheet or galvanized steel may give satisfactory life, as is shown in Australia where galvanized steel tiles have lasted over a hundred years. Zinc coatings form a useful protective coat for steel due to the sacrificial action of zinc which protects small areas of exposed steel such as local damage or cut edges. Galvanizing must be allowed to weather before paint is applied. Zinc rich priming paints can provide a satisfactory technique for restoration.

Copper

Protective treatments are not usually applied to copper or its alloys. If the green 'patina' resulting from weathering is not liked, as in the case of statuary, an acrylic lacquer containing benzotriazole can be applied. 'Bronze disease' caused by organic acids, or other gross outbreaks of corrosion must be treated. Acids from moulds and lichens are destructive but the growth of these is inhibited by atmospheric pollution.

Lead

Lead is protected by a thin layer of lead sulphate which is insoluble. However, after 100 years, about one third of the thickness of a 3–4 mm (0.12–0.16 in) lead roof may have been dissolved (forming lead sulphate and lead carbonate). Lead carbonate is also produced by the attack of acetic acid. This acid (found most commonly in vinegar) occurs in various kinds of timber, especially in oak, where together with tannic acid it produces a vapour that can attack the underside of a lead roof.

Aluminium

Aluminium is highly resistant being protected by a coherent and unreactive oxide film, however, this can be broken down by chlorides or highly polluted atmospheres in industrial areas where pitting is also likely to occur. Pigeon faeces are also destructive.

Anodizing is an electrochemical process by which the natural oxide is thickened and can be dyed and treated with corrosion inhibitors. Contact with some timber preservatives can be damaging to aluminium.

Combating atmospheric pollution

It is hoped that new techniques of 'dry scrubbing' for removal of SO_2 will be developed using pulverized limestone. Wet scrubbing techniques can reach 90% levels of reduction of monthly averages. There is probably an acceleration of the decay of stone and metals, exacerbated by the catalytic action of iron oxides, titanium and vanadium in dust particles. The effect of atmospheric pollution on buildings is cumulative, whereas human beings for whom health standards are established have a remarkable recuperative ability. For cities with fine buildings built of marble, such as Agra, Athens, Rome and Washington D.C., G. Torraca (verbal communication) considers the target annual average for sulphur dioxide should be in the order of 20 $\mu g/m^3$ with a maximum of 50 $\mu g/m^3$. This would also make those cities more healthy.

Design precautions to counter air pollution

Chimneys and fuel

It may not be possible, because of aesthetic considerations, to build the chimney of the heating plant in a historic building high enough to disperse any damaging products of combustion sufficiently to avoid affecting the building. For this reason, choice of fuel to be used can have a direct effect on the life of the building, and natural gas is therefore recommended, with electric storage as second choice.

Choice of materials for repairs

Some building materials are more pollution resistant than others. From this point of view sulphate resistance is one of the properties distinguishing a good limestone from an indifferent one. In Britain, good examples of pollution-resisting limestones are quarried at Portland, Ancaster, Clipsham and Weldon, while the best magnesium limestone has been found near Cadeby in Yorkshire. Although silica, the main constituent of sandstone, is not attacked by carbonic or sulphuric acid, calcareous sandstones, having calcium carbonate as a matrix, are subject to erosion in the same way as limestone and lime mortar. Sandstones such as the excellant Craigleith are not attacked, but unfortunately they collect soot in their pores, which is almost impossible to wash out. Thus highly corrosive hydrofluoric acid, which will dissolve silica, or grit blasting in some form, has to be used if it is necessary to clean such sandstones.

Some preventive measures against air pollution

Atmospheric pollution is so universal that effective preventive measures are bound to be difficult to achieve for whole historic buildings. Obviously, the first step is to see to the reduction of local sources of sulphur dioxide. New industries should not be sited where their emissions threaten a historic building.

167

The second precaution is to ensure that all weatherings, cornices and string courses shed acid-laden rain water clear of the building and do not drip on to valuable features. Regular maintenance and washing of stone in appropriate cases is the third type of precaution. In some cases the application of infrared heating may be useful in preventing condensation in sheltered porches or recesses for by this action the gases in the air remain undissolved and much less aggressive. Indeed, in general terms the prevention of ingress of moisture through joints in masonry by repointing also reduces the damage from pollution.

The internal environment

Gary Thompson, in '*The Museum Environment*' deals with the removal of pollutants by air conditioning plant in museums. Where a building does not have air conditioning it is possible to use sorbents in display cases. James R. Druizik of the Getty Conservation Institute reported: (*Getty Conservation Institute Newsletter*, Vol. IV, No. 3 Fall 1989)

'Tests in both an active mode, in which air was pumped through the sorbent, and in a passive mode, in which the pollutant simply diffused to the reactive surface, were completed. The active mode showed that many sorbents meet the target performance—that is, removing 20 parts per billion of pollutant for one year of continuous use by flowing air at 0.1 litres per minute through 200 grams of sorbent—but that activated carbon and potassium permanganate/alumina are the two most effective, as they removed virtually 100% of all nitrogen dioxide, sulphur dioxide, formaldehyde, and hydrogen sulphide. Activated carbon excelled in ozone removal. In the passive mode where flexibility of design is preferable to active filtration, the efficiency of removal was explored by changing case construction design, varying the amount and surface area of the sorbent, and examining the interactive processes among sorbent, art object, and plexiglas.'

12

Internal environment of historic buildings

Introduction

The main function of architecture is to modify external climatic conditions to suit the occupants of buildings, thus enabling them to better pursue their domestic, social, economic and cultural objectives. As scientific measurement of the external and internal environments of buildings has scarcely begun and as there is also the basic difficulty of measuring the comfort of occupants, the reasons for a rather simplified approach to the study of the internal environment of buildings will be understood; and just as subjective assessments of comfort may be adequate, so it is hoped that a brief discussion of the factors involved will be useful. It should be remembered that numerous microclimates exist within the internal environment, for example damp basements, unheated attics and exposed corners, as well as behind panelling or sculpture.

The internal environment of a building is a complicated interacting system, comprising the movement of air and water vapour, and the transfer of heat. Thus we have to deal with two main factors—relative humidity and temperature—and the ways in which a building modifies the external conditions to create an internal environment.

Moisture exists in the air and in most building materials except metals, glass, paint and plastics. It is added to the environment by a building's occupants and their activities (each occupant can produce over 100 W of heat and 40 ml of moisture per hour, and introduces moisture by activities such as washing). Moisture can also be produced by evaporation from indoor plants, by direct or indirect infiltration of rain water, and by capillarity or rising damp. Moisture is lost by molecular transfer through walls and roofs (if there is no efficient vapour barrier) and by the loss of warm humid air. Provided materials are not saturated, their moisture content tends to adjust when the relative humidity changes, thus providing what is called 'buffer' material. Stone, brick, lightweight concrete, wood (not painted or polished), plaster, cotton and other textiles are good buffer materials and so reduce variations in relative humidity.

Low relative humidity may cause serious damage to the furnishings, fittings and other contents of a building, as well as minor discomfort to the occupants. Hygroscopic materials such as wood and ivory will shrink, while textiles, leather and paper will become brittle. Canvases will tighten and may split. High relative humidity results in expansion of wood, corrosion of metals, growth of moulds and fungi, and prevalence of wood-boring insects. Low relative humidity damages the contents of a building; high relative humidity is destructive alike of the contents and the structure. It is therefore desirable to keep relative humidity within reasonable limits.

Heat in a building is gained from the occupants, from the winter heating and other plant such as refrigerators, from electric lighting and from solar energy. Too large windows are a liability, while thermal mass is an advantage because it reduces the variations of daily temperature change. The albedo factor (see Chapter 7) of external materials is also important. Clearly, the complicated functions of the external membrane of a building are highly important—good insulation, thermal mass and permeability to moisture are beneficial.

The concept of a wall 'breathing' should be considered as a condition that facilitates the transfer of moisture in liquid or gaseous phases more than the passage of air. Tests have indicated that ordinary walls of tufa, brick or sandstone of medium thickness, as used in domestic structures, allow the passage of some 300 g/m² (1 oz/ft²) of water daily, when not protected by a coating that renders them impermeable.

Since the internal environment of a building is such

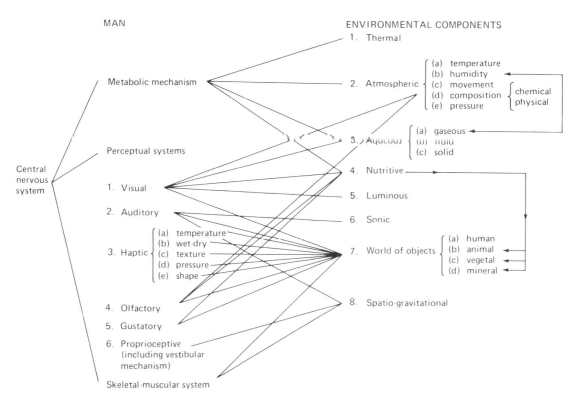

Figure 12.1 Man and his environmental components
(Courtesy: J. Marston Fitch and *Aesthetic Education*)

Human experience takes place across two distinct but complementary levels—metabolic and per-ceptual. The human body's perception of its environment is accomplished by a complex interplay of discrete sensory systems, each responding to the stimuli of its 'own' sub-environment. But this, the highest level of human experience, is totally dependent upon a prior condition—that the perceived environ-ment also provides the required support for the metabolic process

a delicate balance of influences, before undertaking an intervention involving any historic building it is advisable to arrange for readings of internal and external temperatures and humidities throughout an entire year, so as to study the climatic variations and the building's response and performance. Thermo-hygrographs make such readings on weekly charts, but they should be calibrated regularly against measurements taken with an accurate psychrometer.

It is vital that all the effects of an intervention should be beneficial to a building, its contents and its occu-pants. Some new requirements imposed upon a building (such as new forms of heating) may cause damage, and under the altered environmental balance, materials which had been effective for centuries may fail. The building, and the way it has been and will be used or abused, must all be con-sidered together.

In *Figure 12.2* the complicated functions of the external membrane, including windows, of a building are examined. From the environmental point of view, it can be concluded that good insulation, high thermal

mass and permeability to moisture are beneficial characteristics in the external membrane of a build-ing, and that buffer material is helpful in equalizing changes in the internal environment.

Moisture content of air: relative humidity and vapour pressure

Differences of temperature between the inside and outside of a building tend to be equalized by the transfer of heat. Likewise, differences of water vapour pressure tend to be equalized by the transfer of water molecules. Air containing a large amount of water vapour has a higher vapour pressure than drier air, so moisture from the wetter air readily disperses to-wards drier air. This is important for two reasons: first, because it means that a concentration of moist air, such as in a kitchen or bathroom, readily disperses throughout a dwelling, and secondly, because water vapour at higher pressures inside buildings tries to escape by all available routes to what are usually the low vapour pressure conditions outside. Escape may be through ordinary ventilation routes, but vapour can also pass through many building materials. In winter, as warm internal air holds more water vapour than cold external air, the vapour pressure being higher inside a building than outside will cause water to move outwards through permeable walls in vapour form. In summer, the internal and external environments are much more in equilibrium.

Water vapour moves by two methods: first, by bulk transfers of air containing vapour, that is by winds, draughts and convection, and secondly, by the more subtle process wherein the difference of vapour pressure is the driving force through the structure itself. Many modern buildings are constructed with vapour barriers that cause them to act in an entirely different way from a traditional building. For a vapour barrier to be effective it must be impervious to water in both its liquid and gaseous state.

Insulation and condensation

When insulation is added it should ideally be on the warm side. It is a major factor in saving energy. Fortunately, with thick walls most historic buildings are reasonably well insulated. However, roofs are generally areas of major heat loss, although they can be insulated relatively easily. In a cold climate the improved insulation often requires that there be an efficient vapour barrier, which should also be on the warm side.

Warm air at 22 °C (72 °F) may contain 6–8 times as much moisture as the external air at 5 °C (41 °F). This surplus moisture is liable to condense if the air cools. Structural insulation can play a part, but only a part, in reducing the likelihood of condensation. It will be appreciated that no amount of insulation makes a cold room warm, but that a small amount of heat will raise the temperature of a well-insulated room in proportion to the insulation value and thermal capacity of

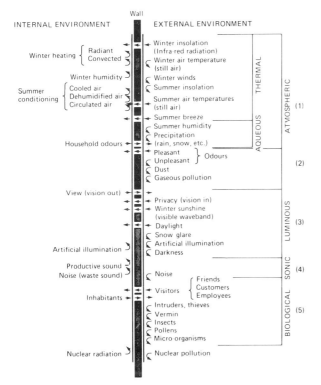

Figure 12.2   Diagrammatic function of a wall
(Courtesy: J. Marston Fitch, with comments by author)

Lightweight construction

(1) Tendency to overheat and trap infra-red rays

Poor insulation value, high heating costs, cold radiation discomfort
Condensation on cold surfaces often in hidden places
Solar overheating compensated for by costly mechanical cooling plant
High overall running costs

(2) Resistant to atmospheric pollution
(3) Lack of privacy
Too much daylight
Too much snow glare

Glare from over-large windows without gradation of light
(4) Difficult to absorb sounds
Difficult to keep out noises
(5) Easily vandalized or broken; difficult to repair, with long delay for deliveries
Vermin, if established, difficult to remove
Generally resistant to microorganisms unless framed in timber, then very vulnerable

Heavy construction

(1) Absorbs heat by day; releases by night—thermal flywheel effect
Good insulation, low heating costs, warm walls

Absorbs and transmits molecular moisture outwards
Balances day and night temperatures and gives pleasant dynamic change
Thermal storage reduces winter heating costs

(2) Some materials vulnerable to pollution
(3) Good privacy
Daylight controlled
Snow glare a pleasant variation of climate
Light gently modulated, giving pleasant internal luminosity by reflection
(4) Easy to absorb sounds
Easy to keep out noises
(5) Easily protected; relatively robust and easy to repair

Vermin easily dealt with

Vulnerable to some microorganisms if badly maintained

171

the structure. Placing the insulating materials on the inner side of the structure will allow the inner surfaces to respond quickly to heating—an obvious advantage in achieving comfort. The overall insulation value affects internal surface temperatures and thus the probability of surface condensation, while the arrangement of the insulation determines the way temperature varies through the structure and therefore whether interstitial condensation is likely to take place within wall material permeable to vapour. As surface condensation depends upon surface temperature, the total amount of insulation is important, unless the surface can be heated by radiant sources.

The occurrence of interstitial condensation within the thickness of the fabric depends upon how easily water vapour can enter and whether it will reach a position where the temperature drops to the dewpoint. With an impermeable vapour barrier at the inside surface to prevent the passage of any vapour, interstitial condensation is prevented, but with an impermeable barrier at the cold exterior surface and the remainder of the construction permeable, condensation within the structure is almost inevitable. This is typical of some non-traditional walling systems, or when historic buildings are painted with an impermeable plastic paint.

Prevention by an internal vapour barrier or arrangements to drain condensed water by a cavity are two methods that may be used. Although completely impermeable vapour barriers at the inside surface are difficult to achieve, a partial vapour check is still useful, if it can be installed easily. Traditionally, birch bark was used for this purpose in Finland.

Condensation and ventilation

A sizable proportion of outbreaks of wet and dry rot are caused by condensation. If a building is left unoccupied, particularly in winter, local condensation of stagnant air when the temperature drops can produce suitable conditions for such fungal growth as moulds on walls and ceilings and dry rot in the structural timbers. Wallpaper often becomes detached due to the dissolution of the glue. Occupants cause air movements by opening doors and windows and, when walking about, by causing floors to deflect, thus moving air through the joints in the floorboards, reducing the danger of stagnant air. Impervious coverings, particularly on the ground floor if there is no damp-proof membrane, increase the risks of dry rot.

Ground floors should never be covered with linoleum unless there is a damp-proof membrane which is also vapour proof. If an old floor without a damp-

proof membrane underneath must be covered, a perimeter band of 200–250 mm (8–10 in) should be left to allow vapour to escape, so avoiding driving moisture into the wall. With suspended wood ground floors it may even be necessary to promote circulation by drilling holes in corners where air may become stagnant. Where a carpet or other floor material needs hardboard underlay in order to provide a flat subfloor, it should be a perforated type if there is the slightest danger of dry rot to the timber subfloor. Air bricks which ventilate suspended ground floors must always be kept open—a point that should be specifically checked on inspections. Air ducts with grills by a fireplace help extract air from the subfloor and also reduce room draughts. Grills under radiators are also worth considering as they assist in subfloor air circulation by drawing air upwards and warming it. Ducting may have to be introduced into subfloors to ensure air movement, assisted by wind pressure differentials, from one side of the building to another.

Excessive internal moisture

Dampness is a common but vague word. It generally means unwanted moisture either in materials or in air which has sufficient vapour content to cause condensation if the surface temperature falls low enough.

Nearly all historic buildings suffer from dampness in their basements because the introduction of damp-proof courses, tanking and vapour barriers is relatively recent. This dampness may be an asset to the contents, as it keeps the relative humidity high, but as it is uncontrollable it may also be a liability. It is always a liability to the fabric because it induces condensation and high moisture contents. If the moisture content of wood is above 20% there is a serious risk of attack by *Merulius lacrimans*, called 'dry rot' because it can carry its own moisture long distances from its source and attack dry wood, or 'champignons' because it smells rather like mushrooms. There are many other forms of decay induced by excessive moisture content in organic materials.

To cure dampness, the source must be found, but it is always wise first to eliminate the possibility of condensation by taking readings on a thermohygrograph which should be properly calibrated and regularly checked. The source may be ground water or wet soil feeding capillarity and assisted by salts dissolved in the ground. In this case, the cure is to cut in a horizontal damp-proof course if possible. The source may also be faulty rainwater disposal, leaking gutter and downpipes or broken drains. It is sometimes caused by rain penetration through a wall. However, a wet wall if dried quickly by wind can become so cool that it causes condensation in the interior.

The interior of each building has a varied micro-climate. If there is lack of ventilation, moisture vapour builds up in recesses and external corners which are liable to be those most exposed to heat loss. Gentle air movement is one of the simplest ways of avoiding condensation and ensuring safe storage for the contents of historic buildings. Excess moisture can be removed from the air of basements and storage areas by using local extractors based on heat pump principles.

Occasionally, when after a long cold spell there is an influx of warm humid air, usually in the spring, the moisture in this air will condense on the walls of an unheated building. Unless heat can be applied, all one can do is close the windows and so reduce the amount of incoming air and cut off the source of moisture.

Windows

Architects generally took great care in placing windows in historic buildings so as to provide natural ventilation in addition to light. An account of the 1860s competition for design of the Law Courts in London shows how carefully ventilation requirements were considered in planning, but windows also admit light with its dangerous ultraviolet components. Our grandmothers knew the danger and kept the blinds down or shutters closed until the room was used and they also used to put dust-covers over the best furniture. Nowadays, an historic building gets more intense use, but we seem to have forgotten the damage that light causes, especially to sensitive water-colours and valuable textiles. Blinds and ultraviolet filters can be fitted to windows to reduce this damage. However, much practical knowledge has now been lost, so a recapitulation of basic factors is desirable. Most historic buildings will continue to rely upon natural ventilation because of the cost and difficulty in installing ducts and plant for air conditioning.

Excessive ventilation, i.e. above 0.3 m/s (1 ft/sec) through windows and doors can be reduced by draught stripping. Such weather stripping may cause an increase of internal moisture content in winter and dehumidification in summer, and if well fitted it is valuable. If not well fitted, it may actually increase rates of ventilation.

Because today we have electrical and mechanical means of solving these problems artificially, we tend to ignore the way a building can help by its own design and construction. The acute condensation problems that now affect contemporary buildings were avoided in traditional architecture by the skill of their designers in using natural ventilation and permeable materials.

Ventilation

Stack effect

Air is moved by temperature as well as pressure differentials. Warm air will tend to rise and escape through high level outlets or vents, and it is replaced by cooler air entering at low level. The greater the temperature difference the greater the rate of the flow. This type of air movement, called stack effect, is greater in winter than summer. Unfortunately, historic buildings used as museums receive far more visitors in summer than in winter, so there is a danger of insufficient ventilation, as happens even in St Paul's Cathedral and Westminster Abbey with over ten thousand visitors on some days. Natural ventilation in buildings depends both on wind pressure and stack effect, singly or in combination. In hot humid climates vernacular designs encouraged natural ventilation for its beneficial cooling effect, through promoting evaporation and thus absorbing heat carried off as latent heat in water vapour. The amount of ventilation achieved in practice is measured by the number of air changes in a given time, which depends on the exposure of the building and such factors as the size of air inlets and outlets and general air-tightness of the building. The main disadvantage of natural ventilation is that it is too variable. In windy weather, undesirably large heat losses may occur due to excessive ventilation.

For good ventilation from the stack effect, outlets should be placed as high as possible on roofs and walls, whereas inlets should be as low as possible. Cracks around doors and windows at low level often provide sufficient infiltration in winter, but it should be remembered that persons near perimeter windows may suffer from draughts while the rest of the room is not adequately ventilated. Outlets on the roof have to be designed so as to draw air out effectively and prevent rain being driven in, even when the wind is blowing strongly. Vertical flues must be considered as outlets, even when no fire is lighted, and they may induce excessive air changes in winter.

Effect of wind on natural ventilation

Air flow rates are normally greatest in rooms on the windward side of a building, from which air will tend to move through the rest of the building. For this reason, when planning alterations, rooms producing odours or moisture should not be on the prevailing windward side—for example lavatories and kitchens.

Control of draughts is partly a matter of detailed design and adequate weather stripping. Attention must be drawn to the danger of cold draughts causing freezing of water in plumbing systems which incidentally is more likely if there is little movement of the water inside the pipes. One of the most vulnerable points is the rising main to the cold water feed tank if this main is run up an external wall and passes close to draughty eaves.

In hot climates the sizing of openings to provide effective air movement is crucial. In Europe it is less important, but nevertheless worthy of design attention, especially in buildings with heat gain from too much glass or 'wild' heat from electric lighting and plant such as refrigerators. Well-fitting vertical sliding sashes have practical advantages for natural ventilation because they have a wide range of control. Not only can they provide appreciable opening areas at low levels to take advantage of summer breezes, but they can also be opened simultaneously at top and bottom to provide stack ventilation in still weather. In winter weather the top part only need be opened, thus avoiding the risk of draughts at low levels. Although they may rattle in high winds they cannot be blown off their hinges like casements, and they do not gather sound from the street below as is the case with centre-hung pivot windows.

Published research on ventilation problems in housing in hot climates is relevant to assessing ventilation performances of an historic building. The objective was to maintain cool interiors in rectangular buildings in a Mediterranean climate, and the findings can be summarized as follows:

(1) With windows on one side only, typical average rates of air movement are of the order of 15–20% of free wind speed, regardless of whether the wind is head on, diagonally on or sideways on. While the size of inlet affects internal velocity, it does so at a regressive rate. The recommended minumum free opening area is one-tenth of the wall area. Above this amount an increase in openable window area has a small, and decreasing, effect on the internal velocities. The rate of heat gain during daytime is directly related to window area, hence the desirability of reducing window area in hot dry climates.

(2) When the inlet and outlet are of different sizes, the internal velocities are governed mainly by the size of the smaller opening. The increase in the larger opening tends to increase the heat gain without producing very much increase in air movement, so it is best to keep inlets and outlets of the same size.

(3) In long blocks with deep, narrow flats extending across the building, with external exposure on opposite sides, it is preferable to orientate the building with its long elevation at an oblique angle to the prevailing wind instead of perpendicular to it (this echoes a recommendation by Vitruvius).

(4) Contrary to common belief, the greatest amount of general air movement is produced when the air flow has to change its direction within a room. The change of direction produces more turbulent mixing than when the flow pattern is straight through, i.e. the whole room benefits from increased air movement rather than only a small part of it.

Effect of height and volume on natural ventilation

With taller buildings, special points will have to be noted, particularly due to the increased exposure at the upper levels. Stack pressure differences can be relatively large because of the height of some internal volumes. Air entering at low levels will move up any central volumes such as domes or stairwells. Vertical service ducts can tend to act as warm air chimneys, so that the sealing off of these at each floor level is desirable to prevent excessive vertical air movement (this is also essential for fire-stopping). Stack effect in tall buildings can produce noticeable pressures on the openings of doors and cause large heat losses when these doors are left open. Strong door-closers should be fitted. Again, in the upper part of tall buildings there is a danger of the wind catching opening lights on windows and swinging them sharply outwards. For this reason conventional side-hung sashes are not to be recommended; sliding sashes or centre-hung sashes are more acceptable as they provide ventilation without these risks.

In temperate climates, most small churches never need to open a window because sufficient air changes percolate through the glazing, roofs and doors to ventilate them adequately, and as they are only occupied for short intervals there is sufficient fresh air in the volume of the fabric to meet all the ventilation need of intermittent human usage. Old buildings are notorious for their lack of air tightness, and accordingly, exposure should be well compensated for in heating calculations. The problem of increasing the number of air changes in historic buildings rarely arises, because of their large volume and low usage, but if the usage increases the demand for fresh air might exceed the supply.

Summarizing, the natural forces inducing ventilation are much greater in tall buildings. Where a building is not in constant use, satisfactory ventilation can generally be achieved by using stack pressure forces, but it should be remembered that these forces are less effective in summer. The location of the terminal outlets for stack systems should be checked particularly to avoid down-draughts due to adverse wind pressure from adjoining parts of the building or adjacent trees or other obstructions to air flow. If the building has an irregular roof silhouette, difficult problems may arise from wind turbulence.

Artificial ventilation

Air conditioning uses mechanical plant to clean and deliver air, as well as controlling the temperature and the humidity. The Capitol, in the USA, was the first building in the world to rely completely on artificial ventilation. Dependence on the process has reached such a state that many modern designers rely upon it entirely and fail to use any of the natural thermal characteristics of a building. This is extravagantly wasteful of energy.

Air conditioning can have side effects which may be totally unexpected if the environmental behaviour of the historic building is not fully understood. If a positive pressure is built up internally the hazards of pollution and dust ingress are reduced, but the danger of interstitial condensation is increased. If a negative pressure is created by recirculation of air or internal air intake, then in a humid climate condensation will occur in parts of the building already cooled below the dewpoint. As air conditioning of individual rooms, to preserve sensitive groups of objects, is recommended on grounds of economy, the side effects must also be assessed.

Air conditioning is useful in museums to control the environment within the precise limits required for certain objects such as paintings on wood. It is also beneficial for historic buildings situated in an unfavourable environment of dust, dirt and sulphur dioxide, as it reduces the damage caused by these agents to furnishings and the contents. The control of humidity prevents wall panelling from shrinking and cracking if central heating is installed. It furthermore assists in dealing with the fluctuating environment created by large numbers of tourists.

However, if the electricity supply is variable and the air conditioning liable to be cut off, a consequent rapid change in the relative humidity of the internal environment can cause severe damage to the contents and wooden elements of the building. Power cuts due to energy crisis are particularly damaging, because they tend to occur when the external temperatures are very low.

Fortunately most historic buildings contain a large amount of buffer material in wood panelling, floors and ceilings and to a lesser extent porous permeable masonry, which give up moisture when relative humidity is too low and absorbs it when too high. The mass of an historic building helps to protect its contents against violent environmental changes by 'damping down' the rate of change. Frequent changes in internal environment are probably more damaging than the wrong relative humidity, so air conditioning if installed must be run continuously.

Lighting

Natural sources

Natural lighting of historic buildings is a subject in its own right. The placing of windows in rooms, and reconciling their internal requirements with the need for order in the external elevation, is part of the stuff of architecture, for the quality of an architect's work depends on how he solves such problems. There are three important aspects of the natural lighting of a building: first, the window/wall ratio in relation to the thermal mass; secondly, the question of heat loss, down-draughts and air infiltration caused by windows; thirdly, the danger of unwanted thermal gain from sunlight.

Besides problems of solar gain in historic buildings with valuable collections, there is generally too much light, as the UV component in particular fades textiles and paintings, embrittles leather and causes textiles to decay. Good housekeeping in the past consisted of drawing blinds and putting dust-covers on furniture and over carpets when the family was absent. Nowadays, historic buildings get far more intensive use than in the past, so reduction of incoming light is a part of the general environmental strategy. Methods of achieving this range from adding blinds or shutters, which should be kept closed whenever possible (i.e. after visitors have departed), to application of UV-resistant varnishes or films to the inside of the existing glass. Experiments have been made with various types of films by C.V. Horie, and he found that a bronze tint was the most acceptable. When fixed to window panes there is generally a thin line of white glass left round the perimeter, but this is not considered objectionable as it throws relatively more light on the architectural mouldings of the window glazing bars and frame. Roof lights were traditionally covered with a layer of whitewash in the spring, which was gradually washed away before winter, providing a simple way of preventing the entry of light and heat. Heat-resistant glass panels can be fixed externally in certain cases; however, the silver reflecting surface or the dead bronze colour of these types of glass are generally unsympathetic to historic buildings.

Artificial lighting

Historically, light levels were very low until incandescent sources, either gas or electric, were developed. Previous to this the candles and lamps that were available emitted a lot of soot. In the past century artificial lighting has developed dramatically and some comments on its use are made in Chapter 19.

Artificial lighting of historic buildings introduces new aesthetic and technical problems. Apart from visual effects, it affects the internal environment by radiation and heat input which, if high, can have undesirable side effects such as timber shrinkage and may even in an extreme case be a cause of the outbreak of fire. To maintain suitable low levels of light and reduce the danger from UV rays, we are nowadays more and more reliant upon artificial light. Research into the environment of the Scrovegni Chapel, Padua, showed that two factors were critical to the health of Giotto's frescoes: the draught entering under the door and the convection currents set up by the heat emitted by the electric lighting. The effect of each could easily be reduced, in the case of the lighting by fitting up-to-date low heat output fluorescent tubes.

In lighting for television a new order of intensity of illumination has to be faced, with consequential gain of heat (about 300 kW for black and white and 800 kW for colour, in the case of St Paul's, London). This tremendous heat input from lighting fittings is dangerous to the internal environment, but luckily is usually only occasional. When the use of television is regular, the heat must be extracted by mechanical ventilation and this can cause the sudden lowering of relative humidity. The heat from electric bulbs, however, must always be dissipated, as otherwise it can become a serious fire risk. Dimmers, which run bulbs at a lower output until their full capacity is required, are useful both in protecting the environment of the building and also in lengthening the life of the electric light source.

Precautions must be taken to control the light falling on most art objects, as damage caused by light cannot be reversed. Paints, pigments and some dyestuffs are the most seriously affected. Textile materials such as wool and silk are degraded by light, becoming brittle and eventually disintegrating when the material is handled. Cotton and linen can deteriorate and discolour. The amount of damage is proportional to the quantity of UV light that the object has received. For equal quantities of light, the following are arranged in order of increasing likelihood of causing damage: tungsten filament, warm fluorescent, daylight and north light, fluorescent, sunlight and blue sky. For valuable objects, the amount of illumination should be measured with a lightmeter, and for objects susceptible to damage, 50–150 lux is generally accepted for display purposes. Glass and plastic filters for fluorescent lights should never be perceptibly yellow. Chemical filters are also available in special fittings, all of which reduce the damage from the UV element in light. Similar filters should be applied to glazing, particularly on north light windows.

Electronic flashes used in photography, being almost instantaneous and producing no heat, need not cause concern, but the strong lights used in cine photography and colour television of say 1000 lux are a more serious problem, together with their associated heat build up, for the radiant heat can cause sudden excessive dryness in wood, ivory, paper and parchment, thus causing cracking and distortion. Rehearsing with dummies and using heat-absorbing filters and air cooling can reduce the impact of the powerful lights required.

The amount of UV light that falls at any point in a building can be compared by using standard blue dyed fabrics as specified in BS 1006:1961. The fading of the fabric is measured against standard shades of grey and thereby classified for comparative purposes.

Heating

Heating is the major environmental factor which can be adjusted or controlled by the occupants. Three states should be considered—no heating, intermittent heating and continuous heating.

M. Koller and W. Beck have reported on an extensive study of unheated church buildings in Austria (preprints of International Institute of Conservation (IIC) Vienna Conference, 1980) and they sum up their study, which excludes very exposed Alpine positions, as follows:

(1) Massively built rooms undergo no rapid alterations of (internal) climate.
(2) Internal temperatures of walls can be taken as between 2 °C and 5 °C (in winter); maximum in summer between 13 °C and 15 °C.
(3) Atmospheric room temperatures in winter have an average minimum of 0 °C and in summer a maximum of around 20 °C.
(4) Relative humidity of non-heated rooms lies above 60–65%, except for a few extremely cold winter days.

A study of this type establishes the environmental baseline against which the value of interventions should be judged.

The choice of heating systems depends on many factors; for instance, if floors have to be renewed then floor panel systems are possible, otherwise the cost may be excessive. On the other hand, an intricate inlay

Figure 12.3 Fireplace in house at Cathedral Close, Norwich, England

A contemporary fireplace with under-floor controlled draught inserted in an early sixteenth century fireplace, which gave evidence of having a smoky chimney. The reduced amount of air required by the new grate and a well-shaped flue cured the smoky chimney

of marble floor of historic value would preclude the possibility in any case. The choice of heating systems must be a three-cornered compromise between the needs of the occupants and avoiding damaging conditions for both the contents and the building itself. For example, in a cold climate to insist on 55–60% RH throughout a long winter may cause frost damage due to freezing of the moisture passing outwards through a wall with no vapour barrier. Convected intermittent heating is not to be recommended, because it does not give real comfort to occupants and induces great stresses in materials due to sudden temperature and humidity variations, and the theoretical savings in cost are usually illusory. Ideally, low but continuous heating should be provided to protect the fabric against frost, but not so much as to lower the RH much below 50% as then wooden furniture may be damaged, and to provide local radiant heating for occupants' comfort.

There is a need to establish ranges of heating that will not cause cycles of crystallization of ground-water salts. A flexible approach relating the inside temperature to the average daily outside temperature is recommended, as the differential can be set at a figure that is unlikely to cause damage to the fabric or contents.

In Austria, temperatures of 10 °C (50 °F) with a maximum of 12 °C (54 °F) are recommended so as to keep RH above 50–60%. If RH drops below 50% some humidification may have to be considered (subject to no interstitial frost damage), or, alternatively, objects which are extremely sensitive to dryness (or moisture) can be put into closed showcases with plentiful buffer material.

Regular maintenance and checks on the operating

controls of the heating system are essential. The best way of monitoring performance is to have recording thermohygrographs, but these must be calibrated every month.

Various types of heating systems have been used:

(a) local radiant heating (open gas or electric heaters with directional effect);
(b) local heating elements (warm water or electric convectors, storage heaters, heating panels attached to walls or fixed seating);
(c) ducted hot air heating, either convected or radiant low temperature floor panel heating.

Defects arising from heating

Defects observed as a result of improper heating of the interior of historic buildings vary according to the nature of the surface finishes. The main ones are listed as follows:

(1) Deposition of dust and dirt together with pattern stains on plaster areas of low insulation and greasy dirt on the inside of windows. Dirt is either brought in by the air or by detritus from the users (i.e. hair and fluff) or by dirt brought in by their feet.
(2) Condensation causing mould growth and decay of painted and stained glass.
(3) Shrinking, warping and cracking of wood and other organic materials.
(4) Blistering, flaking and powdering of paint layers. Changes in chemical composition of some paints and damage by crystallization of salts.
(5) Failure of animal and fish glues, lifting of veneers,

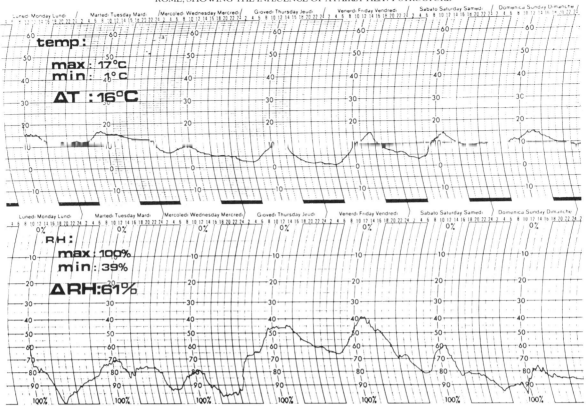

Figure 12.4 External environment, Ospizio di San Michele, Rome, Italy (Courtesy: ICCROM)

Outside temperatures in March vary over 16°C, from 1°C to 17°C, in one week with 14°C change on Friday. External relative humidity varies by 61°C with 50% change on Thursday and 25% change on Friday

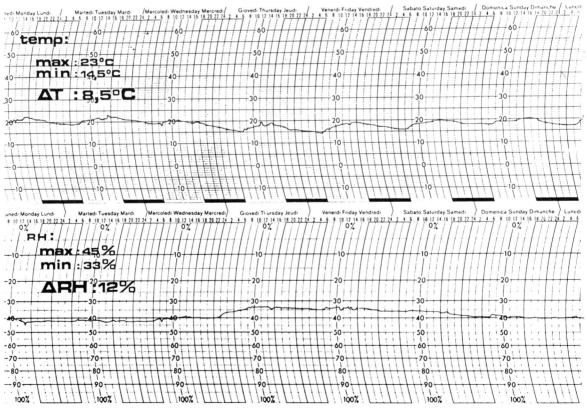

Figure 12.5 Internal environment, Ospizio di San Michele, Rome, Italy (Courtesy: ICCROM)

Inside temperatures vary by 8.5°C, about half the outside temperatures, even though there is no heating, as the heavy walls give up heat. The greatest change occurs on Friday. Relative humidity changes by a maximum of 12%, the maximum change being on Thursday, about 7%, i.e. just over one-quarter of the external change

178

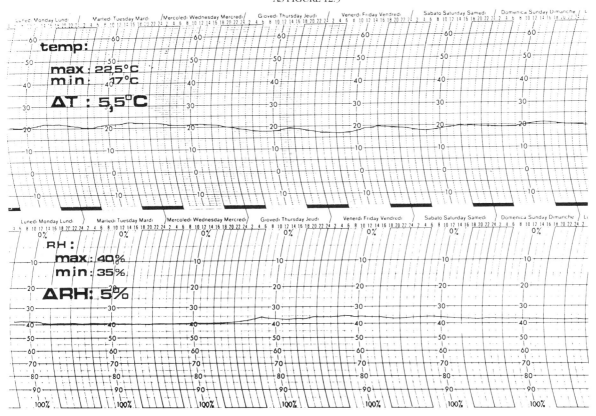

Figure 12.6 Environment inside an unsealed showcase, Ospizio di San Michele, Rome, Italy (Courtesy: ICCROM)

The temperature changes a maximum of 5.5°C in the week, with 3°C on Friday, about one-fifth of the external change. Relative humidity changes by 5% nearly all occurring on Thursday, about one-tenth of the external change

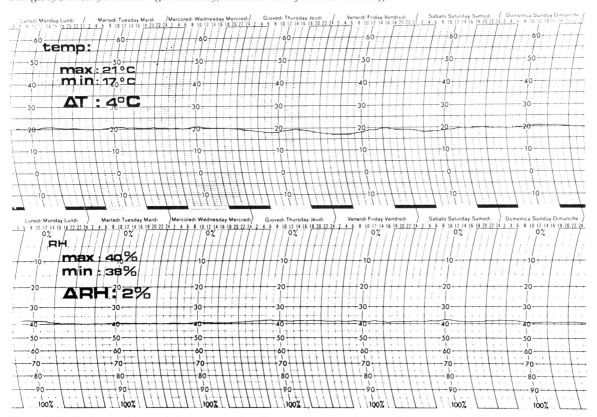

Figure 12.7 Environment in a sealed showcase with buffer material, Ospizio di San Michele, Rome, Italy (Courtesy: ICCROM)

Temperature changes a maximum of 4°C in the week, with gradual fluctuations of 2°C on Thursday and Friday. Relative humidity changes by 2% on Thursday

179

break-down of intarsia work and blooming of polished surfaces.

(6) Breakdown of church organs due to the above reasons and condensation in metal pipes and desiccation of leather valves and bellows.

It is generally the convection component in heat transfer that causes the above defects, although radiant heat from powerful electric light bulbs can also be damaging.

The walls of most historic buildings built of masonry are thick but permeable and generally have good total thermal resistance, although the materials themselves may be poor insulators. Their thermal mass is great, so therefore they do not respond quickly to intermittent heating, but are able to maintain remarkably uniform internal temperatures when heated continuously. In an unheated state there are but few internal air currents; however, when heating is introduced draughts inevitably appear, but this practical problem can be mitigated by skilled design, after investigation using smoke to indicate the paths of air movement.

The tendency to dispense with domestic open fires and the removal or sealing of old-fashioned air bricks has greatly reduced natural ventilation and caused an increase in condensation. Ventilators should be provided for old flues, not only to prevent condensation and hygroscopic salt deposit in the flue itself, which can penetrate through and damage decoration, but also to maintain air changes in the room. Gas heaters with inadequate flues, oil stoves and domestic appliances burning neat fuel produce large amounts of water vapour which may induce condensation. For instance, one litre of paraffin when burnt produces about one litre of water. The explanation is simple: a hydrocarbon, when burnt, forms water and carbon dioxide. Gas-fired boilers produce great quantities of water as a product of combustion and require specially insulated flues to prevent condensation at the top where the gases will have probably cooled below their dewpoint.

In an old damp building or even a recently constructed one, rapid drying out by newly installed central heating can be dangerous to the fabric, especially for the first few weeks. Also, if the building is not kept well ventilated during this period, moisture extracted from the porous fabric will saturate the air within, and in the cool parts of the building, such as unheated roof spaces or attics, heavy condensation may occur. Windows should be opened top and bottom so that the hot moist air may be expelled and temperatures raised only gradually, thus allowing moisture to dissipate slowly and reducing damage by shrinkage of materials and expansion of the structure.

Months, even years, may elapse before equilibrium is achieved in a heavy structure.

Temperature and relative humidity are interdependent in forming the internal climate of a building. This climate affects both occupants and contents; people are rather sensitive to temperature, only achieving comfort when the effective temperature is between 18 °C (64 °F) and 25 °C (77 °F), whereas historical artefacts are more demanding because many require strict humidity control to reduce the rate of deterioration. Effective temperature as an index of comfort has four components: radiant temperature, ambient temperature, air movement and humidity. Air movement is desirable for comfort but too much—a draught—can cause discomfort, and relative humidity if too low can cause discomfort to people and desiccation of leather, wood and other sensitive organic materials.

Preservation of art objects and furnishings in historic buildings

The relative humidity inside a building is the main problem with regard to the preservation of objects. However, it is one of the most difficult to control without mechanical plant. Wood, paintings on wood, horn, ivory, embroidery or weaving in wool or silk ideally require humidities of 55% with a ± variation of 5%. For wood and paintings a constant humidity is important and should not go below 50% or above 60% because of the danger of mould growths at RH over 65–70%, especially if the air is stagnant. With precautions, short periods at a higher RH would normally be safe, but prolonged periods are too risky. There is some evidence that a high RH causes dye-stuffs to fade more readily.

Stone is not affected materially, but with high RH the effect of sulphur dioxide attack would be greater. Paint on stone would be more inclined to become detached or break up in high RH conditions. If paint on stone has weakness then it should be treated as if on wood and kept between 50% and 60% RH.

At relative humidities below 40% organic substances can receive permanent damage; marquetry and veneers are particularly susceptible to over-drying, and paper, parchment, leather and the adhesives used in making furniture can all be affected. Church organs are sensitive to low humidities. At the other extreme, an RH of above 70% will encourage mildew and mould and the formation of corrosion on metals. The absolute limits are therefore 45–65%, but for safety 50% should be aimed at, as measuring instruments and controls are not too accurate.

It is rapid changes in humidity that are most damaging to organic materials, and valuable objects should be kept in a glass case to protect them from temporary changes and, incidentally, from atmospheric pollution. A simple way of reducing the RH is to insert an absorbent such as conditioned silica gel or a quantity of buffer material into the case. Conditioned silica gel can also be used to increase the RH.

Acoustic environment

An historic building may nowadays find itself in an environment of intense noise and vibration for which it was not designed. On a hot day, it may be necessary to close all the windows and forgo natural ventilation because of the external noise—the most common cause of environmental complaints. Intrusive noise and also high levels of background noise may have to be countered and minimized by double glazing, the sealing of all cracks and installation of air conditioning.

The external acoustic environment is measured in decibels using a soundmeter. The internal acoustical characteristics are assessed by the reverberation time of a building, which is a function of its sound absorption and volume. Generally, the reverberation time of large historic buildings is too long for modern usage and there is not enough acoustic absorption, particularly in the lower ranges.

In the acoustical field, problems arise in historic buildings when they are required to perform in a different way from the one for which they were designed and built, a typical example being the Gothic or Romanesque cathedral which was designed for services to be chanted in a language not understood by the laity. So strong is the effect of acoustics on the architectural personality of a building that certain types of music may be said to have been composed for buildings of certain types, e.g. chamber music for small salons and Gregorian chant or plain-song for cathedrals and abbeys.

Nowadays, every word of a sermon must be heard or there are complaints. These complaints can be reduced by the introduction of sound reinforcement. However, in any proposals to improve audibility in an historic building, its acoustic personality should be respected as much as its visual qualities. Illuminating the speaker helps audibility greatly and is a boon to deaf persons who may practise lip reading.

The balance of the internal environment

An attempt has been made to outline factors which affect the internal environment of historic buildings and to show that a delicate balance exists among them. It has been demonstrated that the internal environment is modified by atmospheric, thermal and aqueous influences. Wind causes air movement with consequential pressures and suctions which vary the rate of internal air change, so affecting heat losses and the comfort of the occupants. If changes in methods of usage, heating and artificial lighting are proposed, their effects on the fabric and contents of the building must be carefully assessed. An imprudent alteration of the internal environment may upset a very delicate, long-established equilibrium. It has been shown that this environment is peculiar to each building, depending upon its design, construction, materials, thermal mass buffer effect and insulation and upon its maintenance, condition and usage, as well as its acoustics, lighting, heating and ventilation. In this context the atmospheric, thermal and aqueous components all interact to produce a spatial environmental system which if thrown out of balance may create a new danger for the building and its contents.

Typical examples of interventions which may have an adverse effect are:

(a) Portland cement rendering, external or internal;
(b) Portland cement pointing;
(c) insertion of damp-proof membranes without 'safety valves';
(d) introduction of heating at too high temperatures;
(e) introduction of air conditioning;
(f) application of plastic paints;
(g) sealing up natural ventilation systems, e.g. fireplaces.
(h) preventing air movement by changing tiles or slates to metal or plastic roofing.

Lastly, mention must be made of the effects of building operations which generally introduce large amounts of water into the structure, and internal archaeological excavations which encourage a considerable amount of evaporation of ground water from exposed surfaces. These, however, are exceptional and temporary changes of the internal environment.

Part III

THE WORK OF THE CONSERVATION ARCHITECT

13

Inspections and reports

The methodology of all conservation depends upon making an inspection and report at regular intervals on all items of cultural property, recording the visible defects factually, in order to diagnose the causes of decay and propose an effective cure that involves only the minimum intervention. This meticulous examination requires the ability to appreciate the 'messages' in the cultural property and its values. The extent and nature of the historic building must be defined and its relationship to its setting must be included, as architecture cannot be divorced from its site—it is immovable cultural property which must be seen as a whole. The building must be looked at with a seeing and understanding eye.

Legislation, listing and scheduling cultural property gives the framework and structure of conservation. Inspections and reports give the facts as they relate to each individual building and, if previous reports are available, they are invaluable evidence and helpful in assessing the rate of change and in making decisions. Making an inspection is generally the first encounter the architect will have with an historic building and is an excellent way of getting to know a building well. Inspections are the basis of future action, so it is important that they should be thorough and accurate. The purpose of the initial report is to record and evaluate the significance and condition of the historic building. Most importantly, the report can be used as a basis of the maintenance plan, so it is an essential part of the strategy of preventive maintenance which is the highest form of conservation.

It is important to remember that the report will be read by laymen. Technical words and jargon should be avoided as far as possible, but, if necessary, the words used should be explained in a glossary. Sentences should be short and informative, as precision and clarity are the hallmark of a well-written and well-presented report.

Reports worked up by stages

A full report may be worked up by stages, as follows:

(1) Initial report based upon visual inspection, listing all defects and describing and studying the building.
(2) A maintenance plan. Approximate itemized estimates or immediate urgent and necessary repairs and other desirable works.
(3) Historical research and analysis supported by photographic records.
(4) Recording of the initial state of the building; soil mechanics, humidity studies and opening up suspect parts.
(5) Further studies. Structural analysis.
(6) Final estimates and proposals with specifications and full report for submission for governmental grant covering all the above factors, as they modify each other.

Making initial reports

The conservation architect should have an open mind when making his initial inspection, and be prepared to receive all the evidence of his five senses. Preconceptions are dangerous, as they may blind the inspector to vital evidence. By detailed inspection a trained architect can detect a syndrome of significant evidence before most measuring systems. He must work in four dimensions: length, breadth, height and time, i.e. the history of the site, of any previous buildings and of how the present building came into being and has and will react to the forces of decay.

The report, based upon an initial inspection, may be used for many purposes. Besides being an essential basis for a maintenance plan, a theme developed

Figure 13.1   South choir aisle vault, west bay, York Minster, England
(Courtesy: Feilden & Mawson)

Multiple diagonal cracks indicate settlements of the central tower on the left-hand side. The cracks have been filled and re-pointed several times by masons. The distressed arches have been pushed sideways and strutted with heavy oak props, then later filled with brick. Cracks also show in the vault. The situation is complicated by the eleventh century masonry of an old stair and the 65-year pause between completion of the choir and the tower, which being relatively much heavier settled more

Figure 13.2   Gallery of central tower, York Minster, England
(Courtesy: Shepherd Building Group Ltd)

Repeated filling of this crack did nothing except conceal its ever increasing width. The real cause of the movement lay in the over-stressing of the soil below the foundations some 40m (130ft) down. Such a diagnosis can only be made after inspection of a building as a whole

in Chapter 15 of this book, it is an essential preliminary before embarking upon historical research or any further study of the structure such as structural analysis, including soil mechanics, investigations into moisture, or opening up suspect parts in order to identify all causes of decay. Such studies are only required if the initial inspection shows that they are necessary and they must be kept in proportion to the importance of the problem.

Full reports consolidate all the information collected with regard to the building and identify the causes of decay and propose cures. They should be accompanied by specifications and estimates of cost in the form required for any governmental grants which may be sought. These estimates should include an allowance for recording the conservation work and making a final report.

In making initial reports it is useful to give sketch outline floor plans of the building and, if at all complicated, a roof plan as well. For a full report, measured plans of site, boundaries, rainwater and soil drainage disposal, and mechanical and electrical services, should always be included. The primary aim of the initial report is to record in a factual manner the condition of the historic building. Preliminary opinions, which may be varied later, should be given, but in setting out the report they should be shown explicitly as such, for facts and opinions must not be confused with each other.

Legal aspects

Remembering that further defects can materialize quickly, it should be clearly stated that the defects recorded were those visible at the date of inspection. The limitations of the survey should always be given, i.e. certain roof spaces were inaccessible, floorboards could not be lifted and floor coverings and furniture prevented a full inspection. If a wood ground floor is covered with linoleum or other impervious material, it must be stated that no guarantee can be given that it is not attacked by some form of rot and unless the floor is opened up and examined by a specialist, no estimate can be prepared for repairs. Again, in the inspection, care must be taken to note the location of all insect attacks and whether the flight holes are old or new.

Climate affects the types of insect attack and the incidence of plant growth and moulds. In giving opinions based on experience in one locality, one must remember that in another locality the climate and microclimate of the building may differ and affect performance materially; e.g. exposure can increase chemical actions and fungal attack and proximity to the sea can increase danger from salt aerosols.

Writing the reports

All reports should start with a summary stating the object of the report; final reports should include considerations and alternative courses of action before making a recommendation. The use of upright A4 (normal photocopy size) paper, with drawings folded in, generally makes filing and retrieval easier and should be standard practice.

Reports are working documents and should be as short, concise and specific as possible. Using dictating machines gives a tendency to verbosity, whereas reports written direct on the site in an extended note form are briefer and more accurate. In this way, observation is made more acute, for the act of writing makes one consider the possible complications of the defect that is being noted, and this again suggests further points which can be checked instantly by a more detailed investigation. One can also back-track and easily make insertions in the correct place in a written draft document, whereas this is a very tedious matter with a tape recorder.

The initial report is not a specification and it should be made clear to the client that it is dangerous to attempt to use it as such. Indeed, it is useful to insert the following paragraph in any report:

'This document is a report, not a specification: it lists defects found but does not give detailed instructions for remedying them. Builders should not be expected to quote for or carry out the specialized work required without further guidance; they should be provided with a proper specification, or, if the work is very minor, should be asked to submit their detailed proposals for the architect to check. Even small errors in workmanship or materials can be functionally or aesthetically disastrous.'

Those small works which do not need professional supervision can, in some cases, be indicated in the summary of the report of the survey, and if the builder is available can be gone over while the architect is at the site.

It is undesirable to be too rigid about the form of the report, which must be related to the building and to the purposes for which the report is required. If there is much repetitive detail in a building, a standardized pro forma or schedule can be devised—but a word of warning: complicated pro formas often become an end in themselves, meaningful to the person who devised them, stultifying to those who fill them in and later a curse to those who are trying to decode them. As each building is individual, it is better to use specific words with which to describe it.

Figure 13.3   South transept, east arcade, and tower abutment, York Minster, England

Cracks and distortions are related to the settlement of the tower. The narrow arch was filled in the eighteenth century to improve its stability, but masonry and piers have cracked. When making repairs to the vertical crack (in the flat panel below the roundel), an eleventh century shaft was discovered and left exposed

Figure 13.4 North transept, west arcade, adjacent to north-west pier of central tower, York Minster, England
(Courtesy: Shepherd Building Group Ltd)

The north-west tower pier had settled about 345 mm (13.6 in) and caused severe distortions in the masonry of the three-storey arcading of the transept. Some of the distortions were, however, due to the collapse of the previous tower in AD 1407

Figure 13.5 North transept, west wall, York Minster, England
(Courtesy: Shepherd Building Group Ltd)

The same cracks as in Figure 13.4, from the outside. Their active movement was monitored with a Demec strain gauge. Note attempts to point up with hard cement and a certain amount of superficial straightening up done by masons in previous repairs which concentrated upon appearance rather than structure

189

Making the initial inspection

Equipment for an initial inspection should include a writing-board and note pad, pen or pencil, good electric torch, penknife or awl, measuring tape, plumb bob and bricklayer's level, field glasses with seven times magnification and a large 50 mm (2 in) objective lens, camera with flash attachment (Polaroid if quick results are wanted), a screwdriver for lifting access traps, a short hooked crowbar for lifting manhole covers, a 2 kg (4 lb) hammer for testing masonry and timbers, a magnifying glass, containers for insect samples, a moisture meter, a pocket mirror and overalls or protective clothing; gumboots or even waders are sometimes necessary. Nylon overalls that slip on and off easily are a pleasant refinement; finally, towel and soap for cleaning oneself after a survey are required, as it is unavoidably dirty work.

For buildings with high ceilings or open roofs and for the inspection of roofs and gutters externally, two extending ladders should be provided with men to move them. These ladders are essential to allow the fine adjustment necessary to get close up to inspect and test roof timbers. A builder should be asked to send men who can move one ladder while the architect is using the other. The men should not be kept longer than necessary, but they can be instructed to clean out gutters and blocked drains in their free intervals, so they should be reminded to bring the necessary tools.

Searching for clues

To make an inspection one must be able to understand what one sees, interpreting the meaning of water stains, frass from insects, dust-like spores from fungi, thread-like mycelia and damage to paint films, wallpaper and plaster; one must be able to smell damp from wet earth, mustiness from moulds and fungi and the sour odour of defective drains; one must listen to the note of wood, metal or stone when it is tapped or struck; one must touch and probe and, with due respect for personal safety, jump on floors. All the senses are used in searching for clues.

When inspecting wood members in the structure, one looks for shakes circumferential to the original tree trunk and radial checks and twists and large knots which may cause weaknesses. The open grain at the end of timbers is a danger point, because it can absorb moisture readily and also dry out more rapidly, so detailing here must be studied carefully. Shrinkage of timber can cause defects, longitudinal shrinkage being least and circumferential shrinkage being greater than radial, so causing boards to warp and often causing indirect damage. Rapid wet/dry

sequences fatigue wood, even in small members such as window glazing bars which suffer from daily condensation; abrasion and the wear and tear from heavy foot traffic must be noted; erosion from wind and dust occurs and ultraviolet light causes the breakdown of the lignin making it soluble in rain water. Clear varnishes give no protection against ultraviolet light, however much planing hardens wood surfaces. Wood is always a fire risk and can be set alight by faults in electric wiring, by hot light bulbs and, of course, by lightning.

Rust around nails indicates excessive moisture; nails standing proud may indicate alternate swelling and shrinking. Surface mould may be a prelude to fungal attack, while fruiting bodies of fungus are evidence of advanced decay and real danger to the fabric. Paint areas may fail, particularly if near the vulnerable end grain. Drawn or broken joints must be searched for, as their failure may cause a collapse. In appropriate places timbers may be tested by prodding with a knife, screwdriver or awl. The condition of softwood structural timbers may be tested by lifting up a splinter, which if sound will be a long sliver or if deteriorated a short weak piece.

Procedure on a visual survey will vary according to the problem, but in essence the building must be divided into parts and dealt with methodically. Always work to a standard routine, e.g. vertically, from top to bottom, horizontally clockwise, so that if there are gaps or obscurities of meaning when the report is written out, they can be disentangled. It is usual to start the inspection of a building at the north-west corner, because it is conventional for plans to have the north at the top and because it is customary to read from left to right. If true north is not at the top of the plan it is best to use a notional north so as to simplify descriptions. Jambs (vertical sides) of all openings should be described as 'east' and 'west' or 'north' and 'south', as this description is accurate wherever one stands, whereas left and right can be misleading. The interior of a multi-cell building should be inspected room by room in a similar sequence starting at the ceiling and working clockwise and downwards, inspecting walls, floors and then doors, linings, skirtings and windows in each room.

Inspection of roofs

The inspection will report on the roof structure and how the loads are collected and carried down to the walls. Wind bracing is important to prevent rafters from all tilting in one direction and pushing a gable wall outwards.

In roof timbers, the principal defects in the original timber may be large dead knots leading to partial

Figure 13.6   Choir, north arcade, east end, York Minster, England
(Courtesy: Shepherd Building Group Ltd)

*The foundations supporting the pier and shafts on the left-hand side (west) have settled considerably
more than the east wall, causing distortions and distress in the masonry. The east end has rotated
outwards, causing the vertical elements to lean. The cracks had been mortared over but had reopened*

failure of the member, longitudinal fissures due to shrinkage and radial cracks, only visible at the ends, which together with the fissures may weaken a member and wane due to faulty conversion or decay of sapwood. Fungus and insect attack must be noted and their effect on structure judged. The joints must all be examined carefully as this will give the most helpful information in assessing the roof structure's con-

dition. Tapping with the end of a penknife or hammer will give a great deal of information about the interior condition of structural members, the ends of which must always be carefully inspected for decay by prodding with the penknife blade or drilling, in which case the turnings should be put into an envelope, labelled and kept for future examination.

Eaves and gutters must be checked from ladders.

191

Any deposits therein are evidence of inadequacy, either of design or maintenance. The strength and frequency of fixing brackets should be noted.

The overhang of the eaves is important in shedding rain water clear of the walls, as also are size and slope of the gutters which, if faulty or inadequate, are a source of much trouble. Flashings to abutments and chimneys should be inspected carefully for cracks. Parapet gutters, valley gutters between roofs, are particularly vulnerable, and if snow is common may be a special source of trouble. The slope of all gutters should be checked (using a bricklayer's level) as this affects their performance.

Roof surfaces and hips and ridges should be examined overall to see if any plane is deflecting. The roofing material should be examined for slipping or broken tiles or slates and also previous repairs, which will give an indication of its overall condition. The slope of the roof should be measured to see if it is adequate for the covering. Metal roofs tend to suffer from creep due to fatigue and failure of the nailing at the head of the sheets. Flat roofs are generally easy to inspect, but if there are any faults these are exceptionally difficult to locate. For asphalts, the condition of the surface, if covered with cracks and crazing, indicates age and brittleness. Metal roofs have high thermal expansion which may lead to bulging, and there is also the danger of electrolytic action where two metals join or where nails in the sub-roof have not been punched home. Solder repairs generally fail due to thermal stresses. With flat roofs there is also danger of capillary attraction of water at abutments and joints, particularly in gutter steps. Bitumen felt roofs and other substitutes for lead and copper have such a short life that, in the writer's opinion, they should not be used for historic buildings. If they are found to be split, cracked, wrinkled, puffed up or blistered they must be renewed as soon as possible.

Inspection of chimneys

Chimneys that are cracked vertically have probably suffered from flue fire damage, which would also cause the internal parging to come down. The mortar at the top of chimneys tends to decompose due to condensation from fumes, particularly from gas appliances and slow combustion stoves. Chimneys that lean do so as a result of the decomposition and expansion of mortar upon crystallization of sulphates in the joints on the cold, wet side. Embedded iron cramps may even lift whole chimney stacks due to expansion of rust. Many old stacks are tied back to the ridge with iron ties, but these are useless if rusted through or slack.

Rain can penetrate down old flues, showing at the bends in dark stains of deliquescent salts. The parging of old flues is nearly always defective due to condensation and the salts and tars produced by combustion. Besides gutters, the most vulnerable points for rain penetration in most buildings are the chimneys, which until recently were not built with damp-proof trays, thus allowing water to penetrate down the stack. The joints between roofing materials should always be carefully examined to see that there is sufficient lap or cover to resist climatic exposure and that details do not allow capillary attraction or penetration through porous materials.

Rain penetration will cause rotting of roof timbers at abutments, as these are rarely properly flashed and damp-proofed in historic buildings.

Clogged wall ties in cavity construction can cause condensation spots.

Inspection of rainwater disposal

Ideally, the rainwater disposal system should be inspected in heavy rain as then the defects are self-evident, e.g. gutters overflowing, downpipes blocked and so on. Otherwise, wall staining and rust marks and internal moist patches point to defects.

The fixing of rainwater downpipes should be checked, and so should their condition at the back. Often they are so close to a wall that they cannot be painted. They should be fixed with spacers to make painting easy.

Rainwater drains should be inspected together with the drainage system. Generally it is sufficient if rain water is taken about 3–4 m (10–13 ft) from the foundations. Broken rainwater drains are a threat to foundations and can cause moisture penetration in basements and crypts.

Driving rain will often penetrate doors and windows and cause rot to sills and the base of frames, especially if painting has been neglected.

Inspection for excess moisture

The initial inspection for excess moisture must note the height and where this varies and, if possible, the level of summer and winter evaporation. Most historic buildings do not have horizontal damp-proof courses or underfloor membranes. Any evidence helping to establish the level of the water table and the existence of salts in the soil should be recorded. The amount of rising moisture can be crudely assessed by placing a sizeable glass sheet over a solid floor for a day. Any precautions against rising moisture should be noted, together with the lack of them.

Figure 13.7   Gallery, east window, York Minster, England (Courtesy: Shepherd Building Group Ltd)

The gallery is bowing some 150 mm (6 in) and the window above about 225 mm (9 in). With the very slender structure there was a danger of over-stressing

Good ventilation of wooden sub-floors, avoiding dead pockets of moisture-laden air, is essential. Underfloor ventilation should be at not less than 3.5 m (12 ft) centres and close to the corners of the rooms. Previous repairs and insertions of various types of patent moisture extractors (generally useless) are an indication of whether rising moisture presents problems.

Inspection of windows and doors

Windows and doors are generally inspected at the same time as walls. For windows, the condition of the joinery and ironmongery needs careful inspection. Rot is often found at the bottom of frames and in wooden sills and then may spread into the wall lining or frame. A sagging arch or lintel indicates trouble—either structural settlement or a local defect such as dry rot in concealed timbers.

Defective putties and paintwork are common faults which can lead to more serious trouble. With lead glazing, the mastic may harden and drop out leaving the panes loose and subject to rain penetration. In time, lead windows bulge and creep due to the fatigue of the leadwork which is dependent upon metal tie bars which should be at about 250 mm (10 in) centres. If made of iron, the embedded ends of these bars rust and break the masonry. Bronze bars are to be preferred.

Condensation from windows can also be a serious cause of trouble. This may be the result of insufficient opening lights or the placement of such lights at low level leaving a cushion of moist, warm air in the top of a room. Condensation trays, draining outwards, are desirable. Windows and doors should always be inspected for their fit and draughtproofness and resistance to the climatic conditions to which they are exposed. Doors should also be examined for their fireproof qualities.

Figure 13.8   Choir triforium, York Minster, England
(Courtesy: Shepherd Building Group Ltd)

The creeping movement of the east end, which totalled 610 mm (24 in) over six centuries, was compensated for by the opening of many cracks, of which this in the fifth bay is a large example untouched by previous cosmetic repairs

Inspection of masonry walls

The walls of an historic building need meticulous study on the first inspection. This should be followed by physical tapping, which can give valuable information, for if the note of the tap is dull and there is no rebound in the hammer then the masonry is soft and in poor condition, but if there is a bright ring and the hammer rebounds, the masonry is generally sound for some depth. Listening to hammer taps through the thickness of the wall is also useful. Further techniques are the taking of cores to investigate the method of construction and the condition of the heart of the wall. Water can also be injected into walls in order to test penetration and observe where it leaks out.

All cracks must be recorded and studied. The tendency for movement should be deduced from the tapering and angle of any cracks; many signify nothing more than thermal movement and the slow wearing out of the structure, but a few may be very significant and indicate a likely failure.

In time, dust will tend to settle inside cracks thus indicating 'old' cracks, which will have dark interiors, whereas new ones can be identified by their clean faces which possibly contain loose fragments of masonry. Other clues to the history of structural actions, such as previous repairs to cracks, should be taken into account. Light tapping with a penknife quickly reveals where plaster has come away from a wall.

The preliminary report should merely indicate that a crack exists. Later, suitable measured drawings should be prepared with all cracks marked up, showing their length and width. If the situation is complicated, a perspex model, showing the main features of the building together with cracking recorded on both inside and outside of walls, piers or whatever, is of great help in analysis of the structural actions. Internal cracks can be marked in, say, red ink and external ones in black to show how cracking patterns go through the structural masonry.

It is often convenient to mark the extent of a crack unobtrusively on the building itself with a pencil, giving the date (but this date may be covered up by redecoration). It is important also to record whether cracks are through the mortar joints only or go right through masonry of stone or bricks.

Photographs with a scale included can be made and enlarged to full size in order to record cracks in detail. Photographs of structural elements are invaluable for

Figure 13.9   Al Hadba Minaret, Mosul, Iraq

Like many chimneys this minaret leans, bending its back to the prevailing wind. Wind vibrations have caused loose mortar to drop and cause bulges in the decorative outer casing. There is a shear crack where the flexible tower joins a stiff base

this record; they can be marked up in ink with all pertinent information and the defects numbered for reference. If any of the cracks are considered serious, arrangements should be made for regular recording of their width by means of a 'Demec' gauge or a micrometer reading across three pins. Such measurements should be continued for as long as possible and reviewed each year.

Any necessary structural analysis will follow later; at this stage it is necessary to record the facts. The plane of the wall surface can be tested with a bricklayer's level to see if there is lateral displacement across a crack and the level is also useful for measuring out-of-plumbness. Bulges should be noted most carefully, as they are potentially dangerous.

Even though the condition of the wall can give a great deal of information about the foundations, on an initial inspection it is often wise to have a trial hole dug in order to ascertain the depth of the foundations and the nature of subsoil, and if possible the level of the ground water. Digging such a hole may have implications for an archaeologist, who should be asked to attend and record archaeological information.

If the foundations are on clay and less than 1 m (3.3 ft) deep, soil shrinkage cracks may damage the structure, and adjacent trees and shrubs or wall creeping plants may cause settlement by extracting water from the clay in summer. In cold countries, frost heave is a serious consideration as the water in the soil expands on freezing.

The movement of moisture through the walls must be studied and any impervious surfaces noted. Walls may be composite with rendering, tile or slate hanging externally and linings of plaster on wooden or metal laths internally or even foamed polystyrene, if recent repairs or improvements have been carried out. For an initial inspection, moisture meters give a useful indication of the amount of water in the surface layer, but they are influenced by condensation and can be short-circuited if metal foil has been used in the lining paper.

Penetration of rain water must be carefully noted. Projecting cornices and plinths in the outer face of the wall can cause rain penetration if not properly weathered and flashed. Moisture often penetrates window sills without damp-proof courses; and condensation frequently occurs around windows where the insulating effect of the wall is lower. Cold bridges can be formed by embedded metal cramps and even Portland cement grout.

Inspection of floors and staircases

Floors and staircases may be the elements most likely to collapse and care should be taken if there is any doubt. Scaffold boards can be used to spread the surveyor's weight. Collapse or damage is generally due to fungus and insect attack in the ends of the beams, but beams may have been weakened by walls moving out, thus loosening their end bearing, or by the floor's strutting and wedging working loose.

Many floors in historic buildings deflect much more than in modern structures, due to the use of square-section timbers, yet they are perfectly safe. Floor timbers can be tested in the same way as roof timbers. Damage is often caused by single-minded electricians and plumbers cutting joists at their weakest points to insert cable and pipes.

The floorboards should be carefully inspected. Electricians' traps can be opened and if possible boards alongside each wall lifted to enable the ends of beams to be viewed. A small mirror is useful to look at the sides of beams and also the underside, if the floor is of double construction. The dimensions of structural members and thickness of the floorboards should be recorded. The joints of the floorboards should be noted. Square joints without tongues are draughty and, if wide, allow dirt to accumulate. If the floor has moved down from the skirting baseboards one's suspicions should be aroused.

Staircases in historic buildings are either of wood or in masonry. Sometimes the design of stone staircases fills one with wonder at the daring of the masons

195

Figure 13.10   Mosaics at Jerash, Jordan

Rain penetration causes water erosion which causes soil to leach away forming a depression that collects rain, so accelerating the process. Patching with Portland cement mortar is no answer to the complicated problem of conservation and presentation

whose skill in dispersing floor loadings relied upon anchorage in firm walls. In wooden stairs it is the thickness of treads and condition of the wedges and strength of the undercarriage that counts. If the staircase has an open soffit it is easy to inspect, otherwise one must look carefully for any clues to decay. The joints at newel posts and the stiffness of these members are important as well as the strength and stability of balusters and firmness of handrails.

Tiles and plaster are often used as floor surfaces on suspended floors in historic buildings. Stone/marble tiles and brick are used for solid ground floors where, as has been mentioned, rising moisture through capillary action is probable. The wearing of all floors is a problem in historic buildings, and where this is liable to cause difficulties to future users it should be specifically noted in the report.

Inspection of internal finishes

Most of the defects likely to be found, unless accounted for by structural actions, are due to poor workmanship; shrinkage cracks, plaster detached from lath (quite dangerous in ceilings) and the separation of plaster coats are examples. The cause of all such defects should be analysed.

Mosaics and wall paintings of all types need special consideration, since they are vulnerable to condensation and penetrating water and capillary action. Care must be taken to note canvas linings and wallpapers which may have historic and artistic value. Wallpaper may also have been applied to conceal cracks and other defects.

Ceilings should, if possible, be inspected from above to see if the plaster is still keying. Ornate plaster ceilings are very heavy, so special attention must be paid to the fixing of their armatures. Cornices also present similar problems, particularly if their framing is of wood and liable to decay; cornices were often run in wood which can be deduced when one sees a scarfed joint or mitre.

Previous decoration if its date is known acts as a base line for the assessment of defects and their rate of action. Historic buildings often have many coats of paint and analysis of the colours and types is interesting from the archaeological point of view. Unfortunately, the thickness of the repeated layers may clog decorative detail and spoil the crispness of beautiful plasterwork. Careful scraping will reveal the layers of paint and suggest the colour scheme for restoration. Old gloss paint on joinery becomes brittle and chips easily if knocked, so it is important to recommend in the inspection report whether the existing paintwork must be burned and scraped down to the bare wood, as preparation for complete repainting.

The state of decay of paintwork must be noted with the nature of paint finish. All too often wrong specifications have been used in the past, such as paints made of bitumen or plastic-based paints or varnishes to refresh worn paint, mistakes which pose problems for redecoration. Because they can be renewed easily, only traditional paints should be used. In some cases, the original decoration may exist and its retention may be recommended after special feasibility studies have been made for its conservation.

Inspection of fittings

Wooden fittings and fixtures must be carefully examined and scheduled. Evidence of insect attack must be looked for, which is time consuming. Evidence of an unfavourable internal environment can be found in fittings—shrinkages and blistering of veneers if the relative humidity is too low, and swellings and haze on paint and polish if it is too high, leading to fungal attack. Church organs are particularly sensitive and unless they are of modern construction they are not compatible with relative humidities much lower than 55%.

The fixings of war memorials and tablets should always be checked, as these may be of metal and badly corroded.

Inspection of mechanical and electrical services

Mechanical and electrical services need careful inspection at two levels: first, to see that they do not present a hazard to the fabric of the historic building; secondly, to see if they are functioning adequately. This should be done by a specialist. Remembering that such services generally have a useful life of 15–25 years, they may be obsolescent at the time of inspection; if they are much older than that, they may only have value in the context of industrial archaeology and the history of technology.

Rust spots and blisters inside a galvanized steel storage tank indicate that it should be renewed. Leaks in pipework, faulty taps and valves, faulty connections, particularly of toilet bowls, insufficient supports for pipework of different types and corrosion should all be noted. Dripping taps indicate defective washers and are a hazard in frosty weather.

Protection of pipes and storage tanks against frost must be checked and any lack of precautions against condensation dripping from the cold-water tank noted. The age of the pipework can be assessed from the type, the historic order being: lead (from Roman times), wood (mediaeval), iron, galvanized mild steel tube, copper, stainless steel and polythene. Insuf-ficient supports or a faulty ball valve can cause water hammer. Corrosion and repairs indicate poor condition. The hardness of the water supply may give rise to furring of heating and hot-water pipes and two further special dangers must be mentioned—dezincification (as at Winchester), where zinc leaches out of brass fittings, and impingement attack (as at Cambridge), where copper pipes fail if the bends are too sharp or water velocities too great. Tapping pipework will give some 'hit and miss' information, indicating furring possibly by a dull note.

Heating boilers may be weakened by corrosion and generally only have a life of 20 years. High performance oil fuel boilers need their water tubes renewed even after five years.

The main water supply must be sufficiently deep to avoid frost and salting of roads and protected against traffic. The system must be capable of complete emptying, with isolating valves provided for repair. The water should always be turned off and the system drained down if an historic building is left unoccupied.

The sizing of pipes, condition and performance of the plumbing, hot water and heating systems should be checked by a technical specialist if they are in use. If it is proposed to adapt these installations, experience indicates that it is far better to renew them in their entirety, but material can be salvaged.

Electrical installations are likewise subject to rapid obsolescence, as the material of which the insulation is made decays and becomes brittle. Historically, system followed system, as can be seen from the following:

1880	Cotton-insulated copper wire in wood battens (a fire risk).
1900–1920	Vulcanized india-rubber with cotton braid.
1910–1930	Lead-sheathed cable (vulnerable to rats).
1925–1935	Tough rubber insulation.
1928–1939	Vulcanized india-rubber in conduit with pin grips for earthing (grounding) continuity.
1933–1960	Tough rubber sheathing with earth wire.
1950	Polyvinylchloride compound insulation with two or three wires in conjunction with ring mains wiring.
1950	Mineral-insulated cable.

Insulation to wiring will, if in good condition, be pliable, but even if in bad condition it may give a satisfactory resistance test, so that the architect must wherever possible check the outer condition of the wiring. Workmanship standards can generally be assessed by the proper fixing of wires and the use of junction boxes.

197

Conduit may be rusty and the joints pulled, thereby breaking earth continuity. Drops should always be in conduit embedded in plaster.

The size and position of the electrical intake, the distribution boards, arrangement of circuits and wiring system should be given with readings for their insulation polarity and earthing resistance and continuity. Socket outlets and lights should be checked for polarity. Light pendant cables are particularly liable to decay and short-circuit. The specialist should be asked to report on potential hazards, as poor electrical installations are a major cause of fire in historic buildings.

Inspection of drainage

It is often very difficult to trace drainage runs; electro-magnetic detectors may be found useful for this purpose and also finding other buried services. It is sometimes possible to send sound waves down a pipeline by tapping, using a garden fork as a listening device, and thus find a lost drain.

Almost all old drainage systems are defective and would be damaged by water tests as applied to new work. It is a matter of judgement whether the faults really matter to health or the structure of the historic building. For example, broken drains may leach out soil from under the foundations or cause moisture to penetrate basement walls. Using a smoke test, it may be possible to detect a breakage by the greater volume of smoke percolating through the soil. Other defects will show by smoke emission at joints and between drain and shaft and toilet bowl. To make the test, a smoke machine which pumps smoke into the system is used after all unsealed outlets have been stopped. Another method is the pneumatic test, which uses the same machine but with a pressure gauge and has the advantage that by moving a plug down the drain it can detect where the rate of air leakage is greatest, thus indicating a breakage. The danger points for broken drains are at the point of entry to a building, if settlement has occurred, and under a lightly constructed drive over which heavy loads may have passed.

Visual inspection will show the general condition of drains which should be clean and allow a bucket of water to run freely from manhole to manhole. If there is a delay or only percolation, there is a fault. The condition of manholes should be checked as well as the fit of manhole covers, which may be cracked and rusty and without lifting lugs. They should be bedded in grease and made airtight. Ventilation of the top and bottom of the drain should be checked, together with the condition of the septic tank and sewerage disposal.

Provided that an old drainage system is working without offence, it should be left alone, as otherwise the bacteriological system for disposal of effluent may be upset.

Figure 13.11   Original rain-water disposal system, St Paul's Cathedral, London, England (Courtesy: Feilden & Mawson)

A view along the north branch before cleaning out took place. The drain was found to be blocked, causing storm water to flood over the sensitive foundations of the north-west tower. After cleaning out, the movements of the tower ceased, at least for the time being

Figure 13.12 West porch, St Paul's Cathedral, London, England
(Courtesy: Feilden & Mawson)

A view inside the jack-arch on the middle cornice of the west front porch shows the Lewis bolt which appears to be in good condition: it was not known that the lintel was held up by the Lewis bolt until it was opened up

Figure 13.13 South transept, west wall, St Paul's Cathedral, London, England
(Courtesy: Feilden & Mawson)

Differential settlement in the west wall of the south transept is due to the enormous weight of the dome on the right-hand side

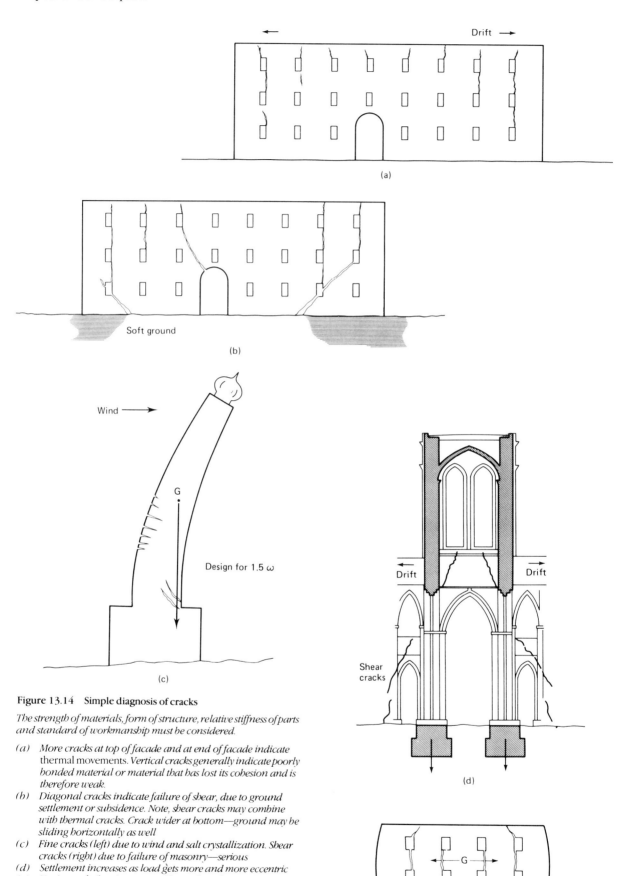

Figure 13.14 Simple diagnosis of cracks

The strength of materials, form of structure, relative stiffness of parts and standard of workmanship must be considered.

(a) More cracks at top of facade and at end of facade indicate thermal movements. Vertical cracks generally indicate poorly bonded material or material that has lost its cohesion and is therefore weak.

(b) Diagonal cracks indicate failure of shear, due to ground settlement or subsidence. Note, shear cracks may combine with thermal cracks. Crack wider at bottom—ground may be sliding horizontally as well

(c) Fine cracks (left) due to wind and salt crystallization. Shear cracks (right) due to failure of masonry—serious

(d) Settlement increases as load gets more and more eccentric

(e) Horizontal vibrations caused by earthquake. Cracks worse in middle. Flexible buildings on hard soils and stiff buildings on soft soils have comparatively more resistance than stiff buildings on hard soils and flexible ones on soft soils

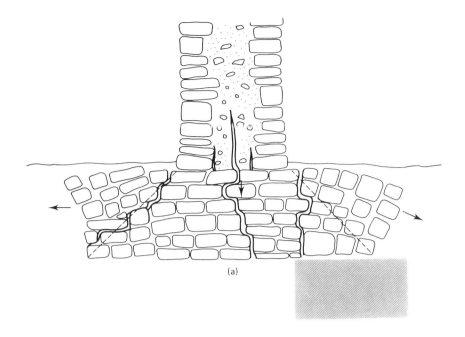

(a)

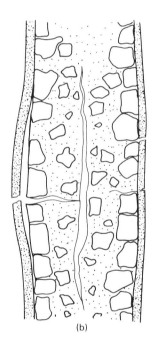

(b)

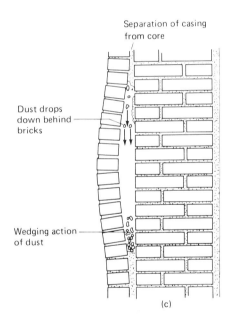

Separation of casing
from core

Dust drops
down behind
bricks

Wedging action
of dust

(c)

Figure 13.15   Failures of walls and piers

*(a)   Column on piers with vertical cracks due to over-stressing of
        poor masonry. Poor foundations spreading under load of
        column*
*(b)   Buckling failure of wall indicated by bulge and horizontal
        crack*
*(c)   Thermal movements and wind vibration give dust the chance
        to drop*

Presenting the initial report

The initial report will have listed all the visible defects such as cracks, poor masonry, rising damp and defective roofs, and these will have been considered and discussed. Then, if further investigation is necessary this will be specified and authority requested. Certain items may need immediate attention, and ideally the architect ought to be authorized to give a builder on-the-spot instructions for such works up to a specified value. This procedure would save a lot of time and prevent damage from spreading; it need not conflict with administrative ideas of accountability, as the architect should be a trusted professional man.

Clear recommendations for action must follow from an initial investigation. The architect must be realistic with regard to the appropriate standard of maintenance and remember that recommending something obviously outside the financial capability of the client is not helpful except in cases of structural danger, when public safety must be the first consideration. Recommendations must be scaled to what is possible in the context of the situation. They should be given in order of priority as follows:

(1) *Immediate work* is what must be done straight away to deal with work necessary for the safety of the fabric or its users.
(2) *Urgent work* is that required to prevent active deterioration, i.e. attack by insect or fungus or penetration by rain water.
(3) *Necessary work* is that required to the 'standard' appropriate for the building and its present or proposed use in the context of the client's resources and includes items of preventive maintenance. This category can be subdivided into 'good housekeeping' 'rolling programme' and 'major works'.
(4) *Desirable work* is what is recommended to enhance the use or appearance of the building or what is necessary for re-evaluation or adaptive use of the building.
(5) *Items to be kept under observation* are, for example, active movements and roofs or installations that are nearing the end of their life and may need renewal within 10 or 15 years.

Considerable skill and knowledge goes into balancing the various factors that lead one to put an item into a certain category. The major consideration is to evaluate the damage that could occur if the repair were not put in hand. Renewal of roof coverings is one of the commonest items of work.

A further consideration is the grouping of the suggested works into logical building sequences; for example, in order to avoid having to work over a

Figure 13.16   Pantheon, Rome, Italy

A detail of a structural crack, probably due to thermal movement. One of only a few deformations visible in this well-maintained monument

recently repaired lead roof, any wall surface above should be repaired first. Work should, if possible, be organized by trades so as to give contractors worthwhile amounts of work that can be carried out at economical prices.

Besides being used as a basis for preparation of a maintenance plan, the initial report may reveal serious defects which require further studies and more detailed reports.

Preliminary estimates

To recapitulate, an initial report should give the client (owner or trustees) a clear picture of the state of the building, the steps necessary to get the building into the condition that is appropriate to its use, and the order in which those steps must be taken. To be realistic, it should also give an approximate estimate of the cost of the proposed work. If estimates are prepared, labour and materials should be calculated separately, for then they are easier to update against inflation as the unit cost of each can be re-worked at current rates. In work of this sort, with so many unknown hazards, giving the possible high and low range of costs provides valuable information for the client. Professional fees and expenses and any taxes (such as VAT in EEC countries) should be included in estimates. Archaeological investigations, art historical studies, research and photography should all be estimated separately.

14

Research, analysis and recording

History of construction

The initial report, dealt with in Chapter 13, should have stated what requires to be investigated in greater depth. The history of the building will have to be unravelled and research may have to be made into site conditions and the building technology of the period or periods of construction. All other relevant historic and archival evidence should be found, digested and recorded, but there is a danger, especially with inexperienced persons, of doing too much research and analysis, treating it as an end in itself and thereby delaying decisions and necessary action.

To understand a building, one must know the story of its phased construction and the whole history of the ground upon which it stands, and have a record of any external environmental changes. Obtaining this information is not always simple. Archaeologically, ground levels tend to rise steadily as the dust and rubbish of generations build up. For instance, Roman historical site levels may average 2–4 m (6–13 ft) in depth and sometimes reach even more than 7 m (23 ft) down. Some prehistoric levels are 14 m (46 ft) or more below the present soil level; in the town of Arbil in north Iraq, which is said to have been inhabited since the time of Abraham, the street level has risen some 16 m (52 ft) above the plain, the city always having been restricted within its walls, with each new building rising upon the ruins of its predecessor. Troy tells a similar story, of seven cities built one above the other on the same site before it was sacked in 1180 B.C. On complex sites, the archaeological levels are often related to documented events such as the capture or burning of a city.

There may be a direct relationship between the historic development of the site and the engineering problems of reconstitution of the fabric; thus it will sometimes be necessary to undertake exploratory archaeological excavations, using properly qualified personnel, in order to get down to original ground levels and uncover buried parts of the structure and possible earlier versions. In this way the sequence of building operations will be more surely established. Such excavation has sometimes revealed hitherto unknown stages in the development of major churches. Examples are numerous, but perhaps Cologne Cathedral, the Basilica of St Denis in Paris and York Minster, England, are noteworthy.

Analytical studies are necessary to ascertain all the features of the edifice, including those which were not executed and those left unfinished. Geometric diagrams indicating modules or proportional systems and indications of design techniques are also of the greatest interest. Old drawings, photographs, models, plans and sketches and general views including those in which the historic building forms a background, bas-reliefs and illuminated manuscripts may give information, even if only of a general nature. Ancient manuscripts relating to the establishment of the building, building accounts, descriptions of modifications, enlargements or demolition should be studied. Information may also be obtained from administrative documents, orders, contracts, sales, receipts, wills, donations and other deeds and grants, as well as censuses and, for churches, accounts of pastoral visitations. Old newspapers and journals, both popular and technical, together with street or trade directories, are excellent sources of information on more recent construction. Records offices, archives and museums should all be enlisted to assist in the search for relevant information.

Information obtainable from the building

The building methods and materials and general style and artistic composition, proportions and aesthetic principles give an approximate dating for many buildings. Stonemasons' and carpenters' marks can also be of assistance, particularly in following the progress

203

of a building, but may be misleading, as it is not certain that the same mason would be allotted the same mark on every building site. The tooling and cutting techniques are a rough indication of the date of masonry. Stamp marks may be found on tiles and bricks. Occasionally, documentation may be concealed within the walls or foundations.

Other information obtainable from the building itself may consist of initials, monograms, signatures, epitaphs, marked dates (particularly in foundation stones), coats of arms, escutcheons, emblems and mural decorations; even casual graffiti accompanied by dates and signatures may give valuable clues. An expert in heraldry can often identify the individual arms of a known armiger and thus provide circumstantial dating evidence.

Recording information

A combination of drawings, both freehand and mechanical, and photographs should provide a clear and exact picture of the building. Although drawings cannot always show ornamental details and may fail to convey shapes, colours, general appearance and perspective, as well as the surroundings and the beauty of the landscape, small sketches are invaluable for attention to a special point. Irregularities of shape and outline, and damaged parts, can be seen more clearly on photographs than by any other means, hence their vital importance for this purpose. Photographs also have many uses for publicity purposes in raising funds for the preservation of cultural property.

Defects can be shown exactly and specifically on annotated photographs. Detailed photographs of cracks, for instance, can provide valuable records if a scale or common coin is included. Another helpful use of annotated photographs is for giving instructions.

Because survey record photographs of elevations require special techniques and lighting, a photographer with experience of this type of work should be employed, using special film which defines linear edges and avoids halation. A 2 or 3 m (6 or 10 ft) scale should be inserted in the plane of the photograph. Photographs are particularly helpful for recording flat subjects. If the camera is set up truly normal to the subject and dead vertical, with two full-sized scales inserted, negatives can be enlarged to a known scale and used as drawings. Such photographs show every stone or brick in the correct position and should be produced when information of this sort is required, as it seems rather wasteful for highly trained personnel to spend time making large-scale drawings to a lesser degree of accuracy. Photographs can be transferred into dyeline negatives for cheap reproduction using special kinds of film.

Survey drawings

It is highly desirable to have an accurate survey drawing of a building before making a final report of recommendations for alterations. This not only assists in identification of features, pricing of necessary works and easy interpretation of the report for someone, possibly a layman, who does not know the building, but can also be a useful working tool in diagnosis of structural defects. Nevertheless, an accurate measured survey of a complicated historic building is usually a difficult and time-consuming job. Idealized drawings often exist together with typical details and these may be sufficient for strategic planning purposes, but to obtain accurate measurements of deformations and to plot all irregularities is a lengthy and costly process, probably involving a specialist firm. However, to embark willingly on any repair or restoration work without accurate plans, sections and elevations is to deny the architect one of his fundamental skills of thinking three-dimensionally and in effect 'seeing through walls'. Without such plans, historical analysis is difficult and co-ordination of mechanical services and design of alterations are almost impossible. Even a humble vernacular cottage should be fully measured and recorded before it is altered. If such plans were sent to a central agency as a matter of routine, they could be made available to those studying aspects of the history of the building, and in time considerable benefit would accrue to the city or nation concerned.

The historic building and its parts should be drawn to scale, with conventional signs to indicate their type, composition and position. The most convenient scales are 1:500 for site plans; 1:100 and 1:50 for general plans, isometric drawings and isometric projections; and 1:10 and 1:5 for details. A 1:2 scale should not be used as it can be confused with 1:1 rather too easily.

As a general rule, one plan should be drawn for each horizontal section being taken 1 m (3.3 ft) above floor level. If inappropriate in relation to the configuration of the historic building, the horizontal section may be varied, but this should be shown with a dotted line on the elevations for the sake of clarity.

A broken line is used to mark any parts not included in the horizontal section that may facilitate an understanding of the building. The intersection points of vaulted surfaces should likewise be marked on the floor plans by a chain dotted line. Higher features can be shown with a dash and two dots. The same method can be used to indicate the soffit profile of barrel or circular vaults.

All the facades should be drawn in orthogonal projection, from a point in infinity in relation to the plan. If desired, faces that are not right-angles can be drawn in true elevation so as to be useful for accurate measurement.

Sections should be taken through the most significant parts of the building so as to reveal the concealed architectural features and show the construction. All plans should, of course, indicate the trace of the predetermined vertical planes through which the ideal sections have been taken. Surveyors should accurately check the curve and thickness of the bearing walls, and all significant structural and decorative details (the latter being drawn large scale or even full size).

Because of a building's particular volumetric characteristics or its special architectural features, the height of the various floors must be given when a detailed graphic analysis is necessary. The survey may be supplemented by key or location plans showing its surroundings, explanatory diagrams or isometric projection drawings.

Field measurements should always be kept and presented with other supporting documentation. The accuracy of a survey should always be proved by taking diagonals or offsets or by using triangulation, both vertical and horizontal, with a theodolite.

Photogrammetry

Photogrammetry offers another method of taking measurements and providing a full recording of the exterior of a building. Although simple in principle, it can be an exceedingly complicated subject in practice. Pairs or series of stereoscopic photographs are used, as in air photography, and from these it is possible to delineate on a plotting machine a plan, section or elevation of the subject and so compute its volume. Photogrammetric technique depends on the accuracy that is desired—the less accuracy required, the simpler the equipment and the quicker the results. Photogrammetry excels in plotting rounded and irregular objects and those that are impossible to measure because of difficulty of access. It has also immense potential for recording and storing all the visual information relevant to a building in such a way that it can be retrieved and specific measurements taken at a later date.

If an historic building has been destroyed, it can be reconstructed from information stored on photograms. The first case of this being done in England was at Castle Howard, by use of two ordinary photographs of the dome before it was destroyed by fire, which were fortuitously available. Needless to say, photographs especially taken for the purpose would have been even more informative.

The main advantages of photogrammetry are, in brief:

(1) Speed in photographic recording (no scaffolding of buildings is needed).
(2) Precision and uniformity in measurements. Gives accuracy of high order.
(3) Can save time and money in survey, especially on curved or irregular objects.
(4) Possibility of measuring fragile or delicate objects. In some cases, X-ray photogrammetry permits measurement of invisible features.
(5) Can survey buildings impossible or dangerous to reach.
(6) Reveals distortions not appreciated by the eye.
(7) Photographs need not be plotted immediately; storage with pertinent data allows for later restitution, if need arises.
(8) Photographs taken at intervals of time (even years apart) can also be used to demonstrate or check the deterioration rate of an object.

Photogrammetric documentation is also very valuable in the case of damage to a building and in special cases can be used for interiors.

Considering the cost of the necessary precision instruments and the need for skilled operators, photogrammetry is most economical if it is used continuously. Groups of users could combine for more cost-effective utilization.

In making any drawing, even in taking measurements, there is an element of interpretation. To be successful, architectural photogrammetric drawings have to be made by people who know about historic buildings so that they interpret them correctly. Photogrammetry can be used to give the co-ordinates of key points with great accuracy and these can be connected together by drawing and filling in detail with rectified photographs.

Photogrammetry reveals in a fascinating way the corrections made by architects and sculptors for acute angles of vision, and even at a simpler level the difference between a roof drawn on elevation and the roof as seen from the ground.

Models

Surveys and photographs give a two-dimensional picture; models and casts can be used to obtain a three-dimensional representation. Whereas it takes much experience to read drawings, particularly elevations, models can be understood by the layman, as the three-dimensional aspects are immediately apparent. An extension of this is the use of perspex models to show three-dimensional relationships and to analyse the effects of structural cracks and their causes. Internal and external cracks can be indicated by different colours and all cracks can be viewed simultaneously.

Models made of wood, wood derivatives, metal, plaster, cardboard or transparent or non-transparent plastic substances can be prepared to illustrate the volumetric and spatial arrangement of urban units or a group of historic buildings, or a general view of ruins and site topography in the case of archaeological excavations. They are useful in visualizing missing parts and even deciding how they might have been constructed, for skilfully illuminated photographs of models can be used to bring the past to life with amazing vividness. Special models can be used for calculating and testing the resistance of existing or projected structures.

Models of historic centres to a 1:500 scale provide invaluable assistance in considering town planning problems and their implications. The 'modelscope', an instrument with a viewing lens at the bottom of a tube and an eyepiece at the top, enables one to see inside models and also take photographs. By its use, the effect of any proposed restoration or alterations for adaptive use may be assessed.

Casts and rubbings

A cast gives an exact reproduction. Into a matrix taken from the original, a fluid substance (plaster, wax or a compound of plaster and synthetic rubber) is poured and removed after it has solidified. This method, excellent as it is, may present serious difficulties when it comes to complicated pieces of sculpture, necessitating a number of carefully made matrices. Another drawback is that making the matrix involves coating the surface with various substances which may harm the colour, the polish, or the surface itself. The surface can be protected by covering it with a thin sheet of aluminium foil or similar material, taking care to avoid folds before making the cast. The foil can easily be removed afterwards. Casts can also be taken to reproduce the shape, position and surface of mosaics, frescoes and epigraphs, or of any section whose surface and structure is to be studied. Papier mâché gives good results; when dampened, it adheres to the surface and carries the imprint when removed after drying.

In some cases, rubbing is convenient; black wax (heel ball) or a small cotton bag containing powdered graphite or a powdered dye is rubbed over thin paper lying on the surface of an area of which a record is required. For small areas such as epigraphs it is often enough to rub a soft pencil gently over a sheet of paper laid on the engraved surface. If a broken memorial slab or piece of sculpture has to be taken down, a rubbing showing all the pieces is indispensable for putting it together again. Stained glass windows are also recorded by rubbings before they are dismantled for conservation and releading.

Recording

When a building has been examined initially 'as a whole' and a preliminary descriptive report prepared, the need for further specific structural and analytical studies may then have to be considered. The preliminary report is essential in order to ensure that all such further studies are properly conceived and will provide highly significant information. It is essential for briefing specialists, especially engineers.

If active movements are suspected, measurements of vertical and horizontal deformations using a theodolite and various types of plumb bobs, and recording of movements in cracks, should be initiated at this stage. Such records should run for at least a year, in order for the effect of seasonal thermal expansion to be taken into account.

One of the benefits of accurate recording and analysis of movements is that one may be able to decide to 'wait and see'. For example, superbly accurate measurements taken over a period of 40 years at St Paul's, London, enable one to predict when future action is likely to be necessary. This subject is dealt with in detail below.

Statical analysis of historic buildings is dealt with more fully in Chapters 2–6. Other major subjects which may require further study are humidity or dampness, vibration and atmospheric pollution. The latter two are dealt with in Chapter 11.

After an initial inspection, the erection of scaffolding for detailed inspection, the making of record photographs and the opening up of suspect areas are some of the first of the additional studies that are recommended. Cleaning, dusting and washing a building all enable an inspection to be more accurate, especially as such work involves only light scaffolding which also gives access for a close study of the fabric. Such a close study enables samples of materials to be taken for laboratory analysis. Woods and metals can then be identified and the geological and palaeographic study of stone made, together with dendrological and carbon-14 studies of timber, if necessary.

Structural analysis method—measurements of cracks and deformations

Poul Beckmann of Ove Arup & Partners writes:

'The two operations (of analysis and recording) must go hand in hand, as without records no meaningful analysis can be made, and without analysis, records have no meaning. For our purposes, structural records include any information describing the structure of the building in the three

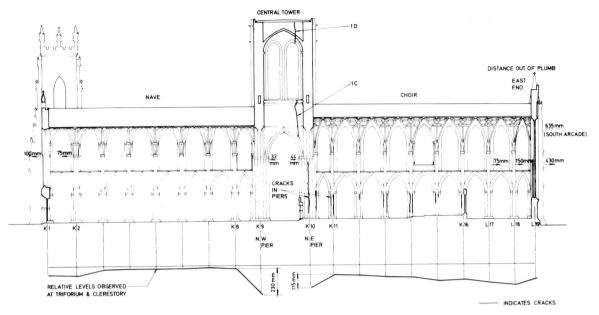

Figure 14.1 York Minster, England, long section
(Courtesy: Ove Arup & Partners)

A simplified drawing to 1/200 scale (now reduced) of a section through nave and choir showing settlements, deformations and some cracks

dimensions of space and the fourth of time. This therefore includes the state of the structure as it exists. Structural analysis will include all methods by which the available data can be processed to produce an assessment of strength, stability and deformations, past, present or future.

'If an ancient building appears in good repair and a visual inspection gives no cause for concern, one would only resort to structural analysis in order to assess the effects of a proposed change of its environment, such as may be caused by major construction or demolition works in the vicinity.

'When an ancient building appears to be in a poor state of preservation, structural analysis can help to assess the following:

(a) the present structural safety;
(b) the effects of any observed defects;
(c) the possible cause of the observed defects;
(d) the remedial works necessary, if any.

'For a structural analysis the first requirement is a complete description of the structure as it stands, warts and all . The most complete record is, of course, the building itself, but in most cases this is too big and too complicated to provide a picture which can be grasped as an entity.

'What is needed before a safe diagnosis can be made is a complete pattern of symptoms. Hence drawings and models are essential. The drawings

should be sections and elevations of small enough scale for the whole of the building to be shown on one sheet. On these should be superimposed all significant defects. Whereas the geographical presentation of cracks is fairly straightforward, deformations are more difficult to depict in a clearly comprehensible manner. Relative levels can be shown under an elevation as a line diagram with exaggerated vertical scale. Out-of-plumbness can be shown with arrows indicating the direction with the magnitude at the level of the arrow superimposed in figures, and where the deformation of a particular line is of special interest, this can be plotted to exaggerated horizontal scale away from the main elevation.

'Cracks are, on the face of it, easily observed, but it is important to ascertain, as far as possible, what the structural gap is. This is often masked by repairs done in the past so that what now appears as a 5 mm crack may in fact signify a structural gap of 25 mm concealed by re-pointing and/or stone replacement. As regards deformations which have taken place between the original date of construction and now, one can obviously only achieve a fairly low degree of precision in the measurements due to the inevitable inaccuracies in the original construction. For this reason, fairly crude methods of measurement suffice; an ordinary levelling instrument will do, but it should have the best possible telescope to assist reading in poor light. As one may have to take levels in triforium galleries and other hard-to-get-at places, the instrument should be as light and compact as possible. When taking and recording levels it should be remembered that any one section of the building which was built as an entity in one period would have been finished as to within ± 10–15 mm on horizontal features such as string courses, but anything built before or after may have been affected by intervening differential settlement.

'For plumbing, simple plumb lines or theodolite-plumbing will be chosen on the basis of which is the easier to do; remembering that plumb lines are not easily fixed to great heights, and they require a calm day to be of any use externally. Where there is more than one storey, and particularly where the work above a floor is of a different vintage from that below, fairly accurate (±25 mm) correlations of pier shapes are necessary to ascertain possible eccentricities. Having thus obtained our description of the structure in three dimensions at one particular point in time, one can perform structural analyses to various degrees of refinement.'

Study of cracks

The age of cracks can only be assessed approximately. If very old, they may be covered by accumulated dust and dirt; if only relatively old, dust may be seen in varying degrees in the length of the crack, and the edges will appear sharper, as they are newer. New cracks have clean interiors and sharp edges. Other clues will be found in careful examination of fixtures and plaster repairs and other incidental features, which, if datable, may indicate whether a crack existed before they were fixed.

In considering cracks it is important to know the sequence of the construction of a building, since initial settlement cracks often remain but are probably of no great significance because they have ceased to move. An example may be seen in St Paul's Cathedral, where quite a large crack exists in the south-west corner but stops below the tower which was built a few years later. Documentation of all previous repairs is of great assistance in the study of cracks.

The movement of cracks can be studied by fixing dabs of plaster to the basic masonry or fixing glass telltales with epoxy resin, but such methods are rather rough and ready. Glass telltales should be only 1–2 mm (0.04–0.08 in) thick, with ends notched to ensure good mechanical bond to the resin, which itself must

grip the masonry: in one recent case a sense of false security was given because the end of the glass telltale was not fixed properly and even though dangerous movements were active in the building, the telltale did not break. Glass telltales are rather slow to react to movements, but can show outward movement as well as the opening of a crack. Pipeclay telltales fixed to knife-edge blocks of precast concrete have been recommended, but the pipeclay is nowadays difficult to obtain, and fixing the knife-edge is difficult. The breaking of a telltale has obvious and perhaps exaggerated significance to the layman, whereas a movement of 0.01 mm may seem to have no such portent but may be of vastly greater significance if the syndrome of the building is fully understood. Furthermore, once a glass telltale has broken, it cannot give much more information. Thus, for proper long-term study of movement in cracks such simple devices cannot be recommended.

An elegant, accurate and not too expensive dial micrometer called the Demec strain gauge is to be recommended. It measures the distance between stainless steel measuring points fixed very easily to the wall masonry with epoxy resin. The dots are set out in a triangle so as to give measurements in two dimensions, but only one plane. The points chosen must of course be firm. They are inconspicuous and, if decorated over, can be cleaned. The gauge is so sensitive that only one man should use it in any scheme of measuring in order to eliminate the personal factor. Measurements are checked against an Invar bar, and after averaging should be corrected for temperature. Micrometers can be used as well, in between plugs set in walls, in much the same way as Demec gauges. The plugs should be protected against damage and corrosion and, if they are substantial, they can measure outward movement in the third dimension. There is also a rather complicated type of plug invented by J. Crockett that enables measurements to be taken in three dimensions with one micrometer.

For most measurements there is an 'envelope of movement', the size of which can only be determined by continued study. If no envelope can be established, the crack is moving actively, but most cracks or points in a building move in accordance with the seasonal expansion and contraction of the fabric. Initially measurements should be taken frequently at, say, monthly intervals; once the envelope is established it is sufficient to take them once or twice a year, but always at the same time of year. In England, for example, spring and autumn are the best times because average temperatures are less variable then. Cracking can be said to be significant if movement is found to proceed beyond the established envelope.

Figure 14.2 Perspex model of York Minster, England
(Courtesy: Feilden & Mawson)

After a visual inspection with a written report, the information was consolidated into drawings and finally a perspex model was made which enabled a three-dimensional simultaneous assessment of the complicated syndrome of cracking and deformation to be carried out, together with an analysis of the structural actions of the building as a whole

Geodetic surveys

A geodetic survey using a theodolite from a fixed base is part of the classic skill of the surveyor and has reached a very high level of accuracy. It can be assisted by use of traditional plumb bobs with some form of damping or optical plummets. Sophisticated equipment such as geodometers and tellurometers has been developed. Such surveys need accurate datum points. Establishing a deep datum may be simple, as at York Minster where rock was found at a depth of some 25 m (82 ft), or extremely difficult as in London where, due to underdrainage of the clay strata, the whole city is sinking at differing rates. A datum should

be permanent and immovable and as close as possible to the building; because it is the relative movements of the parts rather than absolute movements that lead to cracking and deformations, a datum may be simply a pile driven for that purpose or a non-rusting metal rod set inside a protective tube filled with durable oil, sealed and capped with stainless steel.

The objectives of a geodetic survey must be defined, and any assumptions must also be recorded for posterity; provision must be made for continuity of the survey with regular review at suitable intervals. One psychological danger of a long-continued precision survey is that conscientious measuring may become an end in itself and it might be no specific

Figure 14.3 Perspex model of York Minster, England
(Courtesy: Feilden & Mawson)

Using this model enabled information on at least 16 drawings to be absorbed and co-ordinated simultaneously

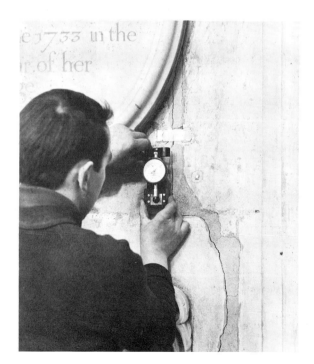

Figure 14.4   Measuring cracks at York Minster, England
(Courtesy: Shepherd Building Group Ltd)

Movement in cracks is measured with a dial micrometer of accuracy (± 3 μm), enabling it to be used as a strain gauge. Because of its sensitivity only one man should be entrusted with making a series of measurements. Five measurements in each of the three directions were taken and then averaged and corrected for temperature

person's job to ask at intervals, 'what does this signify?'. Measurements help those responsible for the building to assess its state of health, and also to avoid doing unnecessary repair work.

To assess these questions it is necessary to make a full study of the building structure and, from analysis of past movements, to formulate projections into the future, so that actual movements can be compared with forecasts. The forecasts enable one to specify the degree of accuracy that is required from the geodetic survey. In the case of St Paul's Cathedral, differential settlements of up to 11 mm (0.4 in) occurred in the 40 years after the great restoration undertaken in 1925–31, while at York Minster, after the work of 1967–72, although there has been an overall settlement of 1 mm (0.04 in) no differential settlement has yet occurred, but 5–10 mm (0.2–0.4 in) is forecast as the maximum that is acceptable. These examples suggest that all measurements should be made to an accuracy of ±1 mm (0.04 in).

When the building has been fully recorded and measured and the structural action has been understood, then the situation should be reviewed, as it may be possible to reduce the measuring programme to a quinquennial check of the most significant points, provided that a full visual inspection of the building is made at the same time. If any further cracks are noted, the initial measurements can be referred to and the change measured.

Soil mechanics

The linking of ground water to the study of foundations through the science of soil mechanics is fully dealt with by Professor E. Schultze in *Techniques of Conservation and Restoration of Monuments*. Certain preliminary investigations should be made before commissioning a costly specialist report by a firm of soil mechanics engineers. It is often easy to have a hole dug down to the depth of the foundation and such an examination is always worth while. It is also possible to probe diagonally to discover the depth of foundation and, if water intervenes, this method may be the only one possible without pumping.

Light hand-augers can probe the ground to a depth of 10 m (33 ft) or so and are useful for extracting samples; similar light equipment can be used to make penetration tests, which give indications of the bearing capacity and thickness of the respective layers of soil.

In commissioning a full-scale soil mechanics survey, it is important to brief the engineers concerned on the problems you have in mind, so that the survey will be as informative as possible. Such surveys are expensive because heavy boring equipment and complicated laboratory tests are involved. Incidentally, the writer has found that an archaeological excavation is one of the best ways of exploring a site.

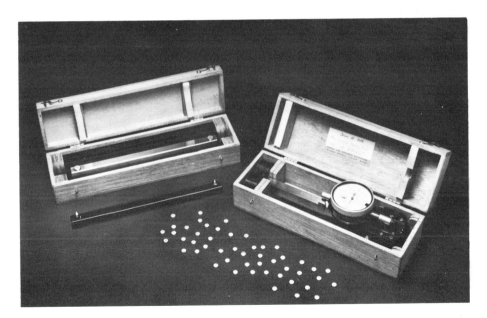

Figure 14.5 Demec mechanical strain gauge
(Courtesy: Ove Arup & Partners)

The standard 200 mm (8 in) gauge is most useful for historic buildings because the stainless steel locating centres can be glued to the surface of the fabric using a locating jig. The extra width of the gauge allows it to span multiple cracks. In practice, it is sometimes difficult to find a firm fixing. Movements in two directions can be plotted

211

Figure 14.6   Principle of the Demec mechanical strain gauge
(Courtesy: Ove Arup & Partners)

The measuring points, a fixed and movable cone, are placed into the locating centres which are glued either side of the crack using a jig to place them sufficiently accurately. Patterns of measurement record that:

(a) *With accurate instruments there is always some background 'noise' due to the person taking the measurement.*

(b) *Periodic oscillation is due to seasonal expansions and contractions. If the fabric expands conversely, cracks will tend to close. Until the annual periodic oscillation has been established (the envelope of movement) it is difficult to assess actual movements.*

(c) *Actual movements show clearly in the long run after the crack has been measured for a year. Note, however, that if judgement were based on the first three months an exaggerated picture would be obtained, and if based on the next six months, a quiescent crack might be diagnosed, whereas the average movement would give a truer picture.*

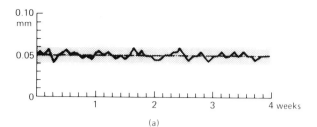

(a)

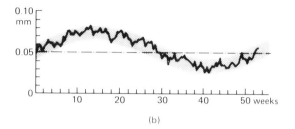

(b)

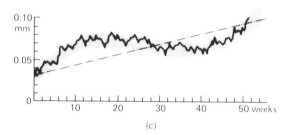

(c)

Figure 14.7   Measuring with a level, York Minster, England
(Courtesy: Shepherd Building Group Ltd)

Light is necessary for accurate reading. For work on historic buildings, levels should have a large objective to gather as much light as possible under difficult conditions. Here, a check on the settlement of the main piers, which moved downwards some 30 mm (1.2 in) in five years, is being carried out

Figure 14.8   Optical plumb bob, York Minster, England
(Courtesy: Shepherd Building Group Ltd)

A plumb bob with illuminated cross-wires is set up in position over a measuring point on the floor to monitor lateral movement in the great east window

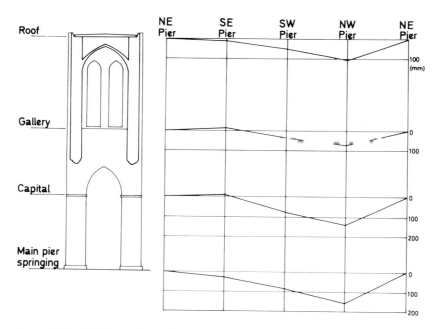

Figure 14.9   York Minster, England, central tower
(Courtesy: Ove Arup & Partners)

A simplified drawing to show the differential levels of the four corners of the central tower measured at different heights. These measurements were used to test assumptions made in the calculations

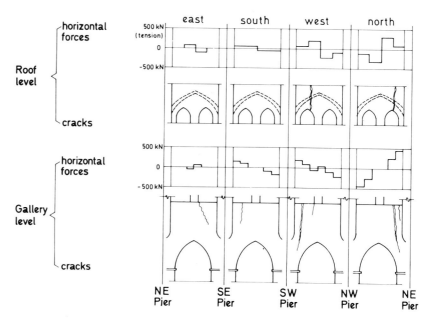

Figure 14.10   York Minster, England, central tower
(Courtesy: Ove Arup & Partners)

An exploded diagram showing observed cracks and the horizontal forces calculated assuming the differential settlement shown above

214

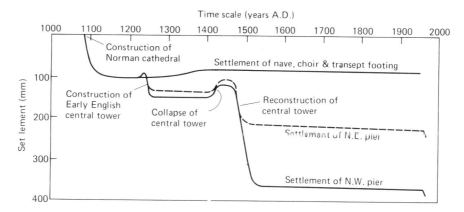

Figure 14.11 Settlements, York Minster, England

A hypothetical reconstruction of settlements since the building of the Norman cathedral in 1080. This diagram is most useful in visualization of the structural history of a building which had reached a crisis due to the foundation, long overloaded, having become sensitive to small environmental changes such as lowering of the water table

Conclusion: making a final report

After the actions recommended in the initial report (Chapter 13) have been carried out and a routine of further inspection established and all historical and environmental information has been absorbed, including measurements and recordings and such further studies as were necessary, the time has arrived for a full report which will cover all factors of decay, and consider how they modify each other.

From the final report a specification of works can be prepared. Again, this is best written on the site in operational form, dealing with the repairs, consolidation and restoration of distinct elements externally, and room by room internally. The writer has to visualize all the work to be carried out and describe it in the order it is to be done. Plumbing and electrical work can be dealt with separately as elements, but attendance must be fully described. Making good and decoration can also be treated separately in a trade specification. The specification and drawings will enable accurate costs to be obtained. Then it is possible to submit the report and scheme for works on the historic building for approval and allocation of such grants as are available.

Estimates of professional fees should show separate figures for both the cost of recording the work as it proceeds and of a final report which, as well as describing the initial condition, should record all work done, with plans and photographs showing the various operations and their results. This final report should also include plans of works, as executed, showing all hidden features. It is of particular importance to give the chemical formulae of any sophisti-cated treatments used, as posterity will not necessarily know the composition of trade name materials. Ideally, samples of these products should be stored in the archives.

After the report has been submitted to the authority commissioning the work, two other copies should be deposited in different places for future reference. The library or archives of the building concerned should have one copy and the other should be placed in a national or local records office.

Non-destructive investigations

Non-destructive technology can be used for:
(a) Evaluation of the total structural performance.
(b) Evaluation of the building envelope.
(c) Analysis of the properties of individual building materials, e.g. moisture content, porosity, permeability, and strength in shear tension, torsion and bending.
(d) Detection of voids, cracks and discontinuities.
(e) Detection of concealed details and elements.
(f) Analysis of the chronology of the fabric for archaeological and historical purposes.
(g) Site exploration, hidden services in the ground.

All techniques and testing procedures have inherent limitations. Interpretation and evaluations of the results needs experience. Field experience is essential in order to choose the most relevant technique.

Some of the more promising techniques are listed below:*

Radiography using X-rays and gamma rays
Infra-red detection, thermography
Ultrasonics
Microwave analysis
Radio detection
Radar detection
Metal detectors
Magnetometry

Fibre optic surveying, endoscope, borescope, flexible fibrescope
Monitoring structural movement, tell tales, gauges
Linear Variable Differential Traducers (LVDT)
Moisture meters
Rectified photography
Photogrammetry

Non-destructive techniques are tools which should be used to answer specific questions. (There are some people who do tests for tests sake!) It should be remembered however, that there is no substitute for observation and the understanding which comes from inspecting many historic buildings.

---

*See Fidler J. *Non Destructive Surveying Techniques for the Analysis of Historic Buildings*. Association for Studies in Conservation of Historic Building, Transactions Vol. 5 1980 pp. 3 –11.

15

Preventive maintenance of historic buildings

The reasons for maintenance

Maintenance is the process by which a building is kept viable for the benefit of its users. With historic buildings, properly executed maintenance is in the public interest. The desirable standard of maintenance depends upon the intensity of the climatic and other causes of decay, as well as upon the needs of the users. Maintenance of historic buildings must have the support of owners and occupants. This is the simplest way of ensuring its conservation, as under constant supervision defects are more likely to be remedied as quickly as they occur.

One of the basic propositions of this book is that a policy of preventive maintenance and preservation work is less expensive in every way than hopeful neglect followed by extreme measures. Human nature being what it is, the latter procedure, although so wasteful, is all too common. It must be remembered that the more sophisticated the building's design, the more essential it is to organize maintenance and the more difficult it is to carry out alterations without the danger of collapse.

A weakness of the architect's professional practice is that he has little experience of the after-care of the very building he conceives. This can be made good by follow-up inspections about seven years after the building has been completed; but unless he has a lawsuit for negligence, usually the pressures of everyday affairs do not allow him to visit and inspect his own creation. Because of this, there is little feedback to designers who, in their ignorance, often repeat the same mistakes.

We can learn so much from mistakes if they are analysed and understood. The pity is that they tend to get covered up, for obvious reasons. In England, a maintenance appraisal should be included in the Royal Institute of British Architects (RIBA) Plan of Work. If this were done, and architects visited their buildings after the glossy photographs had been published, we might get a better building technology.

Historic buildings are a laboratory experience. They can teach architects how buildings are used and abused, how they react to their environment and where design might have been improved, for time is the shrewdest of fault-finders. This digression is meant to emphasize the importance of learning the lessons implicit in the after-care or maintenance of buildings and its importance to designers, especially those who think themselves original and *avant-garde*, but do not understand the wisdom of the ancients.

Skills required for maintenance

Maintenance and preservation work is very skilled and needs responsible and competent craftsmen (who should be rated as technicians). These valuable men are dying off and those that remain are discouraged by the 'stop–go' policy from which the building industry has suffered. Steady, planned, preventive maintenance would keep these specialists continuously employed. Stop–go in the flow of work has seriously embarrassed small firms specializing in high-class work on historic buildings and has contributed greatly to their overheads. This unnecessary increase makes building owners apprehensive about the cost of repairing an historic building. A possible answer to this problem would appear to be in the establishment of building-craft trusts by local authorities on a regional basis; the craftsmen employed by these trusts would treat the materials of historic buildings with a full understanding of the conservation problems involved and of the historic technology of each particular craft. Of course, many interests would oppose such a proposal, but we must put the interest of the building first.

217

Figure 15.1 Ospizio di San Michele, Rome, Italy

As a new use for this building had not been decided, it was neglected for a few years. Blocked rainwater gutters and downpipes initiated decay which led to some parts of the building collapsing

Building maintenance is a subject that tends to fall between several stools and thus to be neglected. It is of importance, for in Britain it absorbs one-third of the building industry output, which fact is scarcely appreciated. Generally, the architect will only be concerned with major repairs and the aesthetics of preservation, whereas the maintenance staff come into action only when something breaks down.

The cleaners who look after a building and come into direct contact with every part of it do not know how to recognize symptoms of incipient problems or to whom they should report. Indeed, large intermediate areas are neglected because no one has been allocated specific responsibility for them. Most building maintenance, as practised, is concerned with tactics, with solving a particular problem, often *in vacuo*, without considering its relationship to the building as a whole. What is required is a co-ordinated strategy involving the owner and users of the build-ing, the maintenance staff and the daily cleaners, all of whom can, by constant vigilance, provide an early-warning system.

A maintenance strategy

If maintenance were well carried out there would be far less need for repairs or renewals. In William Morris's Manifesto of 1877, establishing the Society for the Protection of Ancient Buildings, he enjoined: 'Stave off decay by daily care'. This policy can only be made to work on a basis of regular inspections.

Historic buildings differ from new ones in that they are expected to last for ever—a definition of 'for ever' being 'as long as it is wanted'. An historic building is one that, for various reasons, society has decided shall be conserved for as long as possible.

Electrical and mechanical services, on the other hand, generally have a safe life of about 20 years. Thus

218

the skilful installation of up-to-date services in historic buildings deserves careful study, as a usable structure may be said to be only as up-to-date as its services. Ancient monuments such as ruined castles and abbeys do not have such problems.

A second difference is that the whole building can be considered as an 'environmental spatial system'. We have the advantage that the internal environment can be measured, so any changes can be carefully considered. Nevertheless, improvements which alter the environmental balance may in themselves induce new causes of decay; for instance, traditional building construction 'breathes', i.e. allows the easy passage of moisture vapour, and this should not be prevented by the use of new and impervious materials such as Portland cement. At the same time, old buildings are much more vulnerable to damage from penetrating rain and rising damp and must be protected. The introduction of any vapour checks must thus be considered very carefully in the full context of the building's environmental system. Continuous heating also alters the environmental balance substantially and should be introduced only gradually.

Thirdly, old and decrepit buildings need constant supervision and maintenance, applying the principle that 'a stitch in time saves nine', i.e. *preventive maintenance* should be part of the planned strategic programme. Preventive maintenance includes such acts as reducing traffic vibration and air pollution through the application of town planning controls. As it protects the historic building without any intervention, it is the highest form of conservation activity.

Figure 15.2   Pears Almshouses, Peterborough, England
(Courtesy: Feilden & Mawson)

The slate roof has missing, broken and slipped slates and gutters blocked by debris and grasses, but the roof only needs small repairs, for it is basically sound if work is done in time

Figure 15.3   Pears Almshouses, Peterborough, England
(Courtesy: Feilden & Mawson)

Rainwater penetration through the roof has caused the fall of plaster, and condensation has caused the paint to peel off. The defects are mainly superficial but may lead officials to condemn such buildings

219

Figure 15.4   Living room, Pears Almshouses, Peterborough, England
(Courtesy: Feilden & Mawson)

Local water penetration from the faulty roof has caused reed lathing to rot and the plaster to fall, besides staining the walls. Reed lath was frequently used in East Anglian plasterwork until end of nineteenth century

Figure 15.5   Ground floor, Pears Almshouses, Peterborough, England
(Courtesy: Feilden & Mawson)

Extensive water penetration from faulty gutters has ruined plaster and decoration and caused dry rot

Responsibility for maintenance

The problems of organizing maintenance depends upon an intimate knowledge of the building, its contents and its functions. For a ruin, the tasks are to protect it against frost damage by weathering and re-pointing, to remove plants and control algae and moss, to present it meaningfully to visitors, and to prevent vandalism by providing uniformed supervision. For an abandoned church, the task is to keep it wind and weathertight, to protect it against vandalism and to use it for special occasions. For a house, the task is to keep it wind and watertight, heated and repainted every five years. The owner must see to the repair of defects, and cleaning out of gutters and air vents twice a year, and keep a constant check on electrical defects such as overheated socket outlets.

Although the cost of maintaining and conserving an historic building may seem a burden, it is the duty of owners and trustees to see that the building is handed on to the next generation in good condition. In fact, when compared with the replacement cost of the building, the cost of maintenance will not seem unreasonable, and of course the older an historic

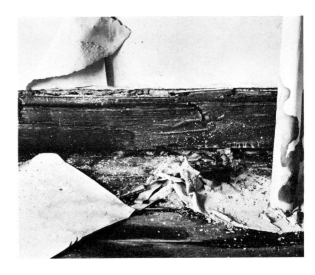

Figure 15.6   Pears Almshouses, Peterborough, England
(Courtesy: Feilden & Mawson)

Rainwater penetration has caused this dry rot in the skirting, which may spread rapidly in an unoccupied building and even reach neighbouring buildings

220

building is, the more valuable it becomes as an artefact whose structural and aesthetic integrity must be preserved. In fact, the cost is low when compared with the 2% of capital cost which modern construction requires.

Maintenance policy

The objective of maintenance policy is to preserve a building so as to secure its uninterrupted use at the users' desired level of activity. This level must be carefully considered, for to achieve it will necessitate a wide range of maintenance actions—from simply preventing damage by wind and weather to providing for inténse use with sophisticated levels of comfort and decoration together with fire and security precautions. The desired standard of maintenance should be agreed upon with those responsible and laid down as a policy appropriate to the building. It must also be economically viable. The problems of organizing maintenance are multifarious, but whether the structure is a museum or an historic house open to the public, a ruined castle, a country parish church or a cathedral, the principles are the same. Regular inspection by staff at specific levels according to their competence should be laid down, culminating in a fully professional inspection at not less than five-year intervals.

The following points are made in a Department of the Environment bulletin on building maintenance which states that the main objective of building maintenance is to keep, restore or improve every facility in every part of a building, its services and surroundings, to an *acceptable standard* and to sustain the utility and value of the facility. The main points are summarized as follows:

(1) The amount of available finance is a substantial influence in determining the acceptable standard.
(2) This standard should be explained to, and agreed with, the owner or trustees of the historic building, as it determines the amount of work necessary. Maintenance expenditure can often too easily be postponed without immediate loss or harm, but such a course will lead to unnecessary deterioration and depreciation. Expenditure on maintenance beyond those things dictated by relevant technical and economic considerations may be wasteful, although high standards can have a general beneficial influence on the attitudes of the users.
(3) Over its life and depending upon its use, the acceptable standard for a building can alter, and this will affect the amount of maintenance work that is required.

(4) Efficiency in the execution of maintenance work depends upon correct diagnosis, followed by effective remedies performed with good workmanship and, it must be added, controlled by good management.
(5) Maintenance is divided into planned and unpredictable work, the former being divided into preventive and corrective maintenance, while the latter has a sub-category of *emergency maintenance*. The less emergency maintenance, the better the maintenance plan.
(6) It should be an important objective of property owners to develop an effective maintenance management accounting system and acquire adequate records and data for forecasting preventive maintenance tasks.
(7) The great majority of buildings provide shelter for people whose wants and needs must be understood and taken into consideration. In fact, the maintenance of buildings involves a social system in which maintenance management, supervisors and operatives, building owners and the occupants all play active parts.
(8) It must be accepted that more rather than less maintenance work is necessary if the value and amenity of cultural property is to be kept at present levels. The author has only seen one building in his lifetime that had been over-maintained, and thousands which had inadequate maintenance.

Each historic building, however small, needs a local custodian who is charged to look around it inside and out, in all weathers, and to note any defects. He must inspect after any severe wind or rain and record his observations in a log book.

If the custodian has the authority to instruct conservation craftsmen to carry out immediate first-aid repairs, needless delays can be eliminated and costs reduced. Problems can arise, however, because it is usually necessary nowadays for skilled guidance to be given to workmen for even very simple repairs, and as the custodian would be unlikely to be technically qualified he will often be unable to offer such guidance. Frequent examples of misguided unsupervised repairs include re-pointing of brick-work or stone with Portland cement mortar, the use of 'patent' gypsum plaster and common sulphate-bearing bricks in damp places. (For an historic building, a good rule is to ban the use of Portland cement and 'fletton' bricks unless specified by a knowledgeable professional.)

The custodian is backed up by the cleaning staff, who can be essential primary trouble-spotters of the internal maintenance operation, for, as part of their routine, they should see every single part of the build-

Figure 15.7 St William's College, York, England

The hard cement pointing stands proud, while the decay of the softer permeable stone has been accelerated. An example of wrong maintenance

Figure 15.8 Parish church, Bedfordshire, England

The poor pointing breaks up because it is too hard. The cement mortar has been spread widely across the joints but not inserted deeply enough—it has accelerated the decay of the stone

ing at regular intervals. Staff must be of a suitable grade for the building they care for, and they should be given simple training in reporting defects. Reliance upon cleaners for front-line intelligence is unrealistic if, as in so many buildings, the turnover of cleaners is frequent or they are simply not interested. Contract cleaning presents other problems. The potential of, and the need for, good grade permanent cleaners for valuable buildings cannot be over-emphasized.

It is most desirable to provide adequate access to the internal structure of roofs by means of walkways, as well as good access externally over roofs and along gutters. Such provision is a good investment because it makes routine checks easy and effective. For the same reason, it is good policy to provide electric lighting within roof spaces; socket outlets for hand-lamps should be provided for viewing difficult places such as the underside of parapet gutters. It is a wise policy to maintain all concealed spaces clean and decorated and in good order, because this encourages a high standard of preventive maintenance.

Budgets

The budget should be divided into two parts: running costs and maintenance costs. Running costs include day-to-day expenses of providing light, heat and water, cleaning the building, security and fire measures, etc., and providing staff for performing these activities. Maintenance costs, on the other hand, include payment for items needed to prevent avoidable damage to, or decay of, buildings and their plant. Doors, windows and gutters and roofs are primarily vulnerable. Also included as maintenance is the cost of replacing any of these items.

Cyclical maintenance

While the simple categories outlined earlier in Chapter 13 are a basis for scientific preventive maintenance, J. Henry Chambers approaches the problem differently, in his book *Cyclical Maintenance for Historic Buildings*, starting with daily routines and working upwards. His book deals with maintenance surveys, the role of conservation craftsmen and conservators, supervision, work records, staffing, and all matters relating to organizing a maintenance programme for buildings in a reasonable state of repair. He makes suggestions as to what should be done by outside contract service and also touches on training, work space planning and maintenance tools, and covers cleaning. These maintenance techniques are based upon the preparation of a maintenance manual which is a sophisticated document giving assessments of work frequencies and calculation of work time units and measurement of areas. Ten different frequencies that are specified are given below:

'A' *policing as required:* Policing is a high-frequency task which is performed during and immediately after the use of the building by large numbers of people, removing conspicuous soil and trash so that it will not have a chance to become permanently embedded in the finish surfaces. The amount of policing will depend upon weather conditions and the building use. Each historic property will have different priorities and different problems.

'B' *routine housekeeping and maintenance:* This is a dry-type maintenance, covering all reachable surfaces so that accumulations do not become permanently embedded due to their oily content. The frequency could be daily, twice a week, or weekly. It may vary for different locations in the building and with the season because of peak visitor periods, or it may vary because of seasonal weather conditions or seasonal air quality.

'C' *periodic maintenance:* This may be a dry, damp or in some instances a wet treatment which cleanses surfaces, removing those accumulations not generally removed by the more frequent methods. If wet, it removes portions of the finish itself which have become chemically changed due to exposure, thereby renewing to a certain extent the surface. The frequency ranges from weekly to monthly.

'D' *periodic maintenance:* The frequency is monthly, bimonthly or quarterly.

'E' *periodic maintenance:* The frequency is quarterly or semi-annually.

'F' *periodic maintenance:* The frequency is semi-annual or annual. Perhaps by a contractor.

'G' *periodic maintenance:* The frequency is annual or biennial. Perhaps by a contractor.

'H' *maintenance:* The treatment is prescribed by a conservator. It may be both routine and periodic at a frequency which would best protect the item. The conservator should suggest means of protection as well as treatment.

'I' *maintenance:* The treatment should be done by a conservator or an outside specialist.

'J' *maintenance:* Irregular frequency; use past experience as a guide; consider outside contractors.

A good deal of expertise and time is needed to prepare such a maintenance manual, but it is undoubtedly well worth while, as scientific preventive maintenance can save large sums of money and reduce the need for costly major works.

Maintenance programming

Having established the importance of maintenance in the care of historic buildings, the methods by which this can be implemented need consideration. In Denmark since 1883, and in the Church of England, quinquennial inspections have long been the basis for maintenance of parsonage houses, and since 1955 the same routine has been applied to parish churches. This is one of the most sophisticated and economical systems in the world, because it involves the users and voluntary cleaners in the overall maintenance strategy as well as professional advisers. The extension of the system to include all important historic buildings is to be recommended.

Maintenance costs should be divided into the following separate categories, which should be recorded in a log book:

(1) Small items (basically good housekeeping).
(2) Repairs to services: (a) heating, (b) electrical, (c) plumbing.
(3) The rolling programme of long-term preventive maintenance carried out year by year and using scaffolding economically.
(4) Major items when in need of renewal, such as (a) roofs, (b) walls, (c) windows, doors and floor coverings, (d) services.
(5) Emergencies. A reserve of about 10% should be allowed for contingencies.

Each of these categories should be budgeted separately. If reductions have to be made, they should be spread equally unless special reasons exist. Just as a doctor keeps a case history for each of his patients, so the log book should be kept by a responsible person.

A routine for the maintenance of an historic building should be laid down, and a year-by-year log book should be instituted with records of costs allocated to headings as given above. Such a procedure will enable rational policies to be established and should ensure a constant feed of data from those with first-hand information. The records should pinpoint weaknesses in design and construction and indicate 'cost-in-use', thus providing the organization (and its architects) with valuable feedback information.

The study of records can lead to an assessment of the frequencies of servicing and repair in the past, and with a detailed survey of the fabric it is possible then to produce a detailed programme as the basis of future preventive work. This may have to be an elaborate document, and the clerical administration and documentation will be considerable. Indeed, in a large operation a computerized programme is the most efficient way of looking after a group of historic buildings with complicated plant such as a college in an ancient university.

A technique of 'resumption by computer' has been developed for St John's College, Oxford. This means that at, say, monthly intervals the computer produces dockets listing that work should be done in each craft skill and, where applicable, how many places need to be checked. (The computer throws up a reminder if a previous docket has been returned uncompleted.) After he has done the job, the craftsman initials the docket and notes on it his time and materials. Most importantly, he also points out anything he is not happy about, and by this means a most valuable source of information is utilized and fed back to the clerk of works or equivalent supervisor, who then should investigate the craftsman's report. The analysis of cost of repairs may indicate which items are deteriorating rapidly. The whole maintenance operation is thus based on survey assessment of frequencies of work loads and on responsible feedback by the staff. Systematic maintenance also facilitates the initiation and programming of major items of repair, reconstruction and restoration, because there is a feedforward of items which may need attention.

For major national monuments, every 30 years (once every generation) it is desirable to clean and overhaul the principal structural elements and make any necessary repairs. This is called the rolling programme and will necessitate the erection of scaffolding, the cost of which dominates the economics of all structural maintenance work, especially on large historic buildings. It enables a close inspection to be made by the professional advisers.

Repair work of a quality to last for at least 30 years should suffice for elements of the fabric of not very great height. On the other hand, towers, which need much more scaffolding, may be taken to justify repair work of a 60-year standard and spires a 90-year standard of durability. It must be remembered that these parts are unlikely to receive routine minor repairs; furthermore, because the cost of reaching inaccessible parts of a building is so great, a higher standard of repair is justified. These figures are fairly arbitrary, but are borne out by study of past records of repairs to historic buildings and are endorsed by the collective wisdom of the 1976 Cathedral Architects' Conference, held at Westminster Cathedral, London.

Maintenance routines

Maintenance should ideally be tackled by routines of daily, weekly, monthly, quarterly, semi-annual, annual and quinquennial inspections, followed by reports.

Checklists have been prepared as an indication of what might have to be done for a cathedral. Other types of buildings might be simpler but, needless to say, each historic building is a special case and needs its own schedules based upon a knowledge of the individual building with its content and of its specific environmental and structural problems. In working out a maintenance strategy, it is desirable to have categories of repair work as defined for the log books, so that the performance of buildings of similar types can be compared on a statistical basis. Such a study might throw up significant facts; for example, the cost of atmospheric pollution or damage from sonic bangs.

Daily routine

First ask cleaners to report any defects they note, i.e. broken windows or ironmongery, leaks in roof, falling pieces of masonry, telltale wood dust from beetle infestation, lime dust from spalling plaster.

Check fire-detection systems to make sure they are functioning properly. A good sense of smell is essential: someone on the staff should make a fire check throughout the building in the morning and evening after work. False alarms are all too frequent in fire-detection and security installations, and it is counter-productive if 'wolf' is cried too often.

Check heating plant, controls, temperature and humidity recorders. A daily check on boilers is very important—as well as a final look before leaving the building at night. The sound of boilers and pumps working sweetly must be made familiar to the ear, for when this sound changes it is a warning that something is amiss. Always make a habit of feeling heating pipes and radiators on a tour of the building; a cold pipe can warn of an airlock or a leak. Fuel oil in tanks should be checked daily. Time spent removing airlocks can be quite costly if boilers are allowed to go out for lack of fuel. The heating feed tank should also be checked, as running water here may indicate a pipe leak.

Do a security check. Windows and doors should be checked for security each evening; in a building used by large numbers of people during the day, one invariably finds doors and windows left open at night, with good intent, but with a real risk to security. Keys borrowed by contractors and workmen must be returned each day. Security installations should be inspected to see that they have not been tampered with.

Change defective light bulbs and fuses and attend to minor faults in the electrical system. Switch off the electricity supply at night (the caretaker or night watchman should have a special circuit for his needs).

Check lavatories and cloakrooms. Report dripping taps (they may cause icing up or an outbreak of dry rot and waste a lot of valuable water).

Weekly routine

Change or clean air filters of the heating or air conditioning plant or organ with humidifier.

Check all thermographs, humidigraphs and other recording instruments, and change charts and study same and report. Correct faults in these instruments' calibration.

Check loudspeaker and microphone units in PA equipment.

Check accuracy of all clocks, including electric and winding mechanisms.

Check all automatic fire-alarm and security devices in addition to the daily check of control systems.

Monthly routine

Have rainwater disposal outlets, gulleys, etc., cleaned out.

Lubricate and adjust all mechanical drives and bearings, e.g. pulley belts, flexible drives.

Check all log books. Report to Fabric Committee or technical supervisor charged with the responsibility for maintenance and other matters in respect of running the building.

Quarterly routine

Inspect roofs (outside and inside), gutters, rainwater disposal outlets, gulleys.

Check glazing. Clean windows and painted surrounds.

Check doors for closing and locking and all means of escape.

Overhaul humidifiers.

Service sound-reinforcement systems, tape machines and turntables, replacing worn drive belts, idlers, etc.

Clean light fittings.

Oil clock bearings. Check ropes and weights.

Oil ball bearings. Check frames and ropes of bells.

Technical supervisor to conduct a maintenance inspection of, say, one-third, one-quarter or one-fifth of the total fabric.

Semi-annual routine

Sound fire alarms and give staff fire-fighting practice exercises.

Clean out all gutters, downpipes and rainwater drains in autumn to remove fallen leaves and in spring to remove winter debris, and leave everything clear to cope with the heavy storms of summer. Grass growing out of gutters is a sign of neglect—if not negligence.

Annual routine

Rod through all rainwater and soil drainage systems.

Overhaul all electric plant. Change fuses, bulbs and tubes, especially where these are not easily accessible.

Inspect boilers and controls, overhaul boiler, clean main stack, renew firebricks. Maintain feed tanks and ease ball valves.

Clean out ducts and fan-assisted heaters, etc.

Oil locks, hinges and replace defective ironmongery.

Service lifts.

Overhaul air conditioning plant.

Fire brigade to test men and plant in mock fire-fighting exercises.

Check problems of fire-fighting access.

Test all fire extinguishers and refill if necessary.

Decorate and clean sections of the interior of the building.

Touch up poor spots on external decoration in autumn.

Test lightning conductors and earth resistance if in an area prone to lightning.

Quinquennial routine

The architect or surveyor must make full reports every five years, especially noting structural defects that should be kept under observation. He should revise and update the long-term maintenance plan after each such inspection, and he should draw attention to any problems that should be kept under observation and studied for the next report. He should divide the proposed work into categories: Immediate, Urgent, Necessary and Desirable (see Chapter 13 for definitions of these terms). Typical quinquennial housekeeping items would be:

Clean out all voids and spaces and report any decay found.

Change tap washers, as a matter of preventive maintenance.

Specialists to clean out sanitaryware to avoid infections.

Check lightning conductors (note that on some buildings with valuable contents annual inspections are desirable).

Inspect and test electric insulation and installation.

Check on mechanical wear, wear of electrical contacts, corrosion and any signs of abnormal deterioration.

Inspect and test the heating installations.

Redecorate externally to a good specification.

For large buildings or series of buildings this quinquennial inspection becomes the basis of a 30-year rolling programme for preventive maintenance of the structure of the fabric.

Building maintenance has unfortunately not been given the status it deserves. It has not been considered at a strategic level but only on an *ad hoc* basis. Skilful management of building maintenance while respecting the principles of conservation is a high-level occupation which deserves respect. Few know the names of the clerks of works and craftsmen who maintain our great monuments, although their job is to interpret great works of art in the face of difficult environmental conditions. As in conservation of all cultural property, the key operation is the expert's inspection.

The hierarchy of skill and organization for efficient and effective maintenance should be examined.

Handymen who can carry out two or three trades competently are invaluable for the maintenance of the numerous buildings that make up an historic district or centre whose values are visual townscape. It is inefficient to wait for one trade to follow another in this work, so multi-trade teams of three of four handymen should work together. They should understand that it is most important for them to use the correct materials and follow traditional workmanship. They should work under instructions of a builder specializing in this field. For important historic buildings, where high-class work has to be maintained and repaired, conservation craftsmen specializing in repair and reproduction work will be required. They must know the history of their craft, understand its technology and the principles of conservation given in the Introduction to this book (Chapter 1). They should work under the supervision of a clerk of works and guidance of an historical architect and should be prepared to advise upon specialist problems.

The productivity of the conservator will be less than that of a conservation craftsman, but he will have greater skills in diagnosis of faults and the application of scientific methods to conservation of historic buildings. He will be asked to advise on maintenance, repair and consolidation of works of art such as sculpture and metalwork, stained glass or wall paintings. To increase productivity, he should work with three or four craftsmen. Part of the skill needed in work organization is to get the right balance of skills for the particular problem. Clerks of works who look after historic buildings should have the skills of a conservator.

Figure 15.9   Kedelston Hall, Derbyshire, England
(Courtesy: D.W. Insall)

A plumber is repairing lead gutters at Kedelston Hall. One trusts men such as this to give good conscientious craftsmanship. If this trust is misplaced it will surely show in the future

Figure 15.10   Kedelston Hall, Derbyshire, England
(Courtesy: D.W. Insall)

Fundamentally, mortar joints in stone should be close in colour to the stone, but should not be made black to match the soot. After re-pointing sandstone the mortar shows up lightly for a few years, but will then darken and harmonize naturally. The colour, thickness and surface texture of pointing are vital to the appearance of a building

Figure 15.11   Bridge, Isphahan, Iran

Maintenance of the bridge includes renewal of brickwork and pointing. A skilled eye can detect a slight colour and texture change in the brick and a slight change in the mortar

Figure 15.12   The Royal Palace, Bangkok, Thailand

Maintenance of such superb roofs presents some problems which are shown in Figure 15.13

Figure 15.13   The Royal Palace, Bangkok, Thailand

Even the ridge pieces of the roof can be attacked by termites. Externally they are protected by thick black natural resin lacquerwork and by pieces of embedded coloured glass which are difficult to reproduce

Figure 15.14   National Museum, Bangkok, Thailand

This eighteenth century structure showed cracks in the plaster, which when stripped off revealed distress in the brick masonry

Figure 15.15   National Museum, Bangkok, Thailand

The cause of distress was found to be that termites had completely eaten away the timber post supporting the roof which was encased by the non-structural brickwork

229

Figure 15.16   Roof spaces, north aisle, York Minster, England
(Courtesy: Shepherd Building Group Ltd)

Before application of preservatives, all accumulations of the rubbish of ages was removed and the roof areas were vacuum cleaned as part of a programme of good housekeeping

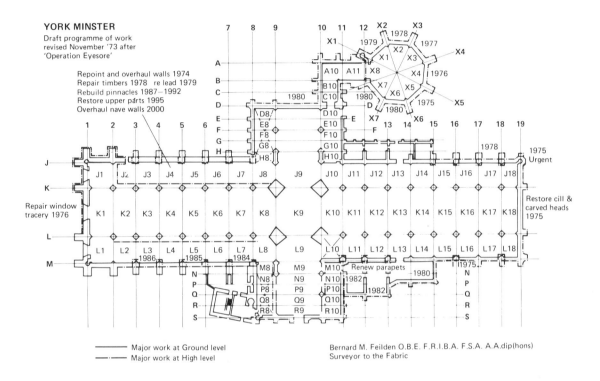

YORK MINSTER

Draft programme of work
revised November '73 after
'Operation Eyesore'

Repoint and overhaul walls 1974
Repair timbers 1978 re lead 1979
Rebuild pinnacles 1987–1992
Restore upper parts 1995
Overhaul nave walls 2000

Repair window
tracery 1976

Restore cill &
carved heads
1975

——————— Major work at Ground level
— · —— · —— Major work at High level

Bernard M. Feilden O.B.E. F.R.I.B.A. F.S.A. A.A.dip(hons)
Surveyor to the Fabric

**Figure 15.17   The rolling programme of preventive maintenance
for York Minster, England**

*This programme was based on two quinquennial inspections; it
should be revised and updated after each regular inspection*

16

Fire

Fire is no respecter of historic buildings, nor do regulations and codes for fire protection respect the cultural and artistic values in a historic building. Their aim is to protect life. The conservationist's aim is to prevent fire and minimize damage caused by disasters and this in effect also protects life.

Morally and psychologically the destruction of any historic building by fire is worse than total loss, for the loss could have been prevented in most cases. It is therefore desirable to examine first the cause of fire and then the means of lessening its extent and effect. It will be found that fire and security precautions must be taken together in order to resolve possible contradictions in their requirements.

The main problems in historic buildings can be summarized as follows:

(1) Failure to consult fire brigade officers and failure to appoint local fire prevention officers and to organize regular fire drills.
(2) Poor standards of management, housekeeping and supervision, e.g. accumulation of dust, dirt and rubbish in roof and storage spaces.
(3) The danger from smoking (11% overall).
(4) The danger from cooking operations (mostly due to frying and fat congealed in ducts 21%).
(5) Faulty electrical installations (21% including faults in wiring).
(6) Flammable decorative materials and furnishings.
(7) Lack of compartmentation, no internal subdivisions, stairways not enclosed, wall linings not fire-stopped.
(8) Deficient fire resistance; walls and floors inadequate, doors not fire resisting.
(9) Inadequate means of escape; doors, passages, staircases have excessive travel distances; no alternative escape routes.
(10) The danger of arson (10% largely in historic buildings, children with fire 9%).
(11) Lack of master keys and mastered locks.

Figure 16.1   Bedford School, Bedford, England
(Courtesy: Bedfordshire Times Press)

Fire breaks out at night; it is too intense to be subdued by firemen with hoses

233

(12) The danger from workmen especially when using 'flame' for repairs.

(13) Possible danger from lightning.

Prevention of fire

One of the most important lessons of major fires, such as York Minster, Hampton Court, Uppark and Windsor Castle, is that every building should have a fire audit at regular intervals. This might well be part of the architect's quinquennial report. Certainly such a review should take place every five years. The participants in this review should cover every aspect of management and maintenance of the historic building and should include:

The building owner or administrator
Fire prevention officer
Architect

Figure 16.2   Bedford School, Bedford, England
(Courtesy: Bedfordshire Times Press)

The burnt-out remains with stone dressings spalled by the heat and all combustible material consumed except for a few charred beams. The cause of the fire was arson

234

Service engineer
Security officer (this may be the police)
Fire fighting organization
Safety officer (this may be a department of fire fighting)
Insurance company
Fire engineering consultant.

The whole building should be viewed jointly; water supply and storage capacity, all weather approaches for fire fighting, the manning of the fire brigade and its response time. The condition of the structure, flammability and disposition of furnishings and condition of electric wiring should all be considered. The audit should cover fire precautions, fire protection measures, rescue, training, salvage and disaster control planning. In conclusion: fire prevention depends on creating awareness in owners, professionals, the public and workmen.

Actions should include:

(1) Appoint a fire prevention officer. Organize fire drills and rescue practice.

(2) Ensure adequate water for fire fighting and good access for fire engines. Alternative routes should be planned in case one is blocked.

(3) Identify important risks and danger of fire spread, and eliminate unnecessary hazards—here the fire brigade can help.

(4) Consult a competent fire engineer (the fire brigade can indicate some of the questions he should study).

(5) See what can be achieved by compartmentation.

(6) Consider what early detection systems can offer.

(7) Consider the merits of sprinkler systems.

(8) Make check lists for monthly, weekly and daily routine inspections.

Fire prevention officer

The most important step in the prevention of fire is to appoint a suitable person as fire prevention manager. He should lay down safety procedures and suitable staff should be appointed to carry them out. Staff may be allocated duties such as fire fighting, rescue work, supervising the evacuation of visitors, assisting the fire brigade, security patrols and monitoring of automatic detection and security systems.

The fire prevention manager should ensure that the arrangements he has made comply with the legal requirements for the uses to which the building is put and the recommendations of the insurers. He should be aware of the various sources of advice available to him, i.e. the local fire authority, the insurance company surveyor, the building control officer, the Fire Protection Association, or Loss Prevention Council (UK), and should work with his architect or surveyor.

The fire prevention manager should:

(1) Establish a system of frequent inspections, using check lists, in order to reduce the likelihood of fire occurring.

(2) Determine the routes of services and identify the positions of isolating switches and valves.

(3) Carry out regular demonstrations and train staff in the effective use of portable fire-extinguishing equipment.

It is the responsibility of the senior management to confirm regularly that these matters are being properly attended to in order to avoid complacency and to motivate all concerned to maintain a high standard of effectiveness.

Management precautions—fire drills

Instruction of the permanent staff in fire drill is essential, so that they should know what to do in case they should discover a fire. When the fire brigade comes out on a practice scheme, the permanent staff of the building should be involved; regular practices at, say, six-monthly intervals are desirable as it should not be forgotten that personnel change. Staff should practise the use of equipment such as hand extinguishers, hose reels, sand and

Figure 16.3 St Paul's Cathedral, London, England
(Courtesy: Feilden & Mawson)

The dome, one of the most perfect, is a major fire hazard due to the amount of timber used (fire load) and its inaccessibility to normal fire-fighting equipment. A lift was installed against the south-west corner to enable four firemen, in full equipment, to be taken up the first 30 m (100 ft). A second lift to the base of the dome has been planned. Repairs to the south-west tower are in progress

235

asbestos blankets. The alarm systems should also be tested.

Alarms range from handbells and triangles to hand sirens. Although manual alarms need little maintenance, they have two disadvantages: the operator may have to retreat from the fire before everyone is warned, and in a large building several alarms will be needed (two being the minimum) and this depends upon a human chain reaction to hearing the first alarm. Electric alarms overcome these disadvantages as they can be linked together and ring continuously. A large number of small bells is more effective than a few large bells. Fire detectors and manual electric systems can be linked together to provide an early warning.

Fire fighting equipment, which should be installed in consultation with the fire brigade, is primarily for immediate action. Areas of special risk should be fully covered. A small fire can reach unmanageable proportions in less than five minutes, so the fire brigade should always be called. The non-public areas of the building should be clearly marked for the benefit of the brigade and plans of all levels fixed on the building and lodged with the brigade.

Common causes of fire and some precautions

The ordinary domestic fire or stove is a common cause of fire, with heat and flame causing the ignition of adjacent wooden members of the structure. Conversion to oil heating reveals latent weaknesses in old construction which might not have mattered with a coal fire. Boiler blowback can cause fire if combustible material is stored in the boiler house. Boiler blowback can also occur in high winds, which then fan the flames of the fire. Sparks from a boiler flue may start a fire either by falling on a combustible roof material or by penetrating cracks in a defective flue. Flues should be swept at least once a year and should be surrounded by 170 mm (7 in) of incombustible material, with any structural timbers kept at least 50 mm (2 in) away from the flue. Wood burning increases the risk of a chimney fire and is banned in the houses owned by the National Trust.

Another common cause of fire is a hot spark, perhaps from defective electric wiring or from welding operations, landing on to a flammable material. Portable electric fires (providing radiant heat) can ignite clothes, curtains or furnishings; likewise powerful modern light fittings can have the same effect.

Lighted candles, if left unattended, should be securely fixed in holders that cannot be blown over or fall. Unattended candles should always stand on a metal tray large enough to contain any candles that may fall over. No candle or naked light should be placed near combustible material.

An accumulation of rubbish or loose combustible material often causes fires or hastens their spread, so tidiness is an essential part of any fire prevention scheme. Rubbish deposited by draughts, or collected by insects or birds or by vermin to form nests, may be a fire risk, as heat can cause this to smoulder or a spark can cause flame. A responsible person should make monthly inspections with this in mind and ensure that any such hazards are removed.

Used polishing rags and mops are liable to heat up and then ignite spontaneously, depending on the type of polish. They are best kept in an outhouse if required for further use. Cleaning materials, oily rags, broken chairs, candle ends, clinker and ash from the boiler house should be disposed of safely. The burning of rubbish should be carefully controlled. No combustible material should be stored in the main volume of the building or areas linked thereto unless proper fire doors or shutters are fitted.

Electricity is a big fire risk; faulty wiring, overloaded circuits and badly maintained or carelessly used equipment have all been known to start fires. Short-circuits in old wiring and defective insulation are a severe hazard. Nothing should be placed close to a convector or tubular heaters so as to restrict air circulation around them and any non-luminous electric heater should have a pilot light indicator by its switch. Storage heaters and the like should have fixed wire guards for safety. Because of these risks, all electricity should be switched off when not in use, particularly at night, and if there is a nightwatchman's room or special plant such as refrigerators which must be continuously connected to the main supply, this should have a special circuit arranged as a safety precaution.

All electrical work should be carried out by competent electricians in accordance with official standards and regulations. In the UK these are given in the current edition of the Regulations of the Institute of Electrical Engineers. The whole of the electric installation should be thoroughly examined every five years and no unauthorized alterations permitted. It is found that 50-cycle frequency vibrations can loosen connections so causing heating and sparks.

The choice of wiring system is most important. Mineral-insulated, copper-sheathed, plastic-coated wiring is undoubtedly the best. Wherever possible all cables should run clear of combustible material such as wood and should not be fixed in inaccessible voids where they cannot be inspected. Electrical plant should be connected by armoured

cables and have isolating switches with indicator lights. Temporary electric lighting and equipment is always a fire risk, particularly as workmen are likely to improvise. Such installations must be of the same standard as permanent work. No loose cables should be permitted at any time.

Before Benjamin Franklin invented lightning conductors, lightning was a major cause of fires in historic buildings. All metal elements and electric wiring in a building should be bonded to the conductor system. The specialist firm responsible for maintenance of the lightning conductor installation should inspect annually and report on any upgrading needed to bond new electrical or structural items into the system and specially considering hazards from side flash. If codes have been revised the maintenance contractor should advise the owner of any additional requirements.

The fire-proofing of fabrics, wood, plastics and paints extends the time to ignition or retards the initial rate of burning. Chlorine, bromide, fluorine, phosphorus and antimony are used to form industrial fireproofing compounds, chlorine being the most important. For wood, ammonium hydroxide, ammonium phosphate pyro-antimonate are used most frequently, and are usually applied by the vacuum impregnation process, but dipping or brushing may be used if the former facilities do not exist.

Fire-retarding paints, varnishes and polishes should be able to fulfil two conditions:

(1) To provide a layer of coating which is neither flammable in itself nor likely to propagate fire, irrespective of the nature of the substrate.

(2) To protect combustible base materials such as wood against the effects of fire by thermal

insulation in the first stage of a fire and then by smothering flames produced by the gases. Intumescent treatments can be effective.

Although no surface treatment can make a substrate absolutely incombustible, it can make a useful contribution by delaying the spread of fire, for when fire breaks out in a building the nature of the interior surfaces may determine the time available for the occupants to escape. Finishes like wax polishes on floors can melt and produce running fire, which can be especially dangerous in a public building. Escape routes should have incombustible finishes. A fire-retardant surface treatment gives fire-fighting personnel more time to save cultural property. The protection of steel in multi-storied buildings is a vital precaution, generally effected by giving a minimum of 13 mm (0.5 in) cover of concrete and up to 50 mm (2 in) to give four hours protection. Plaster and preformed units also give good protection.

Regulations relating to fire and historic buildings

Fire regulations are framed chiefly with the design of new buildings in mind, rather than the improvement of existing buildings, and their primary concern is, quite rightly, the safeguarding of life rather than the safeguarding of the contents of the building. Historic buildings require wider priorities; it is suggested the objective should be broken down into three parts:

(a) To prevent the outbreak of fire.
(b) To minimize the effects of fire by preventing it spreading (passive fire protection).
(c) To enable the fire to be fought efficiently with minimum damage to its contents (active fire protection).

To meet the regulations in the UK the most typical actions are:

(1) Planning alternative protected escape routes. Applications of intumescent paint or fire retardant to combustible materials such as wood panelling. Provision of hatches, crawl-ways and internal ladders.
(2) Forming enclosed staircases, glazed screens and fire doors on magnetic latches. Hardwood treads on stairs.
(3) Upgrading of fire resistance of doors and rebates.
(4) Provision of alarms, detectors, emergency lighting and fire-fighting equipment such as extinguishers, hose reels and hydrants.

Figure 16.5   Norwich Cathedral, Norwich, England

At Norwich Cathedral, fire-fighting drill is practised regularly. A hard standing has been formed so that the heavy fire tender can put its 30 m (100 ft) ladder into position. Rehearsals take place every six months, so that every fireman knows his way in an emergency

(5) Compartmentation with thickening of floor boards or other treatment above the floor joists, fire stopping of cavities and ceiling voids and increasing the fire resistance of ceilings. Sealing of ventilation grilles.
(6) Provision of sprinklers and reserve water storage for fire fighting.

Structural elements must be protected against fire. The amount of protection is specified in notional hours of resistance to a standard fire, but in fact the time the protection will be effective may be less in a fierce fire and longer in a small fire. Load bearing walls must have sufficient fire resistance. The standard required depends on the use of the building, the number of storeys, height, floor area and volume. Compartmentation can reduce the fire protection requirements as well as reducing loss by the spread of fire.

When use of a building is changed from domestic to public often the resistance of specific elements has to be upgraded.

238

Table 16.1   Fire-fighting Agents

| Agent | Effective against fires of class: | | | | | Principle of extinction | | |
	A	B	C	D	E	Cooling	Depletion of oxygen	Catalytic
Water (solid stream)	+ +	–	–	–	–	+ +		
Water spray	+ +	–	–	–	–	+ +		
Foam	+	+	–	–	–	+	+ +	
Dry chemical, regular	–	+ +	+ +	–	+ +			+ +
Dry chemical, multi-purpose	+	+	+	–	±		+	+ +
Carbon dioxide (CO_2)	–	+	+	–	+ +		+ +	
Halons*	±	+	+	–	+			+ +
Metal extinguishing agent	–	–	–	+	–	+	+	

*Only halon 1211 or 1301 is recommended for toxicity reasons. Note instructions of manufacturer.

Classification by material:
Class A   Solid combustible materials — wood, pasteboard, cloth, coal, etc. Soaking the material with water avoids the return of flames. Spray is good because it avoids using too much water.
Class B   Liquid and flammable substances — fuel, lubricants, grease, paint, oil, alcohol, etc. Water must *not* be used as the burning liquid floats on it and spreads. CO_2 is useful in enclosed spaces only.
Class C   Flammable gaseous material — methane, butane, hydrogen, acetylene, city gas, etc. Water is not suitable
Class D   Light metals — magnesium and derivatives, aluminium, potassium, calcium, barium. Water is not suitable
Class E   Electrical appliances and conductors, telephone systems, electric motors. Water and foam must not be used as they are conductors.

The required fire resistance for walls, floors and ceilings and doors depends on the height of the building and its area. The UK legislation demands the following resistances:

Height	Area	Resistance
Single storey	Less than 3000 m²	Half an hour
7.5 m	Less than 500 m²	Half an hour
15 m	Less than 3000 m²	One hour
28 m	1000–7000 m²	One hour
28 m	Over 7000 m²	One and a half hours.

Distance to the nearest protected route should not exceed 20 m.

Vertical compartmentation will involve the introduction of fire doors and screens, and horizontal compartmentation the improvement of the resistance of floors and ceilings. Voids in the floor or ceiling space can present serious problems in fire-stopping, especially when decorative ceilings and valuable floor finishes are involved.

Metal structures in historic buildings are usually of cast iron for columns or wrought iron for beams and trusses. These are generally exposed and will require enhanced protection which can be provided by encasement or application of at least 6 mm of intumescent paint, which unfortunately tends to obscure detail and requires protection against abrasion.

Timber structures can be assessed for fire resistance on the basis of sacrificial charring. As timber beams in historic buildings are often over-sized the amount of timber remaining after the required period may be sufficient for strength; however, if regulations demand a non-combustible floor, serious problems may have to be faced unless a relaxation can be negotiated. Buildings clad with wattle and daub or faced with weatherboarding present special problems in obtaining sufficient fire resistance, the required standard depending on:

the distance between walls and site boundary;
the internal subdivision of the building into compartments;
the occupancy of the building.

Thatch and wood shingle roof coverings are vulnerable to radiation and flying embers, and are only permitted in the UK when the building is 12 m away from its boundary. Timber partitions, especially when panelled on both sides, are liable to have insufficient fire resistance and may have to be reconstructed in order to give sufficient protection, but a half hour standard can often be obtained with intumescent paint. A clear matt fire retardant can be applied to reduce flame spread.

Staircases have to be enclosed by fire-resisting doorways. Sometimes regulations require higher handrails and closer spaced banisters than those existing in a historic building, so it will be necessary

239

to obtain a relaxation in order to preserve its character. The fire resistance of treads may have to be improved by changing softwood to hardwood.

Internal doors are the element most likely to be affected by fire protection regulations, as they are vital to protect escape routes for the safe exit of occupants. Upgrading is then necessary but the work to achieve this has unfortunate side effects. Sheeting over panelled doors radically changes the character of a historic building, so it is not acceptable. Attention must be given to the thinnest portions and to the rebates around the door which often have to be changed to hardwood 25 mm thick. High quality doors have even been sliced in half in their thickness and refixed to a central fire-resisting sheet, so preserving their original appearance yet increasing their fire resistance.

Passive fire protection

Once a flame has started it will spread to any nearby combustible material and so build up until it is checked in one of three ways; by being deliberately extinguished, by running out of combustible materimaterial, or by being confined in a particular compartment with fireproof boundaries.

Compartmentation, to be effective, must have a complete seal. It is preferable for each compartment to have at least two external doors to give access for fire fighting. Roof compartments can be devised with smoke vents operating by fusible links. Passive measures of fire protection, which do not rely on mechanical devices or human intervention, should be given a high priority in historic buildings as they are always on duty.

Automatic devices such as sprinklers can be useful, but it is wise to remember that sprinklers may cause damage to the contents, so their use may be ruled out if the contents are historically valuable. In some cases after a fire, it has been remarked that the fireman's hose caused more damage than the fire itself.

Active fire protection

The strategy for protection of a historic building and its contents depends on preventing the outbreaks of fire, particularly fire caused by human carelessness. A full system of fire warning alarms should be installed, and, if necessary, special detectors can reinforce human vigilance and can be wired by direct line to the fire brigade at the cost of an annual rental. Arrangements should be made for a responsible official to be available by day and night in case of fire; an internal telephone or radio telephone

system is invaluable for this. Closed circuit infra-red television systems which can 'see' in the dark may become more common and be linked with special security systems by direct line to the police station. Locks should be standardized so that the fire brigade can open all relevant doors with one master key. At night all internal doors should be left closed but unlocked, if security permits.

Fire detectors are designed for the following special circumstances:

(1) For hazardous situations such as
    (a) petrol and flammable vapour detectors;
    (b) butane and propane leakage detectors;
    (c) over-heat detection;
    (d) explosion and suppression.

(2) Ionization detectors—to detect combustion.

(3) Visible smoke detectors
    (a) using light scattering techniques;
    (b) using light obscuring techniques;
    (c) using sampling systems.

(4) Flame detectors (either ultraviolet or infra-red).

(5) Ultrasonic and laser detectors.

(6) Combustion gas detectors.

(7) Heat detectors of various types such as
    (a) spot or point detectors;
    (b) solid state detectors;
    (c) thermocouples;
    (d) fusible links (solder or quartzoid bulb);
    (e) line detectors using capillary tube;
    (f) line detectors using cables with flexible joints.

Line detectors are a small but interesting group, useful in rooms with moulded or ornamented surfaces as the capillary tube can be concealed within the architectural decoration. The tube contains a liquid or gas which will expand under heating, thus displacing a diaphragm and activating a fire alarm.

The siting of detectors in historic buildings demands great care especially in large volumes where height reduces the sensitivity of the detectors. Internal air currents can behave differently by day and night when a stratification layer between cool and warm air can form at different levels, so upsetting the functioning of smoke detectors.

Unfortunately the number of false alarms with most detector systems is large—over ten to one—and this is like crying 'wolf' too often. The suppliers of detector systems will advise upon installations and should also put forward proposals for regular maintenance. Additionally they must be asked to state (in writing) the limitations of their equipment, for in historic buildings special problems are frequently met which limit the performance of detectors designed for typical modern buildings having small rooms and low ceilings.

The number of false alarms can be reduced by having detectors close spaced arranged in an 'intelligent self-monitoring system' linked to a microprocessor with a watchdog check and reset system able to identify cable damage or the failure of a detector. Such systems are self-testing and will give maintenance advice. In choosing a system one must consider capital costs, maintenance and running costs in comparison with the cost of equivalent protection from manpower. Generally detection systems are much cheaper and constantly alert.

Escape routes should be protected by lobbies and free of obstructions and combustible material. Glazing in doors and screens must be fire resistant, but even so they present a hazard from radiation transmitting intolerable heat, so preventing escape on the other side of the fire barrier. Additional means of escape, such as external stairs, can disfigure a historic building and so may prevent its beneficial use. Means of escape cannot be dealt with by a series of hard-and-fast rules, but guidance can be obtained from regulations relating to the number, position and width of exits according to the maximum number of people likely to be in the building at any one time. Sometimes the number of persons who may be present in a historic building will be limited by the available means of escape. Signs indicating escape routes can also erode the architectural character of a historic building, as such direction signs must be plainly visible.

The construction of walls, floors and ceilings of escape routes must be 'incombustible'. To prevent the spread of smoke and fire into corridors and stairwells self-closing fire-stop doors must be provided. In historic buildings, fire-stopping of intercommunicating voids must be meticulous. Any report on the fabric should recommend considerable improvements such as fire-stopping at floor levels or behind wall panelling. Roof insulation of glass fibre or rock-wool also gives fire protection, provided that it is not bonded with bitumen.

Precautions during building operations

Repair, consolidation and reconstruction operations present an additional and severe set of hazards in a historic building. In the UK, the Joint Contracts Tribunal form of contract places the onus of informing the fire insurers about proposed works on the building owner, who should be reminded of this by the architect. A special premium may be payable. Workmen busy on repairs generally increase the risk of fire through carelessness or unfamiliarity with the local fire precautions.

Some of the operations carried out by builders and plant engineers involve the use of blowlamps and other equipment that produces flames and heat in areas of appreciable fire risk, for instance on roofs where heat may penetrate to concealed woodwork. This equipment should only be used if no alternative is available, and then the work should be carried out in a safe area if possible. If the work must be done *in situ* the operator should have at hand an assistant with a portable fire extinguisher to watch sparks as and where they fall. Flame should never be used if there is a noticeable wind, and tea or meal breaks must be staggered so as to keep the work under constant supervision.

Combustible materials should be protected by a heat shield. At least two portable water/gas extinguishers should be provided in each area where men are at work, and there should be clauses in the specification of work stipulating these precautions. Neglect of these in one case led to the complete destruction of a thatched house with valuable contents in less than thirty minutes after a painter started stripping external paint on a window with a blowlamp. No operation involving the use of flame should be carried out within one hour of the end of the day, at the close of which the work must be inspected by a responsible person so that any smouldering may be seen before the men leave.

The Fire Protection Association, together with the Society for Protection of Ancient Buildings, have designed a Hot Work Permit, use of which would ensure that workmen carrying out maintenance or rehabilitation of a historic building are subject to proper supervision.

Bitumen and asphalt boiler plants are a hazard, and should be set up well away from the historic building. Tarpaulins used for temporary waterproofing are another fire risk, particularly if a cigarette is dropped carelessly into a fold. When not in use, tarpaulins should be folded neatly. Smoking should be permitted only in the men's mess room and site office; a workman found smoking elsewhere should be subject to immediate dismissal from the site as a term of the building contract.

The Fire Protection Association makes the following comments about insecticides:

'Many insecticides are flammable. They should only be applied by specialists who should be

241

asked to take the following precautions before starting—remove all sources of ignition such as electric fires and naked flames, clear the area of dust, lumber, etc., and take up any fibrous insulating material such as glass fibre. While the treatment is being applied and drying, particular care should be taken to see that there is no smoking in the area. The space should be thoroughly ventilated during the operation and afterwards for at least a week. The glass fibre or other thermal insulating material should not be put back until this time has elapsed. The treated area should not be covered with plastic sheeting. The use of temporary fittings should be avoided and the men should be warned not to spray electric fittings, junction boxes and hot surfaces such as light bulbs.'

17

Presentation of historic buildings

Before a conservation project is started, its objectives should be defined, then the appropriate presentation policy can be proposed. The objectives may be simply to keep a building 'wind and water tight' to preserve it on the one hand, or on the other hand to present it in its full documentary and historical context to be studied for educational and artistic purposes within the context of cultural tourism. This will mean analysing the values inherent in the building. First, as mentioned in the Introduction (Chapter 1), there are the *emotional* values—wonder, a sense of continuity and identity; then the *symbolic* and *cultural* values of art, history, aesthetics, architecture, archaeology and the site landscape and townscape; and lastly there are the *use* values—functional, social, economic and even political.

In the forming of presentation policy these values must be respected, but it may be found that there are conflicts between the claims of some of them which can only be resolved by mature judgement and cultural preparation. Such decisions are too important to be made by one man alone, but once the individual guidelines of policy for presentation have been made, they should be rigorously adhered to in order to avoid aesthetic confusion. This is where the advice of art historians and archaeologists and the wide cultural preparation of the conservation architect are so important. He must see, understand and interpret. The presentation should not destroy historical or archaeological evidence.

It is essential that consideration of the values in cultural property should be assessed objectively and fairly. There is always a danger that the conservation programme will only reflect the bureaucratic objectives of the government department that is responsible.

Therefore, it is wise to insist that the goals and priorities of the presentation programme are established by an interdisciplinary, interdepartmental working group that includes people genuinely interested in all values in cultural property. Their task is to reconcile their purposes as well as the direction of their movement.

W. Brown Morton III, who has had much experience of work within government departments, writes in a personal communication to the author:

Figure 17.1 The Holy Shrine of Al Hussein, Kerbala, Iraq

A building and its setting are inseparable, that is until town planners advise on cutting wide avenues through a dense street pattern applying western ideas of vista and axial approaches to important monuments

243

'The success of this interdisciplinary process to establish a successful . . . conservation . . . programme depends on each member of the team having unquestioned authority to speak for their department or professional discipline and having the unswerving support of their department head. All too often an important value is ranked too low in the order of priorities or ignored altogether, because the person responsible for defending that value in the working group did not have sufficient authority or sufficient confidence in his own department's support of his position to carry the day.

'As you can appreciate, the order in which we rank the Values will dictate the goals and objectives of the environmental design program. If you place the highest priority on archaeological value your program will call for very little new construction or landscape changes. If you place the highest priority on spiritual value your program may severely limit visitor access at certain times and impose very strict controls on the type and frequency of appropriate activities. If you place the highest priority on the economic value, your program may very well exploit the monument at the expense of other values.

'Therefore, it is essential that each of the Values for a given ancient monument and its site be thoroughly researched and evaluated independently before any priority ranking is done.'

When the relative importance of all the values in cultural property has been established then, having examined all the practical alternatives, the 'least bad' solution can be found. If the conservation programme goes forward before all the conflicts of competing values have been thoroughly and thoughtfully resolved, there is the risk of destroying for ever the full integrity of the historic building and its site. Also, if the conservation programme goes forward prematurely, one will face the probability of time-consuming, expensive and professionally embarrassing changes having to be made later. We are indeed only trustees for historic buildings.

Presentation of the message

A piecemeal approach to presentation is disastrous. The conservation architect must guard the 'wholeness' of the historic building in his care, so that it can be presented in an intelligible way to the public.

Presentation must also take into account crowd control, together with security, prevention of crime and vandalism. Museums can show many examples of good presentation.

When proposing the presentation of an historic building or site, it is desirable to consider all the values that have been listed earlier and define the 'message' of the building under each of these headings.

One example is Baguley Hall, an early thirteenth century timber-framed hall, near Manchester, England, which needed structural strengthening to prevent collapse. It proved impossible to strengthen it *in situ* except by consolidation, inserting glass fibre rods and epoxy resin glues, which would have been irreversible, thus preventing any future repairs that might become necessary and contradicting the technological message of the early timber frame. This would make it function in a way for which it was not designed and in a way which might cause even worse defects later on. This scheme was rejected in favour of taking the framed structure down and reforming all the broken joints with small inserts of new material, but this decision involved removing and refixing wattle and daub panels between the timbers with some consequential archaeological loss.

Presenting wholeness by treatment

The treatment of lacunae or gaps in the design and surfaces of historic buildings, which may be caused by the need to renew stone or brickwork, should be given special consideration. Two examples may be considered—the Arch of Titus and the Arch of Constantine. The Arch of Titus was reconstructed *c*.1800–1830 on a core of brickwork in which quite considerable areas of stone were renewed following the original detail in a slightly simplified, less textured manner and using a marble of slightly different colour. The result is that the original work dominates, and only when one looks carefully can the reproduction work be identified. Thus the general effect is of artistic unity.

The reverse is true of the Arch of Constantine, which gives the impression of a lot of holes being filled in, and unnecessary attention being drawn to the lacunae because they are lighter in tone and harder in outline than the original material. The result is an impression of over-restoration and lack of artistic harmony and unity.

At the end of the nineteenth century it became a dogma in Britain that lacunae should be filled in or repairs executed in a different material, so one often found brick patching in stone buildings. This gives some restored buildings a ridiculous patched appearance, which destroys their unity and character.

The treatment of lacunae should reduce neither the artistic wholeness nor the message of the historic site or building or any element therein, and must not aim

*This dramatic site comprises the
ruins of the last mediaeval capital of
Bulgaria and so is of great historic,
educational, touristic and political
value.*

*The whole site is subject to careful
archaeological excavation and recording, but this raises problems in
presentation and preservation of the
ruins. Purely archaeological values
have been overridden by the desire
to make the monument intelligible
to the Communist workers.*

*The cathedral is a reconstruction
on original foundations but otherwise based on conjectural analogy;
the perimeter walls have been raised
using different types of pointing so
as to avoid deception.*

*A coherent theory of conservation
is essential in order to reconcile such
debatable issues*

at deception of trained observers. The general principle is that lacunae should seem to recede visually behind the original material, yet be so harmonious as not to detract but rather add to the whole. At Herculaneum this is done by drawing in the overall lines of the fresco painting on the dull toned and slightly textured plaster that is used to fill in the gaps, thus carrying the eye over and across the lacunae. At some sites in Rome, the filling of lacunae with brickwork has become rather a mechanical formula of using rather dark bricks with broken faces, which in fact become more noticeable than the original material and therefore break the principle of recession. With brickwork, even a slight change of colour to indicate repairs and filling in of lacunae seems preferable to a violent change of texture. The

architect will have to decide each case for himself, but should carefully consider colour, texture and the relative recession of surfaces in order to fill in lacunae. Lacunae should be identifiable on close inspection, new stonework being given a slightly different tooling to differentiate it, while new pieces of stained glass and wood can have the date marked thereon.

Preservation of patina

Patina is acquired by the materials of an historic building through age, by weathering or oxidization and by use. It is something which cannot be produced artificially, for the artificial aging which forgers and

245

Figure 17.3   Arch of Titus, Rome, Italy

This is considered a good reconstruction by Italian experts because it makes the message clear and the missing pieces (lacunae) are restored using a slightly different stone and having less detailed carving so that the intelligent observer can distinguish between original work and that which has been added, but at a distance the unity of the whole monument is not disrupted

Figure 17.4   Arch of Titus, Rome, Italy (detail)

By standing close to the arch, as in this detail, it is quite easy to distinguish the added material which because of its form completes the architectural design, but having less ornament it does not intrude and can be said to recede visually

246

Figure 17.5 Arch of
Constantine, Rome, Italy

*This monument was made up of
pieces from several sources so
perhaps it never had great artistic unity; however, the treatment
of lacunae has not improved its
presentation*

Figure 17.6 Arch of
Constantine, Rome, Italy

*The harsh texture and hard out-
line of the lacunae accentuate
their appearance undesirably, in
that they protrude rather than
recede*

Figure 17.7 The Pantheon, Rome, Italy (detail of brickwork on the drum)

The lacunae are too dark and textured so come forward visually and thus are unsatisfactory. Note the marvellous durability and texture of the second century brickwork with wide joints made of slaked lime and pozzuolana. Age gives material a patina that cannot be reproduced

Figure 17.8 The Pantheon, Rome, Italy

Original work can be recognized with difficulty amid much patching and repairs done in different ways at different times. To devise a presentation policy for such a building is difficult and to explain it to maintenance craftsmen even more difficult, but to ensure continuity of presentation policy over generations may even be impossible

commercial restorers apply will always look false after a short time. For metals, patina is defined as a film or incrustation produced by oxidization, which protects the metal surface and which does not make the message in the design more difficult to read. Corrosion is different from patina in that it does not protect the object. The Pentellic marble of which the Parthenon is built has acquired a marvellous patina through time, which makes new marble from the same quarry look quite out of place. Patina is precious because it can only be acquired by time.

Patina does not include accumulated dirt. When buildings and objects have to be cleaned, it is essential that the processes used should not destroy their patina. Time and circumstance can give an historic building many irregularities: stones may be cracked, edges worn or chipped and spalled and eroded; brickwork may have its arrises softened; wood may be textured by exposure and light; plaster, mosaics and floors may have uneven surfaces. All these irregularities should be conserved as part of the patina of an historic building. This point must be impressed upon craftsmen, for their natural impulse is to make something as good as new, i.e. to destroy patina, because, unless they can be given a sense of history, they will feel it is their duty to eliminate these irregularities. For the true presentation of historic buildings it is essential that patina, in all its forms, is respected.

Presentation and consolidation of ruins

Just as a skeleton is a more acceptable presentation than a decaying corpse, a ruin is a more sanitary state for a building when it is pronounced dead. If the building has incontrovertibly come to the end of its useful life and its cultural values do not justify the cost of re-evaluation and adaptive use, then a ruin should be created. This is particularly necessary in order to discourage vandalism and to avoid the shame of wanton decay.

A complete record drawing of the building should be made and all features and details recorded. Photogrammetry or simple elevational photos to scale can be invaluable. In the case of legal demolition by a developer for profit, logically the cost of recording should be borne by the person making the profit.

Next, all that is valuable should be removed: doors, windows and joinery such as stairs and panelling, then roof covering and timbers, and timber floors (but not vaults). The object is to remove all material that may decay but to leave walls of stone or brick with their openings standing. Some of the typical details should be stored in a library of building elements, as these are invaluable for study purposes.

The walling must be cleaned of all humus, as this

would encourage unwanted plant growth; the newly exposed tops should be sloped so as to shed all rain water and the walls themselves should be repaired and re-pointed if necessary. Usually, loose coats of plaster should be removed. The weathering of the tops of ruined walls needs careful attention, and as this area will be exposed to severe frost attack, asphalt or epoxy resin coatings will have to be applied if the material of the wall is not frost resistant. Holes left by the ends of beams should be filled to within one or two centimetres (less than 1 in) of the surface and then textured. In Britain, timber lintels, which would rot, should be replaced with reinforced concrete, but in some climates such timbers are durable. Vaulting should be retained with the upper surface water-proofed and weathered, provided there is no doubt as to its stability. All exposed surfaces must have good weathering to guide rain water away, and if large flats occur, they should be waterproofed and given rain-water spouts or drains.

The repair of a masonry wall that has lost its facing requires special attention. Often the face is liable to separate from the core, so replacement of some of the ashlar by through-binders may be necessary, but inserting reinforced concrete needles using a diamond-toothed coring drill is probably the cheaper and better method of providing bonding reinforcement. In certain cases it may be possible to insert corrosion-resistant bronze or stainless steel dowels, anchored in epoxy resin grout, if it is possible to conceal the small holes made by the drill. A broken wall should be racked back for stability while protecting the horizontal surfaces against the entry of rain water and frost attack. Stone dressings to copings, sills and cornices all require careful attention, just as in a living building. All ironwork must be removed to avoid rust stains and damage from expansion, and the scars pointed up. The ruin will have to be fully scaffolded in order to get it into good order; however, to avoid repetition of this expense, provision should be made for firm anchorages for cradles or working platforms of an appropriate type to facilitate future inspections, maintenance and repairs.

The layout of the ruin should be made clear to the visitor and this means marking out the alignment of vanished walls. This can be done by inserting lines of chipping between bricks or creosoted board kerbs in mown lawns. Building low upstanding walls which are much more difficult to mow around create a false impression, but box or beech hedges or even flower beds can be used to indicate old alignments.

Lettering and information notices are a matter for the expert and an appropriate type-face should be sought; inspiration may be obtained by looking at the local church monuments or tombstones of the period of the building's greatness, thus enhancing the

Figure 17.9   The Curia, Rome, Italy

The Curia was reconstructed under Mussolini, and it is difficult to determine what was original. Its scale and bulk are much too domineering with regard to excavations in the Forum and the hard outlines make it difficult to think that this building was contemporaneous with the ruins

Figure 17.10   Whitely Court, Worcestershire, England

An opulent Edwardian mansion in its heyday, then neglected and finally destroyed by fire. Was it worth conserving as a ruin? The parkland was an attractive asset for public use. What should the objective of the presentation policy be and how should the ruin be presented?

genius loci, retention of which is one of the objectives in creating a ruin. Ruins are romantic, so the growing of creepers and plants need not be entirely discouraged. Ivy, however, should not be permitted, and it should be remembered that Virginia creeper makes the inspecting architect's task more difficult. Limited amounts of moss and lichen are permissible and small plastic lined cups of soil may be introduced out of view on top of walls or ledges in order to grow wallflowers and stonecrop.

Anastylosis as a method of presenting ruins

The word 'anastylosis' is probably scarcely known to more than a few Anglo-Saxon practitioners of conservation, while on the other hand it is almost equivalent to conservation in the minds of some Latin experts. It is defined as the re-erection of fallen fragments of ruins in their original position. In countries where buildings are suddenly destroyed and towns abandoned by reason of disastrous earthquakes, the practice of anastylosis is general.

It is often difficult to decide whether anastylosis is justified. Meaningless heaps of stones do not give an instructive message to the beholder, but they might do so easily if the stones were re-erected correctly. The anastylosis of a few columns can give the viewer an indication of the spatial qualities of a collapsed building, but on the other hand may prevent an instructed visitor from understanding the historic phases of development of the building. The more interpretation is given before a visitor visits a site, the less anastylosis is necessary. The danger of anastylosis is that it may obliterate one phase of the development of a building at the expense of another: re-creation of a church may obliterate the earlier synagogue or vice versa.

Where a ruin is of one period only, then anastylosis is simpler, but it is never very simple; often, with the given evidence it is possible to proffer two or three probable solutions. Indeed, anastylosis is full of pitfalls, as the re-erection of fallen stones is never certain to be correct. Many examples can be quoted, but one of the earliest is Sir Arthur Evans's attempt to make Knossos more intelligible by re-erecting parts of the palace. Archaeologists now say he was wrong, but boatloads of cultural tourists to Crete have been grateful to him for the attempt, which helps them interpret and understand the site.

Perhaps the most noteworthy example of anastylosis is the re-erection of large parts of the colonnades of the Parthenon, the Propylaea and the Temple of Nike Apteros in Athens. The durability of the Pentellic marble was the saving factor, as most of the materials had been left in a heap after an

Figure 17.11   Whitely Court, Worcestershire, England

The Ancient Monuments Board considered that the historic and archaeological values were sufficient to justify the expense of making a ruin and so recommended this course of action to the Minister. Monuments in the church suggested an appropriate lettering style for the notices

explosion due to a bombardment. The problem now facing the Greek authorities is how to rectify the mistake of the previous restorer, who used techniques and materials that are irreversible and which prevent effective action now that industrial pollution is seeking out all the weaknesses.

It must be accepted that every attempt at anastylosis is potentially wrong; therefore the work must be made reversible, so that later, if more and better evidence comes to light, the former anastylosis can be changed.

Reconstruction as a form of presentation

Many historic monuments have been destroyed in warfare or by earthquake or other disasters. As an

Figure 17.12   South Triumphal Arch, Jerash, Jordan

The South Triumphal Arch was reconstructed leaving a rather hard outline on the right-hand side. The distant skyline must be considered as part of the monument as new buildings out of scale could destroy the message of a walled city, which should not have buildings outside its perimeter

Figure 17.14   Doorway to Byzantine Cathedral, Jerash, Jordan

This doorway and several columns were re-erected thereby giving the visitor a better chance to visualize the volume and architectural character of the building. Unfortunately, Portland cement was used for the work, giving the joints an unpleasant texture

Figure 17.13   The Festival Area, Jerash, Jordan

The colonnade is nearly all the result of anastylosis which helps the visitor visualize the space, but this policy should not be carried to extremes as it can give the impression of being a film set where everything is false. A spare concrete lintel still lies on the right-hand side

insurance against such events, full photogrammetric records are advisable; however, if a disaster occurs it is necessary that immediate action should be taken by first making a full archaeological record, and collecting all the materials including stones, bricks and broken glass that might be redeployed. These should be recorded as to exact location on a grid-lined map and methodically stored and protected against fire, theft, vandalism and neglect, any material needing conservation being given first-aid treatment. Such precautions immediately after a disaster can save great trouble and expense later.

The temples and monuments at Abu Simbel are a special case of reconstruction, as these had to be moved because of the inundation following the building of the High Dam at Aswan. They were dismantled and re-erected on another island site modelled on the original. Although some of their significance has been lost as they are now divorced from their original site, it was the only way in which they could be preserved. It is theoretically wrong to remove entire architectural units to museums, for they lose their poetry and artistic value when taken away from their natural setting. It is always preferable to reconstruct them on the spot, giving adequate protection, as has been done at Lepis Magna in Libya and Baalbeck in Syria and with the Arch of Titus in the Roman Forum.

251

Figure 17.15   Undercroft, York Minster, England
(Courtesy: Shepherd Building Group Ltd)

To help interpret the messages of the site of York Minster a second century Roman wall which was found during the excavations for new foundations was left in position. It was waterproofed by injection. Fragments of plaster found in the mud were put together in three years of patient work and then displayed, as shown on the right, together with a drawing showing the probable scheme of decoration

Figure 17.16   South transept, York Minster, England
(Courtesy: Shepherd Building Group Ltd)

The important discovery of the remains of the second century Roman legionary headquarters basilica under York Minster posed problems of presentation. Where and how should this column drum be displayed and what was the objective of their presentation? An attempt was made to educate visitors and convey the history of the site

Figure 17.17   Undercroft, York Minster, England
(Courtesy: Shepherd Building Group Ltd)

The interpretation was arranged in historical sequence ending up with an exhibition of the work involved in consolidating the fabric between 1967 and 1972. Although the Roman column in the foreground did not conform to the historic sequence of the display, it was re-erected in its original position to show the Roman phase of use of the Minster site

Anastylosis and reconstruction, if over-done or carried out without adequate study and documentation, can turn an historic site into a film set. They are justified if they enhance the message in the monument and make its spatial qualities more easily understood.

Interpretation of the messages

There are many messages to be found in historic buildings and sites, so interpretation may run the risk of manipulation. A good guide will always tell one something worth while, but well-trained guides with the command of many languages are all too rare: generally one has to fight off importunate would-be purveyors of misinformation and mispronunciation, who are more of a liability than an asset. The cultural tourist who has come a long way to visit, see and understand, is entitled to serious consideration and should be willing to pay for interpretation of the site or building. Interpretation can take many forms—simple printed leaflets, plans, illustrated guides and histories, models showing phases of development and museums showing artefacts related to the site. Son et Lumière is yet another form of interpretation, using history in dramatic spoken form with dynamic lighting effects of great variety. All interpretation must be based upon scholarly and accurate information derived from all of the conservation team.

Colonial Williamsburg is a good example of interpretation and the US National Park Service has led the way in showing how much interpretation can add to one's enjoyment in visiting a site. Interpretation facilities, together with restaurants, hotels, car parks and lavatories, need careful consideration in relation to an historic site. The architects who design these facilities must be extremely sensitive to the *genius loci* of the monument, as well as the surrounding landscape.

253

18

Cost control of conservation projects

Causes of increased costs

Efficient cost control systems that favour the conservation of historic buildings are desirable in that they make scarce resources go further. Flexibility, however, is essential, as each historic building is individual and in a sense is the real client or patient—its demands must be taken as paramount if the situation requires it, as in the case of the Leaning Tower of Pisa or York Minster.

Inefficient systems increase the cost by as much as 300%, thus working against conservation in general. In architectural conservation, expensive mistakes can be made due to the lack of an initial inspection which considers the building in its setting as a whole, to wrong diagnosis, to restrictive codes of practice, to clumsy administrative and contractual procedures, to lack of flexibility and poor supervision, and above all to bureaucratic delays, due to lack of specific responsibility.

The effect of faulty contractual procedures may be judged from the following authentic, but necessarily anonymous examples:

(1) A roof was damaged when glazing was repaired, because no protection was specified.
(2) Confusion results because of an unresolved policy of presentation. There are frequent changes of plan as art historical and archaeological ideas alternately prevail when there should have been an architectural synthesis. Changes in plan disorganize labour, reduce productivity and enthusiasm, and cost money.
(3) A building was virtually rebuilt by a contractor, because he was paid for the amount of new stone he incorporated. Supervision was poor.
(4) A contractor strengthening a building inserts concrete beams cutting away wall paintings of great historic value which were concealed by whitewash.

(5) A beautiful dome has to be renewed, because a contractor, who had no knowledge of conservation and no respect for a ninth century masterpiece, was given a 'design and build' contract.
(6) Part of a building fell down after a contractor had been at work several years, because nobody had inspected the building as a whole and warned him that this part was the most vulnerable.

There are many examples of wrong technology, for example the use of cement mortars, wrong cleaning techniques, chemical toxic hazards to occupants by use of dieldrin and chemicals containing dioxin.

Numerous other cases could be quoted, but the ultimate cause lies in faulty contractual procedures and the fact that nobody was responsible. Personal responsibility is the only guarantee that conservation will be efficiently carried out. In bureaucracies, responsibility has the unfortunate propensity of evaporating within a short time.

Preliminary estimates

After the initial inspection has been made, the problems of the building as whole can be presented with preliminary estimates by the professional adviser for the information of the funding authority. Such estimates should express reasonable doubt and be given in two inseparable figures, (a) and (b): (a) the realistic cost of the works, and (b) the worst possible cost of the works.

Inflation, which is a politico-economic problem, makes estimating very difficult as it introduces the time element which is very much in doubt at this stage. Estimates can only be given at current prices (i.e. allowing for inflation in the next six months); therefore, if the funding organization has a system of indexing costs, so much the better. Estimates should ideally be built up with costs of labour, materials, plant and overheads. If any one of these items fluctuates then it is easy to revise. The unit rate method for defined quantities of work is extremely difficult to apply to conservation projects, particularly as rates may not exist for many of the items of work.

Operational specifications necessary

To assist pricing, an operational specification should be prepared, which gives the general order of work on a room-by-room basis for the interior or for each feature externally, under five headings—removals, repairs, alterations, services and decoration or finishing—and describes each operation in detail. From this, the labour can be extracted by trades and a list made of the materials needed. Heating, ventilating, hot and cold water systems, electric installations and plant generally are renewed, and must be designed as a whole so these can be costed separately by specialists, but it is important to specify all the attendance necessary on a room-by-room basis.

Pricing contracts

In normal contracts, building contractors add a substantial element to their price for the risk and are quite legitimately paid for protecting the funding body. In conservation work, the risks are high and often cannot be resolved until the work is well under way. It is considered that the funding body should accept these risks and that is why estimates are given in the (a) and (b) form mentioned earlier. The risk is reduced if full studies of all alternative methods of conservation are made after the initial inspection. They are further reduced if it is possible to open up and explore hidden parts of the building, much as surgeons make exploratory operations.

Scarce materials and skills are another problem that may have to be faced. Shortages of bricks or tiles of the right type, lack of good hydraulic limes and the impossibility of getting wrought iron or matching glass are typical problems that have to be solved. To do so properly assumes professional time and costs money, yet if they are not solved in advance the smooth running of a complicated building contract may be jeopardized and even greater costs incurred.

Programme of works—scaffolding and plant

The programme of works should now be considered. There is a right size of team and right balance of skills for each conservation operation. Archaeological projects, art historical investigations and conservation of works of art have to be given their proper place in the programme. Generally it is better to have fewer highly skilled men working rather longer than too many, for too many men crowd a job and give less flexibility, although too few get lost and overawed by a large building.

Closely linked to programming is the question of supply of scaffolding. Complicated conservation work often needs special scaffolding for a long time, or in a large project scaffolding may have to be moved frequently. Scaffolding should therefore be entirely under the control of the contractor, moved and adjusted by him, as and when required. The contractor must be responsible for and zealous with regard to all safety precautions.

The use of construction plant is another aspect of programming. It is expensive to have hired plant standing by doing nothing. Nowadays, there is such a diversity of plant that a skilled contractor can, by applying it correctly, save considerable costs. The programme and the scale of the work dictate these matters.

On conservation works, because of the number of unforeseeable hazards, flexible programming is essential. The principle is: *continuous work for the right sized team.* Stopping and starting work causes real costs to escalate and leaves expensive plant idle. Programming building work is a specialist skill, but all operations follow the classic time/cost curve, being slow to start, rapid and productive in the middle and slow to finish. In conservation work, even more time should be allowed for finishing, for this is where artists and craftsmen need time to do good quality work. Completion dates, however important, should always be arranged with a good contingency factor so as not to spoil the work.

It is nowadays possible to program a computer with labour and materials, to which can be added costs per hour, plant and overheads, so giving an accurate estimate of the anticipated cost of the operation in print-outs at regular intervals. It should be mentioned that this sophistication is only possible for major operations. Otherwise, simple graphs of cost plotted against time are the most valuable and deception-proof techniques.

Control systems based on regular inspections

Control systems should now be examined. The usual method of governments is to vote so much money for conservation of historic buildings and this is subdivided in various ways, often without any relationship to the actual need of the building or availability of professional staff, so that unco-ordinated projects, carried out in a spasmodic and piecemeal way, result.

Assuming that all documentation has been carried out at a national level, ideally government should have all its classified historic buildings inspected regularly on at least a five-year basis for the purpose of formally estimating their requirements under the headings described earlier, i.e. immediate and urgent repairs and minor works, necessary works (major works or a rolling programme if suitable), and desirable works (whose need is foreseen in 10–15 years)—noting items to be kept under observation.

Such regular formal inspections and reports will be supplemented by frequent supervision and informal visits by professional staff. After 10–15 years, the real cost of the conservation of the historic buildings will be seen to drop, because the principles of strategic preventive maintenance have been applied. Professional staff will get more and more expert in this matter as time goes on. It is important, however, to delegate appropriate responsibility for authorizing immediate and urgent repairs to qualified professionals, as this will save time and administrative costs and above all *prevent further damage*. For example, 1000 US dollars spent on eradicating an attack of *Merulius lacrimans* (dry rot) in good time, can save 40 000 dollars one year later. Grant procedures and attendant bureaucracy can be too slow for the reality of historic buildings.

Long-term planning

'Necessary' and 'desirable' schemes can be handled differently and brought forward by stages from preparation to estimating and approval. Once approved, however, there must be sufficient funds to complete the schemes according to programme. This will mean budgeting a contingency fund. This fund will be necessary, because however well the conservation of historic buildings is planned there will be occasional unforeseeable surprises—for instance, an unexpectedly severe winter may accelerate the decay of stone which it was planned to restore in two or three years' time, or there may be an exceptional gale, a flood or even an earthquake in some countries.

Approval and execution of a project

The funding body will consider the total cost of the conservation project. This should be compared with the cost of building anew on a unit cost per square metre. If the cost is two-thirds or less, it can be claimed that conservation is saving building costs. If more, the cost of a new infrastructure of roads and services, of demolition and delay will have to be considered in economic terms. One must not forget, however, the cultural social and political values of conservation when making a final assessment of the cost and benefits of the scheme.

Also, before a conservation project is approved by the competent authority, the work should be evaluated according to the principles of conservation: (1) is it the minimum necessary—not more; (2) is it reversible (this may not be possible but it should not prejudice future interventions); (3) does it adhere to the Venice Charter (or its equivalent) and the ethics outlined in the Introduction to this book?

The specific objective of the particular conservation scheme should be confirmed and the presentation policy agreed by the competent authority with the responsible professional—the person to whom complete authority, within the budget, will be delegated. Having had his scheme approved he will supervise and co-ordinate the execution of the project. Thereafter, the building becomes his client. These provisions are necessary to ensure: (a) rapid and correct decision-making, which saves money, and (b) coherent artistic treatment, or avoidance of confusion, which also saves money.

The expert in charge can always ask for advice, but his alone must be the responsibility for saving cultural property. He will lead a multidisciplinary team and ensure good communication by regular on-site meetings. He will confirm his instructions clearly in writing. He should report the budgetary situation once quarterly. In his control of his overall budget he should break this down into target costs for recognizable items of work, and so prevent one item from 'robbing' another.

Forms of contract

There are many hazards in a contract for conservation work. One of the techniques should be to reduce the unknown dimension by preliminary opening up and detailed exploration. All archaeological work should be done in advance of a building contract, if this is possible.

Flexibility is therefore necessary in arranging suitable forms of contract. If it is a simple item of fairly common work, not requiring skills that are difficult to obtain, an adjustable 'lump sum' contract with 10% included for contingencies is reasonable. If a large amount of carpentry repair is involved, provisional figures for labour and material can be priced competitively within such a 'lump sum'. 'Design and build' types of contract are totally inappropriate for historic buildings, for with these the architectural conservator abdicates his responsibilities and, in effect, hands them over to a contractor not trained in building conservation. 'Design and build' proposals may lead to the cheapest solution, so are liked by

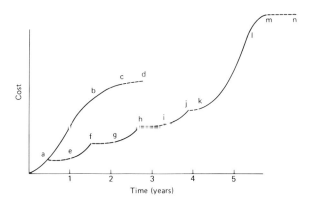

Method A: a, *slow start*; a–b, *major tasks and steady progress*; b–c, *slower progress due to detailed finishes and skilled work*; d, *furnishing and balancing of mechanical services*

Method B: a, *slow start but stop*; e, *start again but stop*; f, *start again but stop*; g, *start again but stop*; h, *start again but stop*; i *start and* j *stop*; k, *somebody says job must be finished that year so it re-starts and is pushed ahead regardless of cost and workmanship, but it cannot be completed by* l; m, *it is now late, and* n *furnishing also needs doing*

A cost/time graph is a simple way of monitoring a complicated job; every contract should use one, even if more sophisticated methods of programming are also applied. Of the two methods shown, method B takes longer, costs much more, gives less job satisfaction to everyone and the workmanship is less good than it should be

Figure 18.1   Two methods of financing a conservation contract: method A (top curve), budget for whole cost; method B (bottom curve), annual budget increments

administrators, but cost is not the only factor to consider in a contract for conservation work.

On anything complicated, it has been found that payment for the actual labour, materials and plant used is the best basis, provided one selects an efficient contractor, whose administration is sound and whose standards of work are known to be good. Such a firm can save 15% or 20% of the costs of conservation work by good organization, so it is not worth quarrelling about 5% in his 'on costs'. The system recommended is that competing contractors of equal quality should give target figures for the cost of the work, based on their assessment of labour, materials and plant, and then should add a percentage for their managerial services. This percentage is the competitive element. There are some subtle and some too-subtle variations of this type of contract. All contracts depend on good and efficient co-operation, but if the builder is treated and trusted as a professional, he will also make his contribution to reducing the cost of conservation.

Conclusion

A good professional will lead and educate his building team. The work may appear to be slow to start with, but once the work-force understand, they will take great pride in the honour of giving good work to historic buildings, which they know also belong to them.

One of the pleasures an architect has in this work is direct contact with skilled craftsmen—together a difficult problem is faced which neither architect nor craftsman can solve independently, so the architect says: 'I do not know how to solve this problem, what are your ideas Mr Craftsman'. A proposal will be put, and discussed and modified by the concepts of conservation which the architect must apply within his vision of the building as a whole. Then, after perhaps an hour, the insoluble problem is solved to each party's satisfaction; the craftsman knows what to do—and he executes the work with real satisfaction because he has been consulted as an equal. As bad workmanship and mistakes cannot be afforded in conservation work, the supervising architect must give his time to this form of consultation, from which he will learn a lot.

Conservation of historic buildings is, as stressed earlier, multidisciplinary teamwork, in which we must respect each genuine contribution and to which we must all give of our best.

19

Rehabilitation of historic buildings

Introduction

In this chapter we will mainly consider the vast number of buildings that are 100 years old or more and which make up the bulk of our urban environment. Historic buildings differ from most other cultural property in that they generally have to be used and also withstand dead and live loadings and resist all the causes of decay.

Often it is necessary to find an appropriate use in order to prevent a building's decay or destruction, this being one of the hardest problems to solve in the practice of architectural conservation. The practice of adapting buildings for new uses is as old as time. A classic example is the Castel St Angelo, which began as Hadrian's Mausoleum, was turned into a fortress, a papal residence, a prison and now is a museum and tourist attraction. Another Roman example are the Baths of Diocletian—Michelangelo made a church out of the main hall and the other parts are now a museum, cinema and planetarium. In England, the King's Manor at York was built in the thirteenth century as the lodgings of an abbot, then used as a king's palace in the sixteenth century, an administrative centre in the seventeenth century, fell on bad times in the eighteenth century as tenements, was used as a workshop for blind persons in the nineteenth century and then as a university building in the twentieth century. In each case, the building was re-evaluated and found useful, so it survived, but with some rehabilitation.

As has been shown historically, rehabilitation was a natural process in the fabric of a living town or in the life of a well-built construction. Nowadays, due to the rapidly changing patterns of life and scale of activities, a more conscious approach must be adopted, especially if all the values in historic buildings and towns are to be recognized, preserved and used.

Rehabilitation has social, cultural and economic advantages. Social, in that people and towns keep their identity; cultural, in that artistic, architectural, archaeological and documentary values can be preserved both for their intrinsic value and their contribution to the identity of the town; economic, in that (a) existing capital is used, (b) energy is saved, (c) demolition costs are avoided, and (d) the existing infrastructure of roads and services is utilized.

In addition, rehabilitation causes far less human upheaval, political friction and physical delay, so it is not surprising that when the total budget is considered, rehabilitation in most cases saves money.

Setting up rehabilitation schemes

How does one start a rehabilitation scheme? A multidisciplinary team is necessary. In the scheme prepared for Chesterfield, England, in which the author participated, the town provided administrators, town planners, engineers, quantity surveyors, a traffic manager and a health officer, to which were added two historic architects expert in conservation, a development architect, a landscape architect and an urban planner, and last but not least a development economist. The team met regularly to discuss their work and to establish priorities (which had to respect all the values in the historic town centre). Two aspects of this teamwork should be emphasized: first, consultations with owners and residents, and representatives of community organizations such as the Chamber of Commerce and Civic Society in the case of Chesterfield; secondly, detailed surveys.

The study of the values in the buildings and spaces that make up an historic district is based on several different surveys, which analyse the historic development, growth, functions, services and amenities of an

area and the condition of each building under consideration. In one word the 'typology' of the action
area or of an individual building is studied. Inspections and surveys of each building involve the making
of measured drawings, preferably to 1/50 scale and a
detailed schedule of all defects that can be noted. This
study is crucial and the work necessary to each building can then be assessed under the main headings,
immediate, urgent, necessary and desirable (which
are defined in Chapter 13), and costed to see that the
proposals can be justified.

In the survey of the building any shortfall in
potential users' requirements should be noted, but in
considering the neighbourhood as a whole it may be
found that these requirements are met in another
way. The rehabilitation team will recommend the
most suitable use for each building after making their
studies. Ideally the new use should involve the
minimum change, as this will preserve the values in
the building and tend to reduce costs, so the closer
the new use is to the original the better, generally.

Rehabilitation policy

When they understand the benefits of rehabilitation,
town planners, building economists and architects
can co-operate to re-use our existing stock of buildings either by reviving their original use or finding
some suitable use in the context of the needs of the
community. Historic buildings with a wide range of
differently sized rooms have survived successfully
because of their adaptability to many different types of
use. It may be found that building regulations for a
proposed new use require floors to be strengthened
and calculations may show that foundations become
overloaded and that costly strengthening becomes
necessary. If this is the case, one should first
reconsider the use and see if a more suitable alternative is possible. It is only by considering all the
relevant factors that the multidisciplinary team will
find the 'least bad' solution.

Often the superficial appearance of buildings leads
people to pessimistic opinions, because they only
judge by appearances and cannot imagine the results
of a rehabilitation scheme. The cost of rehabilitation is
something that seems to frighten people before a
proper examination is made (and this is not helped by
the addition of VAT). It is true that lack of traditional
skills and bad site management by builders without
the flexible organization that is necessary can inflate
the cost. The real cost depends on the structural
condition of the building, the proposed use, the skill
of the architects in devising plans and the most suitable contract procedures, and the skill and organization of the builders. Contract procedures and cost

control need the special techniques dealt with in
Chapter 18.

The ownership pattern will affect the possibilities
and also the design solutions available. Protracted
procedures should be avoided, as these can lead to
planning blight and financial hardship, coupled with
political discontent. Two half schemes are better than
one long delayed whole. Another danger in delay is in
lack of maintenance of the properties, and a lesson
that can be passed on is that someone should be made
responsible for the care of vacant properties and see
that roofs are repaired after gales and that gutters are
not allowed to get blocked or, in case of frost, that the
water system is drained.

No historic building should be pulled down until
every effort has been made to find a beneficial use by
rehabilitation. As cities are living things, the
occasional need for renewal is accepted, but this is
work for architects with special sensitivity and ability
to analyse the problem and design in the idiom of
today, yet respecting the identity and character of the
historic town.

To sum up, to approach this complicated problem
the typology of an historic zone or building must be
studied fully before any proposals are formed, the
principle of minimum intervention must be applied
and authorities must have a presumption in favour of
conservation—then our cities will keep their identity,
character and atmosphere and the communities will
benefit culturally and economically.

Studies and guidelines

To avoid unnecessary and damaging alterations, the
new use should be as close to the original as possible.
The history and archaeology of the building must be
carefully studied, so that the architect is aware of the
sequence in which the fabric was put together. Art
historians and archaeologists should study the fabric
with the architect and advise him on what material is
of special value. The architect must work with
history—not against it.

The US Secretary of the Interior has laid down
Standards for Rehabilitation for certification in order
to obtain tax relief, which incorporate the above
principles. The standards, together with guidelines
amplifying recommended procedures, have been
immensely successful.

Rehabilitation is generally considered a sound
economic proposition if the cost of such work does
not exceed two-thirds of the cost of building anew the
same area. This figure includes an allowance for a less
efficient (but often much more interesting) use of
floor space in the historic building. To meet this
requirement the building should at least have sound

walls and floors. The roof may be defective and need re-covering, rainwater disposal may need redesign and renewal, windows and doors may be faulty and decoration in need of total redoing. It is also to be assumed that all services are defective and obsolete, for it is generally the case that they will need total renewal. It needs understanding of the building as a 'spatial environmental system' and great skill to modernize the mechanical and electrical services of an historic building. Of course, the use of the existing urban infrastructure and avoiding costs of demolition is a bonus for rehabilitation.

Applications of building regulations

New regulations are always more strict and comprehensive than the ones they replace, and this progress represents a danger to historic buildings, as often officials responsible for their application do not consider the fundamental purposes of such regulations, but seek to apply them mechanically in a detailed way, so as to avoid the necessity of making a possibly troublesome decision.

It is often difficult to comply with the details of building regulations, which fall into three groups: structural, fire and security and hygiene. The rehabilitation appraisal should consider each group separately. Structural regulations and codes have been made to help designers of new buildings, so if the building has survived 100 years satisfactorily, it can be deemed to have met the purpose of the regulations.

Building regulations give the superimposed loadings that have to be carried by floors for various types of use. If there is a change of use, strengthening floors to meet increased loadings in offices often presents difficult problems and if storage of paper or books, as in a library, is proposed the greatly increased loads present serious problems first in the floor structure, then possibly in the walls and foundations, in which case the proposal may not be practical for economic reasons. Fortunately, walls and foundations of historic buildings generally have a considerable reserve of load-carrying capacity.

In an earthquake zone, an historic building may need strengthening, which can be put in hand when a suitable opportunity given by rehabilitation occurs, but it should never be condemned to destruction because of failure to comply with regulations. The record of earthquakes in Skopje and Montenegro shows that well-maintained historic buildings are surprisingly earthquake resistant, because of the high quality of their workmanship.

Fire regulations covering fire resistance and means of escape must be complied with fully, but with intelligence, for fire is a deadly serious matter. The risk can be reduced by restricting the uses to which the building is put, and to a limited extent assets such as thick walls and well-constructed doors can be traded off against nominal deficiencies. For safety, much can depend upon the installation of automatic warning devices and sprinklers, as well as the efficiency of the local fire-fighting service, including access for fire fighting, a matter to which town planners responsible for historic quarters in cities should give consideration. Often, additional doors required as smoke checks have to be inserted in such a way as not to spoil the aesthetics of the historic building. The fire resistance of doors may be improved by adding fire-resistant sheets to one side and by making rebates in the frame deeper and of hardwood. Ceilings and floors may be improved by putting fire-resistant sheets under a plaster finish or by thickening the floor covering with plywood and treating timbers with a fire retardant. Joinery and external woodwork should be painted with fire-retardant paints. In such detailed ways the fire resistance and safety of an historic building can be raised to meet modern standards.

Improved hygiene is one of the basic requirements of rehabilitation, yet standards relating to space about buildings, light and air are often not possible to meet and should be waived if forced ventilation and adequate artificial light can be provided. Such standards are not absolute, and experience of historic quarters has proved that excellent living conditions can be had without them, especially if children do not have to be considered. Provision of clean water, good sewerage, gas, electricity, heating, ventilation and efficient rainwater disposal are all necessary. Access must be given for refuse collection, fire fighting and fuel deliveries.

An understanding of the purpose of the building codes and regulations is necessary to deal with them in a flexible way. Limitation of the possible uses and type of tenant may help. If a building has good points in one direction, it may be possible to trade some of its assets for deficiencies in another.

Surviving historic buildings have *ipso facto* 'long life', are 'flexible' and require 'low energy' input in their construction. Insulation values in roofs, wall linings and between floors are generally easy to improve during rehabilitation, so energy requirements in use can be effectively reduced, by inserting glass wool in roofs and floors and linings backed with aluminium foil to walls.

Flexible planning

The suitability of historic buildings for a large number of possible uses, i.e. flexibility in planning, depends to a large extent on the mix of room sizes. Small rooms of 2–3 m² (20–35 ft²) are suitable as lavatories, bathrooms, larders and stores; rooms of 8–12 m² (85–130 ft²) as single bedrooms, kitchens, dining spaces, clerks' offices, etc. Rooms of 12–16 m² (130–180 ft²) can be used as living rooms, dining rooms, double bedrooms, managers' offices, workshops and garages. Above 16 m² (180 ft²) there is a wide range of possible uses, including subdivision. The above figures are entirely subjective, as no proper study is known to have been done.

Measured drawings and full investigation of the building are necessary before starting a rehabilitation project. Ideally, the internal environment should be measured and recorded over a year in order to provide design data. Structural analysis and studies of the moisture content of walls and relative humidity will possibly be necessary. Using drawings to 1/50 scale, in order to show all the existing detail, alternative schemes can be prepared and costed. Drawings show possibilities that could not be visualized in the first instance. Often architects, faced with the difficulties of rehabilitation, find surprising and exciting possibilities which could not be produced when designing new buildings.

Introduction of modern building services

Modern services present a great challenge, so will be dealt with in some detail, for often it is difficult to reconcile their technical requirements with the principles of conservation.

All mechanical, electrical and also acoustical services must be considered together in the rehabilitation of an historic building. In one sense it can be said that nowadays a building is as old as its services; certainly, new life can be given to an old building by renewing the services. However, the fabric of the historic building was not designed to take modern plant, so the installation of new services raises acute technical and artistic problems and will certainly alter the balance of the spatial environmental system.

In designing the services, their eventual renewal and replacement must be considered, as well as accessibility for maintenance. Ducts should always be sized generously in case larger dimensions are required at a later date. It is always wise to insert one extra conduit for 'X', the service that has not yet been invented, or for which a need was not foreseen.

The heating system

Improved space heating is one of the most difficult aspects of rehabilitation, for the effect of this will be to lower the relative humidity and also cause condensation in unheated spaces. There is also danger in the use of old flues which are not capable of withstanding the temperatures produced by modern boilers; ceramic or insulated stainless steel flue liners are probably necessary precautions against the risk of fire.

Continuous background heating at a low temperature is generally best for fuel economy and for the fabric itself. Local heating can then be used to boost the background heat when required. With buildings of large thermal mass, intermittent heating does not produce real comfort, because the walls do not have time to warm up and it has a damaging effect on the contents of the building, particularly if they are art treasures made of wood.

Figure 19.1 St Angelo in Pescheria, Rome, Italy
This building is almost completely made of recycled material

262

The following checklist gives the points that must be considered relating to the user, the building and plant requirements:

User factors
(1) (a) Background, (b) full or (c) intermittent heating.
(2) (a) Temperatures required, (b) air changes, (c) relative humidity.
(3) (a) Cost of heating plant, (b) can running costs be afforded?
(4) (a) Type of control system suitable.

Building factors
(1) Exposure, wind tightness.
(2) Heat loss—can insulation reduce this effectively?
(3) Dampness, humidity, danger to structure and contents.
(4) Thermal mass, internal volumes, window/wall ratio.
(5) Space available for plant and fittings.

Heating plant factors
(1) Cost of fuel and labour.
(2) Size of boiler and expected life of plant and distribution system.
(3) Type of fuel and economic amount to be stored.
(4) Possible methods of production, delivery, dispersal and control of heat output.

Fuel costs depend much on governmental policy and foreign affairs. The era of cheap energy is at an end and since the future is unpredictable, it is advisable to plan for alternative fuels. In Britain, stoker singles have consistently been the least expensive fuel, provided the building owner has sufficient bulk storage and efficient handling arrangements. Anthracite has become expensive, coke difficult to obtain, oil after being very cheap is now becoming costly, and town gas was costly but natural gas was cheap before government policy raised the cost. Electricity has always been costly and is vulnerable to power cuts. In rural areas the amount of power available is often insufficient and, being a high-grade form of energy, electricity should not be wasted on heating unless used to power a heat pump. One of the lessons of the past is that heating plant should be convertible. Light oil is easily converted to gas. Sectional boilers will burn almost anything, but with varying output and efficiency. Labour costs are often critical in formulating a choice for the preferred fuel. Commercial efforts were made by adjusting tariffs favourable to make electric heating popular through storage heaters and underfloor heating, but the latter proved dangerous to the fabric on clay soils as it dried out the ground and caused shrinkage of the soil under

shallow foundations. Solar energy is now being exploited in countries with suitable climate, but with the British climate it is unreliable for heating.

In an historic building, sufficient space may not be available for the heating plant of desired capacity, so choice may be dictated by this factor. Water tube boilers fired by high-efficiency gas or high-grade oil may be found to be the most compact units, taking less space than a sectional boiler with underfeed stoker or conventional oil burner. The space needed to store fuel is another material consideration, it being normal to keep three weeks' supply, but the economics of delivery transport may mean increasing the storage space. Coals tend to deteriorate when stored, while oil does not, although it may precipitate some sludge. Gas and electricity, of course, pose no storage problems, but for this reason the building owner is vulnerable to breakdowns and strikes.

Besides the space needed for fuel storage, space and disposal arrangements must be made for ashes and clinkers. Storage of the products of combustion must allow for the fact that they probably contain a good deal of sulphur which may cause corrosion and decay.

Soot deposit is a sign of poor combustion, which should be checked by flue gas analysis. Good arrangements should be made for cleaning flues and renewing fire bricks in boilers and flues. The size and height of the flue are usually recommended by the services consultant, recognizing the fact that undersizing will reduce the life of the boiler. The air intake for combustion must be at least three times the flue area. The flue should be properly designed to meet the requirements of the fuel and to avoid condensation at the top, which is particularly likely with gas heating.

It should be remembered that flueless gas and oil heaters produce water vapour, which increases the relative humidity inside a building, together with the danger of condensation.

An obtrusive new chimney may be considered objectionable. One way of lowering its height is to divide the flue into several sections, another is to fit an extractor fan. The height in relation to the rest of the building must be considered, as flue gases containing sulphur dioxide can be reduced by careful choice of fuel; some heavy oils having a very high sulphur content of up to 6%, whereas light oils have 1–1½% and natural gas none. The sulphur content of coals varies considerably, but about half is retained in the ash, so the emission of sulphur dioxide is reduced.

Distribution systems for heat consist of pipe runs or ducts for hot air. Hot air heating has the advantage of being capable of upgrading to include humidification and air conditioning, if there is sufficient space for the additional plant. It creates a positive air pressure

Figure 19.2   Theatre of Marcellus (23–13 B.C.), Rome, Italy

The ruins of the theatre were turned into the Orsini strong-hold and later adapted as resi-dential accommodation. All periods of building should be respected

Figure 19.3   Castel St Angelo (A.D. 135), Rome, Italy

Built first as the magnificent tomb to the great Emperor Hadrian, later converted into a papal fortress and prison, now a museum

Figure 19.4 Baths of Diocletian (A.D. 302), Rome, Italy

The frigidarium was converted by Michelangelo into a church, St Maria degli Angeli, in the sixteenth century, so retaining the spatial qualities of the original structure. Other parts of the bath-house the National Museum (c. nineteenth century), a cinema (c. twentieth century), a planetarium and residences

which reduces the ingress of draughts and dust. However, long duct runs are awkward and expensive and difficult to install. The architect must work out all pipe runs in detail, to see that they rise in concealed places such as behind shutters and curtains and generally follow the principles of camouflage. Encasing of pipes is not always to be recommended, as their heat output is valuable and the casing may look clumsier than the pipe itself. The placement of furniture must be planned before radiator and thermostat positions can be settled, after which pipe runs can be confirmed. The cost of the builder's work in connection with heating, normally 10–15%, may rise considerably if special holes have to be drilled in order to pass pipes through thick masonry.

In designing delivery and dispersal systems, the position of doors and windows, which create draughts, is an important factor. In high buildings the introduction of heating by convection will create air movement, resulting in down-draughts from high windows. The path of draughts can be traced by use of smoke. High buildings can have a steep temperature gradient, which is not conducive to fuel economy, so a dispersal system such as radiant heating by overhead panels or floor panels is more efficient. Forced warm air from local heater units can also overcome the problems of down-draught and temperature gradient, otherwise a heating coil or tube must be placed under each high window, which is unsightly.

Heat is mainly dispersed in a building by radiation and convection, conduction playing only a small part in the process. Floor panels and ceiling panels are the usual method of providing radiant heat. Floor panels

put the heat where it is wanted and do not induce draughts to such an extent as other methods, but are sluggish in their response to controls and suitable only for continuous heating. Edge and ground insulation is necessary. With no pipes and radiators showing, floor heating is the ideal proposition for an historic building, especially if the floor needs relaying, but it is expensive.

Radiators, which are really convectors, are the common method of heat dispersal. Cast iron is much more durable than pressed steel, but valves and fittings eventually corrode. Sizing and siting of radiators requires the detailed attention of the architect, as spaces can be ruined by badly proportioned radiators and clumsy pipe runs. Convector radiators are not efficient in tall buildings, as they build up a steep temperature gradient. However, fan-assisted convectors are better in this respect and are more powerful in relation to their size, so are more economical in regard to pipework. The fan enables the radiator to cover a larger area horizontally and hot and cold air is mixed, reducing draughts. An extension of this, using piped cold water in summer, gives a simple type of local air conditioning at the expense of an extra pair of pipes, as was done in the Jefferson Library in New York City. Fan-assisted convectors are flexible in design and can be integrated with the fitting of an historic building in an unobtrusive way. However, they are noisy when the fans are running at high speed and have to be cleaned out at least once a year to remove dust and fluff from the gilled convector tubes.

Heated carpets, electrical tubular heaters and high

265

Figure 19.5   Diocletian Palace (A.D. 300), Split, Yugoslavia

Much of the fabric of the palace remains, but it all has been re-used in many ways; the mausoleum became a cathedral, while shops, offices and residences comprise the remainder

Figure 19.6   King's Manor (13th and 17th cent.), York, England

This was originally the residence of the mitred abbot of St. Mary's Monastery and rebuilt as such, then taken as a palace by Henry VIII and used as administrative headquarters of the Council of the North; after that it became tenements, followed by a school for the blind and now, after rehabilitation which cost 60% of the cost of the same area in new construction, is used by the Institute of Advanced Architectural Studies

Figure 19.7   Gargonza (near Sansovino), Italy

A fortified mediaeval village was no longer inhabited. Being in beautiful countryside, the owner has made a success of turning it into a self-service hotel with houses of a wide variety of sizes and a restaurant which shows in the foreground

266

temperature electric radiant panels, portable oil or gas heaters can all be used for intermittent heating with partial degrees of success where the cost of proper solutions cannot be met.

Electrical services

An historic building generally has a primitive electric installation, which may have been altered and extended by either professionals or amateurs. Early electrical installations with wooden covers or, later, conduit with vulcanized insulating rubber cables, or lead and rubber sheathed wiring, if more than 20 years old, are likely to be defective and impossible to alter safely. Obsolete wiring, bad earthing, over-loaded cables, defective insulation, contact with combustible material giving rise to serious risk of fire, are all to be expected. The first stage is a survey and test by an electrician, who should provide a wiring plan. The standard tests for insulation and earthing often give an optimistic picture, especially as they are made before any rehabilitation work, which could cause a breakdown in brittle insulation.

With rehabilitation, a greater use of electricity is likely. Certain uses of electricity, such as cooking or heating, may well have to be excluded if there is inadequate power supply. The regularity of the power supply should also be ascertained and, with special uses, duplicate supplies may be essential or alternatively a standby generator provided, with automatic changeover gear. If fire fighting depends upon the electric supply, standby plant may be essential, and certainly all fire-detection plant should have a secure supply such as storage batteries with a.c./d.c. conversion charging gear.

New wiring systems may be of polyvinylchloride sheathed cable, or mineral insulated copper cable covered with plastic. The former is cheap, but the latter, costing about 30% more, is much the best because of its long life and remarkable fire resistance. It is neat to use and the reduced cost of the builder's work offsets in part its greater cost. It can be run in old conduit, if this exists. All wiring should be hidden by running it in conduit or, if on the surface, camouflaged by following the mouldings and ornament in the building. The path of all wiring must be approved by the architect and, if possible, none should be allowed to run over wood or other combustible material; in certain places, holes must be drilled to avoid unsightly wiring running across mouldings.

Installation of new lighting in historic buildings is one of the many areas where the architect's artistic skill must be used, for the atmosphere, messages and character of the building can be enhanced by skill or destroyed by clumsy lighting. If lighting has to be used in day time, it may be designed with an emphasis to support the sun and natural daylight. It is a taxing problem to find fittings that are suitable for historic buildings, for often far greater output is required than is usual for domestic products. The writer has found that simple and efficient fittings are to be preferred, even in cathedrals, as they do not date or look false. Fitting should always be tested *in situ*. Pseudo-historic fittings, such as chandeliers originally designed for candlesticks, are unsatisfactory if equipped with too bright electric bulbs, whose heat output may amount to several kilowatts and whose replacement can be costly and tiresome. The heat output of lights may be a fire risk if the fitment is not well ventilated, and will certainly cause dirt streaking above the fitment due to the convection currents induced. Also, the heat output of permanent light installations should be taken into account when designing the heating plant. Dimmers are a highly desirable adjunct to the lighting of the building, which should have both spot and general diffused lighting, usable in a variable way to express the atmosphere and reflect the changes in use of the building. Modern dimmers and switches can be controlled by low-powered relays, so greatly reducing the cost of long cable runs needed previously. The extreme cases of interpretation of an historic building are when floodlighting or Son et Lumière are installed.

When designing the layout of electric installations, the route of the main intake, siting of the distribution room, and of controls for various groups of electrical equipment, such as sound reinforcement and heating plant and ducting for wiring, must all be considered. If provision is to be made for broadcasting and television, it is best to treat this separately, as these may be provided by other authorities who will require their own control rooms. Provision for maintenance and testing is necessary, and bulb changing must not be made difficult or expensive by lack of thought at the design stage. Damage by maintenance men moving ladders is a common occurrence.

Air conditioning

The problem of large ducts and remote plant rooms required for air conditioning is difficult enough in designing new buildings, but in existing historic buildings it is acute unless the ducts can be treated as sculptural forms themselves. In order to avoid the expense of long duct runs, local plant rooms can be planned and they may have an advantage. As, in museums, different groups of objects may require different relative humidities, so the architect should seek out suitable servant spaces adjoining galleries

Figure 19.8   The Patterson House, Leesburg, Virginia, USA, built c. 1762
(Courtesy: Photoworks, USA)

Courtyard elevation in January 1979 before restoration by W. Brown Morton III

Figure 19.9   The Patterson House, Leesburg, Virginia, USA, built c. 1762
(Courtesy: Photoworks, USA)

Courtyard elevation in September 1979 after restoration by W. Brown Morton III, including (a) restoration of original exterior paint colours; (b) re-installation of original eighteenth century window sash in second floor left windows; and (c) construction of new entrance porch. The former house is now used as offices

Figure 19.10   The Maltings, Beccles, Suffolk, England
(Courtesy: Feilden & Mawson)

*These derelict agricultural/industrial buildings provided the shell
for a scheme of rehabilitation*

Figure 19.11   The Maltings, Beccles, Suffolk, England
(Courtesy: Feilden & Mawson)

*After rehabilitation into a holiday house complex with restaurant
and moorings for boats. Note the sensitive treatment of pavings*

Figure 19.12 Houses at Woodbridge, Suffolk, England (Courtesy: Feilden & Mawson)

Badly maintained and derelict housing in the centre of a charming coastal town

Figure 19.13 Houses at Woodbridge, Suffolk, England (Courtesy: Feilden & Mawson)

Rehabilitation of houses with reinstatement of missing windows and doors and general overhaul. The defective chimney belongs to a house not in the scheme

270

**Figure 19.14 The Granary,
Blakeney, Norfolk, England**
(Courtesy: Feilden & Mawson)

*These barns had fine oak roofs
but were no longer required as
warehouses for export of wheat*

Figure 19.15 The Granary, Blakeney, Norfolk, England
(Courtesy: Feilden & Mawson)

*The rehabilitation used the fabric of the granary to provide holiday houses and a shop. The bench,
beloved by old people, was retained*

271

Figure 19.16   The historic centre of Warsaw, which was destroyed in World War II

It has been reconstructed and rehabilitated as a popular tourist attraction with restaurants and museums and other public buildings. There are some residences

when adapting an historic building as a museum or for other public purposes.

There are many ways of manipulating heating by spraying and cooling and recirculating air in what is called air conditioning. This means that air conditioning design should be flexible, but its design depends a great deal on experience and judgement and correct briefing of the specialist engineer by the architect and a client who knows what is needed.

Air conditioning is an important part of museum design; nevertheless, the need for it should be put into perspective, for one should recognize that many countries can use the capital and running costs of air conditioning better elsewhere. Indeed, if the electric supply is spasmodic, an air-conditioning plant could do damage to cultural property. Air conditioning is efficient in reducing sulphur dioxide in museum galleries, but the danger of ozone, particularly in hot urban climates, cannot be ignored. Plenum air heating is often no more expensive than pipes and radiators. It has the advantages of good air distribution and movement and the capability of filter installations, as well as conversion to air conditioning at a future date.

Acoustics

Rehabilitation of historic buildings often involves acoustical problems, for example when a malting or corn exchange is turned into a concert hall. The acoustic characteristics of the building should be measured and compared with the desired requirements. Often the building is required for both music and speech, which have different requirements with regard to reverberation time. Long narrow historic buildings with linked volumes either side give discontinuities in reverberation, while cube and double-cube rooms, domes and barrel vaults have problems with regard to reflections. The materials of which most historic buildings are made have insufficient absorption in relation to their volume, making a long reverberation time unavoidable. For instance, the reverberation time of St Paul's Cathedral, London, is 12 seconds and the Albert Hall required acoustical corrections to reduce its reverberation time. Faults should be identified and corrected where possible by optimum disposition of the sound source and audience and the use of reflectors.

The acoustic specialist should attend typical

Figure 19.17 Darley Abbey, Derby, Derbyshire
(Architects: Wood Newton Partnership, Ripley)
(Courtesy: Civic Trust, London)

Before restoration—This is the last remaining structure from the Augustinian Abbey of St Mary of Darley, outside Derby. It may have been the Guest House of the Abbey, but for almost 50 years since the 1930s its future was in doubt and, in consequence, its condition worsened. Its front wall, which had to be shored up, was as much as 500 mm (20 in) out of true and the building was given up by most as being beyond economic repair.

After restoration—The building was saved through the imagination and courage of new owners who have given it a new lease of life by restoring it and converting it into a public house, not so far removed from its original use. Secondhand materials have been used wherever possible; where new were necessary they have been selected to match or be in character with the mediaeval structure

Figure 19.18   Simpson's Tavern, Cornhill, London (Architects: Michell and Partners) (Courtesy: Greater London Council)

Before restoration—The upper floor of a long-established City lunch house, for years left un-used. It was 'Listed' nonetheless as being of architectural and historic interest and had an interior which retained many of the original fixtures, notably fireplaces, mirrors and eating stalls.

(Courtesy: Michell and Partners)

After restoration—As many of the original fixtures as was possible were retained and refurbished for re-use in such a way as to retain also the character of a City lunch house

274

performances in order to measure the reverberation time, decay patterns, frequency responses, echoes, flutters, resonances and eigentones. By walking round he will find out many of the peculiarities of the historic building. Then he should be able to advise on correction of faults, in the first place by adding reflectors and increasing absorption wherever the design and finishes of the historic building will permit. Failing this corrective treatment, electronic reinforcement will have to be used.

There is much intuitive and some unpublished information on the role of public address engineers, who tend to be linked to firms with predetermined systems which may not suit the special problems of an historic building. For good results, independent acoustic consultants with a wide knowledge of electronic equipment are indispensable, as also are staff specially trained to operate the equipment and having a knowledge of the acoustic characteristics of the building. Siting of microphones, switching arrangements, placing of speakers and location of the central controls can only be decided in consultation between architect, equipment specialist, acoustic expert and the users of the building. With long buildings, time delay systems and multiple speakers will assist in making speech intelligible in spite of long reverberation (Haas effect). If the speaker is illuminated well and clearly seen, he is also more audible. Special short-wave radio circuits and earphones may be considered as an aid to the hard of hearing.

Intrusive noise, both airborne and structure borne, can reduce audibility. With low ambient noise, because of its siting, a Greek theatre had marvellous audibility given by the steep seating and low grazing losses in sound transmission, helped by a polished floor reflector and reflecting surfaces behind the speaker. Most historic buildings, being heavy, can resist intrusive noise, but there are weak points which may need attention. Doors may fit badly, windows perhaps have thin glass and a loose fit, ceilings may be vulnerable to aircraft noise and need extra insulation. Increasing the weight of doors, edge sealing and use of air locks will help reduce intrusive sound penetration, while for windows, double glazing, heavy glass and sealing of edges will also help. The hum from heating plant fans or even electric lights can be intrusive, but one of the major causes of intrusive noise is motor traffic which should, if possible, be diverted.

275

20

Special techniques of repair and structural consolidation

Introduction

In addition to the traditional techniques already described, the repair, consolidation and restoration of historic buildings requires a number of special techniques and some unusual skills such as drilling and grouting. Architects are not generally concerned with scaffolding, shoring and such matters as planking and strutting, yet unless these techniques are skilfully carried out, the conservation of an historic building may not be possible, or at least may be made much more expensive. This topic therefore deserves their attention—just as the building must be seen as an individual 'whole', so the work of conservation must be planned as a totality if it is to be efficient. The source and flow of finance is a major factor in work planning and has been dealt with in Chapter 18.

Grouting, by means of a liquid cementacious mix inserted under pressure after drilling into a building, is a means of consolidating its structure. The special techniques of prestressing with jacks in compression and for post-tensioning reinforcement, subsequently grouted, depend also upon drilling. These are the universal methods of putting strength back into historic buildings in such a way as to maintain their structural integrity and conserve the original materials. Doubtless there will be improvements in these techniques, but subject to whatever adaptations are necessary in an individual project, for a man who understands the principles of conservation, can use a theodolite, aim a drill and instruct labour in the art of grouting and reinforcement and can order materials, keep site records and pay labour, there is a great demand, in order to help save the historic monuments of countries in the developing world.

Planking and strutting

Temporary works to prevent the collapse of excavations or building elements are called planking and strutting. Although they are generally left to the contractor to arrange, the architect should be satisfied that the precautions are adequate—for if they are not, fatal accidents can be the result. Wooden planking should be treated against rot before being inserted.

Scaffolding

Scaffolding is the temporary framework which provides a working platform for the building of new work or which gives access for repair to old. The ancient practice was to lay poles or stout timbers about 150 mm × 150 mm (6 in × 6 in), called putlocks or putlogs, across the wall cantilevered outwards to support the platforms which apparently were made of woven wood hurdles. Similar ramps are still used in the Middle East and are very convenient for carrying loads up. On completion of the works, the horizontal supporting timbers were sawn off and left inside the wall, or they may have been withdrawn, for the holes show clearly in many buildings, e.g. the nave of Fountains Abbey, England, and the Palazzo Sforza in Milan. Old putlog holes now provide a useful fixing for new scaffolding or an easy way of inserting needles for shoring or reinforcements.

Later, scaffolding consisted of independent frames or wooden poles lashed together with wire or rope which in hot weather tended to stretch and slip; refinements were developed using wrought timber and prefabricated frames. Nowadays, metal tubular scaf-

Figure 20.1 Excavations, York Minster, England
(Courtesy: Shepherd Building Group Ltd)

Planking and strutting should follow excavation immediately. This was of heavy steel designed to resist outward thrusts from the heavily loaded masonry and support a temporary floor above. The detail shows the special high tensile steel bolts used to tighten up the strutting. The planking is 50 mm (2 in) thick and with the benefit of experience should have been treated with a timber preservative, as some of it had to remain in position over three years in damp and poorly ventilated positions, and later became affected by dry rot and had to be renewed

folding is almost universal. One of its advantages is that it does not need putlogs, so there is no need to cut into ancient masonry; still, it is necessary to ensure that scaffolding is securely fixed to the face of a building by passing ties through windows and other openings or by forming permanent screwed anchorages drilled inconspicuously into the face of a wall.

Accidents due to collapse of scaffolding are not uncommon, so care in following all safety regulations must be insisted upon. The limitations of the permissible loads on the scaffolding should be clearly understood and a notice posted thereon; these limitations consist of maximum point loads per bay and maximum total distributed loads. Steel scaffolding has the advantage that it can be easily strengthened and adjusted for levels as necessary.

For major restoration works, taking years rather than months, there is no doubt that it is better for the building owner to buy scaffolding rather than pay cumulative hire charges. This may involve the architect in checking the design of the scaffolding, although being temporary work it is the contractor's responsibility. Aluminium scaffolding, although useful for decoration and cleaning contracts, is not strong enough if masons' repairs have to be carried out. Plain steel scaffolding is objectionable because after long use it rusts and stains masonry, but this does not occur if galvanized steel is used. Great care must be taken with the choice of suitable connectors that will not deteriorate. For anastylosis, when weights of several tonnes may have to be lifted, a heavy scaffold made of three rough 225 mm × 75 mm (9 in × 3 in) timbers clamped together and held by friction is sometimes used.

For heavy loads on a steel scaffold, it is not so much the strength of the verticals that limits the design as the weakness of the horizontal members. The thickness of the scaffold boards should be adjusted to the class of work: normal 32 mm (1.25 in), medium

Figure 20.2 Strutting, choir, south aisle, York Minster, England
(Courtesy: Shepherd Building Group Ltd)

Strutting was erected in order to repair an arch. Screw-type struts and wedges hold masonry in position while it is repaired. Such work needs final grouting to consolidate any voids

38 mm (1.5 in), heavy 50 mm (2 in). Extra strengthening can be obtained by laying 9 mm (0.4 in) Douglas fir plywood overall. The ledgers supporting the scaffold boards should be arranged to slope slightly outwards, say 25 mm in 1.5 m (1 inch in 5 ft), in order that rain will run away from the building and drip clear of its face, so avoiding rust stains.

For work at a height in an exposed position, wind is a major nuisance and so slatted wind screens should be provided for the operatives. Because scaffolding is subject to considerable wind pressures, all boards must be tied or clipped down at both ends. There is also a danger of objects being dropped or blown off the scaffold, so fanboards must be provided to protect anyone below. Scaffolding must be well braced diagonally and secured positively to the fabric of the building, or form a stable structure in its own right. Fixing by pressure on to wooden blocks set against masonry is objectionable on two counts; first it might

damage the masonry, and secondly the wood might shrink and the fixing become unsafe. Handrails and toeboards are essential for personal safety. Ladders should be fixed top and bottom and have easy access without the need for gymnastic exercises (which get more difficult with the increasing age of the architect as the work drags on!).

It is the contractor's responsibility to obtain all licences for scaffolding, to arrange for watching and lighting and to prevent unauthorized persons gaining access to the building. This last may mean the use of barbed wire and sticky paint. After work, ladders should either be made unclimbable or removed entirely and locked up by night and at weekends.

Tables 20.1 and *20.2* give ASTM recommended scaffold dimensions for heavy, medium and light duties. Heavy loads are those not in excess of 75 lb/ft²; medium loads are those not in excess of 50 lb/ft²; and light loads are those not in excess of 25 lb/ft².

Table 20.1 ASTM Minimum Nominal Size and Maximum Spacing of Members of Independent Pole Scaffolds (From OSHA Safety and Health Standards 1978, §1910:28, Tables D7, 8 and 9, by permission)

LIGHT DUTY

Member*	Maximum height of scaffold	
	20 ft	60 ft
Pole spacing (transverse)	6 ft	10 ft
Ledgers	1¼ in × 4 in	1¼ in × 9 in
Bearers to 3 ft span	2 in × 4 in	2 in × 4 in
Bearers to 10 ft span	2 in × 6 in	2 in × 9 in (rough)
	or	or
	3 in × 4 in	3 in × 8 in
Planking	1¼ in × 9 in	2 in × 9 in
Vertical spacing of horizontal members	7 ft	7 ft
Bracing (horizontal and diagonal)	1 in × 4 in	1 in × 4 in
Tie-ins	1 in × 4 in	1 in × 4 in
Toeboards	4 in high	4 in high (min.)
Guardrail	2 in × 4 in	2 in × 4 in

MEDIUM DUTY

Uniformly distributed load	Not to exceed 50 lb/ft²
Maximum height of scaffold	60 ft
Poles or uprights	4 in × 4 in
Pole spacing (longitudinal)	8 ft
Pole spacing (transverse)	8 ft
Ledgers	2 in × 9 in
Vertical spacing of horizontal members	6 ft
Spacing of bearers	8 ft
Bearers	2 in × 9 in (rough) or 2 in × 10 in
Bracing (horizontal)	1 in × 6 in or 1¼ in × 4 in
Bracing (diagonal)	1 in × 4 in
Tie-ins	1 in × 4 in
Planking	2 in × 9 in
Toeboards	4 in high (min.)
Guardrail	2 in × 4 in

HEAVY DUTY

Uniformly distributed load	Not to exceed 75 lb/ft²
Maximum height of scaffold	60 ft
Poles or uprights	4 in × 4 in
Pole spacing (longitudinal)	6 ft
Pole spacing (transverse)	8 ft
Ledgers	2 in × 9 in
Vertical spacing of horizontal members	4 ft 6 in
Bearers	2 in × 9 in (rough)
Bracing (horizontal and diagonal)	2 in × 4 in
Tie-ins	1 in × 4 in
Planking	2 in × 9 in
Toeboards	4 in high (min.)
Guardrail	2 in × 4 in

*All members except planking are used on edge.

Table 20.2 Tube and Coupler Scaffolds (From OSHA Safety and Health Standards 1978, §1910:28, Tables D13, 14 and 15, by permission)

LIGHT DUTY

Uniformly distributed load	Not to exceed 25 lb/ft²
Post spacing (longitudinal)	10 ft
Post spacing (transverse)	6 ft

Working levels	Additional planked levels	Maximum height (ft)
1	8	125
2	4	125
3	0	91

MEDIUM DUTY

Uniformly distributed load	Not to exceed 50 lb/ft²
Post spacing (longitudinal)	8 ft
Post spacing (transverse)	6 ft

Working levels*	Additional planked levels	Maximum height (ft)
1	6	125
2	0	78

HEAVY DUTY

Uniformly distributed load	Not to exceed 75 lb/ft²
Post spacing (longitudinal)	6 ft 8 in
Post spacing (transverse)	6 ft

*Working levels carry full loads, while planked levels are for access only.

Figure 20.3   Shoring, choir, north arcade, York Minster, England
(Courtesy: Shepherd Building Group Ltd)

Timber shoring was erected in order to repair a defective arch in the York Minster choir. See also on left side, triple 25 mm (1 in) dia. high tensile steel ties inserted as a safety measure to strengthen the main piers during consolidation of foundations

Planned use of scaffolding in restoration work

During work on an historic building, many people will want to use scaffolding. The restoration programme should be considered, so that time is allowed for all probable operations from the same scaffolding. Even if nothing more demanding than a cleaning operation is envisaged, the possibility must be borne in mind that more substantial work may turn out to be necessary when superficial dirt has been removed and ceases to hide defects. The scaffolding must therefore be strong enough for the heaviest routine work likely to be encountered and it may have to be strengthened to handle exceptional loads, if for instance a decorator's scaffold has to be used for some heavy masonry work. The possible operations that may have to be carried out from one scaffold are given in the following checklist:

(1) Architect's detailed inspection with consultants.
(2) Preliminary repairs and pointing, protection of windows, etc.
(3) Cleaning and removal of lichen and algae.
(4) Masonry or roof repair; repair of rainwater disposal systems.
(5) Re-pointing; renewal of defective plaster.
(6) Electric work, fire alarms, lightning conductors.
(7) Decoration: gilding, mosaic work, restoration of heraldry.
(8) Photography of detail in stone, glass and carving.
(9) Photogrammetry and recording of mouldings, statuary, etc.
(10) Research by art historians, archaeologists and other specialists.
(11) Visits by those interested.
(12) Final inspection by architect.

Figure 20.4 Cradling, north transept, York Minster, England
(Courtesy: Shepherd Building Group Ltd)

A timber and steel cradling was put up in order to hold a thirteenth century archbishop's table tomb and canopy in position while the space below was excavated for foundation works

In major works of restoration the whole programme may depend upon the intelligent planning of the use of scaffolding. It should be remembered that there is a great deal of costly non-productive work in erecting scaffolding, and a programme designed to move the scaffolding sideways—rather than up and down—is more economical. The same scaffolding at York Minster was moved and used eight times over five years.

Shoring

Shoring is a temporary work designed to resist stresses arising from subsidence, overtoppling or bursting and landslip. Although it is a temporary work and therefore the contractor's primary responsibility,

the architect and engineer should check the design and be prepared to comment upon it. In competitive tenders, a contractor may be tempted to skimp the amount of temporary work, while on cost plus contracts he may even over-provide. The correct provision requires judgement and experience and it is better to over-provide than have an accident which may involve loss of life and damage to the very building one is seeking to preserve.

Shoring is of three types: dead shoring, which is designed to take vertical loads and enables walls, piers and columns to be rebuilt, or propping, which is a simple version of dead shoring where only part of the thickness of a wall needs renewal; horizontal shoring or strutting, which prevents bursting and landslip; and diagonal or raking shoring, which can prevent bursting and landslip and overtoppling as

Figure 20.5   Scaffolding, west front, St Paul's Cathedral, London, England
(Courtesy: Feilden & Mawson)

This external scaffolding was put up to effect heavy masonry repairs, so the verticals are just over 1 m (3.3 ft) apart. The diagonal bracing gives stiffness and wherever work is in progress there are scaffold boards and toe-boards. The doorways used by the public are well protected. As such work is likely to take several years it is generally most economical to buy the scaffolding outright, together with an electric hoist in view of the bulk of the work being at heights greater than 25 m (80 ft)

283

Figure 20.6   Scaffolding, nave, York Minster, England
(Courtesy: Shepherd Building Group Ltd)

The scaffold itself is designed for economy, using a central and two side towers linked and braced together. The scaffolding is being moved horizontally from east to west two bays at a time, since a 'rolling programme' is far more efficient than an 'up-and-down programme'. The amount of work in erecting and dismantling scaffolding should not be under-estimated, as in fact one is building a temporary building within a building to gain access to all surfaces. Note the system of bracing which is essential for stability and the toe-boards for safety. Verticals are nearly 2 m (7 ft) apart because this is a light-duty scaffold. The cleaning has exposed local faults which have to be corrected by the masons, while quite serious defects, which had been kept under observation during the consolidation of the foundations, were rectified in the bays immediately adjacent to the central tower

well. When shoring is erected, it is not stressed and consequently some movement must occur before it can carry its load. Because this movement will induce cracks or may cause other damage and in extreme cases may even be quite dangerous, it is highly desirable to tighten up or prestress shoring to its calculated loading. This can be done by jacks of suitable type, either screw or hydraulic. Care must be taken to avoid damaging a tender old building by over-tightening the wedging or over-prestressing.

Figure 20.7   Shoring, east end, York Minster, England
(Courtesy: Shepherd Building Group Ltd)

Raking shores support the wall which is leaning outwards and near collapse. Flying shores act as horizontal struts between the raking shores. The whole wall had to be kept intact in order to avoid damage to the famous early fifteenth century Alpha and Omega window which is as large as a tennis court

Jacking shoring: an example

A refinement of jacking was devised at York Minster where flat-jacks were placed under the bases of 26 m (85 ft) long steel raking shores. These jacks were linked to a constant pressure mechanism which applied a horizontal force of 20.3 t (20 tonf). The shores were able to accommodate movement in the building and the jacks also absorbed the thermal movements in the shores themselves with a total expansion and contraction of about 30 mm (1.2 in). When inserting shores, needles are necessary to transfer the stresses to the masonry, and as has been said it is often useful to find the original putlog holes,

if they exist. Shores should always be removed carefully; if they have prestressing jacks, the procedure is greatly simplified as the pressure in the jacks can be lowered in stages.

Hydraulic jacks

A building contractor with wide experience can greatly assist the architect by suggesting the most up-to-date equipment and plant for any particular project; for example, many uses for hydraulic jacks are being found in restoration works. Post-tensioning of reinforcement and extraction of lining tubes to holes

285

Figure 20.8   Shoring, east end, York Minster, England
(Courtesy: Shepherd Building Group Ltd)

The raking shoring required massive foundations and the base-plate rested on four Freyssinet flat hydraulic jacks which were attached to a constant pressure system. The jacks compensated for settlement of the foundation and thermal movements in the long steel shores, and resisted the thrust of the cathedral while allowing it to settle

Figure 20.9   Shoring, west end, York Minster, England
(Courtesy: Shepherd Building Group Ltd)

The heavy-duty scaffolding devised for the east end was also found necessary to stabilize the west end during the excavation work preparatory to consolidating the foundations. The temporary covers over the excavations prevent rain affecting the foundations; the stoppage of work is also avoided by this precaution

286

Figure 20.10 Enlarged foundations, central tower, York Minster, England (Courtesy: Shepherd Building Group Ltd)

Hydraulic cells or flat-jacks were laid on a large independent pressure pad of concrete and covered with precast slabs. A separate foundation is to be laid above and linked to the existing masonry with post-tensioned stainless steel ties

drilled for reinforcement can also be mentioned; for York Minster, Lee-McCall jacks were used with the equipment mounted on a convenient trolley.

This section, however, deals more fully with flat-jacks of the Freyssinet type, which are made of two parallel circular plates of up to 450 mm (18 in) diameter, joined together at the perimeter by a flexible ring. Hydraulic fluid is pumped into the volume between the plates, which are forced apart according to the load and pressure. The pressure can be measured, so the load can then be calculated by multiplying the pressure by the area of the plate. The pressure can be varied at will or, if desired, kept constant by an automatic hydraulic mechanism.

The use of flat-jacks in a system of needles and dead shoring has great advantages as the jacks can be inflated and the calculated load taken on the shoring before the wall is removed, thus avoiding settlements and consequential cracking when the loads are transferred. It is a safer method of working, too. Dead shores should always be pressurized to take the full weight of a wall before the opening is formed; if flat hydraulic jacks are not available, then a simple screw-jack or even hardwood wedges can be used. However, no automatic compensation is possible with such methods.

Another use of flat-jacks was in the foundations to the central piers of York Minster. These were designed in two horizontal layers with flat-jacks between them (about 400 in all), each connected to an individual inlet with associated pressure gauge. It was planned that when the jacks were inflated the lower layer of the foundations would be pressed into the clay and take up half the overall load, leaving the original foundations with the balance of the load. By measuring the pressure on each plate individually, the loads could be calculated, and if settlements were unequal the necessary adjustments could be made, for the pressures can be adjusted separately by individual piping which is also a precaution against a failure of the jack. In the case above, about 7 out of the 400 jacks failed but there were sufficient reserves. Schemes similar in principle but on a smaller scale have been carried out at St John's, Ousebridge, York, and in the cloisters of Norwich Cathedral. In both these cases, flat-jacks were used on extensions to the buttress foundations in order to ensure proper loading of the additional new supporting areas.

Where rubble fill, in walls, has compressed and the outer skin takes a large share of the load, post-stressing by flat-jacks can be used in maintaining structural equilibrium to new areas of masonry where old defective work has been cut out and replaced.

Drilling techniques

Drilling through masonry and brickwork permits the insertion of both liquid grout and reinforcing steel in a way that is not readily visible afterwards. Such

Figure 20.11   Enlarged foundations, central tower, York Minster, England
(Courtesy: Shepherd Building Group Ltd)

The foundations proper have been cast, leaving ducts for the steel reinforcement on one side and the pipes to the hydraulic cells which will be inflated in due course

Figure 20.12   Enlarged foundations, central tower, York Minster, England
(Courtesy: Shepherd Building Group Ltd)

After drilling through 15 m (50 ft) of concrete, stone, mortar and wood the hole is lined temporarily with a pipe to prevent local collapse and the tensile stainless steel bars inserted These were then stretched and given a final tensioning after two months and then grouted. The probes are all ready to receive the liquid grout injection

288

Figure 20.13 Enlarged foundations, central tower, York Minster, England
(Courtesy: Shepherd Building Group Ltd)

View showing the enlarged foundations and one of the massive piers of the central tower, each of which takes 4064 t (4000 ton) or more, now linked to the adjacent nave pier. As the temporary planking and strutting and floor supports are stripped away the enlarged 16 m (52 ft) square foundations show. They have been designed to eliminate eccentric loadings which gave ground pressures 0f 8 t/ft² (7.9 ton/ft²) which was equal to the ultimate stress of the soil. New loadings were all brought up to 3 t/ft² (2.95 ton/ft²) under the direction of Ove Arup & Partners, the consulting engineers and authors of this elegant design

techniques have opened up new possibilities in the field of building conservation, as they enable old structures to be reinforced in an invisible manner. The technique of drilling and grouting was first developed in the 1920s by Harvey, in his work on Tintern Abbey. It enables the worker in the preservation and repair of historic buildings to comply with some of the essential principles of structural conservation work:

(1) Make maximum use of the existing structure.
(2) Repair the structure in a virtually invisible way.
(3) Adjust the strength of the repairs to the appropriate degree.

Drilling equipment

Drilling equipment is of two main types, powered either by electricity or by compressed air. Portable electric hand drills up to ½ h.p. can drill up to 1–1.3 m (3–4 ft) of hard limestone or brick. For work on remote country sites, a portable 5 kW generator, which will power a high-speed rotary percussive 110 V drill with air-blast waste removal, is very useful. Holes of up to 5.5 m (18 ft) length have been drilled in difficult flintwork with this equipment.

Electric power can be used for rotary cutters, discs, fretsaws and hammers which can save much hard work and, if skilfully used, cause less damage to the

Figure 20.14   Enlarged foundations, central tower, York Minster, England
(Courtesy: Shepherd Building Group Ltd)

A general view showing the enlarged independent foundations of the central piers which are linked to adjacent nave, choir and transept aisle piers. The concrete rings to prevent bursting are above the new foundations proper. Measuring points are fixed on to each foundation, movements being checked each week. Prestressed stainless steel reinforcing rods were inserted diagonally under the main piers, 100 to each pier, in holes drilled through the original masonry

Figure 20.15   Investigation, St Paul's Cathedral, London, England
(Courtesy: Feilden & Mawson)

A core was cut with a diamond-toothed bit in order to investigate the condition of the wall. The sample obtained was much fragmented, indicating weakness of the structure. The core hole was used together with an adjustable sparge pipe to test water penetration in the masonry

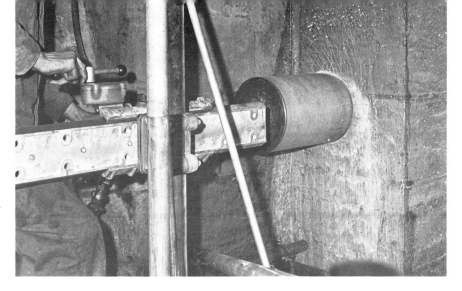

Figure 20.16   Coring, York Minster, England
(Courtesy: Shepherd Building Group Ltd)

A diamond drill coring machine used to insert needles for temporary work or local strengthening. It cuts as a neat hole with negligible vibration

Figure 20.17   Coring, York Minster, England
(Courtesy: Shepherd Building Group Ltd)

This foundation was cored with a 230 mm (9 in) diamond auger to form a hole about 4 m (13 ft) long in order to insert a 200 mm × 100 mm (8 in × 4 in) galvanized steel grillage or needles to consolidate poor masonry

Figure 20.18   Coring, York Minster, England
(Courtesy: Shepherd Building Group Ltd)

Diamond coring was used to cut stone in order to form concealed anchorages for reinforcement. The piece of stone could be re-set, thus respecting archaeological values and patina. Compressed air motors were preferred for all operations as they are lighter than equivalent electric power units and safer on a wet building site

Figure 20.19   Drilling, York Minster, England
(Courtesy: Shepherd Building Group Ltd)

A compressed air drill being set up on a cradle prior to drilling probe holes for insertion of grout on the north-west tower north face. Note the firm rear anchorage to resist the thrust from the automatic screw feed of the drill and the adjustments to scaffold that are required. An electric hoist cage can be seen in the background. Such equipment is essential on large-scale operations with climbs of more than 15 m (50 ft) or for smaller jobs some 30 m (100 ft) height or more simply to save time and energy. Power supply for twin 10 h.p. electric motors is necessary

Figure 20.20   Drilling, York Minster, England
(Courtesy: Shepherd Building Group Ltd)

Accurate drilling horizontally through 15 m (49 ft) of concrete, mortar and stones of various size and condition, with timber baulks set in grout, was difficult. In any horizontal drilling operation it is difficult to keep direction, but much more so if the material is inconsistent. Note the wet conditions and the ear-muffs to protect against the intense and continuous noise

292

Figure 20.21 Drilling, York Minster, England
(Courtesy: Shepherd Building Group Ltd)

A more powerful drill set on a movable cradle which can be adjusted for height was obtained. It was found that a stiff rod helped preserve direction and for most purposes the 'down-the-hole' vole hammer was quickest and most accurate. Auger bits had to be used when embedded wood was met, and occasionally diamond studded bits were used. The operatives acquired a special expertise by continuous work in shifts over nearly three years. Often the holes would collapse, so these had to be lined with a 50 mm (2 in) diameter tube immediately after drilling. Later the steel could be inserted as shown and then the tube was extracted using hydraulic jacks. The drill inevitably breaks out through the concrete, so finished work was planned to cover this

fabric of an old building than cutting with chisel and mallet.

For major works, compressed air supplied by a diesel- or electric-powered compressor is safer, as the great amount of water used in removing the waste in drilling operations tends to be a hazard when using live electric wires, even if only of 110 V. The siting of compressors should be carefully considered, as the large versions are noisy pieces of equipment. Hydraulic-powered equipment is still in the development stage but is reported to be quiet.

For large buildings which have a continuous maintenance programme, a permanent air mains from a compressor is an installation worth considering, especially as it might be possible to arrange for the plant to be used in reverse to act as a central vacuum-cleaning system. Such a plant has been installed and used in Lincoln Cathedral for many years. A permanent air main should cover the ground plan and enable air to be delivered to any point using about 30 m (100 ft) of flexible hose.

Drilling equipment must be matched to the size and difficulty of the task. The power of the drill affects the accuracy of the work, and in general, the faster the rate of penetration, the more accurate the shot is likely to be. Stiffness of the drilling stem is another factor assisting accuracy. High-speed rotary-percussive drills are fast, and in hard limestone, rates up to 135 mm (5 in) per minute can be obtained. Accuracy is improved if a mandrel is inserted behind the head; this mandrel must be able to pass the water-borne waste from the cutting head. Various types of cutting head, based on steel or tungsten carbide, can be obtained. The other type of bit that can be used is a

Figure 20.22 Drilling bits, York Minster, England
(Courtesy: Shepherd Building Group Ltd)

All the drill-head components and assemblies described are powered pneumatically for both rotary and rotary percussive drilling units. Advantages and disadvantages—high-speed rotary percussive is the most economical means of drilling; tungsten carbide tipped bits are much cheaper than diamond crowns. This type of drilling is fast, but demands a homogeneous mass, preferably of like material, to provide for accuracy in operations where long holes are required horizontally in masonry. Diamond core drilling is rather slower and thus more costly, but under adverse conditions in bad materials is more accurate in maintaining alignment

1 Retro-bit, 3 in diameter, incorporating 1⁵/₈ in pilot bit. The assembly as illustrated was used for the purpose of making accurate entry in protecting against drift in the initial stages of rotary percussive long hole drilling.

2 Standard 3 in diameter cross-type tungsten carbide tipped bit used for drilling in homogeneous material by rotary percussive means.

3 Purpose-made 3 in diameter button bit with protruding tungsten carbide inserts, ideal for drilling in limestone, does not require sharpening. Used for rotary percussive drilling, the inserts contain two main components, tungsten carbide, the hard component, and cobalt, the tough component.

4 Standard button bit, 3 in diameter, for drilling in broken ground by rotary percussive means.

5 Standard holbit 1¼ in diameter tungsten carbide tipped, used for short hole rotary percussive drilling.

6 Standard retro-bit 1¾ in diameter tungsten carbide tipped, used for normal drilling operations by rotary percussive action.

7 As above, but 2 in diameter and ditto.

8 Ditto, but 2½ in diameter.

9 Standard holbit, 1½ in diameter.

10 Standard retro-bit, 3 in diameter, used for normal drilling by rotary percussive action.

11 Purpose-made retro-bit incorporating blind pilot, used for reaming 1⁵/₈ in diameter hole up to 2 in diameter by rotary percussive action.

12 Standard drill steel coupler type 408 rope thread for coupling 1 in hex steels for rotary percussive drilling.

13 Standard coupling showing a rope thread coupler used for rotary percussive action.

14 Purpose-made coupler for use with 1 in hex hollow drill steels, designed to provide accuracy when drilling through broken ground, using 3 in diameter retro cross-bits. This type of coupling assembly allows the drill cuttings to pass through internally in suspension and centralizes the drill steels at coupling points, ideal for drilling operations 50–70 ft horizontally.

15 Standard 4¼ in × 1 in hex shank and (water swivel) 408 thread for rotary percussive action.

16 Standard 508 rope thread coupling used for coupling 1¼ in diameter drill steels for rotary percussive action.

17 Standard 1½ in diameter lugged shank and 512 rope thread assembly for 1½ in diameter round drill steels for rotary percussive action.

18 Purpose-made reamer coupling, 3 in diameter, for use with 1¼ in diameter drill steels, ideal for drilling operations in cementatious material.

19/20 Standard walran-type rotary tungsten carbide tipped winged bit used for rotary drilling in timber and decomposed masonry.

21 Standard Trycon roller bit used for rotary drilling in broken ground of material that yields. This type of bit is employed with diamond tubes.

22 Standard Diamond Crown NX with bevelled wall, grade 10 diamonds used for rotary diamond coring and employed with diamond tubes. This bit cuts through masonry, concrete or steel and recovers its core.

All drill head components, drill string assemblies, couplers and drill string centralizers were driven by heavy-duty Drifter chain or screw-fed drilling machines, mounted on portable or purpose-made drilling rigs powered by rotary screw type air compressors.

pure rotary drill with diamond or tungsten carbide cutters. This gives about 20 mm (0.8 in) per minute or less, and is relatively slow and therefore more expensive, but the stiff stem of the rotary shaft assists in accuracy. A rather special type of cutter is a 'down-the-hole' vole, high-speed rotary-percussive hammer with a stiff rotating shaft. Some standard percussive equipment causes far too much vibration to be used satisfactorily on old building structures, so preliminary tests are advisable.

Drilling works

Drilling vertically to great depths through homogeneous materials, however hard, is a comparatively simple and well-established practice, but accurate drilling horizontally through masonry is much more difficult. The tip of the drill has a natural tendency to drop and may be diverted by each fissure, crack, void and joint in the masonry, not to mention embedded timbers and metal. Drilling at an oblique angle to the masonry is even more difficult because the angled joints are more likely to deflect the drill than joints normal to the hole. To assist accuracy, as much grout as possible should be injected prior to the main drilling operation to fill the larger voids and make the masonry more homogeneous. There is a possibility that adjacent drill holes may be filled by this grout and have to be re-drilled. The risk of this happening can be reduced by inserting sleeves in the holes, although the sleeves themselves present a problem, for, if left in position at the time of grouting, they will reduce the bond between the reinforcement and masonry and so must be removed. Ideally the sleeve should be of thin-gauge polished stainless steel pipe. It should be rotated just after the initial set of each grout injection, and then withdrawn when all grouting that is necessary has been done. In practice, galvanized steel is more likely to be available and hydraulic jacks may be necessary to extract the sleeves. If ordinary mild steel sleeves are left in position, there is a great risk that they will rust and cause damage by consequent expansion.

Horizontal shots of up to 20 m (66 ft) length have been carried out effectively on the central tower of York Minster through large blocks of hard limestone, after preliminary grouting. If a shot went off alignment, the drill was withdrawn and the hole was grouted with rapid-hardening cement. The drill used a crown-shaped drilling head with a special guiding mandrel. Horizontal shots of 15 m (49 ft) length in fissured and disintegrated masonry in the Norman foundations had to be re-drilled more than once with a wide range of drill heads. The resident engineer, Norman Ross of Ove Arup & Partners, described the work as follows, and his experience is worth recording for future practitioners:

'The 16 000 ton central tower is carried by four main columns. Each column has, as its effective foundation, a cruciform of Norman strip footings. Taking into account eccentricity, the bearing stresses on the ground are much heavier than desirable. The effective area of each column foundation is increased and the eccentricity reduced by adding slabs of concrete 2.1 m (6 ft 11 in) thick in each re-entrant corner. The whole composite foundation is reinforced by post-tensioned 32 mm (1.3 in) diameter stainless steel rods which form two layers in each elevation. This involves drilling holes up to 15 m (49 ft) horizontally through the Norman foundations with a high standard of accuracy.

'The centres of the rods are 380 mm (1 ft 3 in) apart horizontally and 450 mm (1 ft 6 in) apart vertically in each direction. However, since one layer in each direction bisects the two layers in the orthogonal direction, the actual vertical distance between the layers is only 225 mm (9 in). From these figures it can be seen that the target after 12 to 15 m (40 to 50 ft) of drilling, allowing workable tolerances, is a rectangle only 300 × 225 mm (12 × 9 in). Such accuracy has proved very difficult to achieve—perhaps not surprisingly.

'For several months, before any drilling was attempted on the foundations, similar requirements had been carried out at high levels in the Central and Western towers. The walls of these towers have been protected from further cracking by reinforcing them horizontally in certain areas with stainless steel rods. This involved drilling holes 20 m (66 ft) in length but more tolerance was allowed than was later required for the foundations. The work on the towers, by comparison, went very well and success gave confidence for the drilling below—a confidence which nearly turned to despair when several months after starting on the foundations drilling, only 8 holes had been successful out of a total of 38 attempts (with 400 to do).

'The reason why drilling in the walls of the fabric was easier than in the foundations is not hard to find. Accurate drilling depends basically on two things:

1. The nature of the material being drilled.
2. The use of the correct equipment to suit the material.

The ideal material is a sound, homogeneous rock containing no fissures or voids. Mass concrete, of course, is equally acceptable. The degree by which a material departs from this standard is a measure of the difficulty one can expect in drilling through it. The Minster fabric, in the main, is well-bonded magnesian limestone masonry and where rubble cores occur, they are well compacted and reasonably well mortared. On the other hand, the Norman mortar raft is far from ideal, for several reasons:

(a) It is non-homogeneous. The core has produced various limestones, red sandstone, millstone grits, a few igneous rocks, and even Roman tiles and bricks.

(b) This miscellaneous rubble is held together by a matrix of lime/sand mortar, generally of a very low lime content. In parts the mortar is hard where presumably the proportions were better but usually it can be powdered between finger and thumb, presumably having undergone severe decomposition since it was first mixed in the eleventh century. The soft mortar offers no resistance to the passage of the drill which can thus deflect easily when harder rocks are encountered. Also, since water is used to flush back the drilled material, small voids are often created when the soft mortar is also washed back. Prior to drilling, attempts were made at consolidating the "mortar raft" by drilling holes for grout and pumping in a wet mix under pressure, but, with a few exceptions, only small "takes" have been recorded. To improve the grout penetration Pozament is used at a water/cement ratio of about 0.6.

Pozament is a proprietary cement consisting of roughly equal portions of pulverized fuel ash and ordinary Portland cement. The old mortar absorbs the water but not the solids. Experiments have also been made with epoxy resins as grout and excellent results have been achieved. There was excellent penetration of the mortar by the resin, producing a solid mass. Unfortunately the cost of using resins is prohibitive—blanket grouting of the existing foundations would cost approximately £500,000 (in 1969).

(c) In the vicinity of each tower column the foundations have undergone differential settlements of up to 300 mm (1 ft 0 in). As a result, they have fissured and deformed, producing shear planes which can deflect the drill from its correct alignment.

(d) It was the practice of the Normans to reinforce their strip foundations with a continuous grillage of oak or elm baulks placed centrally. In the Minster the longitudinal members were 450 × 300 mm (1 ft 6 in × 1 ft 0 in) and the lateral distribution members 300 × 300 mm

(1 ft 0 in × 1 ft 0 in). Much of the timber has rotted, leaving voids which have since been filled with sand/cement grout, but some has remained to provide yet another hindrance to easy drilling.

'Compressed air was used for working most of the tools used on York Minster. Two Holman Silver III percussive drills between them completed the work at high level on the towers. The bits used were 63 mm (2.5 in) diameter, with star or cross tungsten carbide cutting heads. The drilling rods were hexagonal and hollow so that the flushing water could pass up through them to the cutting heads. The 32 mm (1.3 in) rods were standard and came in lengths of about 5 m (16 ft). At regular intervals specially designed 63 mm (2.5 in) diameter couplers were used which fitted tightly to the hole yet allowed water and debris to pass through.

'The same rigs were employed initially when the foundation drilling commenced. After a number of "shots" most of which were badly off line, the situation was reviewed. The bits and drilling rods tended to feather which indicated that the rods were curving in profile. More powerful machines of the same type appeared to be the answer. The slightly larger Silver 83 model and the SL 16A drifter were tested in turn. The drifter is a brute of a machine, very popular in mining engineering. At this stage also, experiments were carried out using other types of cutting heads, namely "button" bits and tri-cone or roller bits. In addition all the conventional types and sizes of drilling rods and couplers were tested but without the success we were looking for. Even tube drilling was attempted on the percussive rig, using tubes for greater rigidity. The tubes we produced on the site failed miserably and even specially designed factory-made tubes could not withstand the stresses, especially fatigue, which this type of drilling sets up.

'We now turned to diamond-core drilling which is both slow and expensive. The bits are hollow cylinders whose crowns consist of clusters of industrial diamonds set in a cobalt bed. Each bit cost about £70 and, on average, is good for only 61 m (200 ft) of drilling. The action is purely rotary as a percussive element would obviously smash the diamond crown. However it has proved to be at least one answer to the problem. It is accurate over long lengths through poor material because drilling tubes of 75 mm (3 in) diameter may be used. These are much less flexible than the 32 mm (1.3 in) diameter hexagonal rods used by the Silver III. Even diamonds though, cannot drill through half-rotted timbers (the Norman reinforcement) and, when these are encountered, fly-cutter bits or rag-bits have to be substituted for the diamond crown until the timber has been bored. (Fly-cutters operate on the same principle as a carpenter's auger.) On occasions, a series of as many as five timbers has to be negotiated in this way in drilling just one hole.

'The latest episode of the saga has been the successful introduction of the "down-the-hole" vole hammer. This is a rotary-percussive tool which can be used on the same rig and with the same equipment as for the diamond coring. The percussive element is a hammer bit which has tungsten-carbide cutting edges. The vole hammer drills dry with compressed air passing up through the centre of drilling tubes and forcing back the loosened material. The same air activates the percussive hammer.

'This type of drilling has been accurate, quick and relatively inexpensive. Its secret lies in the stiffness of the drilling tubes and in the fact that the tubes are only required to transmit torque, all the percussion taking place at the cutting face.'

Grouting

The object of grouting is to strengthen and consolidate decayed masonry which is weakened by large fractures and voids. It can also be used to introduce preservatives into stone by vacuum methods of impregnation. Although grouting is a useful preliminary treatment it cannot usually be regarded as a complete structural repair in itself, nor can it be trusted to fill fine cracks. It does, however, consolidate and increase the stiffness of an old structure.

Searching out voids for grouting presents difficulties; often a hit or miss method has to be adopted, with holes drilled in a predetermined grid and water testing used to give advance warning of the existence of and probable size of the void. Other methods involve simple tapping with a hammer and listening to the note, which varies with the solidity of the masonry, or the more complicated use of gamma or X-rays, which can only penetrate about 1 m (3.3 ft) overall, or ultrasonic testing. Each method should be tried, as particular circumstances like multiple fissures or even fine cracks may render the searching out of voids impracticable.

Grouting is the insertion of a fluid cementacious mix, called grout, with good flow characteristics into the cracks and fissures of masonry or concrete. Before inserting the grout it is first necessary to clean out the voids and wet all the surfaces. The grout is inserted under pressure of gravity or by a hand- or air-operated pump. Vacuum grouting is also a hopeful development, but relies on suitable resins for its effectiveness.

Grouting mixes are formulated for each specific project, in order to obtain the desired strength and penetration characteristics. Sand and pulverized fly ash may be added to the cementing material which may be lime, hydraulic lime, Portland cement or various epoxy resins or silane formulations. Proprietary additives are used to promote flow and penetration.

The addition of pozzuolanic material to lime in grouts and mortars is important. Lime itself sets by carbonization—the action of carbon dioxide—and the setting consists of hardening from the surface inwards, so that in thick walls the process may never occur, leaving powdered calcium hydroxide instead of hard mortar. However, carbon dioxide is not needed if pozzuolanic material such as volcanic earth, including alumina and silica or crushed brick and tiles, is added in equal proportions to the lime.

Pulverized fly ash (p.f.a.), which is extracted from power stations, is a pozzuolanic material and can be used with lime to form a hydraulic mortar of attractive colour; but the use of some types of fly ash with a high soluble salt content should be avoided. Two parts pulverized fly ash with two parts lime and, in order to keep the binding material in suspension, one of bentonite clay additive, to promote flow characteristics, is a useful grouting mixture which avoids the excessive hardness and strength of Portland cement grouts. If Portland cement is used, there is a danger that the grout will be too hard and impervious and not marry well with masonry. If hard and impervious material comes too close to the surface of masonry it may promote frost attack and should therefore be cut back at least 50 mm (2 in) before it hardens, and in any case it does not have the necessary resilience to be structurally sympathetic to old masonry.

The simplest form of grouting is practised when large stones that have been set on lead wedges or bits of oyster shell of the correct joint width are grouted with a mixture of sand and lime by pouring this into the open joints; the water percolates away and leaves the solids in position, the stone then being completely surrounded by mortar. A form of gravity grouting can be carried out by forming clay cups against open joints in masonry and filling these repeatedly with grout which flows through the open spaces and consolidates the masonry. The mixture may need some help in its flow, by working a hacksaw blade or similar probe through the joint. Fine sand and the addition of pulverized fly ash assist the flow and, together with lime as the cementatious agent, they make a good grout mix in the proportions 2:1:2; more fly ash can be added along with a little Portland cement if quicker setting is desired.

297

Figure 20.23 Drilling marble shafts, York Minster, England (Courtesy: Shepherd Building Group Ltd)

The shafts were badly cracked, so they were put into splints and encased in plaster of Paris before being dismantled. Then a 40 mm (1.60 in) hole was drilled down the length of the shaft and capital. The shafts were re-erected, having been strengthened with 30 mm (1.25 in) stainless steel rods, and the cracks were repaired with epoxy resin

Figure 20.24 Drilling, York Minster, England (Courtesy: Shepherd Building Group Ltd)

Drilling through decayed eleventh century masonry was difficult as the holes tended to fall in, so tubes were inserted immediately. Then the stainless steel reinforcement was threaded through and the tubes withdrawn using the immense power of hydraulic jacks to overcome friction, and finally each rod was anchored, pre-tensioned twice and grouted into position. Work is shown on one of the piers of the western towers

Figure 20.25 Grouting, west front, St Paul's Cathedral, London, England
(Courtesy: Feilden & Mawson)

A grout mixture is injected by air pressure into the open joints in the stonework. Large areas of walling now need this treatment

Figure 20.26 Grouting, central tower, Norwich Cathedral, England
(Courtesy: Feilden & Mawson)

Holes for the probes were drilled into the wide joints so that their position would not show after making good. During the work at 30 lbf/in², it was found that grout might span a considerable distance and so the protective drapes of polythene were necessary. All the piers of the tower with the arcades and walls above were consolidated by grout

Figure 20.27 Grouting, central tower, Norwich Cathedral, England
(Courtesy: Feilden & Mawson)

The holes drilled ready for insertion of probes show clearly. Lime and fly-ash with a small amount of Portland cement was used as a mix and the amount injected into each hole was recorded. The cracked capitals in the arcade were grouted with epoxy resin which only had a short pot life of 30 minutes

Figure 20.28 Grouting, central tower, Norwich Cathedral, England

Probes are arranged at approximately 500–600 mm (20–24 in) centres with rapid hose connections and valves. The grout is injected and runs both sideways and upwards; when it reaches a probe and runs out the valve is closed and the grout moves further. One hole ran 6 m (20 ft) sideways and received 250 l (50 gal) of grout. Leaks are plugged with tow and masonry washed clean

Figure 20.29 Grouting, south-west tower, York Minster, England
(Courtesy: Shepherd Building Group Ltd)

Consolidating masonry on York Minster's south-west tower by grouting with a weak mixture of cement and fly-ash. Note quick coupling to hose and hand on tap. Grout was hand-pumped at 20 lbf/in² pressure

Figure 20.30 Grouting, York Minster, England
(Courtesy: Shepherd Building Group Ltd)

Large quantities of pulverized fly-ash and sulphate-resisting Portland cement were used to consolidate the foundations of York Minster. Originally there was an oak grillage, but when the water table was lowered these timbers rotted almost completely and left voids which were filled with grout. Note the dark-coloured timber and the stratification in the grout

Figure 20.31 Grouting, foundations, York Minster, England
(Courtesy: Shepherd Building Group Ltd)

After consolidation it is possible to open up masonry. This shows the horizontal strata of grout in the foundations of eleventh century random masonry and also the ancient embedded oaks that had not rotted too much here, being kept wet for centuries until the water table had fallen in recent years

Figure 20.32 Grouting, Ospizio di San Michele, Rome, Italy

The walls, built of random rubble and pozzuolanic lime mortar, were weakened by age and the original workmanship was suspect. Load tests showed them to be very weak. Grouting with epoxy resin, although expensive, greatly increased the strength of the wall. It is, however, a rather messy process

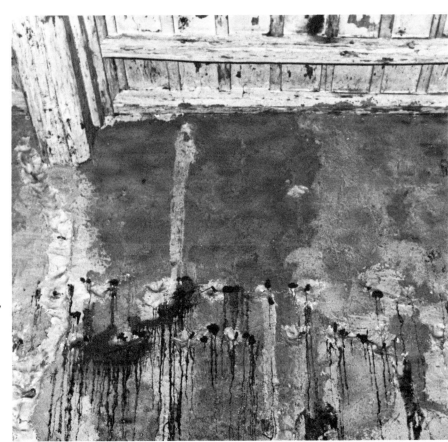

301

Figure 20.33   Reinforcement, central tower, Norwich England

Steel reinforcement for the tensioned ring beams galvanized after bending and cutting. This has to be inserted in short lengths; each piece of steel was hooked on to the next to provide a continuous chain of four 20 mm (0.75 in) bars. The different lengths enabled variations to be dealt with

Figure 20.34   Reinforcement, north-west tower, York Minster, England
(Courtesy: Shepherd Building Group Ltd)

End anchorages of 150 mm (6 in) diameter stainless steel was used. Then the steel was pre-stressed using a hydraulic jack, allowed to stretch for two months and then given final tension. Grout was inserted through prepared probes

302

The mason prepares to make good by cutting out a rectangular shape for the new stone. He should have been consulted about re-setting the piece cored out

Finally, the mason makes good by inserting new stone and grouting it into position

Figure 20.37 Safety precautions for the Alpha and Omega window, East End, York Minster, England (Courtesy: Shepherd Building Group Ltd)

This repair consists of restraining the leaning and bowing east window of York Minster by tensioned cables with suspension rods attached at each strong node point. No other simple way of solving this problem could be found. From ground level the wires are practically invisible, so this can be classed as a permanent repair

For more sophisticated forms of grouting, probe holes are drilled into the masonry at appropriate centres, the spacing of which depends upon the condition of the masonry and the incidence of cracks. For example, on Norwich Cathedral spire, where it was not possible to strut the external surface, holes were drilled at only 300 mm (12 in) centres to reduce the outward pressure loading. In very fissured masonry, probes at close centres are desirable, whereas where large lumps of stone or flint concrete have cracked, it is only necessary to have grout probe holes at 1 m (3.3 ft) centres, following the line of the crack upwards.

The holes having been drilled, water is inserted to wash out the loose materials and wet the masonry so that the grout will adhere. For this, one works downwards, whereas for insertion of grout one must work upwards in order to avoid trapping air in pockets. The probe itself fits into the hole and may be caulked

there, or merely held in position with a foamed rubber washer around it to stop undue leakage.

As all grouting work is liable to be messy, protection of furniture and fitments is essential; if they cannot be removed they should be covered with polythene sheets. The masonry walls themselves must also be protected or at least cleaned down with hoses immediately after a spillage of grout. It is also best to put a protective coating of potter's clay to avoid staining or otherwise damaging precious historic masonry which may be difficult to clean thoroughly. Recent developments of plastics also suggest application of a thin coat that can be peeled off later.

The grout is inserted working first sideways then upwards. When the grout flows out of an adjacent hole sideways, this hole is stopped and the grout allowed to move as far as it can—even up to some 6–7 m (20–23 ft). Then one proceeds to the next hole, and in this manner completes a horizontal row, recording

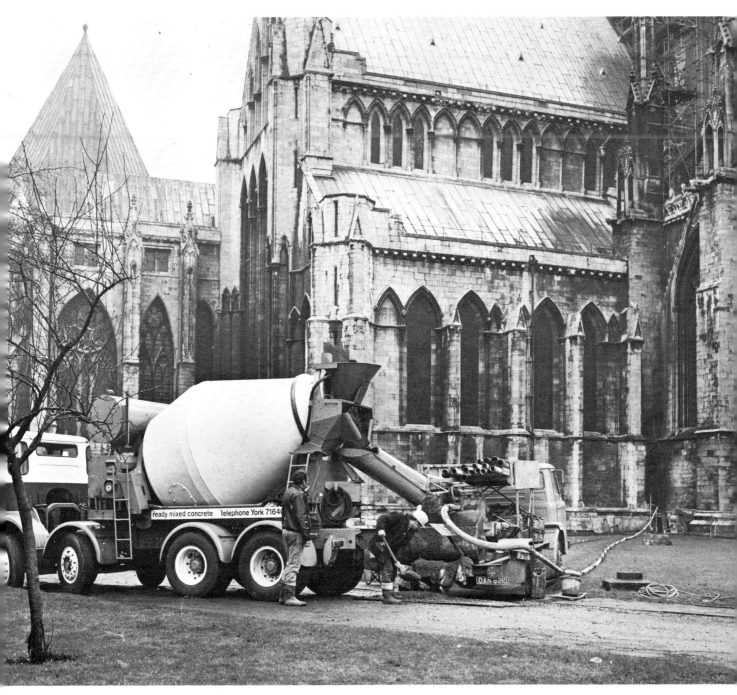

Figure 20.38   Pumping concrete, York Minster, England
(Courtesy: Shepherd Building Group Ltd)

Ready-mixed concrete deliveries can lessen labour costs and save space on a confined site, leaving it cleaner and reducing the noise nuisance from concrete mixers. In combination with a pump unit, concrete can be delivered wherever required by a flexible 100 mm (4 in) pipe

the amount of grout inserted into each hole and the distance of flow. After the horizontal row is complete one moves upwards to the next row and repeats the process.

Gravity grouting with a head of about 5 m (16 ft) is normal practice when consolidating ancient masonry. The advantage over mechanical pumping is that pressures cannot build up if there is a stoppage. The grout is mixed in a raised reservoir, from which it is fed by flexible pipe of about 25–30 mm (1–1.2 in) diameter and controlled by a plunger stopper.

A slightly more complicated method is to use a hand pump with 50 litre (10 gal) reservoir with the mix continuously agitated by an electric or compressed air motor. A hand pump can be used to produce pressures of two or even reaching six or

Figure 20.39 Pumping concrete, York Minster, England
(Courtesy: Shepherd Building Group Ltd)

Shepherd's Contracts Manager organized the pumping of some 80 m³ (105 yd³) of concrete to the top of the central tower, 63 m (207 ft) high. The work of laying this concrete took about five hours. Shepherd's were awarded a special Cembureau prize for this feat. In the conservation team the contribution of the contractor in using plant and equipment efficiently is vital to overall efficiency and economy of the project

seven atmospheres to achieve a deeper penetration of grout. Pressures must be controlled carefully, as there is a danger of blowing stones out of the face of a wall and other damage. The pump operator is supported by at least one man on each side of the wall who stop up leaks as and when they show, and if this is not possible stop the pumping. Sometimes this has to be done very quickly, and if communication by word of mouth is difficult then the use of throat microphones and radiotelephone is the best substitute—telephones are too slow. With hand pumping it is possible to feel the rate of flow and judge the situation and react quickly. This is not possible with mechanically operated pumps, which should not be used on historic building grouting work. However, reservoirs which inject using compressed air, at a predetermined pressure that cannot be exceeded, are probably the most efficient, especially in large operations.

Epoxy resin formulations have been used in much the same way as cementacious mixes to consolidate fissured masonry or cracked stones. The dangers from staining and surface damage are greater, so protective measures have to be more stringent. The pot life of some formulations is short and may cause difficulties in practice. The plant may have to be stripped down and cleaned completely after each injection. As the epoxy resin material is expensive it is not practicable or desirable to use it on large voids, so in some cases it may be desirable to fill the large voids with ordinary grout and then re-grout with a weak penetrating mix of epoxy resin so as to consolidate friable and broken-up areas. In suitable circumstances, vacuum impregnation may be used in order to obtain maximum penetration.

Vacuum impregnation should be carried out by specialist firms with experienced operatives. It is essential to ensure that sufficient vacuum can be obtained on the section to be dealt with, for, unless the object is completely isolated like a statue or pinnacle, there is a danger of air leaks around the perimeter and through the thickness of the chosen section. The object is enclosed in a sheet of impervious polythene. To allow the impregnating mixture to flow and find the crevices, fissures and pores of the masonry, a layer of netting is placed under the sheet which allows visual inspection to make sure that the surface is flooded. When the vacuum is released, the grout is sucked inwards. Various grouts are possible; for the preservation of stone, silane grouts have been used successfully and remarkable penetration has been claimed. As these are monomer resins, they require some six weeks or so to polymerize, before which time the outer sheet cannot be removed. By using vacuum methods it is theoretically possible to obtain deep penetration into

Figure 20.40 Pumping concrete, York Minster, England
(Courtesy: Shepherd Building Group Ltd)

After the enlargement of the foundations had been completed and the active settlement of the central tower stopped, it was possible to reinstate the floor which was of reinforced concrete laid over plastic coffer moulds. The concrete was pumped into position, vibrated and tamped to form a level and smooth finish

the pores of stone as well as fill the cracks and fissures, but there are many problems in practice.

Full records of all grouting operations should be kept and deposited with the archives of a building. The amounts injected are a rough guide to the structural condition of the fabric: up to 2½% of the total volume is by no means uncommon, but far larger amounts have often been injected into areas which have suffered high stresses over a long period of time, which is not surprising as one would expect these parts to wear out more quickly.

After repair of an historic building involving grouting, particularly with Portland cement, serious condensation problems can arise—first, because the water used in the injections may cause damage as it dries out; secondly, because the grout, if different from the wall mortar, may form zones of unequal density and promote cold bridges causing condensation which could result in disintegration of the wall plaster or staining of wall paintings; and lastly, there is always the danger of soluble salts in the cement causing damage by crystallization.

307

Appendix I

Historic buildings as structures

Rowland J. Mainstone D Eng, C Eng, MICE,
FIStruct E, FSA, FRSA, Hon FRIBA

Introduction

Buildings, like people, are individuals—not in the same way, of course, because the differences between buildings are purely physical whatever wider meanings they may have for us. The differences are no less real for that, and they are particularly important for historic buildings. Generalizations about particular 'families' can never take us very far, so I can only hint at a few possibilities in this review.

Like people also, buildings change and age with the passage of time, and eventually die in the sense of ceasing to have any value to us. Structurally the aging process is a progressive narrowing of the range of resistances that can be mobilized to counter the disruptive actions of gravity and the loads imposed by use and by wind, earthquake, etc. 'Death' may be deemed to have occurred when the resistances are overcome in a complete or partial collapse or when the risk of this happening appears to be too great for further use of, or access to, the building. Interventions of various kinds can slow down the aging process and give new leases of life either to the structure as built or by transforming it into something different. But they can also accelerate the process; and this has, too frequently, been the result of past interventions made with insufficient understanding or with too little regard for their possible effects.

In the broadest terms the resistances that can be mobilized depend primarily on two things—on the geometry of the structure and on the characteristic strengths and stiffnesses of the materials used. The main loads to be resisted by most historic buildings are their own dead weights and those imposed by wind and earthquake. These also depend on the geometry and materials, although not in quite the same ways, so that scale is important in the matching of load and resistance.

This dual dependence suggests that we might attempt a first review in terms of either forms (in the geometric sense) or materials. Forms are so varied—

even if we consider only those built before, say, 1850—that the latter seems at first sight the obvious choice, particularly since a material like timber has such very different characteristics from those of brick, stone and concrete. In practice, however, there is an important secondary dependence of the resistances that we cannot ignore. They depend also on the manner, and even on the sequence, in which individual lengths of timber or blocks of stone are joined together. Since joints that could efficiently transmit tension were very rare, a timber structure differs much less from its stone counterpart, for instance, than might otherwise be expected, and the difference tends to diminish with age as joints become progressively looser. Superficially very similar masonry structures may, on the other hand, have markedly different capacities if one—say the triple arcade of the Pont du Gard—is built throughout of closely fitted large blocks of stone while the other—say the triple arcade of a Romanesque church—consists largely of a poor rubble fill behind a thin ashlar skin.

In this review I shall therefore look at several large 'families' of historic buildings, characterized primarily by their uses of particular structural forms. In choosing these families I have concentrated on the forms used to span between vertical supports and enclosing walls, since it is these spanning elements of the total form that differ most and that, through determining what is required of the walls and other supports, have the greatest influence on the overall structural behaviour.

Beams and trusses

Until the introduction of the reinforced concrete beam (or, more questionably, that of the reinforced plate-bande about a century earlier), beams were always cut from single lengths of timber or blocks of

311

stone with little or no understanding of the internal complexities of the bending and shearing actions to which they would be subjected. What was important, from the point of view of overall structural behaviour, was that they were considered as simply weighing down vertically on their supports. This could not be said of the simplest alternative adopted where the span was a little too great for the available timber or stone—that of a pair of rafters or blocks of stone inclined towards one another, which constituted a rudimentary arch. But it could be just as true of a similar pair of rafters whose feet were adequately tied together, and of more complex forms of truss developed from this prototype.

In practice, there are requirements to be satisfied at the supports to achieve this ideally simple transfer of load, and it probably never was achieved until these requirements were better understood. There is a need, in particular, for freedom of horizontal movement at one support. In the absence of this freedom some horizontal loading of the supports is inevitable as a result of expansions and contractions of the beam or truss and of its deflections, even under purely vertical self-weight and imposed load. Especially in trusses, the deflections will often be found to have been considerable, even with ties of adequate strength in themselves, on account of stretching of the ties and movements at their joints. In many more cases the whole design of timber 'trusses' was so poorly conceived and their joints were so inefficient for the transmission of shear and the development of tensile strengths, that it would be much more correct to regard them as framed arches. The English hammerbeam 'truss' should, for instance, always be regarded as a stiffened arch in its original form. Instances are also fairly frequently found of stone beams or lintels that have cracked vertically near mid-span and that are therefore acting simply as three-pinned arches.

Restraint of horizontal movement at the end bearings of an unbroken beam or properly tied truss does, however, allow the beam or truss to act as a bracing element between its supports, and this is a factor that should be taken into account on the credit side in an overall structural assessment.

In any such assessment it is also necessary to consider the effects of non-vertical imposed loads. Wind loads are the commonest example—both wind pressures and wind suctions, which are sometimes more important. These are likely to act directly only on roof trusses but may be transmitted through beams from wall to wall or from column to column. Inertia loads resulting from enforced displacements by earthquakes are fortunately a less common risk; but they can, in some parts of the world, be a more serious threat where roof construction is fairly massive.

The column-and-beam temple and related early forms

In the primitive hut, as envisaged by architectural theorists from Filarete to Laugier, lateral stability was ensured by driving the posts that carried the roof beams into the ground or using as posts the trunks of trees already rooted in the ground. They could thus act as vertical cantilevers fixed at ground level.

In monuments like Stonehenge, a somewhat similar procedure was adopted. The great upright stones were all sunk in pits dug in the ground. But they have depended for their continued stability (where they have not fallen) as much on their large base dimensions, their weight, the good bearing characteristics of the chalk, and the absence of major earth shocks, as on this partial burial. They would probably have stood just as well if they had been set directly on a continuous horizontal base. Some of those that did fall may well have been pushed over by a slowly developed thrusting action of some of the lintels set in a continuous circle. At Luxor there are two considerably taller colonnades carrying massive stone lintels that have stood for the same length of time without relying on any rooting in the ground, and the unfinished Doric temple at Segesta furnishes another example that has stood for well over two millennia.

These structures were not, however, typical of Egyptian and Greek temples and other buildings of these periods. Although all we now have of some of them are lengths of similarly free-standing colonnade, these are only partial survivals or partial reconstructions of structures in which their lateral stability was originally ensured partly by continuous walls to which they were braced by lintels and timber roof beams. In the Egyptian temple and in most other buildings, the principal walls were external and columns were used internally to reduce the spans for the roof and any other beams. In the Greek temple, the walls of the cella were usually completely surrounded by an outer colonnade, with further columns inside in the larger temples. Because of the usual massiveness of construction, additional lateral stability would have been called for chiefly in the event of earthquake, but would also have been valuable if individual columns tended to tip over as a result of a poor foundation. The continuous wall is an excellent means of providing this additional resistance to lateral load because of its ability to carry directly a resultant inclined load in its own plane. Where collapses have occurred and the fallen masonry has been left as it fell, it is notable that it has usually fallen transversely to the line of the colonnade and a parallel wall. Adequate returns were not always provided and spaced sufficiently closely to prevent this transverse collapse, and it was made all the more likely by a common practice of constructing the thicker walls of two ashlar skins with a loose rubble core.

Later buildings with beam floors and beam or truss roofs

Beams or trusses, or both, are probably the major spanning elements of most surviving historic buildings of post-Roman date that are not merely roofless shells. In addition, trussed roofs cover many masonry vaults. I shall leave for later consideration buildings in which this is so and concentrate here on the stability of multi-storey buildings and wide-span single-storey ones in which vaults, if adopted at all, are used in only minor roles. Typically walls, continuous except for window and door openings, provide the main vertical supports with columns, of much more slender proportions than those considered hitherto, used chiefly to reduce internal spans. Such columns are usually capable only of carrying vertical load, so that lateral stability is wholly dependent on the walls. The rigid column-and-beam frame (with moment-resisting connections) was only developed slowly from the 1840s onwards in cast and wrought iron.

The structural action is most clearly defined in the wide-span single-storey buildings, whether single- or multi-bay. If the trusses are adequately tied and have not spread, if they are adequately braced together transversely to their spans, and if they are carried (except where two trusses meet at the same level) by walls capable of resisting any imposed side loads, stability should be ensured. The chief risk is of outward bowing and overturning of the walls if the tying of the trusses is inadequate and the walls do not have sufficient transverse strength to restrain them from spreading. Even with adequately tied trusses, there is a further risk in one particular type of building—the aisled basilica in which the central row of trusses is carried on clerestory walls which stand on open colonnades below the aisle roofs. Such walls are particularly prone to lateral bowing and eventual buckling even under predominantly vertical load. This bowing can be seen in many places today and seems to have been particularly pronounced in the Constantinian Church of St Peter's, Rome, before its demolition in the sixteenth century.

With one exception the action is much less clearly defined in the multi-storey form. This usually has numerous walls running in at least two directions and providing multiple possible paths for the downward transmission of all loads. Inherently it is a very strong form, as is shown by our ability today to build considerably taller buildings using brick bearing walls of a thickness much less than was considered safe in the past. Older buildings may be just as strong, or even stronger, if they are only subject to vertical and wind loads. Their strength may, however, be reduced (usually with a corresponding reduction in the number of paths available for transmitting the loads to the ground) and their stability made more marginal in a number of ways. Inadequate foundations may lead to uneven bearing, differential settlements and other distortions. Poorly constructed walls may crack or bow under these circumstances or as a result of repeated thermal movements, thrusting of roofs, rotting of timber, or weakening by ill-considered alterations. And there may be complete separations between poorly bonded wall facings and everything behind. Generalization is impossible here. Every building must be looked at individually. Where there is a risk of earthquakes, it is also likely that the walls on which survival will principally depend are inadequately tied together. In addition, the masses and stiffnesses of the building may be distributed unevenly and unsymmetrically, so that it will tend, when shaken, to split into sections that will then knock against one another.

The one exception referred to above is the building with completely open or lightly partitioned floors carried entirely by columns except along the exterior, where there is a continuous wall that is usually rectangular in plan. This was a common eighteenth and nineteenth century form for warehouses, mills and, later, for commercial buildings. Initially both columns and floor beams were all of timber, with timber roofs also. From the end of the eighteenth century, cast-iron columns and then cast-iron and wrought-iron beams were progressively substituted. Here again the structural action is clear. Vertical loads are transmitted fairly directly down both the columns and the outer wall; all horizontal load is resisted by the walls on which lateral stability is wholly dependent. This high degree of dependence on the outer walls, coupled often with a considerable interdependence of the lines of internal framing between one wall and the opposite one, is the chief hazard to their stability. Where there is this interdependence (meaning that each line of framing is only connected to, and thereby braced by, the parallel outer walls through its connections to the other lines of framing) there is clearly a risk of a catastrophic internal collapse as a result of a local failure. Such collapses are, indeed, on record.

Arches and barrel vaults

The most important characteristic of the arch is that it does always thrust outwards on its supports as well as weighing down vertically on them. At least it always

313

does so in itself as part of its primary action, although the thrust can be contained by an effective tie between its feet. In the absence of such a tie, it is almost certain to spread to some extent unless its supports are being forced inwards by stronger opposing thrusts. In either case it will be deformed and, since the deformation will affect both its internal action and its action on its supports, we must briefly consider the possibilities. It is convenient for this purpose to consider a stone voussoir arch with well-fitting voussoirs assembled dry, as was the usual Roman practice. With minor differences other arches, even Roman concrete ones, behave similarly—the general mass in the concrete arch being divided into voussoir-shaped blocks by full bricks that penetrate, at intervals, right through its thickness.

All loads acting on the arch are carried sideways, as well as downwards, by means of inclined thrusts passing through the voussoirs and from voussoir to voussoir. If the voussoirs fitted perfectly, were infinitely hard and were unable to slip on one another, it would be possible for the line of the resultant thrusts to pass anywhere within the depth of the arch at any point. Even the smallest inward or outward movement of the supports would then be accommodated by small hinging rotations at three joints or groups of joints, and the resultant thrust line would have to pass through the three 'hinges'. For a small inward movement the hinges would be alternately on the extrados, intrados and extrados. For a small outward movement they would be alternately on the intrados, extrados and intrados. The thrust lines would be, respectively, as flat and as steep as the depth of the arch allowed. It follows that, for a given vertical load, the horizontal thrust at the supports would be a maximum in the first case and a minimum in the second case. This is exactly as it should be to minimize the risk of collapse: from this point of view the arch is an ideal structural form which deforms in such a way as to improve its stability. The extent of the improvement depends on its depth in relation to its rise, being greater the deeper and flatter in profile the arch is. Here, however, all is not for the best because a flat arch will thrust outwards most, other things being equal, and will therefore be more likely to push its support aside.

In practice such ideal voussoirs do not exist. Where the ideal is almost achieved, as again in some Roman arches, a close approach of the thrust line to extrados or intrados of a large arch results in such high local stresses that local crushing or splitting of the stone occurs. This tends to precipitate a local slip, which reduces the effective depth of the arch. In practice also, an arch nearly always has spandrel masonry above it, and it is usually part of a larger structure. Loads from above have to be transmitted through the spandrels. Because these have some stiffness of their own they will press down more heavily anywhere the arch tends to rise and less heavily anywhere it tends to fall. They will thereby stiffen it, or add to its effective depth. Where the arch is also part of a larger structure—spanning an opening in a continuous wall for instance—it may have to accommodate itself to movements of its supports induced from outside as well as to the loads acting directly on it. This it will usually do by a combination of hinging rotations and slips.

The fact that slips as well as hinging rotations do, in fact, occur is both an analytical embarrassment and a factor of some importance in long-term behaviour. Analytically it means that no simple thrust-line analysis can give a clear indication of the margin of safety against collapse. In the long term it is important because slips, unlike hinging rotations, are irreversible (although even hinging rotations may be partly irreversible as a result of the partial jamming of open joints by debris). Spreading of arches as a result, for instance, of seasonal temperature changes tends, therefore, to be cumulative.

Barrel vaults, being merely arches extended laterally, behave in much the same way as arches of the same depth and profile. They have, however, the further capacity to distribute loads laterally. This means that they are likely to deform less and to be somewhat stronger when subjected to very local loads, because these will be distributed sideways to some extent instead of passing, in their entirety, directly to the supports. It also means that they can act in much the same way as walls in resisting side loads that act along their lengths.

Cast-iron arches almost constitute a separate family of forms. They often seem to have been designed with no clear understanding of their mode of action, with the result that they range all the way from close counterparts of the masonry voussoir arch to three-pinned arches and beams or paired cantilevers with arched soffits. Even when they do act as arches, they will usually thrust sideways less than masonry arches of similar spans on account of their reduced weights.

Timber arches usually have some bending stiffness, obtained by lapping the joints between individual lengths of timber. They can thus deform further without collapse in accommodating themselves to imposed loads and support movements. To prevent excessive deformation they were usually braced in some manner, and this bracing stiffens them in much the same way as the spandrels stiffen a masonry arch ring.

Buildings with arcaded walls, vaulted floors, and arch-supported or barrel-vaulted roofs

Arches have been used in place of beams or trusses in most of the types of building referred to above, except the last. Requirements for lateral stability are generally similar with this substitution, apart from an increased requirement for bracing or buttressing where the feet of the arches are not adequately tied or their outward thrusts are not mutually opposed, as in continuous straight arcades. The requirements have also been met in broadly similar ways, although, in compensation for its thrusting, an arch spanning transversely to a wall to carry a roof can assist in bracing the wall if its spandrels are filled. Beams and trusses normally provide no such bracing.

Where barrel vaults have been used in place of beams to carry floors, the extra weight calls for more substantial walls, and these are usually well able to resist any unbalanced thrusts developed by the vaults. It is, in any case, unusual to find heavy barrel vaults so used in the upper storeys of buildings of post-Roman date. Light tile vaults were used here in the eighteenth and nineteenth centuries, with some care taken over their alignments to minimize the unbalanced thrusts at the ends of the building.

Roman arched and vaulted buildings and their derivatives (setting aside for the moment those with domes or large groin-vaulted roofs) are a further type. They are characterized by the use of both arches and barrel vaults on a large scale as the principal elements of construction, including the use of the latter for roofing wide spaces. So used, they inevitably developed large outward thrusts. To a large extent these thrusts seem to have been deliberately countered in the finished buildings by opposing arch to arch or vault to vault including, in the case of principal longitudinal vaults, the use of quadrant vaults alongside at a lower level or the use, again at a lower level, of ranges of barrel vaults aligned at right angles. The need to ensure stability of the incomplete building during construction usually called, nevertheless, for supporting piers and walls substantial enough to resist many of the thrusts at nearer their full magnitude. To this, and to the excellent quality of most Roman masonry and concrete, we owe the ability of many Roman ruins to remain standing in a mutilated state. Examples of impending further collapse may also be observed—for instance at the north-east end of the break in the upper tiers of the outer arcade of the Flavian Amphitheatre (the Colosseum) in Rome, where major voussoir slips and arch distortions have occurred.

Much post-Roman masonry is less sound, including particularly much of that found in West-European Romanesque and Gothic churches. In addition, the testing of the structure in its inherently weaker incomplete state during construction did not extend to its ability—and certainly not to its long-term ability—to contain safely the outward thrusts of the high central vault or vaults. Masonry thicknesses were usually so generous that large vault distortions and associated tilts of their supports could have been accommodated with the resultant thrusts still well within the thickness, if the masonry had been of uniform strength and stiffness. But with walls in which the core is a largely useless rubble fill, the resultant thrusts move much more rapidly to positions dangerously close to the outer faces. It is essential therefore to take into account the nature and present condition of the masonry in appraising the stability of such buildings.

The dome and associated transition elements

Potentially the doubly curved domical form is, from the point of view of strength and stability, ideal. The outward thrusts developed in its upper part can be wholly contained by circumferential tensions lower down, so that it exerts a purely vertical load on its supports. Its double curvature also fits it well to resist side loads from wind or earthquake.

What was achieved, again fell short of the ideal. A few small concrete or flattish monolithic stone domes may have had sufficient tensile strength to have contained the thrusts, if they had been free of horizontal restraints at their supports. But even the single domical slab that roofs the Mausoleum of Theodoric at Ravenna is cracked in two, probably by restraints to its thermal expansion and contraction. The masonry or concrete dome in general certainly lacks both the necessary tensile strength and the necessary freedom of movement at its base.

The typical dome therefore acts, in its lower part, as a ring of incomplete arches. These incomplete arches meet in a crown of continuous masonry under both circumferential and radial compression, this crown often being open in the centre where it may be covered by a lantern. Such arches need to be considerably thicker than an ideal dome of the same diameter if their stability is to be assured, but more than ample thickness was always provided. Like any other arches they thrust outwards at their feet and this thrust must be similarly resisted by the supports or contained by separate ties. Many brick domes have been provided with circumferential ties of timber or iron, but it is unlikely that any of them resist more than a part of the total thrust.

From the present point of view the octagonal pavilion vault is no different from a circular dome. The most notable—that over the crossing of the Cathedral of S. Maria del Fiore in Florence—was deliberately given a thickness sufficient to contain a circular form within and was constructed as if it was a circular dome.

Where the circular form was adopted and the supports were square or polygonal in plan, transition elements had to be used. These have been given many forms, at least on the surface. All can be analysed into either pendentives or squinches, but most of the multiple-squinch forms are closer to pendentives in their overall surface geometry and almost certainly act as pendentives since they contain the pendentive form within their thicknesses. All forms (except for the uncommon merging pendentive) involve some change in direction of the resultant downward and outward thrusts from the dome at the level of its base. The pendentive involves the least change, since the resultant thrusts remain radial or nearly so. But, taking into account again the thickness of the masonry, the differences are unlikely to be of much importance in terms of the overall structural behaviour. All forms will add something to the total outward thrusts to be resisted.

A related form that calls for at least brief mention is the semi-dome. In the complete dome, there is a large resultant horizontal thrust acting in each direction across any notional vertical plane through the centre. If therefore the dome is actually cut on such a plane, it is potentially an excellent buttress. If there is nothing for it to buttress, as when it was used in the apse of a timber-roofed basilican church, its crown moves forward until an internal balance of thrusts is achieved with its forward edge acting as an arch spanning across the diameter in the horizontal sense.

Domed buildings

The complete family of domed buildings includes a primitive form of even remoter ancestry (in all probability) than the column-and-beam temple. This is the widespread beehive hut which sometimes achieved monumental proportions, as in several Mycenean tombs. The fact that the more permanent stone huts and tomb chambers were constructed by laying each ring of stone on a flat bed projecting slightly forward from the previous ring, did not eliminate the radial thrusts. These are resisted in the smaller huts by the ground from which they directly rise or by a very thick wall at the base, and additionally in the large tomb chambers by the earth piled against them on the outside.

In most later domed buildings, where the dome is raised high above the ground, the thrusts are resisted primarily or wholly by the buttressing action of the supports. In the simplest form, typified by the Roman Pantheon, the dome rises directly from a circular or polygonal base, with or without transition elements in the latter case. Usually this base is opened out into a number of arched recesses around the circumference and, since the arches are not in line, their outward thrusts add something to the total that has to be resisted. But the overall thickness of the base, plus that of any projections of the arched recesses beyond it, has clearly been sufficient in surviving structures of this type to provide the necessary buttressing.

In the more complex forms the dome is still carried by arches spanning between four or more piers. But these are now much more deeply opened out, either into a single wider space as in the Church of St Sophia in Istanbul and the Ottoman Imperial mosques, or into the nave, transepts and choir of many domed western churches. In the former examples, the semi-dome is used on the same scale as the central dome itself as a major buttressing element. In the Church of St Sophia, where it was first so used, it clearly demonstrated its superiority in this role over the more conventional arched buttresses used on the north and south sides of the church. In the latter examples, buttressing is provided by arcades extending in two directions from each pier and usually of substantial Roman proportions, although frequently of less than Roman solidity and strength. There is little reason to doubt the adequacy of this buttressing. Where the central dome has shown serious sign of distress, as at St Peter's in the mid-eighteenth century, this has been primarily the result of interposing a tall drum between it and its more substantial base.

Only in the late-eighteenth century Paris Pantheon was the final step taken of supporting a large tall dome on slender piers sufficient only to carry its vertical load, and relying on a combination of circumferential iron ties and masonry struts arching over to outer piers and walls to resist the outward thrusts. This gave again a structure with a fairly simple and determinate overall pattern of action but one which, for this very reason, called for sound construction throughout. The fact that the masonry of the central piers was so constructed that it had an effective strength far below that of the stone from which it was built, necessitated almost immediate strengthening of these piers.

Groined and ribbed vaults

The chief structural difference between groined and ribbed vaults and either barrel vaults or domes is that they bring all loads to a few widely separated points rather than to continuous boundaries. The larger vaults were usually built over rectangular bays and bring all their loads down to the corners of the bays, where they thrust diagonally outwards. They were also usually built in series. This means that in the finished structure (but probably not during construction) the components of the thrusts resolved along two sides of the rectangle are cancelled out by equal thrusts in adjacent bays except at the two ends of the series. The remaining outward components for the whole series of vaults will only be roughly half the total outward thrusts of a continuous barrel vault of the same span and rise and weight. Since ribbed vaults could be made somewhat lighter in relation to their span and rise, there is usually also a further reduction in outward thrust plus a reduction in vertical load on the supports thanks to the exploitation of this possibility.

Much has been written about the extent to which the ribs in a ribbed vault do, or do not, carry the webs. All that can be said with confidence is that the geometric configuration would always allow the webs to stand on their own as groined vaults, but that the ribs will certainly stiffen them and will probably, to a large extent, carry them where the ribs were built first, where the webs are markedly arched up between them, where the masonry of the webs is more compressible and, of course, where there is no continuity of the webs above the ribs. The more complex surface form, as compared with other kinds of vault, means that spreading of the vault is accompanied by more complex patterns of deformation. But, from the point of view of overall structural behaviour, it is sufficient to concentrate on the ribs. These deform by a combination of hinging rotations and slips in much the same way as free-standing arches with heavy spandrel fills only towards their feet (where the space between the converging ribs was usually filled solid).

Gothic churches

Groined and ribbed vaults have been used in many ways in historic buildings, but there have been only two applications of major structural interest. The Romans used large and very heavy concrete groined vaults, sometimes with integrally embedded 'ribs' of brick, to roof a variety of large halls from the early second century onwards. Even in the great halls of the Imperial baths and in the Basilica Nova the resulting structures did not, however, differ sufficiently from those discussed already to justify further discussion in this brief review. I shall concentrate here on the second application—that in Gothic churches and cathedrals.

Gothic builders exploited fully the concentration of all load from the vaults at a few points. Except in some southern churches, the vaults were only fireproof ceilings beneath trussed timber roofs. But the principal roof trusses were placed so that their loads were brought down to the same points, and isolated piers were built up to them to carry the vertical components of the combined loads. Side loads, both vault thrusts and wind loads, were then carried over to outer piers by inclined masonry struts—the flying buttresses that served as a model for similar struts in the Paris Pantheon.

The result was a highly lineal structural form with an unusually clear balance of thrust and counter-thrust throughout. At least this balance is qualitatively clear. Quantitatively it is less clear, because there are numerous points at which the loads can bifurcate and because the forms are not truly linear. The principal piers, in particular, were given sufficient breadth to accommodate resultant thrusts along many different paths. Herein lay the principal margin of safety against collapse, and herein it still lies unless deformations of the structure and differential consolidations of cores and facings of the piers have narrowed the possibilities too far. Where collapses have occurred they have probably been due to excessive eccentricities of resultant thrusts leading to buckling with or without local splitting or spalling of the stone, or to local slips.

Margins of safety

There have been enough recorded collapses of structures that have previously stood for a long time to show that margins of safety can diminish with time, and not only as a result of ill-considered additions or alterations to the structure. Weathering of masonry, rotting of timber, and other similar sorts of deterioration, are one reason, especially today with high atmospheric pollution. Another reason is the progressive increase of deformations to a point where equilibrium is no longer possible or local stresses are too high at critical points and lead to local splitting and bursting or spalling of masonry or other failures. Deterioration of materials and/or deliberate cutting can contribute to this increase by reducing stiffnesses, and it can lower the safe levels of stress. Much of the increase occurs through the accumulation of small irreversible slips and openings of cracks, and through differential foundation movements. The former accumulation is likely to take place at an increasing rate as more cracks form. Differential foundation settlements due to consolidation of the ground should, on the other hand, diminish with time unless the settlements significantly change the distribution of pressures (as in the case of a leaning tower) or the ground conditions change (perhaps as a result of adjacent works or a fall in the water table). Normally they should have reached their final values well within the first 100 years of the life of a building. Further differential settlements may, however, occur at any time as a result of such things as the rotting of piles or bodily ground movements.

It follows that the fact that an historic building is standing today, although irrefutable evidence of its present stability, is no guarantee that it will still be standing tomorrow, and that no analysis that merely assures us of its present stability is of any practical value. The most difficult task for the structural conservationist is to look into the future. He can safely assert that, if it is left alone, the building will one day collapse. But when? The structural designer is accustomed to considering time explicitly only in certain special circumstances, notably when there is a possibility of fatigue failure under cyclic loading. Here we are faced with a situation that has something in common with low-cycle fatigue, but with many complications.

Possibly the best that can be done is to start by ascertaining as fully as possible how the building is at present carrying its loads, how it has been deformed by them, and how the deformations are changing. The present deformations are doubly relevant to the manner in which the loads are being carried; first because it is the deformed structure that is doing the carrying, and secondly because they are often clues to the sequence of construction which is itself very relevant. Also relevant are the details of construction, particularly the nature and condition of masonry or brickwork throughout its thickness and the nature and condition of joints in timber trusses and frames. Only when all of these have been taken into account can useful quantitative analyses be made. To ignore them is to tie one's hands needlessly behind one's back and risk producing impeccable but useless analyses of structures that might have been, rather than the one that is. Realistic analyses should help to identify any potentially dangerous deformations (including cracks and slips). Observations of changes in these deformations should continue over a sufficient period to allow cyclic changes to be differentiated from long-term ones.

Having made his observations and analyses, the engineer should be as well informed as he can hope to be about the structural health of the building. But, except in cases of serious distress and near collapse, he will still usually be forced to make his own judgement about its likely future safety and the need, if any, for his intervention with remedial works.

Possible structural interventions

The correct decision (from the point of view of making the best use of available resources) may well be to leave alone for the present, apart from carrying out normal maintenance to keep out rain or frost. But this is a difficult decision to take when there is any element of doubt, and it is important then that any works undertaken do really increase safety and the expectation of life.

Structural interventions have been made in the past for a variety of reasons, and not always with desirable results. Among the most regrettable have been a number of later additions of tall towers and spires to the crossings of Gothic cathedrals, which have subsequently resulted in major collapses. The outstanding example of this was at Beauvais in the sixteenth century. Many buildings have also been structurally weakened by being cut into to provide more light or space, to open a new entrance, to accommodate new furniture, or for some other similarly non-structural reason. Others, like St Irene in Istanbul, have had columns removed for re-use elsewhere. In this case smaller columns were substituted without apparent damage to the structure. More surprisingly, the entire nave arcades of S. Apollinare Nuovo in Ravenna were lifted, without apparent damage to the clerestory walls, when the floor was raised on account of a rise in the ground level outside.

If we consider only past interventions that have had a primarily structural motive, they can be divided into additions of props, ties or infills; rectifications of leaning walls or columns; consolidation of masonry, partial renewal of facings and patching of decayed timber; and more extensive renewals or rebuildings including partial reconstructions after local collapses. If this list is read as referring only to work above ground, we should add to it consolidation of foundations and underpinning works. Few major historic buildings can have escaped any such attention, and many have achieved their present form only as a result of the later addition of buttresses or ties or as a result of partial rebuilding. This is particularly true of buildings which were innovatory in form or scale, either in an absolute sense or in terms of the experience of their builders. The church of St Sophia in Istanbul is possibly the outstanding example, but many large Romanesque and Gothic buildings are good examples also. Wherever it is true, it is a factor that must be taken into account when assessing the significance of present apparent deformations.

Can we learn anything further from these past interventions? I think that we can draw a few general conclusions, although undoubtedly we could learn more if we were better informed, particularly about the less successful interventions. One lesson, relevant to buildings in continued use, is that visible additions or modifications are not necessarily aesthetically detrimental. It is partly due to the addition of flying buttresses to structures that initially lacked them that we owe the definitive form of the Gothic cathedral. It is also partly due to a series of additions and modifications and a partial reconstruction to a slightly different design that we owe the unique spatial qualities of St Sophia. A more practical lesson that is relevant to all buildings is that props and ties will not restrain further movements as effectively as they might, unless steps are taken to transfer load to them without prior further deformation. Inserted ties were usually fitted with wedge-shaped keys or turnbuckles for this purpose. But buttresses were often simply built against the wall they were intended to prop. They could then do more harm than good, if they were effectively bonded to it, by themselves tilting as the ground beneath consolidated, and thereby pulling the wall further over. In a somewhat similar way, the simple selective replacement of cracked or spalled facings in a wall could merely lead to the cracking or crushing of other blocks, because all load was initially thrown on these other blocks. A further lesson is that the execution of remedial works that involve any cutting away of the existing structure is, in itself, hazardous. A striking demonstration of this hazard was the collapse of the main eastern arch and part of the original dome of St Sophia, not during the earthquakes of A.D. 556 and 557 that both damaged it, but in May 558 while repairs were in progress.

The most desirable action in any particular case today must always be a matter for individual decision and will probably differ according to whether the building is to be preserved only as an historic monument or to be given a further lease of life in active use. In the former case, the minimum interference with the 'original' or 'definitive' form seems highly desirable. In the latter case, additions or modifications may be justifiable.

Given, as the primary objective, the assurance of the continued existence of the structure for a further

period, I should look first (after taking steps to remove any obvious causes of excessive weathering, rot, etc.) for means of limiting further increases in deformation that did not involve any major structural changes. These might include internal consolidation of inhomogeneous and therefore weak masonry; repairs to weak members and joints of timber trusses; and the limited introduction of new ties. In consolidating weak masonry cores, it would be important to ensure the bonding of the core to the facing and to bear in mind the effects of changes in relative stiffnesses if the consolidation was done selectively. Both in repairing joints in timber and in introducing new ties it would be important to bear in mind that some cyclic movements are inevitable as a response to changes in temperature and humidity and that, unless the building is turned into the equivalent of a pre-stressed monolith, some cracks and other similar freedoms are necessary in the absence of deliberately formed expansion joints. This, of course, is also relevant to the treatment of cracks generally. Externally they are undesirable because they provide an entry for water. But filling should preferably be with something of low elastic modulus because, otherwise, it will accelerate the process whereby cyclic movements gradually add to permanent deformations. I should undertake the rectification of leaning walls or columns, partial reconstructions and any other major interferences with the existing form only as a last resort, because I think that they destroy part of the historic value of the building. There are certainly cases, however, where there would be merits, both to reveal what is of chief historic value and to relieve the structure of unnecessary and undesirable weight or mass, in removing later accretions to the original form. Reducing the mass near the top of the building might even be desirable at some sacrifice of the original structure where there is a serious risk of earthquake.

This is really tantamount to a personal plea for respecting the structural as well as the architectural and historical integrity of the building, and therefore for getting to know it as fully as possible before presuming to do anything to it. This knowledge can only be gained in the first place by making a meticulous visual inspection.

Appendix II

Security in historic buildings

Principles

The conservation architect will find himself faced with many practical problems relating to security.

As with fire, security poses difficult problems for the designer. Blind application of the building regulations produces aesthetic disasters so the reasoning behind the regulations has to be understood and trade-offs made in order to find reasonable compromises. Much therefore depends on the quality of the fire service and the architect or surveyor. The fire audit procedure should prove useful. With security one is dealing with a wide range of imponderables and there are no regulations. It is all a matter of judgment for the owner or administrator of the building. Very little has been written on the subject—possibly for security reasons—yet, it is one of which the historic architect must be aware. This Appendix has been added in order to deal with the subject more fully than in the 1st edition.

Standards for fire prevention and means of escape are continually being raised, so that security is becoming more and more difficult to maintain to the standards required by insurance companies, and conflicts which have to be resolved by the designer are becoming more noticeable.

Security is concerned with the prevention of crime, particularly the theft of valuables in the building and prevention of damage to the fabric of the building. There can be conflict between the desired requirements of 'means of escape' for the public and security precautions for valuables—one interest requiring the door to be open and the other shut and securely locked. So it is necessary to treat each case on its merits. First, all possible risks must be identified and the following factors relating to site, construction and equipment should be reviewed.

The site

(1) Climatic hazards such as wind, flood and earthquake.
(2) The environment, pollution, noise, the flight pattern of a nearby airport, military over-flying, sonic bangs.
(3) Access for foot traffic, motor vehicles and their parking locations. Is off street parking available?
(4) Layout, both internal and external. Utilization of spaces, reception areas, visitor control. Note toilet areas are vulnerable. Planning to reduce unnecessary movement and access by careful assignment. Security should increase with depth of access, but escape routes and doors create problems.
(5) Political situation. Incidence of street crime, civil and religious unrest, terrorism, arson.

Construction

Roof structures, walls, partitions, ceilings, floors, doors and locks, ducts, windows and ledges at ground floor and first floor levels where bombs might be placed should be studied. Glazing can be toughened and made bullet resisting. Are curtains capable of stopping flying broken glass? External shutters are useful to protect windows against civil unrest and storms.

Equipment Consider the use of car park barriers, locks and grilles. Review the benefits of combined fire alarm and security systems with computer control to monitor internal movement patterns and the work of security guards, and review the alarms for fire, plant malfunctions, lift breakdowns, and panic alarms for occupants.

In principle there are three types of lock security:

(1) To prevent people entering the building.
(2) To prevent the wrong people entering a room or space.
(3) To protect valuables stored inside furniture.

All valuables should be protected by physical barriers of one type or another including bullet resistant glass.

To overcome the conflict between security and firefighting, one master key for all doors is ideal, but this is easier said than done.

Keys issued by a supervisor must be signed for—however exalted the recipient. Every so often (say at five year intervals) it is desirable that the locks be changed so as to eliminate the number of 'illegal' keys which come into use in the course of time. The mechanism of the locks should be capable of several arrangements to enable these renewals to be done easily and at low cost. This renewal is much easier with electronic coded locks.

Detection systems

The wide range of detection systems available for protection against theft and damage, can be divided into three main groups: (see also *Table 1*)

(1) localized point detection applied to objects
    (a) fixed to a wall
    (b) free standing
    (c) contained in a showcase.
(2) perimeter detection,
(3) volumetric detection.

An electronic alarm system consists of four elements; a detector, a control box, an alarm signaller, and the wires joining them all together. The system is like a chain, it is only as strong as its weakest link; therefore it must be protected against intentional neutralization by cutting of wires, against mechanical or electrical destruction, against masking or changing the alignment or position of the detector, against involuntary neutralization such as by power failure or breakdown.

Good detectors and detector monitoring systems include electronic protection measures to sense any tampering with the detectors, such as cutting of power supply and/or signal lines, and which will also sense mains power failures. Since the technology is readily available and the risk of tampering real, such safeguards should be specified as a matter of course. If an alarm system is monitored by a central station it should signal automatically when a

disaster occurs or if it is intentionally or accidentally disconnected or disabled.

Protection systems are generally designed to give daytime protection based on localized and linear systems, supported at night by volumetric detection. Window and door bars give greater protection if they are wired to anti-tampering devices. More than one complementary system gives greater security against premeditated theft. Control boxes should have a reserve supply of electricity in case of power failure. Alarms can be sirens, flashing lights, closing of doors automatically, taped announcements, and telephone links to the police station via a central station using either the public telephone network or dedicated lines. The malfunction of a sophisticated alarm system can occur at least ten times for one real alarm. Because of the nuisance that these alarms cause, there is a danger that indolent staff may switch them off.

Security personnel

The difficulties of an old nightwatchman dealing with intruders should not be minimized. At night, in addition to electronic alarms, the building should be patrolled by a trained able-bodied person. Uniforms confer some additional authority. The multi-toned internal communication system (bleep) while not being as good as a two-way radio, is a help for internal security when combined with the efficient internal telephone system which may also be linked by direct line to the police station.

One of the easiest ways for an intruder to gain access is via builder's ladders and scaffolding. So, ladders should be removed and locked at night and scaffolding made unattractive by liberal use of barbed wire and sticky paint or grease on the lower parts. Permanent illumination is also another aid to security as any night time intruder would be noticed or anyway run that risk.

The public, who visit historic buildings in ever increasing numbers, produce a range of problems because of carelessness and in particular, illicit smoking and even deliberate arson. Vandalism is common, including name cutting, removing small objects, throwing things from galleries and roof parapets and breaking windows. Rowdyism and aggressive and uncontrollable behaviour are becoming more frequent, particularly with gangs of youths from any distant part. There are problems with unfortunate down-and-outs, methylated spirits drinkers, and would-be or actual suicides; also bomb scares may involve a thorough check of public parts of the building by police and staff. Good internal security reduces these problems.

Table 1 Types of Theft Detection System

Type of detector	False alarms	Remarks
LOCALIZED POINT DETECTORS:		
Mechanical contact	No	Local range of alarm. Cheap installation easy
Magnetic contact	No	Can be used on doors, windows, etc. A small piece of detector must be fixed to the object and this may cause difficulties. Easy to install.
Capacitive system	Yes	Prevents cutting of paintings or tapestries and can deter vandalism if the alarm is sufficiently frightening. Easy to install.
Contact mat	No	Inexpensive. Good for keeping visitors at a distance without using traditional barriers. Useful for protecting works consisting of several pieces. Good 'trap' protection if placed in passages where thieves might walk, but also easily avoided if location is known or suspected. Easy to install.
Variable pressure wire		Invisible when wires are placed directly behind or under the object.
Radio alarm		Can be used with any of the above detectors and avoids the use of vulnerable wires, but the battery must be charged regularly.
Vibration sensor	Yes	Detects attempts to break glass and, as sensitivity can be regulated, can be used to protect walls, ceilings and doors. If too sensitive causes false alarms. Subject to corrosion.
Glass cutting sensor	Few	More expensive than the vibration sensor. The sensor is glued to the glass.
PERIMETER DETECTORS:		
Photoelectric cell	Few	Inexpensive. The light source may overheat and blow out thus setting off a false alrm. Can be bypassed using a torch or cigarette lighter. A mirror system makes the beam zigzag and can make it more difficult to pass.
Laser barrier invisible pulsed emission	No	Based on laser diodes, a low cost technology. The detector cannot be bypassed by supplying another emission source.
Passive infra-red detection, sensitive to rapid changes in temperature	Few	Reliable. Not sensitive to atmospheric disturbance or radio waves. Screens an area 14 m (46 ft) in front of a work but does not detect gradual movement. Can be bypassed by using an insulating cloth as a screen. Also effective for volumetric protection as they are inexpensive in this category.
VOLUMETRIC DETECTORS:		
Ultrasonic detector	Some	Movement in the detector's field of action causes variations in the frequency transmitted and that received. Does not affect materials and can be used in showcases. Solid proven construction. Range limited to 12–15 m (40–50 ft) because false alarms increase as the range becomes greater. Lightning, bells, supersonic booms, air currents and ventilation can lead to false alarms. Low frequency, 16–40 kHz.
Microwave detector	Few	Works at high frequencies, 1–10 GHz, and is therefore not disturbed by lower frequencies. The detection zone can extend to 100 m (328 ft) and can be regulated exactly. High sensitivity can be obtained without risk of false alarms, even by insects. Microwaves penetrate wood, glass and other building materials, so location of the apparatus must be chosen carefully.
PERIMETER PROTECTION:		Line sensing to surround a building or single exhibit, using fibre optic pressure sensing cables or metal wire fencing that can detect vibrations. Many systems available.
CLOSED CIRCUIT TELEVISION:		Cameras covering vulnerable areas relaying back to monitors in the security guard office. Intrusion at night can be detected by infra-red illumination.

The advantages of having able-bodied men to deal with uncontrolled behaviour are considerable. The entrance to a building should be supervised by a uniformed man at all times, for by firm and polite action they can often prevent rowdyism. Thefts of valuables or souvenirs cause a great nuisance, the only antidote being constant supervision; however, pairs of experienced thieves can, by working together, put supervisors off their guard. One historic house has equipped its host guides with whistles to blow the alarm and alert companions to close external exits.

The risk of theft by bogus workmen is considerable, this can be reduced by a system of recording and checking credentials. In historic buildings, workmen generally have to be supervised continuously and this can be a severe problem for the custodial staff.

Additional points on security measures

The U.K. Fire Protection Association provides data sheets intended as an *aide-memoire* for those who have the responsibility for the protection of premises and to help them achieve cost effective security measures. Some of the points that they make are given below.

Control equipment

Controls for alarm systems can usually be operated by non-technical staff and should be contained in a unit within the 'alarmed' area and protected against tampering and have their own detection circuit.

Systems should be divided into zones to assist in identification of devices which have triggered and also for early diagnosis of fault conditions.

Alarms normally operate at 12 volts produced via the mains, with standby batteries in case of power failure. Short circuiting the system will result in an alarm being given.

There should be a maintenance and service agreement with equipment manufacturers. Records of previous inspections, false alarm calls, changes of key holder and servicing should be kept by the user as this can be of considerable use in diagnosing faults.

Wire free systems

Systems using radio transmitters with receivers or transceivers are simple to install but their range is limited. Signals to remote centres are sent conven-

tionally by telephone. Their advantage is that they avoid unsightly wiring and damage to the fabric.

Detection devices

Detection devices need careful siting in historic buildings with large volumes and variable internal air movements, which should be studied using smoke tests. Multiples of a device or different devices in combinations should be used according to circumstances. Wiring for devices and their siting should be supervised to prevent tampering.

The insurer and a fire engineer or security expert should be consulted to advise on the most suitable system.

Surveillance

The effectiveness of patrols and observers can be enhanced by the use of electronic surveillance. Strategically placed, remotely controlled TV cameras improve surveillance possibilities. Movement detectors can be used to activate cameras and security lighting, so alerting the operator. Lenses capable of producing images at extremely low levels of light are available. A further development is the use of infra-red light and television cameras which can read the movements of an intruder.

Access control

Access control is fundamental to security. People are now used to control procedures which involve a body check as well as a baggage check.

Electronic access control systems enable entry to be gained to a secure area by a holder inserting or passing an electric coded card through a reader to a locked door. An electronic lock will be operated allowing entry. Fitting of such locks should not be allowed to spoil the appearance of the door.

Complex facilities to regulate access are possible including:
 Individual code numbers
 Voice recognition
 Signature recognition
 Retina recognition
 Hand, finger or thumb prints.

Perimeter protection

Regardless of their height, most walls and fences, whether topped with barbed wire or other enhancements, can be breached or climbed by intruders within a few minutes. Nevertheless, they present a formidable obstacle for the less determined trespasser. Topping materials on walls and fences must not be so positioned as to be able to injure pedestrians or users of adjacent land. Walls are often perceived as being effective, but are less helpful than fences because they screen buildings from passersby.

When considering walls with a security function:
They should be at least 2.4 metres high.
Avoid providing toe holes.
They should maintain their height throughout their length, regardless of undulating ground.
Be 3 metres from buildings, structures or trees.
Have strong gates and doors of the same height and topping without significant gaps at ground level or between top and keystone if inset.
Deny the use of fall pipes and similar climbing aids by fixing spiked metal collars.
The local fire prevention officer should be consulted before adapting fire escapes and fire doors for security purposes.
Avoid recesses and hidden doorways.

Fences

Many of the requirements which apply to walls apply equally to fences. Only nominal protection is afforded to premises by a standard wire mesh or chain link fence. As wire can be cut or dismantled, additional deterrents including electronic detectors or security lighting may be needed. Welding mesh fences, palisade fencing, reinforced concrete panels and rolled steel palisades improve perimeter security, but will probably spoil the environment of a historic building. Great care must be taken with the quality of any fencing.

Vehicle barriers

In many instances it is important to keep vehicles away from the immediate vicinity of historic buildings, especially at night. Protective measures include, lifting poles, slewing poles, one way plates, and rising steps.

Security lighting

Lighting, unless well planned, installed and maintained may not hinder an intruder but help to light his way or provide shadows in which he can hide. Security lighting should complement physical and electronic security, illuminate the intruder on his approach, conceal a defender from the intruder, completely illuminate protected premises, operate from dusk to dawn and be mounted out of reach of vandals and protected against missiles. It may not be easy to meet all these conditions in a suitable manner. By night, if it is activated by an intruder alarm it is the most effective deterrent as it also gives general alert to staff.

Perimeter lighting

Environmental considerations apart, the aim of perimeter lighting should be to illuminate both sides of a perimeter, especially if it is a wall, without shadows being cast along its length. Columns carrying flood lighting need careful spacing if the maximum benefit is to be obtained. High intensity luminaires providing low level glare towards a perimeter prevents a potential intruder seeing beyond the light, making any intrusions more hazardous. However, it may well be found that perimeter lighting spoils the environment of a historic building.

Vandalism

The potential for vandalism and arson rises if groups are able to gather in unsupervised areas. Extra precautions to safeguard vulnerable areas, such as isolated fuel tanks and flammable stores, need to be considered. Open spaces, e.g. yards, car parks and cleared sites, can be attractive to teenagers for ball games, cycling and similar activities, which can lead to avoidable damage.

Doors

When supervision is at a minimum doors become vulnerable to attack in a number of common ways, such as body pressure, using an instrument, drilling, spreading and removal of panels. Criminals are resourceful and will go to great lengths to force doors which impede them, for example:
Ramming doors with a vehicle.
Using a vehicle to pull a door out.
Sawing through exposed hinges.
Drilling holes to release a panic bar.
Applying torque to a cylinder knob set.
Vulnerability can be reduced by fitting hinge bolts, good rebates, outward opening doors and fitting solid core doors. Quality locking devices at more than one point, such as mortise bolts in the top and

lower third, reduce vulnerability whilst glazing increases the risk of a break in.

Locks and keys

Specifications for thief resistant locks, provide for design requirements such as five levers giving at least a thousand 'differs', end pressure resistance on bolt, hardened steel rollers inset in bolt.

Key security is essential. They should be formally controlled and their whereabouts always catalogued, only be copied as a last resort, labelled by reference to a coded list, issued according to need and *not* status. High security areas should be excluded from key suites.

The architect should understand the merits and dead latches, rim and mortice locks, padlocks and systems of master key suiting and combination locking. Some locks provide thousands more 'differs' plus unique key designs which reduce the risk of unauthorized copying., The most common pin tumbler lock cylinder night catch has little security value. Tumbler locks are more resistant to picking but vulnerable to torque pressures. There are available unorthodox cylinder locks operated by keys for which blanks are not readily obtainable except from the manufacturers.

Master key suiting

A system of locks allowing all to be opened by a master, some to be opened by a sub-master and single doors by their individual keys, is often convenient, but master keying considerably reduces the security of the system.

Combination locking

Combination locking is conveniently used on strong rooms and security cabinets or safes. Sometimes they are combined with key locks. Time locks permit opening only at pre-determined times. On safes and strongrooms they supplement conventional locks.

Windows

It has been observed that large panes are not as often attacked as small ones. Intruders prefer to gain access through an open light rather than a broken window. Secluded windows are most at risk. Leaded lights and puttied panes can be removed without shattering the glass. Windows and skylights accessible from flat roofs, fire escapes and fall pipes need protection. Alternative glazing of polycarbonate or laminated glass having resistance to impact, or toughened glass, although susceptible to pointed objects, may be considered. Acrylic glazing is unsuitable, being flammable.

Anti-bandit glazing

Anti-bandit glazing and bullet resistant glazing are intended to provide protection for staff handling cash or other valuables. It normally consists of laminations of glass and plastics and should be supplied and installed by specialist contractors.

Although windows are not usually part of an escape route, consultation with the fire authority before fitting protective bars and grilles is advisable.

In many cases simple window locks fitted to opening lights and their frames can be a sufficient deterrent, but it should be borne in mind that the keys used in many window locks are easily obtained or duplicated.

Steel bars should be fitted internally, firmly grouted into surrounding masonry or brickwork. Distances between the bars should not exceed 127 mm and the steel rod should not be less than 19 mm in diameter. Tie bars should be fitted at intervals not exceeding 610 mm to prevent springing. Prefabricated welding mesh can be substituted for bars. Proprietary shutters and grilles can also be fitted. The importance of non-return screws, mushroom headed bolts and hidden fixings should be noted when choosing pre-formed protection.

Conclusion

Security is a complex subject ranging from macro considerations to careful attention to detail; it must be studied to be cost effective as any system is only as strong as its weakest link.

Security experts tend to play on our fears and so increase the demand for expensive guards. However, only the owner or full time occupant of a historic building can make a realistic assessment of the risks. The key element is the alertness and vigilance of the caretaking team.

I would like to acknowledge the considerable help received from Mr Stewart Kidd of the Fire Protection Association and Dr E. C. Bell of the Loss Prevention Council Technical Centre in preparing this Appendix.

Bibliography

For ease of reference the Bibliography has been arranged under the various chapter headings of this book. The following list is an explanation of the abbreviations that occur within the Bibliography.

AIA	American Institute of Architects	ICE	Institution of Civil Engineers (UK)
AIC	American Institute for Conservation	ICOM	International Council on Museums
AMS	Ancient Monuments Society	ICOMOS	International Council of Monuments and Sites
APT	Association for Preservation Technology	IIC	International Institute for Conservation
ASCE	American Society of Civil Engineers	I.Mech.E.	Institution of Mechanical Engineers
ASCHB	Association for Studies in the Conservation of Historic Buildings	IOB	Institute of Building (now Chartered—CIOB) (UK)
BISRA	British Iron and Steel Research Association	I.Struct.E	Institution of Structural Engineers (UK)
BRE	Building Research Establishment (UK)	LDA	Lead Development Association (UK)
CCI	Canadian Conservation Institute	NPL	National Physical Laboratory (UK)
CIB	Conseil International du Bâtiment	RIBA	Royal Institute of British Architects
COSIRA	Council on Small Industries in Rural Areas	RICS	Royal Institution of Chartered Surveyors (UK)
DoE	Department of the Environment (UK)	RILEM	Réunion Internationale des Laboratoires d'Essais
DSIR	Department of Scientific and Industrial Research		et de Recherches sur les Matériaux et les
FPA	Fire Protection Association (UK)		Constructions
GLC	Greater London Council	RSA	Royal Society of Arts (UK)
HMSO	Her (or His) Majesty's Stationery Office (UK)	SPAB	Society for the Protection of Ancient Buildings (UK)
IoAAS	Institute of Advanced Architectural Studies (formerly the York Institute of Architectural Study)	TRADA	Timber Research and Development Association (UK)
ICCROM	International Centre for the Study of the Preservation and the Restoration of Cultural Property	UNESCO	United Nations Educational, Scientific and Cultural Organisation
		VAG	Vernacular Architecture Group (UK)

General

Ashurst, J. (1983). *Mortars, Plasters and Renders in Conservation, A Basic Guide*, London Ecclesiastical Architects' and Surveyors' Association. A comprehensive guide to the history, production, use and specification.

Ashurst, J. and Dimes, F.G. (1990). *Conservation of Building and Decorative Stone*, Butterworth-Heinemann, London. A compendium in 2 volumes by several authoritative writers. Gives a comprehensive description of building and decorative stones, introduced by a summary of the history of stone conservation. An explanation of the weathering and decay of masonry is followed by guidelines on treating structural and superficial problems.

Ashurst, J. and Ashurst, N. (1988) *Practical Building Conservation*, Gower Technical Press, Aldershot, England.
Vol. 1. *Stone Masonry.*
Vol. 2. *Brick Terracotta, Earth.*
Vol. 3. *Mortars, Plasters, Renders.*
Vol. 4. *Metals.*
Vol. 5. *Wood, Glass, Resins, Bibliography.*

Ashurst, J. and Dimes, F.G. (1984). *Stone in Buildings its Use and Potential Today*, The Stone Federation, London.

Bates, W. (1984) *Historical Structural Steelwork Handbook*, British Constructional Association, London. A guide to factors to be considered in assessing load bearing capacity of 19th and early 20th century cast iron, wrought iron, and steel framed buildings. Information on properties of materials, profiles, loads and stresses.

Bernard, J. (1972). *Victorian Ceramic Tiles*, Cassell, London. A detailed guide to Victorian tiles.

Bowyer, J. (1981). *Handbook of Building Crafts in Conservation*, Hutchinson, London. A reprint of a large portion of 'The New Practical Builder and Workman's Companion' by Peter Nicholson, 1823, probably the best known book of its kind, to which articles by modern specialists on brickwork, carpentry, joinery, slating, plastering, leadwork, glazing and painting have been added. These give information on the methods which should be used for conservation.

Brereton, C. (1991). *The Repair of Historic Buildings; Advice on Principles and Methods*, English Heritage, London. A wide ranging statement on the policy of English Heritage on maintenance and repair. Covers general principles, day-to-day maintenance and repair techniques related to the principal materials and features of historic buildings. It also advises on situations where reinstatement is necessary rather than repair and where lost original features should be replaced.

Brett, L. 4th Viscount Esher (1968). *York; A Study in Conservation*, HMSO, London.

British Standards Institution, BS 5937: 1981, *Trees in relation to construction*, British Standards Institution, London. A concise introduction to a wide ranging topic.

British Standards Institution, BS 6270: Part I: 1982, *Cleaning and surface repair of buildings; natural stone, cast stone, and clay and calcium silicate brick masonry*, British Standards Institution, London.

British Standards Institution, BS 8210: 1986, *Building Maintenance Management*, British Standards Institution, London.

British Tourist Authority (1980). *Britain's Historic Buildings; A Policy for their Future Use* (Montague Report), British Tourist Authority, London.

Brunskill, R.W. (1970). *Illustrated Handbook of Vernacular Architecture*, Faber & Faber, London.

Brunskill, R.W. (1985). *Timber Buildings in Britain*, Victor Gollancz in association with Peter Crawley, London.

Brunskill, R.W. (1990). *Brick Building in Britain*, Victor Gollancz in association with Peter Crawley, London.

Building Research Establishment (1992). *Recognising Wood Rot and Insect Damage in Buildings*, Building Research Establishment, Watford. A well illustrated handbook to assist with recognition on site with the major wood destroying fungi and insects found in building timbers and appendices on remedial treatment, preservatives including health and safety aspects.

Building Research Establishment, Watford
Digests:
'Control of lichens, moulds and similar growths', Digest 370, 1992.
'Decay and conservation of stone masonry', Digest 177, 1975.
'Painting walls', Digest 192, 1982.
'Repairing brick and block masonry', Digest 359, 1991.
'Increasing fire resistance of existing timber floors', Digest 208, 1988.
'Selection of natural building stones', Digest 269, 1983.
'Cleaning external surfaces of buildings' Digest 280, 1983.
'Influence of trees on house foundations in clay soil', Digest 298, 1985.
'Dry rot; its recognition and cure', Digest 299, 1985.
'Corrosion of metals by wood', Digest 301, 1985.
'Prevention of decay in external joinery', Digest 304, 1985.
'Identifying damage by wood boring insects', Digest 307, 1986 (rev. 1992).
'Insecticidal treatment against wood boring insects', Digest 327, 1987 (rev. 1992).

Butterworth, B. and Flitz, J. (1981). *Dictionary of Building Terms*, English/French, French/English. Construction Press, London.

Charles, F.W.B. and Charles, M. (1984). *Conservation of Timber Buildings*, Hutchinson, London. A description of various types of timber structures and their repair, including detailed case studies.

Charles, F.W.B. and Charles, M. (1987). *Conservation of Timber Building*, Stanley Thornes.

Chitham, R. (1985). *The Classical Orders of Architecture*, Butterworth-Heinmann, Oxford.

Clifton-Taylor, A. (1972). *The Pattern of English Building*, 3rd edition, Faber & Faber, London.

Clifton-Taylor, A. and Ireson, A. S. (1983). *English Stone Building*, Victor Gollancz, London. A well illustrated book describing the use of stone from early times to the present, including recent developments and conservation work.

Coad, J. (1985). *The Royal Dockyards 1690–1850; Architecture and Engineering Works of the Sailing Navy*. (Scolar Press, Aldershot). An authoritative and extensive account of Royal Navy buildings in the UK and abroad. Well illustrated. Bibliography.

Condit, C.W. (1968). *American Building Materials and Techniques from the First Colonial Settlements to the Present*, Chicago University Press, Chicago.

Construction Industry Research and Information Association (1986). *Structural Renovation of Traditional Buildings*, Construction Industry Research and Information Association, London. Structural aspects of renovating 18th, 19th, and early 20th century buildings.

Crafts Council (1982). Science for Conservators, Crafts Council, London.
1   *Materials*
2   *Cleaning*
3   *Adhesives and Coatings*
A series intended to introduce those with no previous knowledge of science to the scientific principles which lie under conservation.

Curl, J.S. (1993). *Encyclopedia of Architectural Terms*, Donhead Publishing, London.

Cutler, D.F. and Richardson, J.B.K. (1989). *Tree Roots and Buildings*, Longman Scientific and Technical, Harlow. The most extensive study into tree roots and buildings in the UK based on an analysis of over 12 000 trees and shrubs, initiated by Kew and completed by Cutler and Richardson. Gives details of 16 major deciduous species, brief reference to 13 lesser species and 6 conifers.

Davey, N. (1961). *A History of Building Materials*, Phoenix, London. (also published in Italian, 1965, Storia del Materiale da Construzione, Il Saggiatore, Milan).

Department of the Environment, (1991). *Environmental Action Guide*, HMSO, London. A guide, following up the 1990 Environmental White Paper, to assist those involved in commissioning works or managing property and ancillary services in dealing with the implications of their activities.

Edinburgh New Town Conservation Committee, (1980). *Care and Conservation of Georgian Houses. A Maintenance Manual*, Architectural Press, London. After explaining the unique qualities of a New Town and the efforts being made to maintain it, the book identifies the weak spots in Georgian construction which need regular attention. A very useful publication, largely applicable to Georgian Houses elsewhere.

Gimpel, J. (1961). *The Cathedral Builders*, Evergreen Books, London.

Gray, A.S. (1985). *Edwardian Architecture, A Biographical Dictionary*, Wadsworth Editions, London. An extensive, well-illustrated production describing the work of over 300 architects and artists of the period. Contains a useful introduction to building at that time.

Harvey, J. (1972). *Conservation of Buildings*, John Baker, London.

Hewitt, C.A. (1980). *English Historic Carpentry*, Phillimore, London. Describes the development of carpentry from the Saxon period to the end of the 19th century. Assists in dating timberwork from framing techniques, jointing methods, and mouldings.

Historic Scotland, Technical Advice Notes:
1   *Preparation and use of lime mortars*
2   *The conservation of plasterwork*
3   *Performance standards for traditional sash and case windows*
Historic Scotland, Edinburgh.

Innocent, C.F. (1916). *The Development of English Domestic Building Construction*, Cambridge University Press, Cambridge, rev. repr. 1971 David and Charles, Newton Abbot.

Insall, D.W. and Associates (1968). *Chester; A Study in Conservation*, HMSO, London.

Insall, D.W. (1972). *The Care of Old Buildings Today*. Architectural Press, London.

Insall, D. (1974). *Historic Buildings, action to maintain the expertise for their care and repair*, European Architectural Heritage Year Study Series 3, Council of Europe, Strasbourg.

Institution of Civil Engineers (1983). *Conference proceedings on the engineering aspects of the repair of historic and recent buildings*, Thomas Telford, London.

Institution of Structural Engineers (1980). *Appraisal of Existing Structures*, Institution of Structural Engineers, London. Describes factors involved in investigating, appraising, and reporting on existing structures. Gives information on nature of and methods of testing structural materials and ways of assessing defects. Useful to architects and surveyors as well as engineers.

Knoop, D. and Jones, G.P. (1933). *The Medieval Mason*, Manchester University Press, Manchester.

Lead Sheet Association (1990–2) Lead Sheet Manual Vol. I, Vol. II *Lead Sheet Coverings to Roofs*, Lead Sheet Association, London. A complete revision of the previous standard work.

Lead Sheet Association, *Lead work* Technical Notes 1–10, Lead Sheet Association, London. Lead Sheet Technical Notes on important developments.

Leary, E. (1983). *Building Limestones of the British Isles*, Building Research Establishment, Watford. Gives information on limestone from British quarries stating quantities available, sizes, and test results.

Leary, E. (1986). *Building Sandstones of the British Isles*, Building Research Establishment, Watford. Gives information on sandstones from 78 quarries including amount available, block size, and test results. Also lists buildings where stones can be seen.

Lee, R. 1987. *Building Maintenance Management*, 3rd Edition, Collins, London. Building maintenance described in a systematic way including the use of computers.

Mainstone, R.J. (1975). *Development of Structural Form*, Allen Lane, London.

328

Martin, D.G. (1970). *Maintenance and Repair of Stone Buildings*, Council for the Repair of Churches, London. A booklet on stone repair.

McKay, W.B. (1963). *Building Construction* Volumes 1–3, Longmans, London. The basic building construction text book dealing principally with traditional construction. The 4th and earlier editions are the most relevant to the construction of buildings in need of conservation.

Michell, E. (1988). *Emergency Repairs to Historic Buildings*, English Heritage, London. A guide to temporary repairs which can be carried out easily and at the minimum expense until permanent repairs are possible. Also covers security protection of empty buildings. Includes case studies.

Nash, W.G. (1986). *Brickwork, Repair and Restoration*, Attic Books, Eastbourne. A practical guide to the maintenance of brickwork, covering the selection of materials, craft techniques, methods of planning and scheduling work, and description of the precise standard of craftsmanship required.

National Audit Office (1991). *Upkeep of Historic Buildings on the Civil Estate*, HMSO, London. A report to the House of Commons on the conditions of buildings on the Civil Estate making recommendations for their maintenance by Departments.

Nature Conservancy Council for England, (1991). *Bats in Roofs—A Guide for Surveyors*, Nature Conservancy Council, Peterborough. A leaflet describing the legal protection for bats and guidance on surveying and carrying out work where bats may be present.

Newmarkkay Gersil (1992). *Mechanical and Electrical Systems for Historic Buildings*, McGraw-Hill, Maidenhead.

Parnell, A.C. (1987). *Building Legislation and Historic Buildings*, Architectural Press, London. Covers Building Regulations 1985, Public Health Acts, Fire Precautions Act, and Housing Act. Examines the legislation in relation to historic buildings and procedures for relaxation. Describes case studies.

Powys, A.R. (1981). *Repair of Ancient Buildings*, Society for the Protection of Ancient Buildings, London. A reprint of the 1929 publication with additional notes and appendices to take account of advantages in technology and provide extra information. It describes methods of repair in accordance with the principles of the Society.

Purchase, W.R. (1987). *Practical Masonry*, Attic Books, Builth Wells (1987 reprint of 1985 publication). Describes practical masonry skills and is also useful to those specifying and supervising work.

Riden, P. (1987). *Record Sources for Local History*, Batsford, London.

Royal Commission on the Historic Monuments of England and English Heritage (1990). *Revised Thesaurus of Architectural Terms*, London.

Royal Society of Arts (1987). *The Future of the Public Heritage*, Royal Society of Arts, London. Verbatim report of a conference in 1986 on the future policy for Government owned historic buildings.

Rykwert, J. (Ed) (1955). *Ten Books on Architecture by Leone Battista Alberti*, Trans. J. Leoni, London, 1776. Facsimile edn, Tiranti, London.

Salaman, R.A. (1975). *Dictionary of Tools used in Woodworking and Allied Trades c. 1700–1900*, Allen & Unwin, London.

Schwicker, A.C. (1972). *International Dictionary of Building Construction*, Technoprint International, Milan; McGraw-Hill, New York; Dunod, Paris.

Scottish Civic Trust (1981). *New Uses for Older Buildings in Scotland. A Manual for Practical Encouragement*, HMSO, Edinburgh. Gives general guidance on possible new uses, describes case studies, and provides information on technical and financial aspects of conversions.

Scottish Conservation Bureau (1991). *Edinburgh; Historic Scotland*. A comprehensive guide to organisation: whose work relates to the conservation of historic objects and buildings.

Scottish Natural Heritage (1988). *An Inventory of Gardens and Designed Landscapes in Scotland*. In 5 volumes available from the Scottish Natural Heritage, Battleby, Redgoston, Perth PH1 3EW.

Smith, L. (1985). *Investigating Old Buildings*, Batsford, London. Describes materials and methods of construction of post-medieval buildings and techniques for recording them.

Smith, R.J. (1990). *A Dictionary of Specialist Crafts for Architects and Builders*. Robert Hale, London. A classified directory of firms and individuals practising the various professions, trades, and crafts required in conservation of buildings and their contents.

Society for the Protection of Ancient Buildings, Basic Information Leaflets:
IN/1 *How to make limewash*
IN/2T *Timber Treatment – A Warning about De-frassing*
IN/3 *Surface Treatment of Timber Framed Buildings*
IN/4T *The Need for Old Houses to Breathe*
IN/5 *Removing Paint from Old Buildings*
Society for the Protection of Ancient Buildings, London.

Society for the Protection of Ancient Buildings, Technical Pamphlets:
MacGregor, J. *Outward Leaning Walls*
MacGregor, J. *Strengthening Timber Floors*
Williams, G. *Chimneys in Old Buildings*
Ashurst, J. *Cleaning of Stone and Brick*
Williams, G. *Pointing of Stone and Brick Walling*
Parnell, A. and Ashford, D. *Fire Safety in Historic Buildings*
Thomas, A. *Treatment of Damp in Old Buildings*
Hunt, A. *Electrical Wiring in Old Buildings*
Brockett and Wright *Care and Repair of Thatched Roofs*
Society for the Protection of Ancient Buildings, London.

Stagg, W.D. and Masters, R. (1983). *Decorative Plasterwork, Its Repair and Restoration*, Orion Books, Eastbourne. An introduction to assist craftmen and supervisors in plastering in traditional materials and methods and to guide architects restoring decorative plasterwork.

Stone Federation *Handbook and Directory of Members* (revised annually) Ealing Publications, Maidenhead. Includes tables of members engaged in quarrying, stone supply, and cleaning.

Stone Federation *Natural Stone Directory* (published every three years), Ealing Publications, Maidenhead. Lists members engaged in quarrying giving details of stone produced.

Suddards, R. (1988). *Listed Buildings; The Law and Practice*, (2nd Edition) Sweet and Maxwell, London. A detailed examination of the Law relating to Historic Buildings, Ancient Monuments, and Conservation Areas.

Thompson, M.W. (1981). *Ruins, Their Preservation and Display*, British Museum, London. An exploration of the care of ruined buildings—retrieval of remains, preservation of masonry, laying out for display, representation of missing parts, restoration of ancillary parts and interpretation.

Viollet-le-Duc, E.E. (1854–68). *Dictionnaire raisonné de l'architecture française du XIe an XVIe siecle* (The analytical dictionary of French architecture from the 11th to the 16th century), 10 vols, Bance, Paris (see trans. article 'Restauration' in Vol. 8).

Viollet-le-Duc, E.E. (1875). *On Restoration*, trans. Charles Wethered, Sampson Low, Marston, Low and Searle, London.

Warland, E.G. (1986). *Modern Practical Masonry*, Stone Federation, London. (reprint of 1929 publication by Pitman Books). This was the standard work on masonry. It illustrates the methods used earlier this century for cladding steel framed buildings with stone which are now causing trouble in some instances.

Weaver, M.E. (1993). *Building Conservation. Guide to Techniques and Materials*, Wiley, New York, USA. A scientific study which also defines the work of conservators.

Introduction to architectural conservation (chapter 1)

Australia ICOMOS (1981) *The Burra Charter*. Pamphlet.

Bowyer, J. *et al.* (1981). *Handbook of Building Crafts in Conservation*, Hutchinson & Co. London.

Bibliography

Committee on Historic Resources (1983). *Preservation Practice*, AIA Handbook, C-1, American Institute of Architects, Washington, D.C.

English Heritage (1986). *Public Sources of Grant Aid for the Repair, Adaption and Reuse of Historic Buildings and Monuments*. Historic Buildings and Monuments Commission for England, London.

Fitch, J. M. (1982). *Historic Preservation. Curatorial Management of the Built World*, McGraw-Hill, New York.

Fram, M. (1988). *Well-preserved: The Ontario Heritage Foundation's Manual of Principles and Practice for Architectural Conservation*, The Boston Mills Press, Extracts from 'The Inheritance' and 'Careful Conservation', Erin Ontario.

ICCROM (1982). International Meeting of Co-ordinators of Training in Architectural Conservation. UNESCO Rome.

ICOMOS (1966). *The Venice Charter (1966)*, International Charter for the Conservation and Restoration of Monuments and Sites. Paris.

ICOMOS (1984). *Florence Charter for Historic Gardens and Landscape*, Paris.

ICOMOS (1987) *Washington Charter for the Conservation of Historic Towns and Urban Areas*, ICOMOS/INFORMATION, April/June, Paris.

ICOMOS (1990) *Lausanne Charter for Archaeological Heritage*, Paris.

ICOMOS (1993). *Guidelines for Education and Training for Conservation of Monuments, Ensembles and Sites*, Paris.

Insall, D. (1972). *The Care of Old Buildings Today*, Butterworth-Heinemann, Oxford.

Litchfield, M.W. (1982). *Renovation a Complete Guide*, J. Wiley, New York.

Maddex, D. 1985. All About Old Buildings. The Whole Preservation Catelog. The Preservation Press, Washington D.C.

Miller, H. *et al.* (1986). *Skills Development Plan for Historical Architects in the National Park Service*. US Department of the Interior (NPS), Washington D.C.

Philippot, P. (1972). *Restoration, Philosophy, Criteria, Guidelines*, ICCROM, Rome.

Powys, A.R. (reprint 1981). *Repair of Ancient Buildings*, Society for the Preservation of Ancient Buildings, London.

Smith, J. (1978). *A Critical Bibliography of Building Construction*, Mansell, London.

Snowden, A.M. (ed) (1990). *Maintenance of Brick and Stone Structures*, E. & F.M. Spon, London.

Thompson, M.W. (1981) *Ruins, their Preservation and Display*, Colonade Books, British Museum Publications, London.

Tschudi, M.S. (1976). *Restoration and Anti-Restoration*, (2nd Edition), Universiteforlaget, Oslo.

UNESCO World Heritage Convention (1985). *Conventions and Recommendations of UNESCO Concerning the Protection of Cultural Heritage*, UNESCO, Paris.

UNESCO (1968). *The Conservation of Cultural Property*, UNESCO, Paris.

Structural actions of historic buildings (chapter 2)

Beckman, P. (1977). 'Structural Analysis and Recording of Ancient Buildings', in papers on the *Seminar on Structures in Historic Buildings*, ICCROM, Rome, also *Arup J.* 7 (2) 2–5 July 1972, London

Building Research Establishment (1988). 'New Site Tool for Testing Masonry Strength', in *BRE News of Construction Research*, Watford.

Fitchen, J. (1986). *Building Construction before Mechanization*, MIT Press, Cambridge MA USA.

Innocent, C.F. (1971). *The Development of English Building Construction*, (Cambridge University Press, 1916, reprint), David and Charles, Newton Abbot, England.

Jandl, H. Ward (ed.) (1983). *The Technology of Historic American Buildings*, Foundation for Preservation Technology, Washington, D.C.

Lemaire, R. N. and Van Baless, K. (eds) (1988). *Stable – Unstable? Structural Consolidation of Ancient Buildings*. (24 lectures) Leuven University Press, Leuven.

Reid, E. (1984). *Understanding Buildings; a Multidisciplinary Approach*, Construction Press, London.

Torraca, G. (1982). *Porous Building Materials. Science for Architectural Conservation*, ICCROM, Rome.

Viollet-le-Duc, E.E. (1881). *Lectures on Architecture*, 2 Vols, translation, Sampson Low, Marston, Searle and Rivington, London.

Beams, arches, vaults and domes (chapter 3)

Fitchen, J. (1961). *The Construction of Gothic Cathedrals; a Study of Medieval Vault Erection*, Oxford University Press, Oxford.

Heyman, J. (1966). 'The Stone Skeleton', *Int. J. Solids & Structures* **2**, 249–279, Pergamon Press, Oxford.

Heyman, J. (1967). 'Spires and Fan Vaults', *Int. J. Solids and Structures*, **3**, 243–257, Pergamon Press, Oxford.

Heyman, J. (1969). 'The Safety of Masonry Arches', *Int. J. Mech. Sci.*, **11**, 363–385, Pergamon Press, New York.

Heyman, J. (1976). 'The Strengthening of the West Tower of Ely Cathedral, *Proc. Inst. Civ. Engrs.* pt. 1. pp. 123–147, London.

Heyman, J. and Threfall, B.D. (1972). 'Two Masonry Bridges: (1) Clare College Bridge, (2) Telford's Bridge at Over', *Proc. Inst. Civ. Engrs*, **52**, 319–330, London.

Macgregor, J.E.M. (1973). *Strengthening Timber Floors*, (Technical Pamphlet 2), Society for the Preservation of Ancient Buildings, London.

Viollet-le-Duc, E.E. (1854–68). *Dictionnaire raisonné de l'architecture française du XIe au XVIe siecle*, Paris, 10 vols. Translation of the article 'Construction' in Huss G. M. (1895), *Rational Building*, Macmillan, New York.

Trusses and frames (chapter 4)

Bailey, M.W. (1961). *The English Farmhouse and Cottage*, Routledge and Kegan Paul, London.

Brunskill, R.W. (1970). *Illuustrated Handbook of Vernacular Architecture*, Faber & Faber, London.

Charles, F.W.B. (1984). *Conservation of Timber Buildings*, Hutchinson, London.

Fletcher, J. (ed.) (1978). *Dendrochronology in Europe*, 139–161, BAR International Series 51.

Goodall, H. and Friedman R. (1980). *Log Structures. Preservation and Problem Solving*, American Association for State and Local History, Nashville, USA.

Hewett, C.A. (1969). *The Development of Carpentry 1200–1700*, David and Charles, Newton Abbot.

Insall, D. (1973). *The Care of Old Buildings Today*, Butterworth-Heinemann, Oxford.

Rempel, J. (1980). *Building with Wood*, (revised edn), University of Toronto Press, Toronto.

Tokyo International Research Institute of Cultural Properties (1983). *The Conservation of Wooden Cultural Property*. Internal Symposium on Conservation and Restoration of Cultural Property Nov. 1982. Tokyo and Saitma. Tokyo National Institute of Cultural Properties, Veno Park, Tokyo. CALMSC.

Walls, piers and columns (chapter 5)

Ashurst, J. (1983). *Mortars, Plasters and Renders in Conservation*, Ecclesiastical Architects and Surveyor's Assoc., London.

Ashurst, J. and Ashurst, N. (1988). 'The Repair and Maintenance of Cob, Chalk Mud, Pise and Clay Lump', in *Practical Building Conservation*, English Heritage Technical Handbook, Vol. 2, *Brick, Terracotta and Earth*, Gower Technical Press, Aldershot.

Building Research Establishment (1983), *The Selection of Natural Building Stone*, Digest 269, HMSO, London.

Knoop, D. and Jones, O.P. (1933). *The Medieval Mason*, Manchester University Press, Manchester.

Ross, K.D. and Butlin, R.N. (1989). *Durability Tests for Building Stone*, Building Research Establishment, Watford.

Schaffer, R.J. (1985). *The Weathering of Natural Building Stones*, Building Research Establishment Special Report No 18, Garston, BRE (1932) (facsimile reprint), HMSO, London.

Foundations (chapter 6)

Aboricultural Journal, (1985) A series of articles:
Pryke, F.S. 'Trees and Buildings'
Biddle, P.G. 'Trees and Buildings'
Coutts, M.P. 'Tree Root Damage to Buildings'
Flora, T. 'Physiological Characteristics of Tree Root Activity'
Flora, T. 'Trees and Building Foundations'
The series covers arboricultural aspects with some thoroughness.

Bowen, R. (1984). *Geology in Engineering*, Elsevier Applied Sciences Publishers, London.

Dowrick, D.J. and Beckman, P. (1971). Paper 74155, *York Minster Structural Restoration*, ICE, London.

Dunham, C.W. (1962). *Foundations of Structures*, McGraw-Hill, New York.

Schultze, E. (1970). *Techniques de conservation et de restauration des monuments, terrains et fondations* (Techniques for conservation and restoration of historic buildings, soils and foundations). Publication No. 3, ICCROM, Rome.

Climatic causes of decay (chapter 7)

Addleson, L. (1982). *Building Failures (non structural); a Guideline to Diagnosis, Remedy and Prevention*, Butterworth-Heinemann, Oxford.

Building Research Establishment (1971). *An Index to Driving Rain*, BRE Digest 127, 2nd ser., HMSO, London.

Building Research Establishment (1976). *Roof Drainage*, Digests 188–9, HMSO, London.

Building Research Establishment (1982). The *Durability of Steel in Concrete* Parts I, II, III. Digests 263, 264, 265, HMSO, London.

De Angelis d'Ossat, G. (1972). *Guide to the Methodical Study of Monuments and Causes of their Deterioration*, ICCROM, Rome.

Holmström, I. and Sandström, C. (1975). *Maintenance of Old Buildings*, Document D 10, National Swedish Institute of Building Research, Stockholm.

Kendrew, W.G. (1963). *Climate of Continents*, 5th edn, Clarendon Press Oxford.

Mather, J.R. (1974). *Climatology; Fundamentals and Applications*, McGraw-Hill, New York.

Plenderleith, H.J. and Werner, A.E.A. (1971). *The Conservation of Antiquities and Works of Art*, 2nd edn, Oxford University Press, Oxford.

Simpson, J.W. and Horrobin, P.J. (eds) (1970). *The Weathering and Performance of Building Materials*, Medical and Technical Publishing, Aylesbury.

Thomson, G. (1974). *The Museum Environment*, Butterworth-Heinemann, Oxford.

Earthquakes and historic buildings (chapter 8)

Anon. (1976). *Guidelines for Disaster Prevention*, Office of the United Nations Disaster Relief Co-ordinator, United Nations, Geneva.
Vol. 1 *Pre-disaster Physical Planning of Human Settlements.*
Vol. 2 *Building Measures for Minimising the Impact of Disasters.*
Vol. 3 *Management of Settlements.*
Anon. (1978). *Disaster Prevention and Mitigation; a Compendium of Current Knowledge*, Vol. 3, *Seismological Aspects*, Office of the United Nations Disaster Relief Co-ordinator, United Nations, Geneva.

Cestelli, G.C. *et al* (1981). *Salient Aspects of the Behaviour of Buildings under Seismic Shaking*, Associazione Italiana Tecnico Economica del Cemento, Rome.

Dowrick, D.J. (1977). *Earthquake Resistant Design—a Manual for Engineers and Architects*, Wiley, London.

Feilden, B.M. (1987). *Between Two Earthquakes*, ICCROM with Getty Conservation Institute, Rome/Marina del Rey, USA.

Pichard, P. (1984). *Emergency Measures and Damage Assessment after an Earthquake*, UNESCO, Paris.

UNESCO (1985). *Earthquake Risk Reduction in the Balkan Region*, Final Report, Sofia.
UNESCO (1985). *Building Construction under Seismic Conditions in the Balkan Region & Post-Earthquake Damage Evaluation and Strength Assessment of Buildings under Seismic Conditions; Seismic Design Codes*, United Nations Development Programme, Vienna.

Botanical, biological and microbiological causes of decay (chapter 9)

Allsopp, D. and Seal, K.J. (1986). *Introduction to biodeterioration*, E. Arnold, London.

Building Research Establishment (1985). *Dry Rot. Its Recognition and Control.* Digest 299, HMSO, London.

Insects and other pests as causes of decay (chapter 10)

Bletchly, J.D. (1967). *Insects and Marine Borer Damage to Timber and Woodwork*, Forest Products Research Laboratory, HMSO, London.

Bravery, A.F. Berry, R.W. Carey, J.K. and Cooper, D.E. (1992). *Recognising Wood Rot and Insect Damage in Buildings*, Building Research Establishment, Watford.

Building Research Establishment (1980, rev. 1992). *Reducing the risk of pest infestation: design recommendations and literature review* Digest 238, HMSO, London.

Building Research Establishment (1986). *Controlling Death Watch Beetle*, Information paper 19/86, BRE, Garston, Watford.

Building Research Establishment (1986, rev. 1992). *Identifying Damage by Wood-boring Insects*, Digest 307, BRE, Garston, Watford.

Building Research Establishment (1987, rev. 1992) *Insecticidal Treatments against Wood-boring Insects*, Digest 327, BRE Garston, Watford.

Leigh, J. (1972). *Bats, Birds, Bees, Mice and Moths; the Control of Occasional Pests in Church Buildings*, Council for Places of Worship, London.

Man-made causes of decay (chapter 11)

Building Research Establishment (1989) *Brickwork: Prevention of Sulphate Attack (Design)*, DAS 128, BRE, Garston, Watford.
Building Research Establishment (1990). *Damage to Structures from Groundborne Vibration*, Digest 353, BRE, Garston, Watford.

DoE Building Effects Review Group (1990). *The effects of acid Deposition on Buildings and Building Materials*, HMSO, London.

Kapsa, I. (1971). *Protection of Housing Estates against Unfavourable Effects of Traffic*, Research Institute for Building and Architecture, Prague.

Steffens, R.J. (1974). *Structural Vibration and Drainage*, BRE, Garston, Watford.

Internal environment of historic buildings (chapter 12)

Brommelle, M. Thomson, G. and Smith, P. (eds) (1980). *Conservation within Historic Buildings*, IIC, London.
Building Research Establishment (1949). *Pattern Staining in Buildings*, Digest 4, 1st ser., BRE, Garston, Watford.
Building Research Establishment (1951). *The Principles of Natural Ventilation in Buildings*, Digest 34, 1st ser., HMSO, London.

Cunnington, P. (1984). *Care for Old Houses*, Prism Alpha, Sherborne, Dorset.

Department of the Environment (1970, 1971). *Condensation in Buildings*, pt, I 'Design Guide' pt. II 'Remedial measures', HMSO, London.

Hughes, P. (1986). *The Need for Old Buildings to 'Breathe'*, SPAB Information Sheet No 41, London.

Leiff, M. and Trechsel, H.R. (eds) (1982). *Moisture Migration in Buildings*, Symposium Philadelphia Oct 1980. ASTM Special Technical Publication 779, American Society for Testing and Materials, Philadelphia, USA.

Plenderleith, H.J. and Werner, A.E.A. (1971). *The Conservation of Antiquities and Works of Art*, 2nd edn, Oxford University Press, Oxford.

Straaten, J.F. van (1967). *Thermal Performance of Buildings*, Elsevier, Amsterdam.

Thompson, G. *The Museum Environment*, 2nd edn, Butterworth-Heinemann, Oxford.

Inspections and reports (chapter 13)

Becker, N. (1980). *The Complete Book of Home Inspection*, McGraw-Hill, New York.
Beckman, P. (1972). Structural analysis and recording of ancient buildings. *Arup J*, **7** (2) 2–5, Arup and Partners, London.
Bowyer, J. (1970). *Guide to Domestic Building Surveys*, 3rd edn, Architectural Press, London.
Building Research Establishment (1991). *Why do buildings crack?* Digest 361, BRE, Garston, Watford.

Building Research Establishment (1986). *Rising Damp in Walls; diagnosis and treatment*, Digest 245, BRE, Garston, Watford.
Building Research Establishment (1972). *Condensation*, Digest 110, BRE, Garston, Watford.
Building Research Establishment (1976). *Site use of the theodolite and surveyors level*, Digest 202, BRE, Garston, Watford.
British Research Establishment (1989) *Simple measuring and monitoring of movement in low rise buildings*, Digest 343, BRE, Garston, Watford.
Burnav, S.G. Williams, T.L. and Jones, C.D. (1988). *Applications of thermal imaging*, Adam Hilgar, Bristol.

Carson, A. and Dunlop, R. (1982). *Inspecting a House; A Guide for Buyers, Owners and Renovators*, General Publishing, Toronto.
Council for the Care of Churches London (1980). *A Guide to Church Inspection and Repair*, CIO Publishing, London.

De Angelis d'Ossat G. (1972). *Guide to the Methodical Study of Monuments and Causes of their Deterioration*, Issued jointly by ICCROM and the School of Architecture, Rome University, Rome (text in English and Italian).

Ecclesiastical Architects and Surveyors Association (1985). *Quinquennial Inspections: notes for Members undertaking quinquennial inspections of Churches and Church premises and for the preparation of reports on such inspections*, Newcastle upon Tyne.

Hart, J.M. (1990). *A Practical Guide to Infra-red Thermography in Building Surveys*, BRE Report 176, Garston, Watford.

Mainstone, R.J. *Evaluation of Actions in the Field of Protection and Restoration of Cultural Monuments 1960–85*, UNESCO, Paris.

Seeley, I.H. (1985). *Building Surveys, Reports and Dilapidations*, Macmillan, London.
Smith, L. (1985). *Investigating Old Buildings*, Batsford, London.

Research, analysis and recording (chapter 14)

Beckamn, P. (1972). Structural analysis and recording of ancient buildings, Arup. J. **2**, 2–5, Arup and Partners, London.
Borchers, P.E. (1978). *Photogrammetric Recording of Cultural Resources*, US Department of the Interior (NPS) Washington D.C.
Bray, R.S., Dale, W., Grainger, W. and Harrold, R. (1980). *Exterior Recording Training Manual* (rev. edn) Parks Canada (CIHB), Ottawa.
Buchanan, T. (1983). *Photographing Historic Buildings*, HMSO, London.
Building Research Establishment (1971). *Devices for Detecting Changes in Width of Cracks in Buildings*, Information sheet TIL5, BRE, Garston, Watford.
Busch, A. (1987). *The Photography of Architecture*, Van Nostrand Reinhold, New York.

Chambers, J.H. (1973) *Rectified Photography and Photo Drawings for Historic Preservation* (draft) US Department of the Interior (NPS) Washington D.C.
Chitham, R. (1980). *Measured Drawings for Architects*, Architectural Prees, London.
Colvin, H.M. (1954). *A Biographical Dictionary of British Architects 1600–1840*, revised edn, 1978, John Murray, London.

Falconer, K. and Hay, G. (1981). *The Recording of Industrial Sites. A review*, Council for British Archaeology, London.
Fladmark, K. (1978). *A Guide to Basic Archaeological Fieldwork. Procedures*, Simon Fraser University, Burnaby.
Fleming, J. *et al.* (1991). *The Penguin Dictionary of Architecture*, 4th edn, Penguin, Harmondsworth.

Hart, D.M. (1975). *X-ray Examination of Historic Structure*, Office of Archaeology and Historic Preservation, National Park Service, US Dept. of Interior, Washington D.C.
Harvey, J.H. (1974). *Sources for the History of Houses*, British Records Association, London.

McDowall, R.W. (1980). *Recording Old Houses; A Guide*, Council for British Archaeology, London.

Poppeliers, J.C. *et al.* (1983). *What style is it?* Preservation Press, Washington D.C.

Salzman, L.F. (1952). *Building in England down to 1540; a documentary history*, Clarendon Press, Oxford.

Smith, J.T. and Yates, E.M. (1974). *On dating English Houses from external evidence*, (reprint) E. W. Classey Ltd, Faringdon, Berks.

Teutonico, J.M. (1986) *Laboratory Manual for Architectural Conservators*, ICCROM, Rome.

Preventive maintenance of historic buildings (chapter 15)

Anon. (n.d. late 1940s) *The Treatment of Ancient Buildings damaged in Wartime*, SPAB, London.

Anon. (1985). *Proceedings of symposium on building appraisal, maintenance and preservation*, University of Bath, Department of architecture and engineering, Bath.

Anon. (1986). *Wood decay in Houses and How to Control it*, rev. edn, US Department of Agriculture, Washington D.C.

Architect's Journal (1976). 'Damp Proof Courses. In Handbook of Housing Rehabilitation, Repair and Maintenance', Information Sheet No. 2, 21 July pp. 139–141, London.

Ashurst, J. (1977). *Cleaning Stone and Brick*, Technical pamphlet 4, Society for the Preservation of Ancient Buildings, London.

Beard, G. (1975). *Decorative Plasterwork in Great Britain*, Phaidon, London.

Beard, G. (1983). *Stucco and Decorative Plasterwork in Europe*, Thames and Hudson, London.

Brereton, C. (1991). *The Repair of Historic Buildings (Advice on Principles and Methods)*, English Heritage, London.

Building Technology Standards (1975), *Graffiti Removers; evaluation and preliminary selection criteria*, MB SIR 75–914, Division of Energy, Washington D.C.

Building Research Establishment (1962—88), Garston, Watford
Advisory papers:
'Diagnosis of rising damp', TIL29, 1977.
'Electro osmosis damp proofing', TIL35, 1975.
'Rising damp: advice to owners considering remedial work', TIL47, 1976.
Digests:
'Condensation', Digest 110, 1972.
'Drying out buildings', Digest 163, 1974.
'Failure patterns and implications', Digest 176, 1975.
'Preventing decay in external joinery', Digest 304, 1985.
'Rising damp in walls', Digest 27, 1962.
Current papers:
'Protection of buildings against water from the ground', CP 102/73
Information papers:
'House inspection for dampness. A first step in remedial treatment for wood rot', IP 19/88.

Building Research Advisory Service (1985). *Diagnosis of Dampness*, BRE, Garston, Watford.

Central Council for the Care of Churches (1960). *Bats and Birds; damage by; notes on its preservation and cure*. 14th rept, Central Council for the Care of Churches, London.

Central Council of Church Bell Ringers (1966). *A Handbook of the Installation and Repair of Bells, Bell Frames and Fittings*, 6th edn, Council for the Places of Worship, London.

Central Council of Bell Ringers (1973). *The Towers and Bells Handbook*, Brackley Smart & Co. for the Council, London.

Chambers, J. H. (1976). *Cyclical Maintenance for Historic Buildings*, U.S. Department of the Interior, Washington D.C.

Clements, R. and Parker, D. (1965). *Manual of Maintenance Building Services*, Business Publications, London.

Clutton, C. (1951). *The Parish Organ*, 11th rept, Central Care of Churches, London.

Council for the Care of Churches (1951). *The Treatment and Preservation of Monuments in Churches*, 11th rept, Council for the Care of Churches, London.

Council for the Care of Churches (1957). *Church Timberwork, Books and Fabrics: Damage and Repair*, A special report. Council for the Places of Worship, London.

Council for the Care of Churches (1962). *The Care of Monuments, Brasses and Ledger Slabs in Churches*, Council for the Places of Worship, London.

Council for the Care of Churches (1963). *Damage to Organs through abnormal Atmospheric Conditions*, Council for the Places of Worship, London.

Council for the Care of Churches (1970). *Church Organs*, Council for the Places of Worship, London.

Council for the Care of Churches (1970). *How to look after your Church*, Church Information Office, London.

Council for the Care of Churches (1971). *Church Clocks, Maintenance and Repair*, Church Information Office, London.

Council for the Places of Worship and Monumental Brass Society (1973). *Monumental Brasses and Brass Rubbing*, Church Information Office, London.

Davey, A. Heath, B. Hodges, D. Milne, R. and Palmer, M. (1978). *The Care and Conservation of Georgian Houses; a Maintenance Manual for the Town of Edinburgh*, Paul Horns Publishing, Edinburgh.

Department of the Environment (1972). *R & D Bulletin: Building Maintenance*, HMSO, London.

Department of the Environment (1972). *Efflorescence and Stains on Brickwork*, Advisory Leaflet N 75, HMSO, London.

Department of the Environment (1976). *Current Information on Maintenance*, pt F, 'Preservation and Restoration of Buildings, a Bibliography', 2nd edn, Library Bibliography, Property Services Agency Library, London.

Department of the Environment (1977). *Current Information on Maintenance*, pt. B 'Design and Maintenance, a bibliography', 3rd edn, Library Bibliography, 140, Property Services Agency Library, London.

Gayle, M. Look, D. Waite, J.G. (1980). *Metals in America's Historic Buildings, Uses and Preservation Treatment*, Heritage Conservation and Recreation Service, Washington D.C.

Gettens, R.J. and Stout, G.L. (1966). *Painting Materials—a Short Encyclopedia*, Dover Publications, New York.

Grimmer, A.E. (1988). *Keeping it Clean. Removing External Dirt, Paint Stains, Graffiti from Historic Buildings*, US Department of the Interior, Washington D.C.

Harley, R.D. (1982). *Artist's Pigments c. 1600–1835*, 2nd edn, Butterworth-Heinemann, Oxford.

Holmström, I. and Sandström, C. (1975). *Maintenance of Old Buildings*, Document 10 D, National Swedish Institute for Building Research, Stockholm.

Hurst, A.E. and Goodier, J.H. (1980). *Painting and Decorating*, 9th edn.

Hutchinson, B.D. Barton, J. and Ellis, N. (1975). *Maintenance and Repair of Buildings and their Internal Environment*, Butterworth-Heinemann, Oxford.

Insall, D. (1972). *The Care of Old Buildings Today: A Practical Guide*, Architectural Press, SPAB, London.

Insall, D. (1974). *Historic Buildings: actions to maintain the expertise for their Care and Repair*, Council of Europe, Strasbourg.

Locke, P. (1986). *The Surface Treatment of Timber Framed Houses*, SPAB Information Sheet No. 3, Society for the Preservation of Ancient Buildings, London.

Locke, P. (1986). *Timber Treatment*, SPAB Information Sheet No. 2, Society for the Preservation of Ancient Buildings, London.

London, M. (1988). *Masonry; How to care for old historic brick and stone*, National Trust for Historic Preservation, Washington D.C.

Massari, G. and Massari, I. (1974). *Risanamento Igienico del Locali Umidi*, (Hygienic Improvement of Humid Buildings), 4th edn, Hoepli, Milan (English Translation ICCROM, Rome).

Michell, E. (1988). *Emergency Repairs for Historic Buildings*, English Heritage, Butterworth, London.

Mills, Edward D. (1994). *Building Maintenance and Preservation*, 2nd edn, Butterworth-Heinemann, Oxford.

Mora, P. Mora, L. and Philippot, P. (1984). *Conservation of wall paintings*, (English translation), Butterworth, London.

Newton, R. and Davidson, S. (1989). *Conservation of Glass*, Butterworth-Heinemann, Oxford.

Newton, R.G. (1982). *The Deterioration and Conservation of Painted Glass, a Critical Bibliography*, Oxford University Press, Oxford.

Oxley, T.A. and Gobert, E.G. (1984). *Dampness in Buildings; Diagnosis, treatment, instruments*, Butterworth-Heinemann, Oxford.

Richardson, B.A. (1980). *Remedial Treatment of Buildings*, Construction Press, Lancaster.

Sandwith, H. and Stainton, S. (1984). *The National Trust Manual of Housekeeping*, Allen Lane, London.

Saunders, M. (1987). *The Historic House Owner's Companion*, B. T. Batsford Ltd, London.

Schofield, J. (1984). *Basic Limewash*, Pamphlet available from the Society for the Protection of Ancient Buildings or the Council for the Care of Churches.

Stagg, W. and Pegg, B. (1976). *Plastering: A Craftsman's Encyclopedia*, Crosby Lockwood Staples, London.

Stahl, F. (1984). *A Guide to Maintenance, Repair and Alteration of Historic Buildings*, Van Nostrand Reinhold, New York.

Stambolow, T. and Asperen de Boer, T.R.J. van (1972). *The Deterioration and Conservation of Porous Building Materials in Monuments. A Literature Review*, (rev. 1975), ICCROM, Rome.

Sugden, A.V. and Edmonson, J.L. (1925). *A History of English Wallpaper 1509–1914*, Batsford, London.

Thomas, A.R. (1992) *Control of Damp in Old Buildings*, Technical pamphlet 8, Society for the Preservation of Ancient Buildings, London.

Torraca, G. (1981). *Porous Building Materials. Materials Science for Architectural Conservation*, ICCROM, Rome.

Webster, R.G.M. (ed.) (1992). *Stone Cleaning and the natural soiling and decay mechanisms of stone*, Donhead, London.

Wingate, M. (1985). *Small Scale Lime Burning*, Intermediate Technology Publications, London.

Wright, A. (1986). *Removing Paint from Old Buildings*, SPAB Information Sheet No. 5, Society for the Preservation of Ancient Buildings, London.

Fire (chapter 16)

Allen, N.L. (1988). *Protection of Churches against Lightning*, Council for the Care of Churches, London. A booklet which gives guidance on protection from lightning with references to BS 6651: 1985 'Protection of Structures against lightning'.

Anderson, H. and McIntyre, J.E. (1985). *Planning and disaster control in Scottish libraries and record offices*, National Library of Scotland, Edinburgh.

Butcher, E.G. and Parnell, A.C. (1979). *Smoke Control in Fire Safety Design*, E & FN Spon, London. Explains the principles governing the behaviour of smoke and its control in building design.

Butcher, E.G. and Parnell, A.C. (1983). *Designing for Fire Safety*, John Wiley, Chichester. Describes the nature of fire, and the precautionary measures to be taken in the design of buildings.

Council of Europe (1986). *The Protection of Cultural Heritage against Disasters*, Doc. 5624E, Strasbourg.

Jones, B. (1986). *Protecting Historic Architecture and Museum Collections from Natural Disasters*, (ed.) B. G. Jones, Butterworth, London.

Building Research Establishment (1987). Digest 320. *Fire Doors*, HMSO, London.

Department of the Environment (1992). *Fire Standard E. 13*. Department of the Environment, Fire Branch, Construction Policy Directorate, HMSO, London. Provides guidance to government departments in the precautions to be taken against fire in historic buildings.

Department of the Environment (1991). *Guidance for the Design of Government Buildings*, HMSO, London. Provides important guidance to departments on the design of new buildings and the alterations to existing buildings and the consultants.

Department of the Environment (n.d.) *Standard Fire Precautions for Contractors*, HMSO, London. Revised periodically. The precautions which should be applied to all building contracts by government.

Fire Protection Association (1981). *Fire Safety Bibliography (Fire and the Architect; Fire Protection Design Guide)*, FPA, London.

Fire Protection Association (1990). *Fire and Historic Buildings*, FPA, London.

Kidd, S. (ed) (1990). *Heritage under Fire*, Fire Protection Association, London.

National Fire Protection Association (1985). *Recommended Practice for the Protection of Libraries and Collections*, NFPA, Quincey, MA USA.

National Fire Protection Assocation (1985). *Recommended Practice for the Protection of Museums and Museum Collections*, 911, NFPA, Quincey, MA USA.

Parnell, A. and Ashford, D. *Fire Safety in Historic Buildings*, Part 1, Technical Pamphlet 61, Society for the Preservation of Ancient Buildings, London.

Withers, M. (1975). *Fire Protection of Panelled Doors*, Bath Preservation Trust, Bath.

Presentation of historic buildings (chapter 17)

Alderson, W.T. and Low, S.P. (1976). *Interpretation of Historic Sites*, AASLH, Nashville, USA.

Bosselman, F.P. (1978). *In the Wake of the Tourist*. The Conservation Foundation, Washington D.C.

Brown. C. (1983). *The Mechanics of Sign Control*, American Planning Association, Chicago.

Denhez, M. (1978). 'Heritage in Action; A Case Study', in *Heritage Fights Back*, pp. 184–277, The Heritage Canada Foundation, Ottawa.

Fitch, J.M. (1982). *Two Levels of Interpretation. Historic Preservation; Curatorial Management of the Built World*, McGraw-Hill, New York.

Kerr, J.S. (1982). *The Conservation Plan: A Guide to the Preparation of Conservation Plans for Places of European Cultural Significance*, The National Trust of Australia, Sydney.

Longstreth, R. (1987). *The Buildings of Main Street; A Guide to American Commercial Architecture*, Preservation Press, Washington D.C.

Serageldin, I. (1986). *Financing Adaptive reuse of Culturally Significant Areas; The Challenge to our Cultural Heritage; Why Preserve the Past?* (ed. Yudhishthir Raj Isar), Smithsonian Institution Press and UNESCO, Washington D.C.

Worskett, R. (1969). *The Character of Towns; An Approach to Conservation*, Butterworth-Heinemann, Oxford.

Cost control (chapter 18)

Davey, K.J. (1992). *Building Conseravtion Contracts and Grant Aid—A Practical Guide*, E & FN Spon, London.

Thorncroft, M.E.T. (1975). *The Economics of Conservation*, RICS, London.

Rehabilitation of historic buildings (chapter 19)

Aldous, T. (1990) *New Shopping in Historic Towns. The Chesterfield Story*, English Heritage, London.

Advisory Council on Historic Preservation (1976). *Adaptive Use: a survey of construction costs*. Report, special issue IV(4), Advisory Council on Historic Preservation, Washington D.C.

Advisory Council on Historic Preservation (1979). *Assessing the Energy Conservation Benefits of Historic Preservation*, US Government Printing Office, Washington D.C.

Advisory Council on Historic Preservation (1979). *The Contribution of Historic Preservation to Urban Revitalization*, US Government Printing Office, Washington D.C.

Benn, B. Karma, D. and Denhez, M. (1979). *How to Plan for Renovations*, Heritage Canada Foundation, Ottawa.

Benson, J. and Stone, E. (1981). *Restoring Victorian Houses, and turn-of the-century Structures*, Architectural Press, London.

Cantacuzino, S. (1975). *New Uses for Old Buildings*, Architectural Press, London. Old buildings are categorized and several examples of new uses are given for each category.

Cantacuzino, S. and Brandt, S. (1980). *Saving Old Buildings*, Architectural Press, London. Describes nearly 100 projects for converting old buildings to a wide range of new uses in Europe and the United States.

Council for the Places of Worship (1972). *Lighting and Wiring of Churches*, revised, Church Information Office, London.

Cunnington, P. (1988). *Change of Use*, Alpha Books, A. Black, London.

Chudley, R. (1981). *The Maintenance and Adaption of Buildings*, Longman, London.

Department of the Environment (1971). *Aspects of Conservation 1. New Life for Old Buildings*, HMSO, London.

Heritage Conservation and Recreation Service (1979). *Federal Tax Provisions to encourage Rehabilitation of Historic Buildings*, US Department of the Interior, Washington D.C.

Hunt, A. (1985). *Electrical Installations in Old Buildings*, Technical Pamphlet 9, Society for the Preservation of Ancient Buildings, London.

Levitt Bernstein Associates (1978). *Supervisor's Guide to Rehabilitation and Conservation*, Architectural Press, London.

Lumsden, W.K. *et al.* (1974). *Outdoor lighting Handbook*, Gower Press, Epping, London.

Markus, T.A. (ed.) (1979). *Building Conversion and Rehabilitation: Designing for Change in Building Use*, Butterworth-Heinemann, Oxford.

Mitchell Harris (1982). *How to Hire a Contractor*, CMHC, Ottawa.

Royal Institute of Chartered Surveyors (1976). *The Economics of Conservation*, RICS, London.

Sabnis, G. (ed.) (1985). *Rehabilitation, Renovation and Preservation of Concrete Masonry Structures Symposium*, American Concrete Institute, Detroit.

Thompson, E.K. (1977). *Recycling Buildings, Renovations, Remodelings, Restorations, and Reuses*, McGraw-Hill, New York.

US Department of the Interior (1983). *The Secretary of the Interior's Standards for Rehabilitation and Guidelines for Rehabilitation of Historic Buildings*, revised 1983, US Department of the Interior, Washington D.C.

US National Park Service (1982). *Respectful Rehabilitation. Answers to your questions about old Buildings*, The Preservation Press, Washington D.C.

Special techniques of repair and structural consolidation (chapter 20)

Anon. (1972). 'Moving House after 350 Years', *Contract Journal*, February, London.

Beard, G. (1975). *Decorative Plasterwork in Great Britain*, Phaidon, London.

Beckmann, P. (1974). Flatjacks and some of their Uses. *Arup J.* **9** (3), 10–14, Arup and Partners, London.

Borchelt, J. G. (ed.) (1982). *Grout for Reinforced Masonry*, Symposium Orlando Dec. 1980, ASTM Special Technical Publication 778, American Society for Testing Materials, Philadelphia.

Bowen, R. (1981). *Grouting in Engineering Practice*, Applied Science Publishers, London.

Braun, H. (1954). *The Restoration of Old Homes*, Faber & Faber, London.

Building Research Establishment (1944—46). *Repair of Damaged Buildings series*, Notes 1–24, BRE, Garston, Watford.

Building Research Establishment (1945). *Shoring and Other Precautions against the Collapse of Damaged Buildings and Adjacent Property*, Repair of Damaged Buildings series, Note 17. BRE, Garston, Watford.

Hayden, R.S. and Despont, T.W. (1986). *Restoration of the Statue of Liberty 1984–86*, Harper and Row, New York.

Lizzi, F. (1982). *The Static Restoration of Monuments*, Sagep editrice Genova.

Peterson, S. *et al.* (1980). *Mortars, Cement, Grouts used in the Conservation of Historic Buildings*, Symposium, Rome, IC-CROM, Rome.

Simpson, J.W. and Horrobin, P.J. (eds) (1970). The *Weathering and Performance of Building Materials*, Medical and Technical Publishing, Aylesbury, England.

Stumes, P. (1979). *The WER System Manual*, APT, Ottawa.

Zander, G. (1971). *Methods of Consolidation*, (Text in Italian and English), ICCROM, Rome.

Bibliography

Principal magazines and periodicals in conservation and restoration

Conservation

Archaeometry, Oxford University, England
Bollettino dell'Istituto Centrale del Restauro, Rome
Bulletin de L'Institut Royal du Patrimoine Artistique, Brussels
Bulletin du Laboratoire du Musée du Louvre, Paris
Denkmalpflege in Baden-Württemberg, Stuttgart
Deutsche Kunst und Denkmalpflege, Munich-Berlin
Jahrbuch der Bayerischen Denkmalpflege, Munich
Maltechnik, Munich
Monuments Historiques, Paris
Osterreichische Zeitschrift für Kunst und Denkmalpflege, Vienna
Restauro, Naples
Studies in Conservation, London
Technical Studies in the Field of the Fine Arts, Harvard, Boston, Mass.
Technische Mitteilungen für Malerei und Bildpflege, Munich
Urbes Nostrae, Amsterdam
Zeitschrift für Schweizerische Archaeologie und Kunstgeschichte, Zurich

Restoration

Annual Report of the Society for the Protection of Ancient Buildings, London
Annual Reports of Ancient Monuments Society, Civic Trust, Georgian Group, Society for the Protection of Ancient Buildings and Victorian Society, London
Bulletins and Newsletter of Association for Preservation Technology, Ottawa
Transactions of the Association for Studies in the Conservation of Historic Buildings, London

Principles and norms for the protection of movable and immovable cultural property: relevant UNESCO statements and definitions

UNESCO documents which contain statements of principles concerning the above are listed below. Many legal texts contain *definitions* of what is meant by cultural property, some of which overlap considerably, but generally speaking the Conventions do not contain very much statement of what is ethically or technically desirable since their main emphasis is the provision of legal cover.

Text	Cover
1. Convention for the Protection of Cultural Property in the Event of Armed Conflict (The Hague), 1954	Definitions of cultural property, protective action and rules for military authorities in the particular case of armed conflict
2. Recommendation on International Principles applicable to Archaeological Excavations, adopted by the General Conference at its Ninth Session, 1956	Definitions, extensive statements of principle and guidelines on archaeology
3. Recommendation concerning the most effective means of rendering Museums accessible to everyone, 1960	Definitions, statements of principle and guidelines on the museum in the community
4. *The Organization of Museums—practical advice*, Museums and Monuments, IX, 1960	Wide-ranging coverage of museum practice
5. Recommendation concerning the safeguarding of the beauty and character of landscapes and sites, 1962	Definitions, statements of principle and guidelines on landscapes, natural sites, parks, reserves, etc.
6. Recommendation on the means of prohibiting and preventing the illicit export, import and transfer of cultural property	Definitions of cultural property, legal and institutional arrangements
7. Recommendation concerning the preservation of cultural property endangered by public or private works, 1968	Definitions of cultural property, wide-ranging guidelines on administrative, technical measures, etc.
8. *The Conservation of Cultural Property*, Museums and Monuments, X, 1958	Wide-ranging coverage of conservation practice—some aspects now out of date or innacurate
9. Convention on the means of prohibiting and preventing the illicit export, import and transfer of cultural property	See 6 above
10. Convention concerning the protection of the World cultural and natural heritage, 1972	Definitions of 'cultural and natural heritage', institutional arrangements
11. Recommendation concerning the protection, at national level, of the cultural and natural heritage, 1972	Definitions, guidelines on practice and institutional, legal arrangements
12. *Preserving and Restoring Monuments and Historic Buildings*, Museums and Monuments, XIV, 1972	Wide-ranging coverage of building conservation practice; certain elements out of date

13. Recommendation concerning the international exchange of cultural property, 1976

Definitions of cultural property, general institutional arrangements for exchange

14. Recommendation concerning the safeguarding and contemporary role of historic areas, 1976

Definitions of historic areas, general principles and guidelines for planners and conservators, institutional and legal arrangements

15. *The Manmade Landscape*, Museums and Monuments, XVI, 1977

Wide-ranging coverage of landscaping principles

16. Recommendation for the protection of movable cultural property, 1978

Definitions of movable cultural property, general principles, institutional and legal arrangements

17. *Introduction to Conservation*, by B.M. Feilden

Wide-ranging introductory explanations of basic principles of conservation

18. *Conservation Standards for Works of Art in Transit and on Exhibition*, Museums and Monuments, XVII, 1979

Self-explanatory

N.B. A collection of international and national legislative texts has appeared in French: *La protection du patrimoine culturel mobilier*, 1979.

Index to buildings, persons and places

Subject index

345